The Sola Scriptura Challenge

The Sola Scriptura Challenge

Understanding Revelation

by
BRIAN E. BARNES

WIPF & STOCK · Eugene, Oregon

THE SOLA SCRIPTURA CHALLENGE
Understanding Revelation

Copyright © 2022 Brian E. Barnes. All rights reserved. Except for brief quotations in critical publications or reviews, no part of this book may be reproduced in any manner without prior written permission from the publisher. Write: Permissions, Wipf and Stock Publishers, 199 W. 8th Ave., Suite 3, Eugene, OR 97401.

Wipf & Stock
An Imprint of Wipf and Stock Publishers
199 W. 8th Ave., Suite 3
Eugene, OR 97401

www.wipfandstock.com

PAPERBACK ISBN: 978-1-6667-4595-5
HARDCOVER ISBN: 978-1-6667-4596-2
EBOOK ISBN: 978-1-6667-4597-9

VERSION NUMBER 102622

Scripture quotations marked (NIV) are taken from the Holy Bible, New International Version®, NIV®. Copyright © 1973, 1978, 1984, 2011 by Biblica, Inc.™ Used by permission of Zondervan. All rights reserved worldwide. www.zondervan.com The "NIV" and "New International Version" are trademarks registered in the United States Patent and Trademark Office by Biblica, Inc.™

Scripture quotations taken from the (NASB®) New American Standard Bible®, Copyright © 1960, 1971, 1977, 1995 by The Lockman Foundation. Used by permission. All rights reserved. www.lockman.org

To Amy, Emily, Joel, and Dad

Contents

1. Chaos and Confusion | 1
2. Two Questions, Too Many Answers | 18
3. Let There Be Light: Keeping Things in Context | 46
4. Daniel: Parallel Dreams and Visions | 62
5. Zechariah: Two Messiahs and a Final Battle | 85
6. Ezekiel: The Aftermath of Gog | 126
7. Joel: The Valley of Decision | 165
8. The Background Context of Revelation | 185
9. The Structure of Revelation | 197
10. Revelations About Jesus | 207
11. Revelations About Satan | 231
12. Revelations About the Beast | 240
13. Revelations About Babylon | 255
14. Revelations About Judgment | 263
15. Revelations About Eternity | 272
16. What Does All This Mean for Us Today? | 275

Bibliography | 287

1

Chaos and Confusion

"If we want revivals, we must revive our reverence for the Word of God. If we want conversions, we must put more of God's Word into our sermons; even if we paraphrase it into our own words, it must still be his Word upon which we place our reliance, for the only power which will bless men lies in that." —Charles Spurgeon

IN THE BEGINNING THERE was chaos and confusion over the interpretation of the book of Revelation. As the teachings of the Apostles took hold in their disciples in the early church, two major schools emerged in early Christianity with conflicting interpretations. The school in Antioch held to a more literal interpretation, while the only other major Christian school of the early church, the school in Alexandria, held to an allegorical interpretation. A literal interpretation is a straightforward view that claims a text means what it directly says. An allegorical interpretation is a spiritualized view that claims a text means something other than what it directly says. In other words, the early church argued about how to interpret Revelation. One main view was a literal approach, while the other was allegorical. Since that time a great variety of interpretations have arisen, each claiming an origin in the teaching of the Apostles, each claiming to be rooted in the scriptures, and each conflicting in some way with the others.

> The early church argued about how to interpret Revelation. One main view was a literal approach, while the other was allegorical.

The first part of this book will introduce you to these conflicting traditional interpretations and propose that all Christian denominations should agree on a common starting point. But what is that common starting point we should all agree with? The scriptures themselves. This is the Sola Scriptura challenge. We should begin only with the scriptures themselves as a starting point, setting aside all other sources of information until we at least first understand the plain sense of the scriptures.

MANY CONFLICTING VIEWS

To introduce you to the great variety of interpretations consider the vision John has of the Throne of God in Revelation chapter 4. John looks up and sees a door opened in Heaven. He is taken up in the Spirit and sees a vision of the Throne of God.

> "5 From the throne came flashes of lightning, rumblings and peals of thunder. In front of the throne, seven lamps were blazing. These are the seven spirits of God. 6 Also in front of the throne there was what looked like a sea of glass, clear as crystal. In the center, around the throne, were four living creatures, and they were covered with eyes, in front and in back. 7 The first living creature was like a lion, the second was like an ox, the third had a face like a man, the fourth was like a flying eagle." (Rev 4:5–7, New International Version)

Who are these Four Living Creatures? We see a similar vision in the Old Testament (hereafter referred to as the Hebrew Bible) in Ezekiel's visions of God.

> "4 I looked, and I saw a windstorm coming out of the north—an immense cloud with flashing lightning and surrounded by brilliant light. The center of the fire looked like glowing metal, 5 and in the fire was what looked like four living creatures. In appearance their form was human, 6 but each of them had four faces and four wings. 10 Their faces looked like this: Each of the four had the face of a human being, and on the right side each had the face of a lion, and on the left the face of an ox; each also had the face of an eagle." (Ezek 1:4–6,10, NIV)

If you read different commentaries, you will get many different explanations. Some will lean toward a straightforward interpretation and say these Living Creatures seen in Revelation are the same as those seen in Ezekiel. Other commentaries lean toward a spiritualization of the text and say the Four Living Creatures represent other things. Various explanations include:

- The Four Gospels (Matthew, Mark, Luke, John)
- The Four Great Apostles (Peter, James, Matthew, Paul)
- The Four Principal Angels (Gabriel, Michael, Raphael, Uriel)
- The Four Patriarchal Churches (Alexandria, Jerusalem, Antioch, Constantinople)
- The Four Doctors of the Church (Augustine, Pope Gregory I, Jerome, Ambrose)
- The Four Ancient Elements (earth, air, fire, water)
- Four Motive Powers of the Soul (reason, anger, desire, conscience)

- Four Orders (Pastor, Deacon, Doctor, Contemplative)
- Four Attributes of Divinity (wisdom, power, omniscience, creation)
- Four Orders of life (human, ox/domesticated animals, lion/wild animals, eagle/birds)
- And many more

Theologians have their reasons for insisting on the above interpretations. But the text of the Bible does not actually tell us who these four living creatures are. So how are we to move forward? How do we gain an understanding of the text?

The Sola Scriptura approach in this book will use only the scriptures. Without denying any of the above possibilities (though some seem very unlikely), it does not cling to any of them either. The above explanations depend on the thinking of theologians. In other words, they do not depend on the Bible, but rather interpretive speculation. Nowhere in the Bible will you find the verse that says the four living creatures are the authors of the four Gospels. Nowhere will you find the verse that says they are the four great Apostles, the four ancient elements, or the four patriarchal churches. And the four principal angels listed above do not even all appear in the Bible. Nowhere in the Bible are Raphael or Uriel named. Raphael is found in an apocryphal book (Tobit), and Uriel is found in later Rabbinic and Gnostic writings. The Bible itself never explains who or what the four living creatures are. All explanations come from outside scripture.

> The Bible itself never explains who or what the four living creatures are. All explanations come from outside scripture.

Immediately we are presented with a challenge to understand the book of Revelation. Where will we draw our firm understanding from? From the Bible alone (Sola Scriptura), or from sources outside the Bible such as the speculations of theologians, apocryphal books, or even non-Christian writings? The Bible never names the Four Living Creatures directly, so why do theologians attempt to do so? Is it embarrassing to say we do not know? Do we need to have every question answered? Are we less informed than people who claim to have an answer, even if that answer is from outside scripture? And what does it really matter who or what the Four Living Creatures are? Is it going to change your life? The result of all this speculation has only been arguments and division, resulting in church splits and even the formation of cults. These things have led the secular world to laugh at Christians, suggesting that one or another interpretation is ridiculous, and Christians believe in fanciful and impractical things. As Christians, should we continue down this path of discord, argument, and blame? Or should we instead be peacemakers and start over, going back to the beginning, going back to the scriptures themselves? We should, with humility, begin again. At the very least, we should agree on what the plain sense of the scriptures is. At the

WHO IS THIS BOOK FOR?

This book is intended for anyone who desires to better understand the book of Revelation. It is for anyone who has encountered confusing explanations, or worse, conflicting opinions like the above example. Mainstream Christianity is clear about who Jesus is, the Son of God who saves us from our sins because of his sacrifice on the cross. Mainstream Christianity is clear about our need for salvation from sin, and that the Blood of Jesus covers our sins. Mainstream Christianity is clear that whoever believes that Jesus died for their sins will not perish but will have eternal life. However, it is not at all clear about the meaning of the book of Revelation or the working out of the prophecies of Daniel, Ezekiel, Zechariah, Zephaniah, Isaiah, Joel, or other prophets that spoke of the end times. This book is intended to help provide clarity on these matters for anyone who wants to understand what the Bible says directly.

> This book is ultimately not about helping you win arguments. Instead, it is about showing you the great variety of interpretations and driving you into a deeper study of the Word of God.

This book is ultimately not about helping you win arguments. Instead, it is about showing you the great variety of interpretations and driving you into a deeper study of the Word of God. The answers provided in this book are those provided directly in scripture, not according to any specific denominational tradition. After reading this book, if your tradition lines up with what the scriptures say then you can be joyful. If, however, it does not seem to line up, then you have work to do and should seek a deeper conversation with your religious teachers. A win for reading this book is that you go deeper in the scriptures. A win for you is that you take the time to better understand the wide range of interpretations and go deeper in your study of the scriptures. A win for you is that you step back from the chaos and confusion, follow the light of scripture, and seek God in prayer for understanding. You will be spending time in the Word, so no time is wasted. All scripture is profitable.

WHAT IS THE SOLA SCRIPTURA CHALLENGE?

Sola Scriptura is really one simple idea: what do the scriptures say by themselves? There are several traditions that have developed throughout history about how to interpret the book of Revelation. Some lean toward a more literal interpretation that takes the words at face value, while others lean toward an allegorical interpretation that says the words have a deeper spiritual meaning than the plain sense reading. Some views also mix these two approaches.

Sola Scriptura is a Latin phrase that means "by scripture alone." The early Protestant Reformers believed that scripture itself should overrule church traditions. We should set our beliefs based on what scripture says, over and above what any traditional church teaching holds. The reformers fought against church teachings that were based on human traditions rather than canonical scripture, such as paying indulgences, working your way to salvation, the infallibility of the Pope, or praying to Mary. The Roman Catholic tradition is that these teachings were handed down orally since the time of the Apostles. They say if the Roman Catholic church teaches something different from what the Bible says, the Catholic teaching is correct. You cannot understand scripture on your own and need Catholic teaching to interpret it for you.

A similar thing happened in Judaism. After the time of Jesus, a split occurred within Judaism regarding "new" teachings, which became the Talmud. One part of Judaism, the Karaites, fought against the other part, led by the Rabbis (the successors of the Pharisees). The Karaites said that the Talmud, the Oral Torah, the traditional teachings of the Rabbis, should not overrule scripture. The written canonical Hebrew Bible should be the sole authority for doctrine, and it should be interpreted in its plain sense of meaning. The teachings of the Rabbis in the Talmud were not to be placed above scripture, especially if they were different from the plain sense of the meaning of the text. The Karaites lost that battle and Judaism today is predominantly Rabbinic. They say if the Rabbis teach something different from what the Bible says, the Rabbinic teaching is correct. Rabbis teach that God gave the judges who came after Moses the authority to make decisions, and that authority has been handed down along with oral teachings since that time to the Rabbis today. You therefore cannot understand scripture by itself and need Rabbinic teaching to interpret it for you.

Though various religious groups teach their own interpretations; they all claim to be rooted in the scriptures. The Sola Scriptura approach asks only: what exactly do the scriptures say by themselves? Sola Scriptura has been fought against throughout the ages and the fight is still underway today. This book proposes to use Sola Scriptura as our common starting point. Though Roman Catholic theologians and Rabbis both teach their own evolved traditions, they also both believe their teachings are rooted in the original texts of the scriptures. Therefore, we should all be able to start from this common point: what is the plain meaning of the scriptures as they would have been understood by their original audience? While the denominations will continue to disagree on interpretations of the meaning of those texts, we can all start at the common point of understanding them in their original plain sense. And that is the focus of this book, to show that common point.

> Though various religious groups teach their own interpretations; they all claim to be rooted in the scriptures. The Sola Scriptura approach asks only: what exactly do the scriptures say by themselves?

This book will put scripture above all traditions. While there are several interpretations held by different Christian denominations, the intent of this book is not to disprove them. The intent of this book is to look at only what the scriptures directly say and see where that takes us. Some interpretations of Revelation depend on underlying assumptions that are built from an analysis of theological themes understood from a study of the entire Bible. From a lifelong study of thematic arcs across scripture, theologians assemble them into various theories of what Revelation is saying. However, there is an uncomfortable truth with some of them that the Bible nowhere actually says exactly what they propose. Some of these theologians suggest that if you don't agree with them because the Bible does not say it directly, then you are not smart enough to understand the Bible. Some even attempt to shame and belittle others, but they ultimately cannot "prove" their point by showing where their assertions are directly stated in the Bible. Recall all the examples above of the theological positions on the four living creatures in Ezekiel. Not even one of those is directly stated in the scriptures.

When challenging some of these views to show just one verse that directly says them, you may hear a response that John was afraid to say things directly. For example, a teacher may say that John used symbols in Revelation, such as the name Nero Caesar coded as 666 to hide the truth because he was afraid of Roman punishment. This is actually a claim that John used a mystical practice called Gematria (which is like astrology) to hide spiritual secrets such as the name of the beast. This is an interesting theory, but John was already in prison on the Island of Patmos for preaching Christ as the Messiah (Rev 1:9). So we know he wasn't afraid of speaking his mind or else he wouldn't have been in prison to begin with. And are we to believe that John practiced Kabbalah, an ancient occultic practice still taught today that uses Gematria to "reveal" the deep hidden secrets of the Bible? Those are heavy accusations to place against John. Who would accuse John of being fearful or practicing the occult? Moreover, if this was the vision revealed by Jesus to John (Rev 1:1), then why would John suddenly be afraid to proclaim what God Almighty has revealed and write down something different that only a few could understand? Why would Jesus intentionally cause unlimited controversy within the church for ages to come? Is it God's will that there be chaos and confusion? Is God the author of confusion? Does that lead anyone to Christ?

Unprovable theological assertions like the above can lead to great trouble. As another example, one tradition holds that Jerusalem was destroyed in 70 AD by the Romans because God divorced the Jewish people and punished them for rejecting Jesus Christ as their Messiah. Because they rejected his Son, then God divorced them and married (or will marry) the bride which is the church. But there is not a single verse in Revelation that actually says this. No, not one. Search the scriptures for yourself. This view is only arrived at by combining numerous parts of the Bible. Yet it is likely you have heard this taught before as if the Bible stated it directly.

Moreover, saying that God divorced the Jewish people because they rejected his Son, and that God will marry the bride, which is the church, should give us pause. They are saying that God had a Son with another woman, and his first wife rejected that Son. Because the first wife rejected the Son by another woman, then God divorces her and marries the other woman. Isn't that adultery and the ultimate betrayal and shaming of a wife? The Bible nowhere says this, and it certainly raises some questions about the morality of God.

You can see just how quickly, and ugly, the debate over the meaning of Revelation unfolds. Therefore, our approach will be to look at only what the scriptures directly say and see where that takes us. We will not support any theories from outside the scriptures. However, we will briefly review the major denominational views for your consideration and edification. Though you may become confused or bewildered by all the different interpretations, remember that all time spent studying the scriptures is profitable. And as all these interpretations claim to originate in the scriptures, then you should at the least try to understand what the scriptures plainly and directly say.

WHY IS THIS CHALLENGE IMPORTANT?

Revelation is a book that many Christian denominations do not teach in depth. Few go verse-by-verse and study numerous commentaries. And if they do go verse-by-verse, they will likely only teach one particular view (their denominational view). On the other hand, some denominations have an intense focus on it, often resulting in either scaring away new potential congregants, or worse: spiraling into internal debate resulting in church splits. With all the conflicting interpretations, general confusion, complex symbolism, and a secular culture that tends to focus only on doomsday scenarios and end times cults; where is the blessing promised in the first chapter?

> "Blessed is the one who reads aloud the words of this prophecy, and blessed are those who hear it and take to heart what is written in it, because the time is near." (Rev 1:3, NIV)

As Christians we all generally agree on the prophecies about the Messiah as referring to Jesus. And we all generally see them in the same way. For example, the prophecies said the Messiah would be despised and rejected, and then put to death to make atonement for the sins of others. He would bear the sins of others and make intercession for us with God. We look at what Isaiah and other prophets had to say about the Messiah, and we take their prophecies seriously, as written. Shouldn't we, at the very least, begin our approach to Revelation in the same way?

> We look at what Isaiah and other prophets had to say about the Messiah, and we take their prophecies seriously, as written. Shouldn't we, at the very least, begin our approach to Revelation in the same way?

The Sola Scriptura Challenge

The Sola Scriptura approach challenges us to read the prophecies in Revelation the same way we read the prophecies about the Messiah. A surprising number of prophetic symbols are actually explained in the Bible. Instead of theorizing about what the symbols mean, we should at first see what Revelation actually says they mean. A surprising number of symbols are explained to John, just like we see in the earlier prophets like Daniel, Zechariah, Ezekiel, Joel, and Zephaniah. Before listening to any theologian's suggestions about what the symbols mean, we should at first hear what the Bible tells us they mean. What the Bible has to say should be more important to us as Christians than what any theologian, doctrine, or church tradition has to say. We should first take the Bible seriously, and then later we can evaluate what the theologians think.

> A surprising number of prophetic symbols are actually explained in the Bible.

This call to look at what exactly the scriptures say, and what they do not say, should be important to all Christians. For our faith is in God and not mankind. He has given us his Word, which has been consistent over the centuries. The Dead Sea Scrolls and the Textus Receptus have shown us the remarkable accuracy of the transmission of the scriptures, unlike the varying theological opinions that seem to blow wherever the wind takes them.

Is it right for us to place scripture above church traditions, above the teachings of theologians smarter than we are, above the doctrines that our local church may hold dear? What did Jesus think about the accuracy of the scriptures?

> "For truly I tell you, until heaven and earth disappear, not the smallest letter, not the least stroke of a pen, will by any means disappear from the Law until everything is accomplished." (Matt 5:18, NIV)

Have heaven and earth disappeared? Has everything written in the scriptures come to pass? Has death been taken away? Has God already wiped away every tear from all faces? Is there already only one God over all the earth that all people acknowledge as the one True God? No, these prophecies of Isaiah (Isa 25:8) and Zechariah (Zech 14:9) have not come to pass. A multitude of tears are shed every day. Wars, oppression, and selfishness continue. The whole world does not acknowledge God. If the smallest letter will not disappear, according to Jesus, then should we not pay attention to all the details written in scripture? What did Paul say about this matter?

> "2 Preach the word; be prepared in season and out of season; correct, rebuke and encourage—with great patience and careful instruction. 3 For the time will come when people will not put up with sound doctrine. Instead, to suit their own desires, they will gather around them a great number of teachers to say what their itching ears want to hear. 4 They will turn their ears away from the truth and turn aside to myths." (2 Tim 4:2-4, NIV)

It is right and good to place the scriptures above all man made interpretations. Jesus spoke of the accuracy and power of God's Word in all its details. God's Word does not go forth and return empty, without fulfillment. Paul warned of the days to come when people will not pay attention to the scriptures, but instead turn to teachers with different teachings. We should keep the scriptures at the center. Let them be a fence all around us, a hedge of protection.

> "9 'As the heavens are higher than the earth, so are my ways higher than your ways and my thoughts than your thoughts. 10 As the rain and the snow come down from heaven, and do not return to it without watering the earth and making it bud and flourish, so that it yields seed for the sower and bread for the eater, 11 so is my word that goes out from my mouth: It will not return to me empty, but will accomplish what I desire and achieve the purpose for which I sent it.'" (Isa 55:9–11, NIV)

If these arguments aren't enough to encourage you to look at what the scriptures actually say, setting aside the conflicting commentaries and theological opinions about their meaning, then perhaps a warning from Revelation itself might inspire your study:

> "18 I warn everyone who hears the words of the prophecy of this scroll: If anyone adds anything to them, God will add to that person the plagues described in this scroll. 19 And if anyone takes words away from this scroll of prophecy, God will take away from that person any share in the tree of life and in the Holy City, which are described in this scroll." (Rev 22:18–19, NIV)

OBJECTIONS TO THE SOLA SCRIPTURA APPROACH

When you read something that someone else wrote, questions can arise about what they meant exactly. Having witnesses that knew the author and spoke with them about their beliefs can shed a great deal of light on what the author actually meant. For example, in the Law of Moses it is written that if an ox gores someone to death, then the owner of the ox will not be held responsible, unless the ox had the habit of goring. If the ox is known to have had a habit of goring and it kills someone, then the owner of the ox is to be stoned and put to death (Exod 21:28–29). That seems straightforward. But what if the ox was loaned out to someone and that other person was careless with keeping the ox tied up? Should the owner be put to death if the other person was negligent in controlling the ox and the ox gored someone to death? Perhaps not. However, what if the ox had a habit of goring and the owner did not tell the other person about it? Or what if the other person did actually tie up the ox, but the rope they used was weak and the person that sold them the rope lied about the strength of the rope? Should the owner still be responsible and put to death? The Bible does not explain these situations, and so oral traditions have arisen to provide answers. An entire approach to law has developed around taking the Law of Moses, expounding it, and creating a system of justice to decide cases that arise in the courts. This system is still meticulously maintained today by the Rabbis.

Church tradition holds that a similar approach has been taken with understanding key books like Revelation. The early church leaders, who lived closer to the time of the Apostles, passed down their understanding of biblical texts. Points of confusion and questions about meaning were passed down from teacher to student over time. A criticism of the Sola Scriptura approach is that it looks only at the Bible itself and ignores these early church teachings. How can we, being roughly 2,000 years separated from the time of Jesus, claim to better understand the authors' original meaning than the people who lived nearer to the time of the Apostles and handed down explanations and judgments from teacher to student?

This criticism that Sola Scriptura is a wrong approach because the Bible doesn't provide all the answers as in the case above of an ox goring someone to death, and ignores how early church leaders understood the Bible, is a powerful argument of those opposed to Sola Scriptura. Not only that, but who decided what books constitute the official "scriptures" used in Sola Scriptura anyway? Nowhere in the Bible does it actually say which books are canonical and which are not. That is a church tradition and not in the scriptures, yet Sola Scriptura depends on this very teaching which is not found in the Bible itself. Ironic indeed.

The trouble with this criticism however is that we have been handed down conflicting traditions. Throughout the New Testament we see the Apostles arguing against false teachings within the church. Already by the time of the disciples of the Apostles we see a major difference in how the scriptures are interpreted: literally or allegorically. The church in Antioch, where disciples were first called Christians (Acts 11:26) taught a literal approach to scripture. While the church in Alexandria, traditionally believed to have been founded by the author of the Gospel of Mark, developed an allegorical approach to interpreting scripture. And there are major differences in which books are even canonical according to different ancient church traditions. For example, the books of the Maccabees may or may not be included in your Bible.

So, we cannot look to church tradition for answers, because there are conflicting viewpoints since the beginning of church history. Several ancient denominations all claim to have the original teachings (such as Roman Catholic, Greek Orthodox, Egyptian Coptic, and Ethiopian Orthodox). Not only that, but conflicting viewpoints already existed within Judaism as well about understanding the scriptures. You may recall the famous debates over resurrection between the Sadducees and the Pharisees, and how they tried to trap Jesus in their arguments. The dialogue Jesus had with these different groups takes on a deeper meaning when you understand the difference in beliefs they held. For example, you can see that Jesus responded to his critics from the scriptures they actually believed in, because the Sadducees and Pharisees disagreed on many things including the canon. You can see differences in which part of the Hebrew Bible that Jesus quotes from depending on which Jewish group he is speaking with. These different traditions and decisions about which scriptures are canon go back throughout Israel's history and predate Christianity. You may recall the day when they were repairing the Temple and the High Priest found a lost book (2 Chr 34:14–21). Although modern scholars disagree over which writings were contained in this "Book of the Law" that was found, the priests of the First Temple apparently had lost some official scriptures. Since the arguments over which books belong in the Bible predate Christianity, and conflict arose across the most ancient Christian denominations, we cannot look to traditions for our answer.

> Since the arguments over which books belong in the Bible predate Christianity, and conflict arose across the most ancient Christian denominations, we cannot look to traditions for our answer.

The traditions that have been handed down about the interpretation of the scriptures, and which scriptures are the real ones, are conflicting. We cannot look to the interpretations of mankind, the traditions of mankind, for our beliefs. Jesus even warned specifically against that. When Jesus was accused of breaking the Law because he and the Disciples did not wash their hands before eating, Jesus quoted Isaiah 29:13 and called them hypocrites for following the traditions of men while breaking the actual laws of God (Matt 15:1–9).

> "The Lord says: 'These people come near to me with their mouth and honor me with their lips, but their hearts are far from me. Their worship of me is based on merely human rules they have been taught.'" (Isa 29:13, NIV)

The oldest church tradition was a literal interpretation of Revelation. This was given by Ignatius of Antioch, a disciple of John himself, as well as Irenaeus who was a disciple of Polycarp, another disciple of John. The allegorical approach developed later in the fourth century under the influence of Greek Philosophy (Hellenism in Alexandria). Even though the earliest church tradition was to interpret Revelation literally, and the allegorical approach developed later, we cannot look to church tradition because since the beginning there have been conflicting opinions.

> Even though the earliest church tradition was to interpret Revelation literally, and the allegorical approach developed later, we cannot look to church tradition because since the beginning there have been conflicting opinions.

However, we do know we have accurate scriptures. Since the discovery of the Dead Sea Scrolls, we have scientific evidence of the authenticity of the scriptures. We can read Isaiah, Daniel, and other key Hebrew texts with confidence. Even though some scholars and other religions have said the Hebrew scriptures were changed (both by Jewish people to "not support" Islam, as well as by Christians to "find" Jesus in them), when the Dead Sea Scrolls were found and analyzed by scholars years later, it turns out we have extremely accurate scriptures and neither the Jewish people nor Christians changed them since before the time of Christ. While there are small typographical differences among different copies (such as spelling of certain words), there are no meaningful differences. And with the thousands of Greek fragments of the New Testament we have, known as the Textus Receptus, there is more evidence of the authenticity of the New Testament than to any other ancient literature in existence. In fact, the Bible is more accurate than our copies of the works of Homer.

The Sola Scriptura approach depends on the accuracy of the scriptures, rather than the conflicting church traditions that have evolved over time. We do not have to decide which church tradition is right. We can instead begin with only the scriptures and see where that takes us. And as you will see, explanations abound inside scripture itself. Scripture truly does interpret scripture. And then, after seeing what the scriptures directly say, let the Holy Spirit testify in your own spirit what the scriptures mean.

A WARNING ABOUT PERSONAL ATTACKS

If you study the history of the Sola Scriptura idea in the Protestant Reformation you will find plenty of arguments against it as we saw above. Some will argue that their view is the one originally held. Others may even question the integrity of the proponents of Sola Scriptura, suggesting they have ulterior motives. And still others may even attack theologians by accusing them of being sinful people.

As you have seen in the previous section, no denomination can truly claim to have the "original" view because there are several ancient traditions that all go back to the time of the Apostles. Moreover, these views are conflicting, so there was no uniformity and no single "original" understanding believed by the whole church throughout history. The oldest interpretation we have of the book of Revelation comes from a disciple of John himself, as well as a disciple of one of John's disciples. These men taught a literal interpretation only. Allegorical interpretations in Christianity developed later in history and swept up much of the theological developments afterward (as also happened in Judaism). Yet what is the same in both interpretations is the scriptures themselves. We can set aside these claims of an "original" view because there are too many of them that are plausible. Without denying any of them, we can point to the scriptures themselves which all interpretations claim to be founded on. There are many "original" views, but they don't agree so we must set them all aside.

> There are many "original" views, but they don't agree so we must set them all aside.

Another major tactic opponents of Sola Scriptura will take is to attack the character of the theologians who use it. If you spend time reading their views you are likely to see character assassinations of Luther, Zwingli, or Calvin. In truth everyone is a sinner. The one who claims to be without sin is a liar. So all theologians are sinners. To attack the character of your opponent is to avoid defending your own theology. It is a distraction, and a technique people use to scare others away from competing ideas. But if we knew the deepest thoughts, desires, and secrets of everyone around us then we would see that we are all sinners. We should only argue about ideas, not about the guilt of specific theologians. That matter is already settled: we are all guilty of sin.

The clarion call to go back to the scriptures instead of our evolved traditions is nothing new. Luther's call to go back to the scriptures during the Protestant Reformation was not the first time this ever happened. Ezra did the same thing millennia before with his reforms of the Israelite religion, as did many high priests throughout Israel's history. Pope Leo X, who opposed Luther, was not the first person to claim to have an older tradition that gives the true meaning of scriptures. The Pharisees did the very same thing with their "Oral Torah," and we all know how Jesus felt about the Pharisees.

> It's not about people. Our arguments should not be about the integrity of people, but rather just what the scriptures directly say. Attacking the credibility of theologians is playing dirty.

It's not about people. Our arguments should not be about the integrity of people, but rather just what the scriptures directly say. Attacking the credibility of theologians is playing dirty. Though the scriptures cannot completely contain God and interpretation is necessary, they are the right place for us to begin to seek him out. Though all the things Jesus did weren't written down, what was written down is a great place to start. Before we read a commentary, we should read the Bible passages first. They are very revealing.

A WARNING ABOUT EMOTIONS

People many times form specific opinions about unfulfilled prophecies, and when other viewpoints arise it can make people angry. Look at what happened to Jesus when the prophecies of the Messiah were applied to him. They crucified him. Many of the religious leaders at the time had other ideas about what those prophecies meant. Different interpretations of scripture can trigger our emotions. Fear, anger, and contempt easily come out if we are not careful.

> Different interpretations of scripture can trigger our emotions. Fear, anger, and contempt easily come out if we are not careful.

As we take this Sola Scriptura approach together, we must recognize that it may trigger some strong emotions in us and in others. I have personally experienced this many times when just trying to explain what the different views are, without taking a specific position. Nobody likes to be wrong, think they are wrong, or question their beliefs. Few people have done an in-depth study of the book of Revelation, let alone examined beliefs across different denominations. This is a blind spot for us as Christians, and one in which cults and conspiracy theories run rampant.

Many churches simply do not emphasize teaching from the book. The ideas are vivid and can sometimes be scary. Some people have only heard "fire and brimstone" preaching on the book and do not get taught the Good News and the blessing promised in studying the book (Rev 1:3). Several cults have sprung up from misunderstandings of Revelation, and therefore many people are rightfully afraid and skeptical of teachers of Revelation. Numerous false predictions of the return of Christ, the end of the world, and conspiracy theories have risen from well-meaning but wrong interpretations.

Martin Luther (founder of the Lutheran church) thought that the Antichrist was Pope Leo X and Babylon was the church in Rome. John Wesley (co-founder of the Methodist church) opined that the expansion of Islam under Mohammed was foreseen at the 6th trumpet of Rev 9. John Calvin (founder of the Reformed church movement which includes Presbyterian, Reformed Baptist, and Evangelical Anglican) wrote a commentary on the entire Bible, except he refused to write one on the book of Revelation. Calvin thought we should only set doctrine based on the plain sense of scripture, yet the Calvinist Reformed Church today embraces an allegorical interpretation instead. All the false predictions about the return of Christ and who the Antichrist is, with their changes in interpretation over time, have caused great anxiety in the churches.

We must be aware that our study of Revelation may trigger anger in us if we hear a teaching different from what we have heard before. It may trigger fear in us to think that our denomination, our favorite teachers, our favorite commentaries, or our own personal thoughts might not align with what the scriptures actually say. I know from my own experience that this can be maddening. It can be disheartening. But as we study the scriptures, we join theologians throughout history in trying to better understand them. As we study, we develop an appreciation for the different interpretations, and the people who hold them. And as we study, we test our own mettle in properly dividing the Word of Truth, engaging with other people, and watching over our own heart as we honestly consider what the Word really says. Therefore, enter this study aware of your emotions. And when discussing these things with other people, be aware of their emotions. I have personally encountered more fear and anger over the passages in this book than in any other I have studied and taught over the years.

A WARNING ABOUT BACKGROUND BIAS

A wise person once said that wherever you begin your study of Revelation is likely where you will end up. In other words, if you come into a study of Revelation with a

Premillennial Dispensational viewpoint, an Idealist Amillennial viewpoint, or a Preterist Reconstructionist viewpoint, then you are likely to end up just reinforcing your presupposed beliefs. Depending on where you grew up or lived a significant amount of time, that culture may also impact your views without your knowing. Popular movies, books, and cultural myths may unknowingly be rolling around in your mind and influencing what you hear. Chances are, you already have some bias. Therefore, try to have an open mind and think only about what the scriptures are actually saying. Do your best to put aside what you "already know," which is the influence of the culture in which you live. The scriptures provide ample evidence of what they are saying, often repeating the same idea many times in the same book and across the Bible itself. While extra-Biblical writings can help us better understand the Bible (hopefully like this book), do your best to lean heavily into just the scriptures.

> Do your best to put aside what you "already know," which is the influence of the culture in which you live.

Most importantly, know that your view of Apocalyptic Literature does not impact your salvation. Your salvation rests solely on faith that Jesus died for your sins. For whoever believes in Jesus will inherit eternal life (John 3:16). So don't let your bias, your emotions, or your thoughts about Revelation worry you. Clearly the denominations have argued over its meaning throughout the ages, so just have faith in Jesus. He is the way, the truth, and the life.

A WARNING ABOUT JUMPING TO CONCLUSIONS

In a book like this it is tempting to jump to the conclusions at the end. Sometimes we just want to know what the conclusion is, to know if we should even read the book. But what does that say about our open-mindedness? Unless a book agrees with what we already "know," then we are not going to read it? That says we only want to reinforce what we already believe, and we do not want to be challenged. When I began a serious study of the book of Revelation, I had an advantage. The denomination I grew up in rarely ever spoke about the book. So I only had a few "official" ideas about its meaning. On the other hand, the culture around me in movies and popular books, as well as the prevalent denomination in the area I grew up in turned out to hold a very different interpretation than my home church. I basically had a lot of loosely connected and conflicting ideas about the book without a formal teaching. After teaching about the prophecies of the Messiah in the Hebrew Bible for several years I had the good fortune of taking a non-denominational class through the book of Revelation verse-by-verse. It is there where I learned of the variety of interpretations and took a systematic approach to understand all the major views and present them equally to our class. For well over a year, we went verse-by-verse of both the book of Revelation as well as the relevant Hebrew Bible references, looking at each major interpretation and discussing them in turn as a group. This experience of not holding a specific view and equally considering all of them in a deep study was a wonderful, and often maddening, experience. Some dropped out of the class along the way, but a core group stuck it through to the end and were glad to have had the experience. Moreover, when working on my Master of Divinity degree we were taught that proper exegesis (critical explanation of scripture) always starts with the scriptures themselves and not the commentaries. I encourage you to read this book straight through, building up your knowledge, before you get to the conclusions. I encourage you to take the journey and do not jump to conclusions. It will be worth your time, and you will also sharpen your own interpretation skills.

> Take the journey and do not jump to conclusions.

This book only supports what the scriptures plainly say. While there are a variety of possible interpretations, if the Bible does not directly say something, and ideally in more than one place, then this book does not take a position. No theological speculations are made, only the scriptures are shown. And some things are, indeed, mysteries and not explained directly in the Bible. God's ways really are above ours, and we cannot know everything.

STUDY LIKE DANIEL

Consider only the scriptures and think about what they mean. Daniel found himself in the direst of circumstances. He lived in captivity in Babylon after the Southern Kingdom of Judah was overthrown by Nebuchadnezzar. Although the Hebrew prophets had warned them before that captivity was coming, they also promised a return from exile once the punishment for disobedience was over. Daniel studied the writings of Jeremiah to understand prophecy. He prayed. He confessed his sins and that of his people. He pleaded with God in prayer and petition, in fasting, and in sackcloth and ashes (Dan 9:1–27). Approach Revelation in the same way as Daniel did the prophecies of Jeremiah. Study what the scriptures say. Plead with God for understanding. Confess your sins. And in humility ask God for understanding.

> Approach Revelation in the same way as Daniel did Jeremiah. Study what the scriptures say. Plead with God for understanding. Confess your sins. And in humility ask God for understanding.

Remember that other "prophets" in the time of Jeremiah spoke against Jeremiah. Jeremiah was ridiculed and not taken seriously. When God reveals his Word there are others who think they know better. We are surrounded by voices that claim to know what God says. And just like Daniel took Jeremiah seriously even though others didn't, we too should listen to what scripture actually says even though there are differing traditions that have grown up around it. We should earnestly lean into the

Word of God and set aside our human traditions. We should fear the Living God more than we fear the views of other people. For in the end, we will stand alone in judgment. Only the Blood of Jesus can truly save us from shame and everlasting condemnation.

2

Two Questions, Too Many Answers

"Nothing therefore can be more absurd than the fiction, that the power of judging scripture is in the church, and that on her nod its certainty depends."—John Calvin

THE BIG QUESTIONS ABOUT REVELATION

When is Jesus returning? Is there a Beast? If so, who or what is it? What does the number of the Beast mean? Who are the Four Horsemen? Who is the rider on the white horse? Who are the 144,000 that are sealed before the trumpets are sounded? Will there be a rapture? If so, when? Before, during, or after the tribulation? What is the tribulation? Will there literally be a Millennium? Why does John refer to Gog and Magog? Who is the Prostitute that sits on the Beast? Do the Jewish people have an end-time destiny? Does the land of Israel figure into the end times? Is there really a Hell? Is there really unending torture or do wicked souls eventually end their existence? Does everyone eventually end up in Heaven? What is the "New Heaven and New Earth"? What does it mean to reign with Christ? Are Christians reigning right now while Jesus reigns in Heaven?

These are some of the intriguing questions that have occupied the minds of Christians throughout the ages. But underlying the answers that the various denominations provide are some more fundamental questions. Different answers to two fundamental questions of interpretation will produce a variety of interpretations. You will see in the next section how these different answers result in the different interpretations commonly taught today. In this section we will explore just what these two underlying questions are.

Different answers to two fundamental questions of interpretation will produce a variety of interpretations.

UNFULFILLED PROPHECIES OF THE HEBREW BIBLE

One of the uncomfortable truths in Christianity is that not all of the Hebrew Bible prophecies have been completely fulfilled yet. It seems as though many popular Christians teach that the Hebrew Bible isn't worth studying because everything has already been fulfilled in Jesus. And the New Testament is all there is going forward. But that just isn't true.

> One of the uncomfortable truths in Christianity is that not all of the Hebrew Bible prophecies have been completely fulfilled yet.

It's not true that the whole Hebrew Bible points exclusively to the First Coming of Christ, and the Jewish People missed the whole point of the scriptures. Consider the prophecies of Daniel about the resurrection of the dead on the Day of Judgment (Dan 12:2–3). Did that happen already? Consider the prophecies of Isaiah about the day when the nations will no longer learn war and will beat their swords into plowshares (Isa 2:3–4). No, that clearly hasn't happened yet. Or what about Joel's vision that Judah and Jerusalem would receive the outpouring of God's Spirit and be restored forever (Joel 2:28–3:21)? Ezekiel says the same thing in chapters 36–37. Zechariah not only says Judah and Jerusalem will receive God's Spirit, but they will also look upon the Messiah who was slain and mourn for him as if for an only Son (Zech 12:10–14). There are many more examples like this which we will explore later.

The Hebrew Bible still has prophecies remaining to be fulfilled. And that's a problem for some Christian theologians. For Christian theologians who hold that all Hebrew Bible prophecies are already fulfilled in Christ, they have challenges explaining passages like those mentioned above. Some interpretations hold an allegorical view which understands those prophecies to mean something other than the plain sense of the words. They find an underlying deeper, sometimes hidden, spiritual meaning that explains how those prophecies have already been fulfilled. In other words, the prophecies don't mean what they plainly say, they mean something else "spiritually" so that they can appear to be already fulfilled in Christ.

Some interpretations reinterpret Hebrew Bible passages to substitute Christians for mentions of the Jewish People, a "Spiritual Israel" that replaces Ethnic Israel. They then go on to explain those prophecies in terms of fulfillment through Christians instead of through the Jewish People. And still other interpretations hold a more literal understanding of those older prophecies and look forward to a future time when God will fulfill them exactly as they are written.

Recall earlier in this book when you were warned about emotions. Some of yours may already be at work just hearing about these different interpretations. There are a variety of ways these prophecies are explained, but the underlying questions are the same: have these prophecies already been fulfilled or not? And in light of Christianity, how do we understand the prophecies related to the Jewish People? This is why you will find denominations that focus intently on the newspaper headlines of the day and others that don't, denominations that encourage their congregations to support modern Israel and others that are Anti–Semitic, and denominations that have regular prophecy seminars while others that completely avoid the book of Revelation. And you will find everything in between, even within the same denominations, even within the same individual churches.

ACCURACY OF PROPHECIES

Given the variety of interpretations of prophecy, we must ask ourselves why it is this way. If as Christians we claim all prophecies are true, then we end up needing to explain how they are true. If they haven't come to pass as plainly said, then we either 1) say they are for a future time, 2) say they are already partially fulfilled in the past, or 3) say they are both fulfilled in the past and will be fulfilled yet again in the future. In explaining how some prophecies are already fulfilled, but not as literally written, some will provide an alternate explanation presented as a secret few people know. But if what a prophet said has not come to pass just as that prophet spoke, should we accept an alternative explanation for the meaning of the prophecy? Is it Biblical to do that? Does the Bible ever speak about the accuracy of prophecies?

> "If what a prophet proclaims in the name of the LORD does not take place or come true, that is a message the LORD has not spoken. That prophet has spoken presumptuously, so do not be alarmed." (Deut 18:22, NIV)

Recorded above in the Law of Moses is a test for prophets. Anyone who speaks in the name of the Lord must be tested. And if what they say does not come to pass then they are not a true prophet. It does not say, if you know them to be a prophet of God and their message has not come to pass, then you have misunderstood the message and need a deeper underlying secret way of understanding it. It does not say the prophets misunderstood the prophecies because they were before the time of the Messiah. In fact, we take the prophecies of the Messiah clearly and plainly, because they do really point to Jesus. They plainly described his rejection, his salvation of others from sin, his death, and his resurrection. What those prophets said did literally come to pass.

If we say those prophets were blinded by Judaism, misunderstood the prophecies because they weren't Christian, or were simply wrong because everything was contingent on the Jewish people accepting Jesus, then we dishonor those prophets. If these things are true, then those are not true prophets of God according to the Law of Moses. If Daniel, Ezekiel, Zechariah, Isaiah, Jeremiah, and the Psalms spoke plainly of the Messiah, but in riddles or misunderstanding of the end times, then by the Law of Moses they are not true prophets. And if they are not true prophets, as Orthodox Judaism holds regarding Daniel by not placing his book among the prophets (his book is organized into a lesser collection of writings), then we must reject everything they say. Including what they say about Jesus. We cannot pick and choose verses we like and claim they show Jesus is the Messiah, then interpret the other prophecies (often in the same passages) differently because we don't like what they say about the End Times.

> We cannot pick and choose verses we like and claim they show Jesus is the Messiah, then interpret the other prophecies (often in the same passages) differently because we don't like what they say about the End Times.

No, Daniel was truly a prophet. His book belongs with the prophets, as Christians have placed him in our Bibles. And the prophets spoke of both the Messiah and the end times. Either we take all of the words seriously, or we are fooling ourselves. We are inconsistent. We cannot pick and choose what things we want to plainly believe because they sound like Jesus, and then reinterpret verses we don't like to mean something else. If these are true prophets, then everything they said will come to pass, according to God, according to Moses.

UNDERLYING QUESTIONS

Given the unfulfilled prophecies from the Hebrew Bible, and our belief that the words of a true prophet will come to pass, then we are left with two underlying questions about apocalyptic prophecies. These two fundamental questions are worked out by each interpretation: 1) Are these passages to be taken literally or allegorically? And 2) when will these events come to pass? In other words: 1) Do we depend on a plain sense interpretation of the prophecies, or do we redefine them with an alternate meaning that provides a "more satisfactory" spiritual answer? And 2) regardless of our answer to #1, can we assign a time of fulfillment to them? For example, like is commonly done with the prophecies about the Messiah and the First and Second Comings of Jesus?

> These two fundamental questions are worked out by each interpretation: 1) Are these passages to be taken literally or allegorically? And 2) when will these events come to pass?

We can view answers to both fundamental questions as a range from one extreme view to the other. The first question ranges from a strictly literal view to a strictly allegorical view, with a mixture of views somewhere in the middle. The second question ranges from all prophecies being fulfilled in the past to all in the future, with a mixture of views somewhere in the middle. We can generally map all views of revelation along these two spectrums.

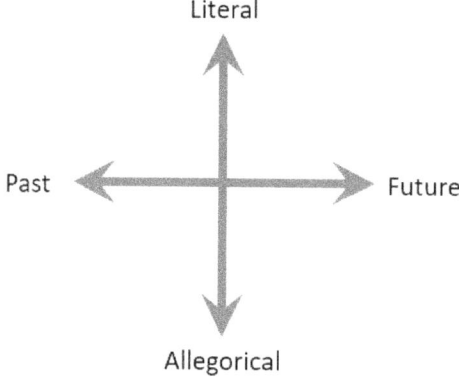

For example, a pure Preterist view holds that all prophecies are fulfilled in the past, such as is taught by some Jesuits in the Roman Catholic church. They are on the left end of this diagram. A pure Futurist view holds that the prophecies in Revelation are all in the future, they are to the right of the diagram. A pure literal view, which includes interpreting symbols just as they are explained in the scriptures directly, is on the top of the diagram. And a pure allegorical view which holds the entire book of Revelation to have a deeper secret meaning other than what it directly says is to the bottom of the figure. They tend to view the book of Revelation as teaching timeless truths and not any specific historical events. Some theological interpretations such as the Progressive Dispensational view hold that select events repeat. The first instances of select events occurred in the past and there will yet still be a future instance.

Hopefully these brief examples help you see the large field of interpretations we have, and how they range along these two dimensions. Behind all the interpretations you can see these two questions being worked out. The more conservative denominations tend to be closer to the literal end of the spectrum while the more liberal denominations tend to be closer to the allegorical end of the spectrum (though there is variety within denominations). Each of these ends of the spectrum has a range of views on the events being in the past, future, both, repeated, or never at all. Regarding the interpretation of the prophecies in the Hebrew Bible this is true for both Christianity as well as in Judaism, which we will explore in the next section. And we will suggest an approach forward that can serve as a starting point for all discussions of the book of Revelation.

HOW DOES THE NEW TESTAMENT VIEW HEBREW BIBLE PROPHECIES OF THE END?

As we begin to explore the different viewpoints people have about Revelation it is important to begin with how the Bible itself views these end times prophecies. The Sola

Scriptura approach begins its discussion with the scriptures themselves. As discussed above, there are unfulfilled prophecies in the Hebrew Bible. Does the New Testament refer to these? And if so, how? Does it view them as events that will still take place? Does it view them as allegories with some underlying secret meaning? We will take a look at how Jesus viewed these prophecies first. Then we will look at how Paul, Peter, and the angels viewed them. The way that the New Testament views the Hebrew prophecies should matter to us, especially if we hold a different view.

> The way that the New Testament views the Hebrew prophecies should matter to us, especially if we hold a different view.

Jesus Teaches About the Second Coming

While in Jerusalem, Jesus disputes the meaning of the Law with the religious leaders. He routinely points out their hypocrisy. And one day as he is leaving the Temple, he predicts that it will be destroyed (Matt 24:2). He then goes to the Mount of Olives which is just outside the city and overlooks the Temple complex. As he and his Disciples are seated overlooking the city and the Temple, they ask him about his prediction of the destruction of the Temple, the sign of his coming, and the end of the age (Matt 24:3). Jesus gives an answer that many theologians see as parallels to the warnings and judgments found in Revelation (wars, famines, earthquakes, martyrdom of the saints, false prophets, and false messiahs). These warnings of Jesus are general enough to sound like they could apply to most times throughout church history. Some theologians apply these general warnings to today's headlines. In the past some theologians who applied the warnings to the events of their day also made false predictions about the timing of the return of Christ. Still other theologians see the general nature of the warnings and teach that Jesus was referring to repeated events that happen in every generation. So what did Jesus really mean? Notice that Jesus makes a direct reference to the prophecies of Daniel. And those are not generic prophecies at all. The vision shown to Daniel, which Jesus referred to, was very specific.

> "15 So when you see standing in the holy place 'the abomination that causes desolation,' spoken of through the prophet Daniel—let the reader understand— 16 then let those who are in Judea flee to the mountains. 17 Let no one on the housetop go down to take anything out of the house. 18 Let no one in the field go back to get their cloak. 19 How dreadful it will be in those days for pregnant women and nursing mothers! 20 Pray that your flight will not take place in winter or on the Sabbath. 21 For then there will be great distress, unequaled from the beginning of the world until now—and never to be equaled again." (Matt 24:15–21, NIV)

Jesus refers to this episode in Daniel as an actual event that is going to happen. He is not referring to it as an allegory of repeated events that happen in every generation of believers. Instead, he warns his Disciples to flee Judea when they see it happen. Moreover, he says it is a single event, unequaled from the beginning of the world, and never to be equaled again (Matt 24:21). It is a singularity, an event which happens only one time according to Jesus. Jesus views the prophecies of Daniel as literal events that will take place. And we have as an anchor in time this specific event, for it is unequaled by anything before or forever after.

> Jesus refers to this episode in Daniel as an actual event that is going to happen.
> It is a singularity, an event which happens only one time according to Jesus.

Jesus also warns that at the time of this event there will be false prophets and false messiahs.

> "23 At that time if anyone says to you, 'Look, here is the Messiah!' or, 'There he is!' do not believe it. 24 For false messiahs and false prophets will appear and perform great signs and wonders to deceive, if possible, even the elect. 25 See, I have told you ahead of time." (Matt 24:23–25, NIV)

And then Jesus tells his Disciples what happens next, quoting from the prophecies of Isaiah (Isa 13:10, 34:4) and Daniel (Dan 7:13).

> "29 Immediately after the distress of those days 'the sun will be darkened, and the moon will not give its light; the stars will fall from the sky, and the heavenly bodies will be shaken.' 30 Then will appear the sign of the Son of Man in heaven. And then all the peoples of the earth will mourn when they see the Son of Man coming on the clouds of heaven, with power and great glory. 31 And he will send his angels with a loud trumpet call, and they will gather his elect from the four winds, from one end of the heavens to the other." (Matt 24:29–31, NIV)

This is another singularity (single one-time event): the Second Coming of Our Lord. As you can see above, Jesus views the end time events as literal events that will take place, not a secret allegorical teaching about events that repeat in every generation. This is important for us to remember as we explore Revelation and listen to the variety of viewpoints that theologians offer us.

> Jesus views the end time events as literal events that will take place, not a secret allegorical teaching about repeated events in every generation.

Paul Teaches About the Second Coming

How did Paul view the Hebrew Bible prophecies? Did he, like Jesus, view them as actual events that would happen? Did he think that since the Jewish people rejected

Jesus then their prophecies were broken and would not be fulfilled? Did he think that there was a secret underlying spiritual meaning to the prophecies?

Paul sent letters to the early churches to encourage their faith, as well as to explain his views about the different topics they grappled with. It is believed that Paul's very first letter was sent to the church at Thessalonica about 20 years after Jesus' resurrection while Paul was living in Corinth (Acts 18:11,18). Paul wrote it in response to the good news from Timothy about their church (1 Thess 3:6, Acts 18:5). Timothy also had shared with Paul that some of his teachings had been misunderstood, so Paul set out to correct their views in these letters. In particular, the church at Thessalonica thought Jesus' return was imminent, so Paul set out to correct them.

> "1 Concerning the coming of our Lord Jesus Christ and our being gathered to him, we ask you, brothers and sisters, 2 not to become easily unsettled or alarmed by the teaching allegedly from us—whether by a prophecy or by word of mouth or by letter—asserting that the day of the Lord has already come. 3 Don't let anyone deceive you in any way, for that day will not come until the rebellion occurs and the man of lawlessness is revealed, the man doomed to destruction. 4 He will oppose and will exalt himself over everything that is called God or is worshiped, so that he sets himself up in God's temple, proclaiming himself to be God. 5 Don't you remember that when I was with you I used to tell you these things?" (2 Thess 2:1–5, NIV)

We see in this letter that Paul also refers to the coming of Christ as a singularity. It is a single one-time event that had not happened yet, as some other teachers were telling this church in Thessalonica. Paul also shares that the Second Coming will not happen until a "man of lawlessness" appears who sets himself up in the Temple to be worshiped as a god. Although Paul doesn't quote Daniel directly here, you can see the indirect reference. Also, Paul tells the church that it is at the Second Coming of Jesus that this man of lawlessness is overthrown. Paul is not talking about a person of the past as some Rabbinic interpretations of Daniel hold (Nebuchadnezzar, Darius, or Antiochus Epiphanes), because this "man of lawlessness" is overthrown by Jesus at his Second Coming, not his first nor in the past.

> "And then the lawless one will be revealed, whom the Lord Jesus will overthrow with the breath of his mouth and destroy by the splendor of his coming." (2 Thess 2:8, NIV)

> "35 Some of the wise will stumble, so that they may be refined, purified and made spotless until the time of the end, for it will still come at the appointed time. 36 The king will do as he pleases. He will exalt and magnify himself above every god and will say unheard-of things against the God of gods. He will be successful until the time of wrath is completed, for what has been determined must take place. 37 He will show no regard for the gods of his ancestors or for

the one desired by women, nor will he regard any god, but will exalt himself above them all." (Dan 11:35–37, NIV)

As shown in Paul's letters to the Thessalonians, he believed that Jesus would literally return. He believed the Second Coming would not happen until this man of lawlessness is revealed, whom Jesus will overthrow. Paul did not view these Hebrew prophecies as allegories with an alternative hidden secret meaning. Paul did not appreciate those who taught that Jesus had already returned, and the prophecies had already been fulfilled. Paul, like Jesus, viewed the Hebrew prophets literally as events still yet to come, not as secret allegorical teachings about events that repeat throughout history.

> Paul, like Jesus, viewed the Hebrew prophets literally as events still yet to come, not as secret allegorical teachings about events that repeat throughout history.

Peter Teaches About the Second Coming

In Peter's second letter to those who were exiled from Jerusalem (1 Pet 1:1) he writes to clear up their understanding of the scriptures. He specifically warns about false teachers who follow their own desires rather than what was spoken in the past by the holy prophets.

> "1 Dear friends, this is now my second letter to you. I have written both of them as reminders to stimulate you to wholesome thinking. 2 I want you to recall the words spoken in the past by the holy prophets and the command given by our Lord and Savior through your apostles. 3 Above all, you must understand that in the last days scoffers will come, scoffing and following their own evil desires. 4 They will say, "Where is this 'coming' he promised? Ever since our ancestors died, everything goes on as it has since the beginning of creation." (2 Pet 3:1–4, NIV)

Not only does Peter encourage the faithful to cling to what the prophets had spoken, he also speaks directly of a singularity: the Second Coming of Jesus. Peter, like both Paul and Jesus, viewed the Hebrew prophets literally, not as secret allegorical teachings that repeat in the hearts of every believer in every generation throughout history.

> Peter, like both Paul and Jesus, viewed the Hebrew prophets literally, not as secret allegorical teachings that repeat in the hearts of every believer in every generation throughout history.

Like Paul, he describes the Second Coming as a single future event, not an allegory like the advent of Jesus in the hearts of all believers in every generation.

> "But the day of the Lord will come like a thief. The heavens will disappear with a roar; the elements will be destroyed by fire, and the earth and everything done in it will be laid bare." (2 Pet 3:10, NIV)

Peter says that not only should the faithful cling to what the prophets of old have said, but the false teachers to come would even go so far as to deny Christ himself.

> "1 But there were also false prophets among the people, just as there will be false teachers among you. They will secretly introduce destructive heresies, even denying the sovereign Lord who bought them—bringing swift destruction on themselves. 2 Many will follow their depraved conduct and will bring the way of truth into disrepute. 3 In their greed these teachers will exploit you with fabricated stories. Their condemnation has long been hanging over them, and their destruction has not been sleeping." (2 Pet 2:1–3, NIV)

We can see that Peter, like Jesus and like Paul, took the Hebrew prophecies seriously. Peter looked at them as things to be literally fulfilled in the future. And he warned of false prophets and false teachers that ultimately would even deny Christ.

The Angels Teach About the Second Coming

Even the angels testified to a literal Second Coming of Christ on the clouds in glory, just as Daniel spoke about (Dan 7:13). After Jesus rose from the dead, he appeared among his Disciples and taught them more about the Kingdom of God. And at the last they gathered around him as he ascended into heaven.

> "6 Then they gathered around him and asked him, "Lord, are you at this time going to restore the kingdom to Israel?" 7 He said to them: "It is not for you to know the times or dates the Father has set by his own authority. 8 But you will receive power when the Holy Spirit comes on you; and you will be my witnesses in Jerusalem, and in all Judea and Samaria, and to the ends of the earth." 9 After he said this, he was taken up before their very eyes, and a cloud hid him from their sight. 10 They were looking intently up into the sky as he was going, when suddenly two men dressed in white stood beside them. 11 "Men of Galilee," they said, "why do you stand here looking into the sky? This same Jesus, who has been taken from you into heaven, will come back in the same way you have seen him go into heaven." (Acts 1:6–11, NIV)

> "13 In my vision at night I looked, and there before me was one like a son of man, coming with the clouds of heaven. He approached the Ancient of Days and was led into his presence. 14 He was given authority, glory and sovereign power; all nations and peoples of every language worshiped him. His dominion is an everlasting dominion that will not pass away, and his kingdom is one that will never be destroyed." (Dan 7:13–14, NIV)

As Jesus is literally taken up into Heaven in a cloud two angels appear and tell the disciples that Jesus will return in the same way. The angels do not say Jesus will return in an allegorical way, rising up spiritually in the hearts of new believers in every generation, influencing world leaders through the philosophies and values of Christianity, nor in working through governments throughout history to bring about a fairer and more just world. No, the return of Christ is a literal single event. A singularity that will occur in the future.

> Like Jesus, Paul, and Peter, the angels speak of specific literal events to take place in the future, not of secret allegorical teachings about an inner experience in new believers, nor in events that repeat throughout history.

Like Jesus, Paul, and Peter, the angels speak of specific literal events to take place in the future, not of secret allegorical teachings about an inner experience in new believers, nor in events that repeat throughout history. The Apostle's Creed bears witness to this, for "We believe that Jesus will return to judge the living and the dead" and "We believe in the resurrection of the body and in the life everlasting." The Bible, and even early church tradition, views the Hebrew Bible prophecies as describing literal events of the future, not as already fulfilled events of the past, and not as allegories of secret hidden spiritual meanings for all believers in all generations throughout history.

WHY ARE THERE DIFFERENT TRADITIONAL VIEWS?

Remember our two fundamental questions that divide the Christian denominations today:

1) Do we take these passages allegorically or literally?

2) Are these events of the past or future, both (repeated events), or never?

The primary mode of interpretation (allegorical or literal) has examples throughout the Bible as well as church traditions that support each. But in fact, it is more complicated than just allegorical versus literal. Historically there are actually four different types of biblical interpretation, and we can see each of these being used in the New Testament. The four traditional views (interpretative modes) of scripture that originated in Judaism and continue in Christianity are:

1. the literal and plain "simple" (*peshat*, פְּשָׁט) meaning,

2. the allegorical and hidden meaning just beyond the literal that "hints" (*remez*, רֶמֶז) at another truth,

3. the comparative meaning found by comparing the passage to other similar passages and "expounding" (*drash*, דְּרָשׁ) on arcs and absolute principles found throughout scripture, and

4. the "mystical" (*sod*, סוֹד) meaning which is completely different and given through a vision or revelation by God or an angel.

The author of the book of Hebrews quotes from the Hebrew prophecies in chapter 1 to demonstrate that Jesus is the Messiah and is the Son of God. These references, primarily to the book of Psalms, use all four of these interpretive modes. We also see Jesus teaching in Parables in the Gospels, which are not understood as literal events. For example, the story of the Good Samaritan teaches us about morality but is not understood as an actual story about an actual Samaritan that helped someone who was attacked. Likewise, the Parable of the Prodigal Son is not generally understood as a literal person either. The New Testament is not limited to only a literal interpretation of events, and there are plenty of examples where passages in the Hebrew Bible are not interpreted literally. The question before us is: among the four different interpretive modes, as used in the Bible itself, which one do we use for the book of Revelation?

> The question before us is: among the four different interpretive modes, as used in the Bible itself, which one do we use for the book of Revelation?

The timing of specific events is also a key interpretative consideration. There have been many who searched the history books for past fulfillment of prophecy and have found several examples that come really close. However, none seem to fit every single detail provided in scripture when it comes to end times prophecies like Daniel, Zechariah, Ezekiel, Joel, Isaiah, Zephaniah, or Revelation. This therefore leads to three possibilities: 1) the scriptures were visions and we shouldn't look for every detail to be answered, for now we see only as if looking through a dark glass, 2) the events were partially fulfilled in the past and will find their final fulfillment in the future in another similar event, or 3) past similar events are foreshadows of what is to come in a final future fulfillment. In other words: 1) prophecies about specific events are not going to be fulfilled literally and exactly, 2) some events will repeat, or 3) unfulfilled events do not repeat and await their future fulfillment.

John Wesley, co-founder of the Methodists, held an allegorical view of Revelation. He believed in a "mystical" (*sod*, סוֹד) interpretation of the book.[1] In this view the beast is a governmental system that exists throughout the generations until Christ's return. It represents all governments throughout history that oppose Christ. But literalists would ask Wesley: on whose authority do you create a meaning different from what the scriptures literally say? Who says your mystical interpretation is right, since scripture nowhere says exactly what you are saying, and some of the details of scripture cannot be explained in your view? If your mystical interpretation does not make sense of all the details in the text, you should question your interpretation, not ignore those details.

---

1. Wesley, *Explanatory Notes on Rev 13:1*.

Martin Luther, Protestant Reformer and founder of the Lutherans, held a literal view. In his 1546 preface to the book of Revelation he said the allegorical interpretation was a heresy brought in by an early Church Father named Origen (184–253 AD).[2] Origen mixed Greek philosophy (allegorical interpretation, known as Neo-Platonism) with the scriptures and corrupted the church teachings. Luther held that those who taught an allegorical view were heretics. Instead, Luther believed the scriptures would be fulfilled exactly as they were written. But allegorists would ask Luther: when has history ever fulfilled the details of all these prophecies? Revelation uses symbols to express ideas, not specific events. Only the less intelligent hold a literal view. You must be enlightened through reason.

You can see how this could get ugly between the denominations, and between people. It can lead to arrogance by the teachers of any particular interpretation. Allegorists can assert that their view is the enlightened and reasonable view, while putting down the baser literal view. They can claim that only wise people who understand the broad arcs found across scriptures can put together the true meaning. Only people of intense and broad study can come to the truth. Literalists are not smart enough to put everything together.

On the other hand, the literalists can also become just as arrogant, asserting that one must stick closely to the scriptures and any idea that doesn't match the details of every prophecy must be rejected. Any idea, no matter how smart sounding, and even if given by angels, should be rejected if it doesn't completely line up with scripture. The allegorists are caught up in their own imaginations. Disagreements over interpretation can lead to arrogance, accusations of heresy, and further division with the church.

> Disagreements over interpretation can lead to arrogance, accusations of heresy, and further division with the church.

The Sola Scriptura approach should be agreeable to everyone. It asserts that we should begin our study of Revelation by looking at only what the scriptures say. And then once we have done that work, we can assess the different interpretations that have been offered. We should notice that in the prophecies the prophets are frequently surprised, shocked, or confused. And then they are given explanations of what things mean. We should start right there, with the explanations already given in scripture. But we don't. Revelation is confusing and so we naturally turn to commentaries. Unfortunately, most commentaries have a bias they don't tell us about, let alone mention other possible interpretations.

> Revelation is confusing and so we naturally turn to commentaries. Unfortunately, most commentaries have a bias they don't tell us about, let alone mention other possible interpretations.

---

2. Luther, *Preface of 1546*, 1.

It is only when we read other commentaries, or one that explains multiple views, that we begin to understand all of this variety of interpretation. Instead, the Sola Scriptura approach sets the starting point with the scriptures, not a particular commentary. It should not dishonor our own tradition to want to begin with the scriptures. It should not be offensive to suggest we want to first form an understanding based on the scriptures alone. We always reserve the right to afterward compare our favorite commentaries to what we learn.

HOW OLD IS THIS ANCIENT CONTROVERSY?

Martin Luther, in his 1530 preface to the book of Revelation, states that Origen corrupted the interpretation of the scriptures with Greek philosophy and reason.[3] Origen, an early church theologian born in the second century, lived in Alexandria where Hellenism held sway over the culture. Hellenism was the cultural influence of Greek ideas from the time of Alexander the Great. The Hellenistic approach to interpretation was a Greek philosophical approach to searching for deeper spiritual truths underlying specific texts. This allegorical approach to understanding religious texts made it possible to explain how the apparent bad behavior of the Greek gods was meant to teach deeper spiritual truths. They were not to be taken literally but rather allegorically. This enlightened allegorical view of the Greek religious texts allowed Greek philosophers to claim a hidden spiritual meaning for texts that would have otherwise been embarrassing for enlightened people to hold. Greek gods that rape and murder seemed unappealing unless you understood those acts to be teaching deeper spiritual truths about life and not seen as literal things that happened. In other words, who wants to worship a god that raped someone? But if the rape never actually happened and it is only a story that makes a point about morality, then an enlightened person can be more comfortable believing in that god or goddess. Origen used Greek philosophical interpretation (allegory) to interpret the Bible. This changed the literal meaning of the texts into something that was more appealing to an "enlightened" mind.

> Origen used Greek philosophical interpretation (allegory) to interpret the Bible. This changed the literal meaning of the texts into something that was more appealing to an "enlightened" mind.

This philosophical approach has its roots in the teachings of Plato. He taught that everything we see in the world is just an imperfect version of an ideal "Form." If you know something about this spiritual Form, then you are "informed." If what we see is a damaged version of a perfect Form, then it is "deformed." If we try to put something deformed back into its proper shape it is "reformed." If we don't know quite what to think, or don't have the right information, then we are "uninformed." This approach to viewing ultimate reality permeates much of Western thinking to this day.

3. Luther, *Preface of 1530*, 1.

According to this philosophy, what we see and experience are allusions to a greater secret reality. For example, consider the great variety of dogs. How do you know they are all actually dogs and not cats? The Platonic answer is that there is an underlying and perfect Form of "dogness," what the truth of a dog is. We subconsciously know these Forms and so we recognize dogs we have never even seen before for what they truly are: a dog. The Forms are truth.

A famous analogy is that it is like we are sitting inside a cave unable to ever go outside. We see shadows on the wall of the cave made by objects passing by the entrance outside in the light. We only see the shadows, and not the reality of what those objects really are. We see their shadow on the wall inside the cave, but the shadow is not the truth. The truth is what is actually passing by outside the cave. Similarly, religious texts were not to be taken literally and the real truth is hidden beneath them. We must look with spiritual eyes to see the hidden truths.

Philo, a Jewish philosopher who lived from 20 BC to 50 AD (during the time of Jesus), was already at work applying this Greek philosophical approach to the Torah (Genesis through Deuteronomy). He lived in Alexandria and was one of the first to combine Jewish study of the scriptures with Greek philosophy. He leveraged both the Greek allegorical interpretive mode as well as Greek numerology which explained the significance of special numbers. Origen, who lived just after Philo (184–253 BC), followed in his path. He interpreted the Christian Bible in the same way. His prolific writing and influence on one of the early Christian schools in Alexandria made a tremendous impact on early Christianity. His teachings and speculations on the deeper spiritual meanings of texts beneath the literal meaning created great controversies, and he was eventually declared a heretic in 543 AD. Though Origen was eventually declared a heretic, his writings heavily influenced later important theologians down through the ages. Tyconius, who lived in the late 300s AD, wrote a book called the Seven Rules of Interpretation and then applied it to the book of Revelation thus producing a defense of the allegorical interpretation. These writings are quoted by Augustine (354–430 AD) in his defense of the allegorical view, "De Doctrina Christiana."

> Though Origen was eventually declared a heretic, his writings heavily influenced later important theologians down through the ages.

Opposed to this allegorical approach taken in Alexandria was the rival school in Antioch. This opposing Christian school of thought was at the church where Barnabus and Saul taught (Acts 11:25–26). This was the place where Christians were first called Christians. The school in Antioch opposed the allegorical approach being taught in Alexandria. Instead, they held to a literal interpretation of the scriptures and claimed teachings directly from Peter and Paul. Other Church Fathers such as Ignatius of Antioch (who died around 108 AD) and Polycarp (69–155 AD), who were both disciples of the Apostle John were from Antioch. Irenaeus (130–202 AD), a disciple of Polycarp, also taught a literal view. He is most famous for his work called

"Against Heresies" in which he lays out the literal view of Revelation as well as speaks against the heresies swirling around early Christianity. Before the allegorical approach was applied in Christianity, early Christian leaders who were students of the Apostles taught a literal view and fought against numerous heresies.

> Before the allegorical approach was applied in Christianity, early Christian leaders who were students of the Apostles taught a literal view and fought against numerous heresies.

The point in reviewing this history of interpretation is not to make either sound ridiculous, or either sound more legitimate. The point is that this controversy between allegorical or literal interpretation goes all the way back to the disciples of the Apostles. Each tradition claims direct descent from the Apostles themselves. Each tradition has Church Fathers that can be pointed to for their appeals to authority, such as Origen and Augustine, versus Ignatius, Polycarp, and Irenaeus. It is not true that Christians have throughout history held a single view, or that one view is the most commonly held throughout church history. In fact, throughout history Christians have argued about Revelation. So how are modern people to decide which approach is right, given the controversy goes all the way back to the start of Christianity? We should begin with the scriptures themselves and set aside both approaches for the moment. We should look to only what the scriptures explain and put speculation and tradition on the side. We should begin with a Sola Scriptura approach.

> Throughout history Christians have argued about Revelation. So how are modern people to decide which approach is right, given the controversy goes all the way back to the start of Christianity? We should begin with the scriptures themselves and set aside both approaches for the moment.

A BRIEF REVIEW OF MAJOR CHRISTIAN VIEWPOINTS

Applying our two basic questions about interpretation, let's briefly review the various viewpoints of Revelation which have unfolded over time. Note that as there are thousands of Christians denominations, and within the same denomination there are often multiple views of Revelation, there can be no comprehensive guide to all the views. However, by considering the possible answers to our two basic questions we can arrive at the prevalent mainstream views held today. This book will not get into the esoteric views held by cults, of which there are numerous.

Recall our two fundamental questions that sadly divide the Christian denominations today:

1. Do we take these passages allegorically or literally? (mode of interpretation)
2. Are these events of the past or future, both, or none? (timing of specific events)

The first question creates a nice division between those who interpret scriptures in the plain sense versus those who hold an alternative meaning that is not directly written in the text but revealed as the underlying hidden meaning (allegorical).

The Amillennial View

The allegorical view holds that the events described in Revelation are not literal events. The symbols within the book such as the one-thousand year period, the beast, the dragon, the woman, the harlot, the 144,000, the 24 Elders, the Four Horsemen, Babylon, etc. all represent something. They all represent an underlying spiritual truth. The explanations of what these underlying spiritual truths are vary greatly, but all generally fall into what is known as the Amillennial view. This moniker is taken from Revelation chapter 20 which speaks of a one-thousand-year period, typically referred to as the Millennium.

When the letter "a" is placed in front of a word it changes its meaning to its opposite, like "atypical" is the opposite of "typical" or "asymmetric" is the opposite of "symmetric." Thus, Amillennial is the opposite of Millennial, and is the belief that Revelation 20 is not speaking of a literal one-thousand-year period, but instead is symbolic of some other time period. Theologians provide several different explanations of what time period it refers to, sometimes using numerology in their explanations of the number one thousand. Although you have to read through nineteen chapters of Revelation (most of the book) before ever seeing the one thousand years mentioned, this is a good name to summarize how the various symbols are given alternative meanings to the plain sense of the text.

> Amillennial is the opposite of Millennial, and is the belief that Revelation 20 is not speaking of a literal one-thousand-year period, but instead is symbolic of some other time period. Theologians provide several different explanations of what time period it refers to, sometimes using numerology in their explanations of the number one thousand.

The view holds that "one thousand years" does not mean "one thousand years." Explanations include: one thousand means the "Christian Era" since the birth of Christ, or the time from the Ascension of Christ until the end of time, or the time from the Day of Pentecost until the Second Coming, or time everlasting without end. But it in no way means literally one thousand years. Besides, a thousand years for us is to the Lord as a day, so we could be in for quite a long wait. Using the Jewish lunar calendar John would have been using when Revelation was written, one thousand years of three hundred and sixty days, where each day represents a year would be interpreted to mean $1{,}000 \times 360 = 360{,}000$ years (excluding the slight difference for the leap months used in the Jewish calendar).

When reading Amillennial commentaries you can recognize both the Greek philosophical approach as well as numerology in use. This mode of interpretation also shows up in explanations of the corresponding prophecies in the Hebrew Bible, as you will see when we explore those below.

Amillennialism is typically found in Reformed Presbyterian, Anglican, Episcopalian, Roman Catholic, and some Methodist churches. Again, note that viewpoints can vary widely within the same denomination and not all members hold the same view. In the Jewish world, an allegorical approach to end times prophecies is typically found in the more liberal Reformed Judaism Movement. Famous Christian proponents include Origen, Tyconius, Augustine, John Calvin, and R.C. Sproul.

The Millennial Views

Opposed to the idea of one thousand years meaning anything other than one thousand years, because the Bible never says that, are the various literal interpretations of Millennialism. Our second big question now comes into view, asking when the specific events described in the book of Revelation will (or did) occur. For the literal views we can divide the answers to our second question into three major groups. Specific events occurred 1) in the past, 2) in the future, or 3) both the past and the future.

Preterism is a view that the specific events described in Revelation are literal events that have all happened in the past. The general assertion is that John was writing in a cryptic format to hide the truth of what he was saying for fear of Roman government suppression or retribution. This view holds that the tribulations and destructions described in Revelation all refer to the Roman destruction of Jerusalem in 70 AD. You are most likely to find Preterism taught by some Roman Catholic Jesuits.

While Preterism holds that the events described in Revelation all occurred in the past, different Dispensational views place them in the future. Classical Dispensationalism, the early version of this view also known as Futurism, holds that the specific events in Revelation are literal events that will happen in the future. The Antichrist has not yet come, and when he does, he will lead a worldwide government to attack the nation of Israel right before the Second Coming of Christ. This view was made even more popular when the nation of Israel was formed once again after nearly 2,000 years of extinction. Before 1948 when there was no Israel, since the time of Roman dispersion of the Jewish people around the first century, it was almost laughable to think that an Antichrist would come to attack a nation that did not even exist. Some theologians even held that God divorced the Jewish people for rejecting Jesus, and so Israel had no future destiny. But when Israel was born again in 1948 people stopped laughing. At a minimum, their existence today causes theologians to wonder. You are most likely to find Dispensationalism taught at the Moody Bible Institute and the Dallas Theological Seminary.

Progressive Dispensationalism, a theology that built on and modified Classical Dispensationalism, holds that the events in Revelation are literal events as well. But instead of placing them only in the future, it teaches an "Already and Not Yet" view that says some events already happened in the past and they will repeat again in the future. For the Bible does say there will be many false prophets, many false messiahs, and many antichrists. Progressive Dispensationalism might best be described as a mix of Preterism, Futurism, and Amillennialism. This view mostly arose from further theological development at the Dallas Theological Seminary in the 1980's.

> While Preterism holds that the events described in Revelation all occurred in the past, different Dispensational views place them in the future.

Millennial viewpoints are typically held in Evangelical, Baptist, Pentecostal, some Lutheran, and some Methodist churches. Again, note that viewpoints can vary widely within the same denomination and even in the same church congregations. In the Jewish world a literal approach to end times prophecies is typically found in the more conservative Orthodox Movement. Famous Christian proponents include Ignatius of Antioch, Irenaeus, Martin Luther, John Wesley, John Nelson Darby, C.I. Scofield, Charles Spurgeon, and David Guzik.

Pre, Mid, and Post-Tribulation with Millennialism

The question of a literal one-thousand-year period begs the question of when Jesus will return. Those who hold that he will return at the end of the one-thousand-year period are called Post-Millennialists. This view generally best aligns with the Amillennial view that the one thousand years is not to be taken literally. But instead of denying that there is a literal Millennium, the Post-Millennial view holds that the one thousand years of Rev 20 represents the Christian Era, and when Christ returns it will be the end of the Christian Era. Hence the moniker "Post"-Millennialism, or "after" the Millennium is over. While Post-Millennialism holds that Christ will return after a literal Millennium, Pre-Millennialism holds that Christ will return before it.

> While Post-Millennialism holds that Christ will return after a literal Millennium, Pre-Millennialism holds that Christ will return before it.

The view that the one thousand years is a literal one thousand years and Christ will reign during this time period teaches that Christ returns "before" the one thousand years begin. This is a "Pre"-Millennial view. Within the Pre-Millennial views is another subset of beliefs regarding the timing of the return of Jesus before the literal one thousand years begin. Essentially, does Christ return before, during, or after the period of tribulation leading up to the one-thousand-year Messianic Era known as the Millennium?

In answering this question, one typically learns about the concept of the Rapture, which is when Christians are taken up into Heaven. This is not normally taught from Revelation, but rather from Paul's first letter to the Thessalonians (1 Thess 4:17). Paul says Christians will be caught up into Heaven to be with Christ forever. The Greek word Paul uses for "caught up" is *harpazo* (ἁρπάζω), which was translated by Jerome into the Latin Vulgate as *rapiemur*, from which we get the English word "rapture." Paul's letters to the Thessalonians are combined with observations about the book of Revelation to teach the concept of the rapture.

These teachings can be divided around the question of "when does Christ return to rapture his church"? There are typically three answers given. The answers to when Christ returns to rapture his church are given with respect to what part of the book of Revelation this happens in. Views that teach the rapture occurs before any tribulations begin are called Pre-Tribulation Pre-Millennialism. Some other views teach that he returns to rapture the church in the middle of the tribulations (known as Mid-Tribulation Pre-Millennialism), or that he returns at the end (known as Post-Tribulation Pre-Millennialism). Teachings about the rapture are commonly Pre-Millennial and derive mostly from Paul's letters and not the book of Revelation. It is not clearly stated in Revelation when such an event would occur, which leads to three different interpretations: Christ returns either before, during, or after the tribulation.

> Teachings about the rapture are commonly Pre-Millennial and derive mostly from Paul's letters and not the book of Revelation. It is not clearly stated in Revelation when such an event would occur, which leads to three different interpretations: Christ returns either before, during, or after the tribulation.

Summary of the Major Christian Viewpoints

Remembering all these different viewpoints can be confusing. But recall that all these views spring out of two basic questions (mode of interpretation, and timing of events). The different views can be said to be organized around these two key questions as follows:

1. Do we take these passages allegorically or literally? (mode of interpretation)
   - Amillennialism vs. Millennialism

2. Are these events of the past or future, both or none? (timing of specific events)
   - Preterism vs. Futurism (timing of all the events)
   - Classical vs. Progressive Dispensationalism (timing of some of the events)
   - Pre-Millennialism vs. Post-Millennialism (timing of Christ's Second Coming)
   - Pre, Mid, or Post-Tribulation Pre-Millennialism (timing of the Rapture)

Note again that these are only the mainstream views. There are many more, and some esoteric views have led not only to church splits but offshoot cults. There is also a rich history of allegorical versus literal interpretation found in Judaism (Orthodox, Conservative, and Reform movements), so Christians are not alone in how they argue about prophecy. And there are famous theologians from both the early church as well as in the modern church that argue against the opposing views.

Are you confused by all the different viewpoints? You are not alone. Proponents of each view will typically argue that it goes all the way back to the Apostles. Each side will argue they are the original view, and the others are corruptions. Each side will try to convince you that what they teach is the most original, or most authentic, or most widely believed, or most common, or most enlightened and rational viewpoint. Teachers who claim that their view is the oldest, most commonly held, or most reasonable are making claims from tradition and not from actual verses in the Bible. Those are unscriptural claims by definition.

But the Sola Scriptura approach asks you to put all these views aside. Begin with just what the scriptures actually say. That should be the starting point for all views. And the moment an explanation for something is given that is not immediately backed up with a direct Bible verse, we have to set that aside until another day. And once we have fully studied the entire book of Revelation as well as all relevant Old and New Testament passages, done fully in the context of the original book in which it is found, only then can we say we are ready to begin our consideration of the different church traditions. Until then we must cling only to the scriptures.

> Teachers who claim that their view is the oldest, most commonly held, or most reasonable are making claims from tradition and not from actual verses in the Bible. Those are unscriptural claims by definition.

A BRIEF REVIEW OF MAJOR JEWISH VIEWPOINTS

Many Different Movements Within Judaism

One of the most important keys to understanding scripture is to first understand the context. Who wrote the text, to whom, and why? Otherwise, we run the risk of taking words out of context and applying them inappropriately in a way they were never intended. One does not have to look far to see how many different denominations and church splits there have been over conflicting interpretations of scripture. You may be surprised to know that Judaism also has a wide range of interpretations of the scriptures. There is not a single Jewish viewpoint, just like there is not a single Christian viewpoint, just like there is not a single viewpoint in any group of human beings.

There is not a single Jewish viewpoint, just like there is not a single Christian viewpoint, just like there is not a single viewpoint in any group of human beings.

For example, in America there are large different movements within Judaism such as Orthodox, Conservative, Reform, and Reconstructionist. While in Israel there are the Haredi, Zionist, Masortim (traditional), and Hiloni (secular) groups.[4] From the outside you can observe a wide range of appearances in dress, hairstyles (including facial hair), as well as in adherence to wearing special religious items such as kippahs (yarmulkes) or tzitzit (fringes) with or without tallits (prayer shawls).

Just as there is a wide variety of appearance, there is also a wide variety of interpretation of scriptures. If you listen to a Rabbi from an American Reform Congregation you are likely to hear different opinions about the Messiah than if you listen to an Orthodox, Conservative, or Lubavitch Chasidic (Haredi) Rabbi. You will also likely hear different opinions about the modern Israeli government, the Temple Mount, the desire to build another Temple (and if it is the legitimate Second or Third Temple), and even if animal sacrifices should be restarted if another Temple is built on the Temple Mount. This is just like in Christianity where you will hear different interpretations of the meaning of the scriptures if you listen to Baptist, Roman Catholic, Pentecostal, Methodist, Lutheran, Presbyterian, Unitarian, etc. preachers.

Different Views of Atonement and a Future Temple

One major point of disagreement among both Jewish movements as well as Christian denominations concerns the potential rebuilding of a temple on the Temple Mount where the Al-Aqsa Mosque and the Dome of the Rock stand today. With no Jewish Temple on the Temple Mount today, there is no way to offer sacrifices and thus fulfill many of the commandments in the Hebrew Bible. In other words, for religious Jewish people who want to do everything the Bible asks (in a literal sense), they are unable to offer a sacrifice of any kind in the Temple since there is no Temple. This issue is similar to the times when the Jewish People were in captivity in Babylon after the First Temple in Jerusalem was destroyed, and so could no longer offer sacrifices in the Temple. How did they receive atonement then? How do Jewish People receive atonement today without the ability to offer Temple sacrifices? This is one of the largest points of disagreement among the various Jewish movements today.

> How do Jewish People receive atonement today without the ability to offer Temple sacrifices? This is one of the largest points of disagreement among the various Jewish movements today.

---

4. Sahgal et al., *Israel's Religiously Divided Society*, 6.

Even though there are ways to receive atonement without performing sacrifices in the Temple (such as through prayer, charity, service, lovingkindness, and the study of the scriptures), as was done while they were in captivity in Babylon, it is not the ideal way for some Jewish believers. Orthodox Jewish People, for example, want to see a new modern Temple built and animal sacrifices to resume.[5] In the liturgy of an Orthodox service, you will find prayers for the restoration of Israel, rebuilding the Temple, and for sacrifices to once again be offered. There is a Yeshivah (school) in Jerusalem focused on the Order of Kodashim today, in which people are studying the laws of sacrifices to be prepared to offer them again when the Messiah comes.[6] They are looking to build a new Jerusalem Temple and to restart the sacrifices.

Reform Judaism (the largest Jewish movement in America) is on the opposite end of the spectrum and does not want to resume animal sacrifices nor do they typically focus on a return to the land of Israel. Their interpretation of the scriptures claims an evolution away from what they consider to be more primitive ideas, and the Messianic hope has become a universalist idea instead. In fact, they even removed the prayers for these things from their liturgy.[7] They are not looking for a new Jerusalem Temple. They are not looking to restart the animal sacrifices.

Conservative Judaism is in the middle of the spectrum between the Orthodox and the Reform movements when it comes to the interpretation of scripture. While not holding everything as literally as the Orthodox, they also do not adhere to the more liberal Reform theology. They retain the prayers in the liturgy for the restoration of the Temple, however they do not think that the animal sacrifices will be restarted.[8] They look to build a new Jerusalem Temple, but not to restart sacrifices.

Depending on which Jewish viewpoint you take (and there are more than the THREE major ones explored above), you will find a range of answers relating to how the Jewish People understand atonement today without a Temple in Jerusalem. These different expectations have a significant impact on their views of the future and how they interpret Apocalyptic Literature. These different eschatological views are also found expressed in the various Christian denominations, ranging from the most literal to the most allegorical.

Different Views on the Appearance of the Messiah

The Reform Judaism movement does not look for a literal Messiah to appear and instead sees an evolution of theology away from primitive animal sacrifices to a universalism where humankind itself judges what is right and wrong, and self corrects based on reason. All human beings are created in the image of God, and it is our role

---

5. Kogan, *Atonement Sacrifices*, 1.
6. Jacobs, *Jewish Religion*, Sacrifices, Kodashim.
7. Jacobs, *Jewish Religion*, Sacrifices, Liturgy.
8. Jacobs, *Jewish Religion*, Sacrifices, Liturgy.

to partner with God to improve the world. "The repairing of the world" (*Tikkun Olam*, תיקון עולם) is the chief aim of Reform Judaism, striving "to bring about a world of justice, wholeness, and compassion" just as foretold in the Hebrew Bible.[9]

Some Jewish movements look for the Messiah while others do not. For those who look for the appearance of the Messiah, for example Orthodox and Conservative Jewish People, the issues of the restoration of the land of Israel, rebuilding the Temple, and the appearance of a literal Messiah are cherished ideas. But what will bring about the appearance of the Messiah? Is it something that occurs because the world is so bad that he needs to appear to save us? Or does he come as a reward because we have done such a great job in making the world a better place? Does he appear to put in place the Messianic Kingdom of everlasting peace, or does he appear once humanity has done the work required to build the world up to that point? In other words, does the Messiah come to lead us in the work, or after the work has already been completed?

> Some Jewish movements look for the Messiah while others do not. But what will bring about the appearance of the Messiah?

The Hebrew Bible presents two very different views of the coming of the Messiah. In one view he comes lowly riding on a donkey (Zech 9:9), an embarrassing and humble entry. In another view he appears coming on the clouds in glory (Dan 7:13). Is this a contradiction in the Bible? Does he come lowly on a donkey, or in power on the clouds in glory?

For the Jewish movements that believe in a literal Messiah, they are awaiting his coming. While waiting they are performing good deeds, studying the Torah, and offering praise and prayer to God. Some strive to repair the world in any way they can, in the hopes that when the world is good enough then the Messiah will appear. And they believe the Messiah is already prepared to appear in any generation but is just waiting for the one which is good enough to merit his appearance.

Others believe the Messiah will appear and usher in an everlasting kingdom of peace. Instead of working to "cause" him to appear as above, they study and follow the Torah, help others, and offer prayers and praise to God because they seek to fulfill the Mitzvot (commands in the Torah). They don't try to bring about the appearance of the Messiah, but instead believe that perfection will only occur when the Messiah arrives.

The Orthodox Rabbis teach that how the Messiah arrives shows how well the people did in their efforts. If he comes appearing on the clouds in glory, then the people have done well. If he appears lowly and riding on a donkey, then the people did not do well. So the debate within Judaism over the literal appearance of the Messiah is both a debate over "if" there is a literal Messiah, as well as how the Messiah will appear. On the clouds in glory, or lowly riding on a donkey? As Christians we should reflect on what that means for the arrival of Jesus on Palm Sunday. A Messianic Rabbi who believes in a literal Messiah, Jesus, would see his arrival on the donkey as

---

9. Jacobs, "Reform Judaism", 1.

signaling that the people were not prepared for his arrival. We as human beings have failed to prepare the world for the Messiah, so he appeared in the midst of our failure to save us.

> "6 The disciples went and did as Jesus had instructed them. 7 They brought the donkey and the colt and placed their cloaks on them for Jesus to sit on. 8 A very large crowd spread their cloaks on the road, while others cut branches from the trees and spread them on the road. 9 The crowds that went ahead of him and those that followed shouted, 'Hosanna to the Son of David!' 'Blessed is he who comes in the name of the Lord!' 'Hosanna in the highest heaven!'" (Matt 21:6–9)

Different Views of a Messiah Who Dies

Within the Hebrew Bible there are passages that speak of a Messiah who dies, and passages that speak of a victorious Messiah. The idea of a Messiah who dies is not exclusive to Christianity and can also be found within Judaism. However, given the historical interfaith hostility around this topic it is something not often discussed. Within the Pogroms of Europe, the Crusades, the Inquisition, or the Holocaust, the Jewish people have been mistreated by Christians and the wider world. We must approach this particular topic with sensitivity given our past, however we also must approach this topic in truth because the witness of history bears out this truth. There are, in fact, passages in the Hebrew Bible that speak of a Messiah who dies.

The Talmud, one of the most important writings of the Jewish people and written after the time of Jesus, shows that the Sages (the religious leaders dating back to the time just after the crucifixion of Jesus, the destruction of the Second Temple, and the expulsion of the Jewish people from the land of Israel by the Romans) taught there were two Messiahs.[10] In other words, prevailing Jewish belief around the time of Christ held the belief in a Messiah who dies. The Jewish Sages recognized there were passages that referred to the death of a Messiah and commonly referred to that Messiah as "Messiah Ben Joseph" (*Mashiach Ben Yosef*, מָשִׁיחַ בֶּן יוֹסֵף). The name Ben Joseph, which means son of Joseph, recalls the famous son of Jacob who was rejected by his brothers and left for dead, but eventually was the one who saved them though they did not recognize him at first.

> Prevailing Jewish belief around the time of Christ held the belief in a Messiah who dies. The Jewish Sages recognized there were passages that referred to the death of a Messiah and commonly referred to that Messiah as "Messiah Ben Joseph" (*Mashiach Ben Yosef*, מָשִׁיחַ בֶּן יוֹסֵף).

---

10. Ashi and Ravina, *Babylonian Talmud*, Sukkah 52a:6.

The other Messiah, recognized in passages referring to the victorious son of David who is the king who rules the world from Zion with an iron scepter, is referred to as "Messiah Ben David" (*Mashiach Ben David*, מָשִׁיחַ בֶּן דָּוִד). A fascinating discussion between Messiah Ben David and God recorded in the Talmud suggests that Ben David asked only one thing from God. After Ben David saw that Ben Joseph was killed, he asks God for eternal life. And his request is granted.[11]

While the Sages held specific beliefs about a Messiah who dies before the time of Jesus, we can see that much later Jewish Theologians, such as Rashi (Rabbi Shlomo Yitzchaki), sharply disagreed with the sages after the time of Jesus. For example, in Rashi's commentary on Psalm 2, which had been earlier viewed by the Sages as a Messianic Psalm[12], Rashi says he clearly disagrees with the Sages that it is a Messianic reference.[13] Psalm 2 discusses the nations raging against the Messiah who is the Son of God.

We can see that the Talmudic Sages held an earlier view around the time of Jesus of a Messiah who would die. However, after the introduction of Christianity, later Jewish theologians disagreed with the Talmudic Sages, and the later Jewish view became the predominant one taught today. As a Christian, you are not likely to run across this earlier Jewish viewpoint unless you study the Talmud. So not only are there different Jewish viewpoints today about prophecies, but the prevailing view itself has changed over time.

> The Talmudic Sages held an earlier view around the time of Jesus of a Messiah who would die. However, after the introduction of Christianity, later Jewish theologians disagreed with the Talmudic Sages, and the later Jewish view became the predominant one taught today.

As Christians we see these two types of Messianic prophecies, one collection about a humble Messiah who appears riding on a donkey and is rejected and put to death for the sins of others, and the other collection about a victorious Messiah who appears on the clouds in glory and will rule the entire world, as a single person. Instead of two different Messiahs coming at different times, it is the same Messiah coming at two different times. A First and a Second Coming. First in humility to save us by offering his soul as a sacrifice for our sins because we have failed to keep God's laws, and Second to defeat all evil and establish an Eternal Messianic Kingdom where nations no longer learn of war and where God wipes away every tear.

---

11. Ashi and Ravina, *Babylonian Talmud*, Sukkah 52a:6.
12. Ashi and Ravina, *Babylonian Talmud*, Berakhot 7b.
13. Rashi, *Commentary of Tanach*, Psalm 2.

Other Jewish Messiahs

Jesus warned his Disciples that false messiahs and false prophets would appear (Mark 13:21–22, Matt 24:23–26). While most, but not all, Jewish people today do not accept Jesus as the Messiah, have there been other Jewish Messianic figures? Yes. In fact, numerous.

In the second century the prominent Talmudic scholar, Rabbi Akiva (who contributed much to the Mishna of the Talmud and was called the "Chief of the Sages") identified Simon Bar Kokhba as the Messiah. Bar Kokhba led a Jewish revolt against Rome around 132 AD. He was initially successful, but later killed by Rome.

In the fifth century a leader named Moses of Crete led a diaspora group back toward Israel. When reaching the Red (Reed) Sea, he told them to jump in and it would be miraculously parted. It was not, and many people died. Moses of Crete disappeared afterward.

Over the centuries numerous people have been identified as the Messiah. A recent example in modern times is Menachem Mendel Schneerson (1902–1994). The Chabad Judaism movement today believes Schneerson is the Messiah. Although he died without ushering in the Messianic Era, some believe he will rise from the dead and return for a second coming.

The Orthodox Jewish Millennial View

While there are a variety of Jewish movements with differing views about eschatology, an interesting viewpoint taught in Orthodox Judaism regards a one-thousand-year Messianic period. As you saw above in the Christian views, the understanding of the one-thousand-year period mentioned in Revelation chapter 20 varies so much that entire eschatology systems are named after them (Pre-Millennial, Post-Millennial, and Amillennial).

Orthodox Judaism teaches that Daniel is literally about specific kingdoms, not an allegory to all kingdoms which are opposed to God throughout history. One of the most famous Jewish Theologians (Rashi) names Babylon (Nebuchanezzar), Persia (Darius), Greece (Antiochus Epiphanes), and Rome (Titus) as specific kingdoms Daniel speaks of, in his commentary on Hebrew Bible. The Talmud clearly states that the fourth kingdom of Daniel is Rome (Avodah Zarah 2b:2, Shevuot 6b:13).[14] Rashi also teaches that the coming of the Messiah is a day in the future, and prior to those days there will be the war of Gog and Magog as prophesied by Ezekiel.

> Orthodox Judaism teaches that Daniel is literally about specific kingdoms, not an allegory to all kingdoms which are opposed to God throughout history.

---

14. Ashi and Ravina, *Babylonian Talmud*, Avodah Zarah 2b:2, Shevuot 6b:13.

One of the most famous Jewish theologians, Maimonides (known as the "RaMBaM"), teaches in his commentary on Genesis that the Messiah will have a literal one-thousand-year millennial reign.[15] According to Orthodox Jewish teaching, we are currently closing out the 6th Millennium, the one right before the 7th which will be the one-thousand-year millennial reign of the Messiah. But before you calculate the Rabbinic date of the coming of the 7th Millennium, the Messianic Age, remember that Jesus said, "But about that day or hour no one knows, not even the angels in heaven, nor the Son, but only the Father." (Matt 24:36).

Summary of the Major Jewish Viewpoints

As you can see above there are many different viewpoints within Judaism about how to interpret scripture. Just like in Christianity, we can see a range of views from the most literal to the most allegorical. These different views produce different understandings of the Messiah, the Messianic Age, a future Temple in the land of Israel, and the end of time as we know it. The prevalent view of interpreting prophecies around the time of Jesus, according to the Talmudic Sages, was a literal view. But those views changed after the crucifixion of Christ, after the destruction of the Second Temple, and after the dispersion of the Jewish people from the land of Israel. The prevalent view in modern Israel is different from that found in America, which are the two largest populations of Jewish people in the world today. There is no single Jewish view of prophecies about the end times, just like there is no single Christian view.

> There is no single Jewish view of prophecies about the end times, just like there is no single Christian view.

---

15. Rambam, *Commentary of Mishnah*, Gen 2:3.

3

Let There Be Light
Keeping Things in Context

"When I was young I was sure of everything; in a few years, having been mistaken a thousand times, I was not half so sure of most things as I was before; at present, I am hardly sure of anything but what God has revealed to me." —John Wesley

IN THE LAST CHAPTER we explored the great variety of viewpoints about prophecies of the end times. We examined the chaos of conflicting opinions across both Christianity and Judaism, and we looked at the fundamental ways in which the views are different from each other. Next, we will look at examples in the Bible where God tells us how he views the prophecies. We will see how the New Testament looks at many of these prophecies. And we will challenge ourselves to be consistent in how we interpret scripture, so as not to mix our method of interpretation based on the outcome that we personally desire.

To understand the context of the book of Revelation we will look at who wrote it, to whom, and why. Then in subsequent chapters we will turn our attention to the Hebrew prophecies that John and his audience were well aware of when Revelation was written down. We will build up our knowledge of what the people at the time of Christ were expecting, as well as how the New Testament views ancient prophecies about the Messiah and the end times. Altogether we will seek to understand Revelation within the context in which it was written, within the expectations of the original audience, and in line with the greater arcs of scriptures as demonstrated in the New Testament.

DANIEL'S VIEW OF PROPHECY

While studying prophecy, we see that Daniel pleaded with God in prayer and petition, in fasting, and in sackcloth and ashes (Dan 9:1-27). In that case he wanted to know what Jeremiah meant in his prophecy of the Babylonian Captivity only lasting for seventy years (Dan 9:2, Jer 25:11-12, 29:10). Three times in Jeremiah he says that the captivity will only last for seventy years.

> "11 And this whole land will become a desolate wasteland, and these nations will serve the king of Babylon for seventy years. 12 But when seventy years are complete, I will punish the king of Babylon and that nation, the land of the Chaldeans, for their guilt, declares the LORD, and I will make it an everlasting desolation." (Jer 25:11-12, NIV)

> "For this is what the LORD says: "When Babylon's seventy years are complete, I will attend to you and confirm My promise to restore you to this place." (Jer 29:10, NIV)

Daniel clearly wanted to know when the end of the seventy years would be. When would his people be set free to return to the land of Israel?

> "2 in the first year of his reign, I, Daniel, understood from the Scriptures, according to the word of the Lord given to Jeremiah the prophet, that the desolation of Jerusalem would last seventy years. 3 So I turned to the Lord God and pleaded with him in prayer and petition, in fasting, and in sackcloth and ashes." (Dan 9:2-3)

Daniel read Jeremiah's prophecies in a straightforward and plain way. Seventy years meant, well, seventy years. And that is how our Sola Scriptura approach will read scripture as well. But what if Daniel took a different approach?

An Amillennial view generally denies a literal interpretation of scripture and instead finds an allegorical and deeper spiritual meaning underneath the text. If Daniel took that approach, then he perhaps would have understood Jeremiah to be saying not a literal seventy years, but until such time as God was good and ready. Seven, representing godliness, and ten, representing perfection and completion, could imply that the seventy years were seven times ten, or the perfect completion of God's will. In other words, not literally seventy years but whenever God was good and ready to end the captivity in the fullness of his time.

A Preterist view generally takes a literal interpretation and seeks to find fulfillment in past historical events. A Dispensational view also usually takes a literal approach but finds fulfillment in either the past or the future (or perhaps both as in the case of Progressive Dispensationalism). If Daniel interpreted in either of these ways, then he would have understood a literal seventy years. Scholars disagree on the exact dates due to historical record differences, but the first deportation of the Judeans to Babylon occurred around 609-598 BC. Their return from captivity was marked by the decree of Cyrus to free the Jewish slaves, dated 538 BC. This is a range of 60–71 years, depending on which scholarly view you take.[1]

> Daniel interpreted Jeremiah literally and historical facts support that view.

So at least in the case of Daniel interpreting the prophecies of Jeremiah, we see both a theological and historical value to interpreting scripture first in the plain sense. And if the plain sense of the text is understandable and historical facts support it, why would we seek an alternative explanation? Indeed, it is possible that the allegorical approach is most appealing only when the historical facts do not seem to line up with scripture. In Daniel's case of the seventy years, it worked out well. Daniel interpreted Jeremiah literally and historical facts support that view. So how should we interpret the rest of Daniel? And how should we interpret other apocalyptic literature like Daniel? And last, how should we interpret the book of Revelation, especially when it references Daniel? Or Jesus when he too references Daniel?

EXPLORING ALLEGORICAL VERSUS LITERAL APPROACHES

Symbolism

One of the first challenges you run into when interpreting Revelation is if what the words say are literally true, or if they refer to a deeper spiritual meaning underneath the text (allegory).

We do find allegory used in many places in the Bible. Jesus taught in parables and there is a rich church tradition of interpreting Revelation as allegory. With all the strange symbols we see in Revelation, it naturally causes us to look for some underlying meaning. On the other hand, John is told directly what most of the symbols mean. Some examples are:

> "The mystery of the seven stars that you saw in my right hand and of the seven golden lampstands is this: The seven stars are the angels of the seven churches, and the seven lampstands are the seven churches." (Rev 1:20, NIV)

> "The beast who once was, and now is not, is an eighth king." (Rev 17:11a, NIV)

> "The ten horns you saw are ten kings who have not yet received a kingdom, but who for one hour will receive authority as kings along with the beast." (Rev 17:12, NIV)

> "The woman you saw is the great city that rules over the kings of the earth." (Rev 17:18, NIV)

---

1. Albertz and Becking, *Yahwism After Exile*.

Since John is told what the symbols mean, an allegorical interpretation to say they mean something else is giving a second interpretation. For example, most commonly an allegorical interpretation says the beast represents all antichristian governments and powers that are opposed to God throughout history. But that explanation is not what the Bible really says. And it is a different explanation than the one John is given. John is told the beast is a king. To say the beast is not a king is saying something different from the explanation in the Bible. If the Bible gives us an explanation for a symbol, we should not ignore that. An alternative explanation that is different from the Bible is unscriptural, but common in some interpretations.

> If the Bible gives us an explanation for a symbol, we should not ignore that. An alternative explanation that is different from the Bible is unscriptural, but common in some interpretations.

Sometimes an allegorical interpretation sounds right because it does make truthful claims. For example, Jesus will defeat evil, and we should not follow any antichristian governments or powers that are opposed to God. These things are true. Yet, the Bible says the beast is a king. This is the conflict we get into. It's an argument not about the truth of the principles being claimed (God will defeat evil, so don't follow evil rulers), but an argument about what the text is actually saying. Sola Scriptura does not argue against general principles which may be true. It only argues for what the text actually says.

> Sola Scriptura does not argue against general principles which may be true. It only argues for what the text actually says.

God's View of Prophecy Interpretation

Regarding our example of the beast above, does the Bible tell us if the Hebrew Prophets were predicting a specific king (the literal view), or instead referring to all antichristian governments throughout history (the allegorical view)? Hear what God tells Gog through the prophet Ezekiel.

> "17 This is what the Sovereign Lord says: You are the one I spoke of in former days by my servants the prophets of Israel. At that time they prophesied for years that I would bring you against them. 18 This is what will happen in that day: When Gog attacks the land of Israel, my hot anger will be aroused, declares the Sovereign Lord." (Ezek 38:17–18, NIV)

Notice that God is saying two things here: 1) he says he spoke through the earlier prophets, and 2) that he was speaking of a specific king (Gog). God does not say that the earlier prophets were told an allegory about a constant battle in your heart to choose to follow his Will instead of the antichristian governments, powers, and principalities throughout all history. While it is a true principle that we should follow God in our hearts and not antichristian leaders, that is not what this passage is saying. God tells Ezekiel that the earlier prophets were speaking of a specific king who would come, not a general principle about all bad world leaders throughout history. God's own words about the prophecies support a literal interpretation. And that interpretation is the same that John is given about the beast, the beast is a king (Rev 17:11) as shown above. Revelation also specifically mentions Gog.

> "7 When the thousand years are over, Satan will be released from his prison 8 and will go out to deceive the nations in the four corners of the earth—Gog and Magog—and to gather them for battle. In number they are like the sand on the seashore. 9 They marched across the breadth of the earth and surrounded the camp of God's people, the city he loves. But fire came down from heaven and devoured them." (Rev 20:7–8, NIV)

> God plainly tells Ezekiel that the earlier prophets were speaking of a specific king who would come, not a general principle about all bad world leaders throughout history.

Who are the earlier prophets that God says he spoke through? Since God tells Ezekiel they were speaking of Gog, the king to come, then who are these earlier prophets? None other than Daniel, Zephaniah, Isaiah, Jeremiah, Joel, and the Psalmists. Zechariah came after the time of Ezekiel but also spoke of a specific king, not an allegory of all antichristian powers throughout history.

We will explore these relevant prophecies later in this book in detail. For now, it's enough to know that the allegorical interpretation gives a different explanation than what John is told the symbols mean, and different from what God told Ezekiel they mean. God himself declares through Ezekiel that the prophets were speaking of a specific king and not an allegory about something in your own heart, and not allegorically about all bad rulers down through the ages.

Mixed Hermeneutics

Another dimension of this argument is the way in which sentences themselves are interpreted. Since the Bible does use allegory, we need to examine the scope of an allegory. In other words, how much of a passage is allegorical, and when does allegory stop?

An allegory is a story or brief prose that is meant to reveal a hidden meaning. For example, when Jesus teaches with parables, he is telling a story that has an underlying moral spiritual truth. The Parable of the Sower (Matt 13:3–9) is famous for telling a story about a farmer who went out to sow his seed. The kind of soil it was thrown on had different results. And Jesus explains the parable to be about a deeper spiritual meaning: the way in which you receive the Word gives different results. If you receive scripture correctly, then you will produce an abundant crop.

The scope of the allegory is limited to the story itself. When Jesus later explains what the symbols mean, that explanation itself is literal, not allegory. In other words, the allegory is limited to the story of the parable and not the later explanation. In the same way, when John sees visions and is later told what they mean, the explanations he is given are literal and not allegorical thus needing a re-explanation.

You would not switch between allegory and literal in the middle of a parable. It would not be the case that Jesus spoke allegorically of a farmer who was sowing seed, while the soil was literal. That makes no sense and is not how allegories work. Thus, the span of an allegory is limited to the story itself. All of an allegorical story is to be interpreted spiritually, not switching to literal half the way through. Switching mid-story is called using a "mixed hermeneutic."

> All of an allegorical story is to be interpreted spiritually, not switching to literal half the way through. Switching mid-story is called using a "mixed hermeneutic."

A mixture of allegorical and literal approaches within the same story is the wrong way to understand scripture. As the example above shows, all the different types of soil that the seed is thrown onto are to be taken allegorically. It would not be the case that the first types are allegorical, but the last type is literal soil. That just makes no sense.

You cannot switch your interpretive mode (hermeneutic) in the middle of a narrative, and certainly not in the middle of a sentence. If the first part of a sentence is literal, then the second part must also be literal. Here are some examples of beliefs that Christians hold to be literally true. These same literal beliefs are in the very same passages that allegorical interpreters will take part of the sentence to be allegorical instead of literal. But you cannot mix hermeneutics like that. You cannot interpret sentences as half literal and half allegorical. In other words, if it is allegorical, then it is not literally true. Read the passages below and ask if you believe they are literally true. If so, then the other part of those exact same passages must also be taken literally. An allegorical interpretation would suggest the following are allegorical and not literally true:

- Ps 2:7 The Messiah is the Son of God.
- Rev 19:16 Jesus is King of Kings and Lord of Lords.
- Dan 7:13, Rev 1:7, Matt 26:24, Acts 1:9 Jesus will return on the clouds.
- Zech 12:10 The Messiah was pierced (crucified).
- Psalm 2:6 God will install his King in Zion.
- Rev 19:15, Ps 2:9 Jesus will rule the nations.
- Joel 2:3 The Day of the Lord is unlike any other day, ever.

- Rev 19:20, 20:10 There is an eternal lake of fire with ongoing punishment (hell).
- Rev 20:9 Fire will come down from heaven as part of God's judgment.
- Zeph 3:8 The whole world will be consumed by God's anger.
- Rev 17:11 The beast is an eighth king.
- Rev 17:12 The ten horns are ten kings.

Consider this: in Daniel 7 we are told that the beast is a king that oppresses the people of God. And we are also told that the Messiah will appear on the clouds.

> "24 The ten horns are ten kings who will come from this kingdom. After them another king will arise, different from the earlier ones; he will subdue three kings. 25 He will speak against the Most High and oppress his holy people and try to change the set times and the laws. The holy people will be delivered into his hands for a time, times and half a time." (Dan 7:24-25, NIV)

> "13 In my vision at night I looked, and there before me was one like a son of man, coming with the clouds of heaven. He approached the Ancient of Days and was led into his presence. 14 He was given authority, glory and sovereign power; all nations and peoples of every language worshiped him. His dominion is an everlasting dominion that will not pass away, and his kingdom is one that will never be destroyed." (Dan 7:13-14, NIV)

In this passage Daniel is given an explanation of the symbols. As Christians we take literally that Jesus will return on the clouds of Heaven at his Second Coming. We take literally that he will rule all nations and peoples of every language will worship him. We take literally that his kingdom will be everlasting. So when we are also told the beast is a king, why would we believe that explanation is wrong and instead is allegorical of all antichristian governments and powers throughout history? In other words, Daniel tells us the Messiah will return on the clouds in glory and all nations and peoples will worship him. We take that literally. Yet in the very same passage Daniel tells us there is a king who will arise and oppress the Holy People of God. This king, this lawless one, referenced by Jesus, Paul, and Revelation is not explained as an actual man in the allegorical interpretation. The allegorical interpretation instead says he represents all kingdoms and governments opposed to Christ throughout history. Thus the allegorical interpretation takes part of the passage in Daniel as literal, and part as allegorical. The part which fits the allegorical theology of the victory of Christ is taken literally, yet the other part which doesn't align is re-explained allegorically.

The allegorical interpretation cannot say that Jesus will literally return on the clouds, but the beast is allegorically not a king. Not only is Daniel told directly that the beast is a king, but we are also told that Jesus will literally return on the clouds. Surely you have seen the pictures and stained-glass windows. You can't take one part of a passage and say it is literal and another part of the very same narrative and say it is not literal. That is a mixed hermeneutic and misinterpretation of scripture. Moreover, we should ask if the New Testament has anything to say about this matter. Indeed it does.

> "9 After he said this, he was taken up before their very eyes, and a cloud hid him from their sight. 10 They were looking intently up into the sky as he was going, when suddenly two men dressed in white stood beside them. 11 'Men of Galilee,' they said, 'why do you stand here looking into the sky? This same Jesus, who has been taken from you into heaven, will come back in the same way you have seen him go into heaven.'" (Acts 1:9–11, NIV)

A literal interpretation of these passages is consistent. John, Daniel, Ezekiel, and other prophets were told what symbols meant. And this understanding lines up with the rest of scripture: the Hebrew prophets, the Gospels, and the letters of the New Testament.

An allegorical interpretation must mix hermeneutics within the same passage, otherwise it would deny that Christ is the Son of God, deny that he will return on the clouds just like the angels told the men of Galilee, and deny he will have an everlasting kingdom. To be consistent, they would have to interpret those passages allegorically too. If Jesus is the Son of God is actually allegorical, what does that mean? If Jesus will not literally return on the clouds, then how (perhaps only in your hearts when you think of him)? And what did the angels mean when they spoke to the men of Galilee about his return? Recall again our earlier discussion on emotions. If you have been taught (or hold) the allegorical view, then you may be feeling anger at this moment. We should simply cling to what the Bible itself says, wherever that leads us.

> An allegorical interpretation must mix hermeneutics within the same passage, otherwise it would deny that Christ is the Son of God, deny that he will return on the clouds just like the angels told the men of Galilee, and deny he will have an everlasting kingdom.

Why Interpretation Matters

As you can see above, the way in which we interpret scripture matters. An allegorical view gives us an explanation of symbols that can be different from what the scriptures themselves say they mean. It says the Hebrew prophets were speaking of something that God himself said meant otherwise. And it must mix hermeneutics in the middle of a passage, otherwise it would deny that Jesus is the Son of God and will return on the clouds just like the angels told the men of Galilee.

As Christians who believe that Jesus is the Son of God, he will return just as he left on the day of his Ascension into Heaven, and the Bible is the inspired Word of God, then we must first look within the Bible for explanations before we look outside of scripture. That is the Sola Scriptura approach.

THREE WAYS TO FIND AN ANSWER

How does the Sola Scriptura approach find answers to our questions? By looking directly at the scriptures. If something is answered by scripture, then we depend on that answer. If something is not directly answered, then we do not venture a guess. For example, in Revelation 12 John has a vision of a woman, her child, and a dragon. We are told directly in Rev 12:9 that the dragon is Satan. We are told directly in Rev 12:5 that the child is the Messiah, by reference to a Messianic prophecy in Psalm 2:9. However, we are not told who the woman is.

> "The great dragon was hurled down—that ancient serpent called the devil, or Satan, who leads the whole world astray. He was hurled to the earth, and his angels with him." (Rev 12:9, NIV)

> "She gave birth to a son, a male child, who 'will rule all the nations with an iron scepter.' And her child was snatched up to God and to his throne." (Rev 12:5, NIV)

> "6 'I have installed my king on Zion, my holy mountain.' 7 I will proclaim the Lord's decree: He said to me, 'You are my son; today I have become your father. 8 Ask me, and I will make the nations your inheritance, the ends of the earth your possession. 9 You will break them with a rod of iron; you will dash them to pieces like pottery.'" (Ps 2:6–9, NIV)

The identity of the woman has caused a great deal of speculation and argument among the denominations. Some say the woman is the mother of the Messiah, so she is Mary. That view also is taken to support the Roman Catholic teaching on the Assumption of Mary's body taken into Heaven, because in Rev 12:6 the woman is taken to a place prepared for her by God away from the reach of Satan. Another view held is that the woman represents Israel, the Jewish nation that first gave birth to the Messiah. Rev 12:17 says that the dragon goes off to wage war against the rest of the offspring of the woman, meaning the Christians – who are the spiritual children grafted into the family of Abraham. A third view of the identity of the woman is that she represents Christianity. She is thought to be an opposite figure to that of the prostitute who shows up in later chapters. People with this view may say God previously divorced the Jewish people because they rejected the Messiah, and he instead marries the bride, which is the woman, which is the Christian church.

However, the Sola Scriptura approach does not take a position on the identity of the woman. We are never told who she is in the passage. And while there are several great possibilities as explained by the different denominations, it is not central to our understanding of the message of Revelation to know the identity of the woman. We are not told, so why should we add anything to the scriptures that is not there? And why should we engage in a discussion that would be divisive to the body of Christ? Especially on a topic that is not critical to anyone's salvation. If you believe the woman is Mary, or Israel (either Ethnic Israel or Spiritual Israel), or exclusively Christianity, it doesn't change the fact that Jesus died for your sins, and he is the Promised Messiah. Your view of the identity of the woman has no impact on your salvation. And there is no single verse in the Bible that will answer this question for you, unlike the identity of her child and the dragon. If the Bible does not explain something, the Sola Scriptura approach does not either. Why should we create an argument that causes division? Why should we argue about things that are not even necessary for salvation?

> If the Bible does not explain something, the Sola Scriptura approach does not either. Why should we create an argument that causes division? Why should we argue about things that are not even necessary for salvation?

To better understand scripture the Sola Scriptura approach looks only at 3 things:
1) Context

What do we know about the author of the book? What do we know about the original audience the author was writing to? And what do we know about the situation of those people at the time of the writing? With the Sola Scriptura approach, we will limit ourselves to only what the scriptures directly say on these matters. Because again, there are conflicting opinions held in different church traditions about all these things. Authors are debated, audiences are argued over, and purposes for writing are theorized. Instead, we look to only what is written in the scriptures.

2) Primary Support

We will look at passages in Revelation primarily. Starting with the specific passage we are questioning and expanding outward to the rest of Revelation, we will look at what things are repeated in multiple places. Instead of setting our belief on a single verse, we will look at multiple passages about the same idea or topic to ground ourselves in the meaning of the text.

3) Secondary Support

We will also look across the entire Bible, but again only the Bible and not conflicting church traditions and extra-biblical writings. Revelation has many parallels in the Hebrew Bible, as we will see. For example, Jesus quotes from Daniel while talking about the end times (Matt 24:15) so it is incumbent upon us to also understand the corresponding passages in those last two visions recorded in Daniel (Dan 9:27, 11:31, 12:11). They are part of the context of what Jesus is saying.

However, we will only look at what the passages say directly and not develop our own hypotheses about the arcs of scripture, the themes and ideas that span the Bible. For again we have many conflicting traditions about what those arcs actually are, and their meaning and implications for Revelation. As these biblical references are secondary support, then they must fit under and inform the primary references in Revelation. Not only should we not develop a hypothesis that means the opposite of what the scriptures say because of some arc we envision across the Bible, we also should not make a doctrine out of a secondary reference if that conflicts with the primary reference. In other words, not only do we place the scriptures above all traditions, but we place scriptures within the same book and passage above those found in other books.

> Our approach begins first with the actual book a passage is found in. We look for other passages of a similar topic in the same book. Secondarily we look across the rest of the Bible for related passages. We do not look outside the Bible.

Our approach begins first with the actual book a passage is found in. We look for other passages of a similar topic in the same book. Secondarily we look across the rest of the Bible for related passages. We do not look outside the Bible. For example, there are several places in the Bible that refer to the bride of the Lamb. But the explanation given of the bride is different in different places. This is an example where a symbol is used in different ways in different books. To say the given meaning of a symbol in one book is its meaning in another book would be to take that first meaning out of context. Take, for example, Paul's use of the symbol of a bride used in his letter to the church at Ephesus.

> "31 'For this reason a man will leave his father and mother and be united to his wife, and the two will become one flesh.' 32 This is a profound mystery—but I am talking about Christ and the church." (Eph 5:31–32, NIV)

In this example Paul is alluding to the church as being the bride of Christ. In Revelation John also uses the symbol of a bride.

> "1 Then I saw 'a new heaven and a new earth,' for the first heaven and the first earth had passed away, and there was no longer any sea. 2 I saw the Holy City, the new Jerusalem, coming down out of heaven from God, prepared as a bride beautifully dressed for her husband.
>
> 9 One of the seven angels who had the seven bowls full of the seven last plagues came and said to me, 'Come, I will show you the bride, the wife of the Lamb.' 10 And he carried me away in the Spirit to a mountain great and high, and showed me the Holy City, Jerusalem, coming down out of heaven from God." (Rev 21:1–2, 9–10, NIV)

In Rev 21 John says the bride is the New Jerusalem, the Holy City, which comes down from Heaven. To say that the bride referred to in Rev 21 is the church is to mix how a symbol is used in a different book (and different author) with how it is used in another. While a theological argument can be made about this, it is not what Revelation directly says. Nowhere does Revelation say the bride is the church. The Sola Scriptura approach looks only at what the scriptures directly say. Incidentally, some theologians not only say the bride John sees (Rev 21) is the church, but so is the mother of the Messiah from our earlier example (Rev 12). So the bride of Christ and the mother of Christ are both the church in that view. Neither Rev 12 nor 21 actually say that, and having your mother also be your wife is just plain confusing, as Oedipus tragically found out.

Here is where paying attention to the details really matters. God does not change. God is consistent. The Truth is the same now, as it was from the beginning, and as it will always be. If our theology does not line up with every detail of the scriptures then we should question our theology, not ignore the details. A simple question for the above verses would be: If the bride is the church, then how does the church come down from Heaven? And what does it mean further in the passage when Jesus says those who have the right to go into the city are blessed, if the city is the church?

> "Blessed are those who wash their robes, that they may have the right to the tree of life and may go through the gates into the city." (Rev 22:14, NIV)

Those who wash their robes are believers in Jesus. If the city (the bride) is the church, then how do the believers in Jesus (the church) have the right to go into the city (the church)? How do they have the right to go into themselves? That makes no sense at all.

Without disputing the theology of saying the bride is the church, you can see that it does not line up with how the symbol of the bride is plainly used in Revelation 21-22. So the Sola Scriptura approach will not claim the bride of Rev 21-22 is the church, but only admit that the bride is the New Jerusalem which comes down from Heaven, into which believers washed in the Blood of Jesus will have the right to enter. Because that is what the scriptures directly say. To bring in other references to the symbol of the bride of Christ from other books in the Bible and ignore the obvious conflicts in the details of what Revelation actually says is just confusing.

Other books in the Bible are used as secondary support for the understanding of Revelation, but what Revelation says itself is primary. When the secondary support conflicts with the primary, then the primary is what we hold to. Otherwise, we are doing what is called Eisegesis, a fancy word for bringing outside meaning into a text. In other words, adding something to a text which is not really there.

These are our three ways to find answers to what Revelation says: 1) We look at the context of who wrote the book, to whom, and why, as described directly in the scriptures (not according to later interpretations). 2) We look at the primary text itself, the book of Revelation. 3) And then we look across the entire Bible for principles and things that are absolutely true for all people in all times and in all places. But those principles and absolutes are secondary to what the primary text says. We bring in support from other books if they support a principle or absolute that is already defined in the primary text. We do not add things to the primary text if they are not already there, and especially not if it conflicts with what is there. We never ignore the details of the primary text.

> We do not add things to the primary text if they are not already there, and especially not if it conflicts with what is there. We never ignore the details of the primary text.

SOME ANSWERS ARE HIDDEN

Since not everything is explained in the primary text, as shown above in the example of the woman in Rev 12, the Sola Scriptura approach does not have an answer for every question. This might make some people uncomfortable. Some preachers, teachers, scholars, or Bible students might not want to appear to not have all the answers. That might make us look like we don't know the Bible very well, especially if another person claims to have an answer and shames us. It also might be embarrassing, and our pride might not let us admit we don't know. But we must ask: is it God's plan for us to actually know everything right now? No. That is not God's plan. John was even told not to write down some of what he saw.

> "And when the seven thunders spoke, I was about to write; but I heard a voice from heaven say, 'Seal up what the seven thunders have said and do not write it down.'" (Rev 10:4, NIV)

This is not new to Apocalyptic Literature. Daniel also saw things that were sealed.

> "But you, Daniel, roll up and seal the words of the scroll until the time of the end. Many will go here and there to increase knowledge." (Dan 12:4, NIV)

Even the prophets did not always understand what they were seeing. And that sometimes caused them great distress.

> "I, Daniel, was worn out. I lay exhausted for several days. Then I got up and went about the king's business. I was appalled by the vision; it was beyond understanding." (Dan 8:27, NIV)

So, all things have not been revealed yet. If we say we have all the answers, then we are claiming to know things that John did not write down. And we are claiming to know things that only God knows, as Jesus said to his Disciples on the Mount of Olives when teaching about the End Times:

> "But about that day or hour no one knows, not even the angels in heaven, nor the Son, but only the Father." (Matt 24:36, NIV)

We are not meant to know everything. Those who make claims but cannot back them up with scriptures that say exactly what they are claiming are stepping outside of what God has revealed. They are venturing into what has been sealed until the end. The Sola Scriptura approach does not do this. God has not revealed all things yet.

When Jesus returns, let us be found helping the poor and needy, rather than imagining we know the secret things of God.

> God has not revealed all things yet. When Jesus returns, let us be found helping the poor and needy, rather than imagining we know the secret things of God.

> "42 Therefore keep watch, because you do not know on what day your Lord will come. 43 But understand this: If the owner of the house had known at what time of night the thief was coming, he would have kept watch and would not have let his house be broken into. 44 So you also must be ready, because the Son of Man will come at an hour when you do not expect him. 45 Who then is the faithful and wise servant, whom the master has put in charge of the servants in his household to give them their food at the proper time? 46 It will be good for that servant whose master finds him doing so when he returns." (Matt 24:42–46, NIV)

CONTEXT OF THE PRIMARY SOURCE

Authorship

As we seek to better understand the book of Revelation, we begin with looking at who actually wrote it. The name of the author of the book of Revelation is John as given at Rev 1:1,4,9, and 22:8. However it is not known which John it was.[2] He says he is a prophet (Rev 1:3) and is living in exile (Rev 1:9). He also seems to have had authority and recognition enough to author a letter to the seven churches and had prominence enough that he was exiled by the authorities. The author's use of the Hebrew Bible suggests he may have been a Jew from Palestine rather than a native Greek speaker; however, he was an adept user of the Greek version of the Hebrew Bible.[3] Moreover, many themes used in Revelation also appear in the Gospel of John, therefore it is generally asserted the author was the Apostle John. Church tradition holds it was authored by the Apostle, and Irenaeus testifies to this under the authority of his teacher Polycarp who personally knew the Apostle John. Modern critics would at least assert the author came from a Johannine community, if not John himself.[4] The Sola Scriptura approach will hold only that it is written by a prophet named John who is living in exile, as is directly said by the text.

---

2. Wolvaardt, et.al., *Interpret the Bible*, 304.
3. Beale and Campbell, *Revelation Short Commentary*, Rev 1.
4. Thompson and Macchia, *Revelation Commentary*, Rev 1.

Audience and Purpose

To really understand the context of a letter we need to know not only who wrote it, but to whom they sent it and why. The purpose of this letter from John is to reveal the revelation of Jesus Christ to show his servants what must come to pass (Rev 1:1). The letter is addressed to the seven churches in the province of Asia (Rev 1:4). Early church fathers held that the time of writing was during the reign of Domitian (81–96 AD). Domitian set up an imperial cult to worship himself and persecuted those who did not obey. John directly addresses Christians who were being forced to participate in the emperor worship (Rev 2:9,13,14, and 13:15). However late twentieth-century scholars have shown that no Christian persecution occurred under Domitian.[5] An earlier persecution did occur under Nero, and some place the time of writing between the suicide of Nero in 68 AD and the fall of Jerusalem to Titus in 70 AD. The Sola Scriptura approach will hold only that the letter was a revelation of what was to come, sent by Jesus to the seven churches through the prophet John.

Type of Literature

The book of Revelation is in the genre of Apocalyptic literature (e.g., Revelation, Ezekiel, Daniel, Zechariah). The word "apocalyptic" comes from the Greek word for "revelation" (*apokalypsis*, Ἀποκάλυψις), meaning an unveiling, uncovering, or a revealing of something previously unknown. The book contains three different kinds of writing: apocalyptic, prophecy, and epistle. It also draws heavily on Hebrew Bible prophetic literature. Of the four hundred and four verses, two hundred and seventy-eight of them (roughly two-thirds) refer to the Hebrew Bible and there are over five hundred allusions to it.[6] The book uses several literary devices such as repeated words, phrases, and images, to tie multiple sections together into a single vision.[7]

The genre of Apocalyptic literature is characterized by an intensified focus on prophecies about the end times.[8] Literature of this type often begins with a vision of God sitting on his Throne in the Heavenly Temple (Rev 4:1–11, Ezek 1:1–28, 1 Ki 22:19) revealing to the author a vision of what must come to pass (Rev 1:1, Dan 11:35, 12:1–4,9). This relays the authority of the vision as coming directly from God, as well as highlights the importance of the message and its relationship to God's ultimate plan for the world (Rev 11:15–19, 14:14–20, 21:1–8, Dan 12:1–3). Apocalyptic literature may also be used to expose false teaching and ungodly behavior, reveal divine judgments for the unrepentant, and exhort believers to persevere in the face of

---

5. Wilson, *Revelation Commentary*, Rev 2.
6. Beale and Campbell, *Revelation Short Commentary*, Rev 1.
7. Thompson and Macchia, *Revelation Commentary*, Rev 1.
8. Beale and Campbell, *Revelation Short Commentary*, Rev 1.

persecution.[9] It is not a Gospel account, historical narrative, nor traditional Epistle, but a wholly different work describing what God has revealed to the author. It is imaginative and invites the readers to experience the feelings and emotions evoked by the symbols used therein.[10]

CONTEXT OF THE SECONDARY SOURCES

Secondary sources are other books in the Bible besides the book of Revelation. These are still scriptures and so are applicable to our Sola Scriptura approach. The nearness of passages in the primary source, the book of Revelation itself, gives us our first and immediate understanding. The other books in the Bible give us a larger perspective that God has revealed through many people over time. For example, Revelation has much to say about the coming Kingdom of God, the New Heaven and the New Earth, but so do the other prophets in the Bible. We will take all of these things into consideration and look at what the prophets had to say which form the background context into which the Revelation to John occurred. In other words, John and the people living at the time of Jesus had their Messianic expectations set by these other writings. We will look at them in detail to better understand the context of Revelation. When John sees the beasts, the war against God and his Messiah, or a New Jerusalem, he is seeing things already familiar because of earlier prophecies such as those found in Daniel, Zechariah, Ezekiel, Joel, and others. Before we delve into Revelation in detail, we need to know its background context.

Another way to look at it is this: at the time of the Revelation to John there had been many unfulfilled prophecies. John and others would naturally have wanted to know how those would be worked out. God's revelation to John provides answers to these questions.

---

9. Wilson, *Revelation Commentary*, Rev 1.
10. Reddish, *Revelation Commentary*, Rev 1.

4

Daniel
Parallel Dreams and Visions

"In certain ways they, the prophets, were greater than him, Daniel, and in certain ways he, Daniel, was greater than them. They were greater than him, as they were prophets and he was not a prophet."—Talmud Megillah 3a

CONTEXT OF THE BOOK OF DANIEL

WE READ IN THE New Testament that people were expecting the arrival of the Messiah at the time when Jesus came. We see that in the first few interactions of Jesus with his Disciples, as well as in the narratives about John the Baptist. The people knew it was the right time for the Messiah to appear. But where did they get that idea? From the scriptures, of course.

The book of Daniel is one such source of prophecies about the coming of the Messiah. It contains prophecies that Jesus himself quoted. And it also has symbols that we see being used in Revelation. It is important for us to understand Daniel's prophecies, as they provide some of the background context to understanding Revelation, in addition to demonstrating how Jesus was the long-awaited Messiah. Jesus and the Apostles quote Daniel, so we need to really understand it.

> Jesus and the Apostles quote Daniel, so we need to really understand it.

DANIEL

You may remember that ancient Israel wandered away from following God, and so God warned them through several prophets about their impending doom if they didn't return to him. They did not return and what the prophets declared came to pass. The kingdom of King David's son, Solomon, was split into two. The northern kingdom (then called Israel) was conquered by Assyria. And the other half of Solomon's kingdom, called Judah, was conquered by Babylon. The Judeans who were conquered were deported to Babylon and served as slaves to that kingdom led by Nebuchadnezzar.

It is in this experience, the captivity in Babylon, that we find the book of Daniel. Daniel lived in the time of Judah's fall to Babylon. He grew up in the beginning of the Babylonian Captivity. God's judgment on the nation of Israel, both the Northern Kingdom that went captive into Assyria, and the Southern Kingdom that went captive into Babylon, was taking place. Daniel's name means "God is my judge" (*daniyel*, דָּנִיֵּאל) which is truly appropriate for his nation and his life. For God had judged Israel and Judah, and his punishment was underway. As you might expect, a big question on every Judean's mind would have been: when are we going to get out of here? When will God be done judging us? When can we return to our homeland? God provided them answers through visions and dreams during the time of Daniel. And typical to God's answers, he not only answered their immediate questions, but he also provided a much longer view of God's ultimate plan for the world way beyond their own time. That is where we find some of the prophecies about the Messiah to come and the Messianic Kingdom to come at the end of the world as we know it.

> God had judged Israel and Judah, and his punishment was underway. As you might expect, a big question on every Judean's mind would have been: when are we going to get out of here? When will God be done judging us? When can we return to our homeland? God provided them answers through visions and dreams during the time of Daniel. And typical to God's answers, he not only answered their immediate questions, but he also provided a much longer view of God's ultimate plan for the world way beyond their own time.

The book of Daniel can be divided into roughly two parts: chapters 1–6 describe the major events in his life chronologically, and chapters 7–12 document a dream and three visions that Daniel had along the way. His dream of the four beasts and the Messiah in chapter 7 is fundamental to understanding the book of Revelation, as is the dream of Nebuchadnezzar in chapter 2 and the three visions Daniel had in chapters 8–12.

The vision in chapter 9 gives specific insight to the predicted destruction of Jerusalem and the predicted death of an Anointed One (generally seen as the death of a Messiah in both the Jewish Talmud and in the Christian New Testament). It also contains a famous "Seventy Weeks" prophecy that some theological interpretations of Revelation revolve around. The last vision in chapters 10–12 ends with the resurrection of the dead after the time of Israel's greatest distress. The Archangel Michael appears in order to protect Daniel's people at that time, and we also find him in Revelation chapter 12 when a great spiritual battle takes place in Heaven.

Daniel's life in the Babylonian captivity, his desire to be set free and return to the land of Israel, and the prophecies God gives him regarding all these things are key to understanding the book of Revelation. They provide the context in which Revelation is set. This is one of the places where people at the time of Jesus looked for prophecies about the coming of the Messiah. And it is one of the places that Jesus, the Disciples, and the book of Revelation looked at for prophecies about what was, what is, and what is to come.

While Christians love the book of Daniel, and Jesus himself referred to it directly, the modern Jewish viewpoint is surprisingly that Daniel was not a prophet.[1] His book does not appear alongside other "prophets" (*Nevi'im*, נְבִיאִים) in the Jewish Canon, but is relegated to a lesser status in a different collection in the Hebrew Bible called the "writings" (*Ketuvim*, כְּתוּבִים). Daniel is front and center in the New Testament but tucked away in the Jewish Canon. Daniel is front and center in some theological interpretations of Revelation but tucked away in others. It is crucial for us to understand just what he said, regardless of how we decide to view him (as a prophet or not, to be taken literally or not).

> Daniel is front and center in the New Testament but tucked away in the Jewish Canon. Daniel is front and center in some theological interpretations of Revelation but tucked away in others. It is crucial for us to understand just what he said, regardless of how we decide to view him (as a prophet or not, to be taken literally or not).

HAS DANIEL BEEN FULFILLED YET?

There is a lot of historical evidence that lines up nicely with Daniel's prophecies. However, there are two major events that Daniel speaks of that have not happened yet. The first is that Daniel speaks of the resurrection of the dead and the final judgment.

> "2 Multitudes who sleep in the dust of the earth will awake: some to everlasting life, others to shame and everlasting contempt. 3 Those who are wise will shine like the brightness of the heavens, and those who lead many to righteousness, like the stars for ever and ever." (Dan 12:2–3, NIV)

Clearly the multitudes who sleep in the dust of the earth have not awoken to everlasting life or shame. This time of judgment where the dead rise to either everlasting life for ever and ever, or to shame and everlasting contempt has not happened yet. As Christians we believe that Christ will return to judge the living and the dead. And

---

1. Shurpin, "Daniel and the Prophets," 1.

Christ has not returned yet. We await his Second Coming and the resurrection of the body to everlasting life.

The second reason Daniel has not been fulfilled yet is because God has not yet completely established his Eternal Messianic Kingdom which destroys all other kingdoms.

> "44 In the time of those kings, the God of heaven will set up a kingdom that will never be destroyed, nor will it be left to another people. It will crush all those kingdoms and bring them to an end, but it will itself endure forever. 45 This is the meaning of the vision of the rock cut out of a mountain, but not by human hands—a rock that broke the iron, the bronze, the clay, the silver and the gold to pieces. The great God has shown the king what will take place in the future. The dream is true and its interpretation is trustworthy." (Dan 2:44–45, NIV)

How do we know this hasn't happened yet? How do we know this isn't a reference to Christ reigning in Heaven today, with his Kingdom already established after his Crucifixion and Resurrection? Because he sits at the right hand of the Father while his enemies are being made a footstool (Ps 110:1, Matt 22:44, 26:64, Acts 2:34–35, 1 Cor 15:25, Heb 10:13). Jesus taught us to pray for the coming of the Kingdom, "Our Father who art in Heaven, hallowed be Thy Name, Thy Kingdom come, Thy Will be done on Earth as it is in Heaven." It is not here yet, at least not completely. And lastly, other kingdoms clearly exist today. All other kingdoms have not been destroyed yet. They have not come to an end like Daniel predicted. And many kingdoms on Earth today are clearly not trying to follow Christ.

> Because we have not had the resurrection of the dead, the final judgment to everlasting life or contempt, and because all kingdoms opposed to Christ have not yet been destroyed, we can say with certainty that Daniel has not been completely fulfilled yet.

Because we have not had the resurrection of the dead, the final judgment to everlasting life or contempt, and because all kingdoms opposed to Christ have not yet been destroyed, we can say with certainty that Daniel has not been completely fulfilled yet. Moreover, we see that references to Daniel in the New Testament are seen as a future (not past) fulfillment, which we will explore further below.

DANIEL IN THE NEW TESTAMENT

Having established above that Daniel has not yet been historically fulfilled (because we haven't had the resurrection of the dead, nor have all the non-Messianic kingdoms been defeated yet), we will next take a look at how Daniel was viewed in the New Testament. Did the people in the New Testament think that Daniel had been completely fulfilled? Did they think past historical events fulfilled Daniel, like those events described in the apocryphal books of the Maccabees found outside the Bible?

Jesus predicted that the Second Temple standing at his time would be destroyed. His Disciples asked him when that would happen and what would be the sign of his coming and the end of the age (Matt 24:3). In Jesus' reply to them while sitting on the Mount of Olives, he made a reference to a prophecy of Daniel as something that was coming in the future, not as something already past. This is key as some interpreters want to put the book of Daniel as having been completely fulfilled in the past before the time of Christ (specifically during the time of the Maccabees). Without getting into those details let us again take the Sola Scriptura approach. What do the scriptures actually say? What did Jesus say? Jesus clearly spoke of a future time, not a time in the past, when he was teaching on the Mount of Olives.

> "15 So when you see standing in the holy place 'the abomination that causes desolation,' spoken of through the prophet Daniel—let the reader understand— 16 then let those who are in Judea flee to the mountains." (Matt 24:15-16, NIV)

Jesus quoted Daniel. Jesus warned of something that was coming, not past. Is this a double fulfillment? Was Daniel fulfilled in the past as well as again at some future point, as some theologians might suggest? Look again at what Jesus actually said. "When you see [it] . . ." the thing spoken of by Daniel, "then . . . flee." Jesus did not say, when you see "again" what Daniel said. Jesus did not say, just like was fulfilled in the past and will be again in the future. No, Jesus said that when you see it happen then flee. He is clearly speaking of Daniel in a future and as yet unfilled sense.

We also see the book of Revelation making a clear reference to Daniel. In the opening of the book John points us directly to the vision in Daniel of the Messiah coming on the clouds. He also points us to a prophecy in Zechariah.

> ""Look, he is coming with the clouds," and "every eye will see him, even those who pierced him"; and all peoples on earth "will mourn because of him." So shall it be! Amen." (Rev 1:7, NIV)

> "13 "In my vision at night I looked, and there before me was one like a son of man, coming with the clouds of heaven. He approached the Ancient of Days and was led into his presence. 14 He was given authority, glory and sovereign power; all nations and peoples of every language worshiped him. His dominion is an everlasting dominion that will not pass away, and his kingdom is one that will never be destroyed." (Dan 7:13-14, NIV)

> "And I will pour out on the house of David and the inhabitants of Jerusalem a spirit of grace and supplication. They will look on me, the one they have pierced, and they will mourn for him as one mourns for an only child, and grieve bitterly for him as one grieves for a firstborn son." (Zech 12:10, NIV)

Revelation also references the Archangel Michael, which is again a clear reference to the book of Daniel.

> "Then war broke out in heaven. Michael and his angels fought against the dragon, and the dragon and his angels fought back." (Rev 12:7, NIV)

> "At that time Michael, the great prince who protects your people, will arise. There will be a time of distress such as has not happened from the beginning of nations until then. But at that time your people--everyone whose name is found written in the book--will be delivered." (Dan 12:1, NIV)

Lastly, the vision of the beasts in Revelation are also clear references to the imagery in Daniel. We will explore those parallels in detail further below. Thus, Daniel is clearly referenced in the New Testament, which views the complete fulfillment of Daniel as a future event. From the point of view of Jesus and John in the early part of the first century, Daniel had not been fulfilled. Daniel was taken literally. The Messiah will be pierced and mourned as if for an only Son. God will pour out a spirit of grace and supplication. The Messiah will appear on the clouds in glory and every eye will see him. The Messiah will have authority and dominion over all nations and peoples and tongues. The Messianic Kingdom is everlasting and will never be destroyed. All of these are literal interpretations, plain and direct understanding of the scriptures, and generally held by most Christian denominations.

> From the point of view of Jesus and John in the early part of the first century, Daniel had not been fulfilled. Daniel was taken literally.

REASONS WHY DANIEL HAS NOT BEEN FULFILLED COMPLETELY

In the previous two sections we looked at key passages within Daniel referring to the resurrection of the dead, eternal judgment, and the Eternal Messianic Kingdom. Then we looked at how both Jesus and the book of Revelation referred to Daniel's prophecies. In summary, here are the reasons why Daniel has not been completely fulfilled yet:

1. Daniel spoke of the Day of Judgment and the Messiah coming on the clouds of Heaven.
   - We believe that Jesus will return to judge the living and the dead.
   - Zechariah tells us every eye will see him coming on the clouds, but that has not happened.
   - Jesus sits at the right hand of the Father while his enemies are being made a footstool.
   - Jesus and John viewed Daniel as having future events from their day.

2. Daniel spoke of the Messianic Kingdom destroying all other kingdoms.

- Kingdoms opposed to Christ still exist today and have not been destroyed.
- Jesus taught us to pray for the coming of the Kingdom of God on Earth as it is in Heaven.

3. Daniel spoke of the resurrection of the dead.

- We believe in the resurrection of the body to eternal life.
- The dead have not been resurrected yet. Their bodies are still in the grave.
- The final judgment to everlasting life or contempt has not happened yet.

Next, we turn our attention to Daniel's visions of the kingdoms before the Eternal Messianic Kingdom.

PARALLEL VISIONS AND DREAMS

The book of Daniel is not a continuous sequential narrative. It does not tell a story straight from beginning to end, with each succeeding chapter describing later events as you might read in a novel. Instead, Daniel has two major sections. The first section, chapters 1–6, primarily speak of Daniel's life experiences. The last section records one dream and three visions that Daniel had about the coming of the Kingdom of God.

This is important to know, because we don't have a chronological sequence of events from chapter 1 to chapter 12. Instead, we have dreams and visions of the end that are parallel to each other. God gave Daniel the interpretation of dreams as well as visions that all spoke about the coming of the Eternal Messianic Kingdom.

> The book of Daniel is not a continuous sequential narrative. It does not tell a story straight from beginning to end, with each succeeding chapter describing later events as you might read in a novel. Instead, we have dreams and visions of the end that are parallel to each other.

The first dream comes in the first section of the book. In chapter 2 we see the dream King Nebuchadnezzar had and the interpretation of it that Daniel is given. This is the famous dream of the statue of gold, silver, bronze, iron, and clay. This dream ends with the Messianic Kingdom destroying all the previous kingdoms.

In chapter 7 Daniel also has a dream, a dream of four beasts. In this dream he sees one like a Son of Man coming in glory on the clouds. He sees the everlasting Kingdom of God established after the destruction of those earlier kingdoms. Chapter 8 of Daniel is yet another vision. He sees a struggle between Greece and Medo-Persia, which are specifically named, followed by another kingdom which oppresses the People of God.

One of the most famous visions is recorded in Chapter 9. In that vision Daniel asks God when the Judeans will be set free from captivity in Babylon. Daniel is praying and fasting, wearing sackcloth, and confessing both his sins and the sins of his people. He reads in Jeremiah where God promised to end the Babylonian captivity, and so Daniel prays in great earnest for when that would happen. God answers Daniel in a vision, which not only tells of their release from captivity, but also the rebuilding of Jerusalem. However, God goes further than Daniel's immediate concern. The vision also says that after Jerusalem is rebuilt, the Anointed One (the Messiah) will come and be put to death. And the people who kill the Messiah will also destroy the city and the sanctuary. So the Judeans will return from Babylon and rebuild the city and the sanctuary. Then the Messiah will come and be put to death, and afterward those who killed the Messiah will destroy that rebuilt city and sanctuary (the Second Temple). God's answer was perhaps more than Daniel wanted to know.

The last vision recorded in the Daniel spans chapters 10 through 12. The vision ends with the resurrection of the dead for final judgment to everlasting life or to shame and everlasting contempt. But before that happens the People of God are oppressed, and the abomination is set up in the Temple. This is the same abomination that Jesus referred to when he taught his Disciples on the Mount of Olives. You'll recall from above that Jesus was answering their question about when the Second Temple would be destroyed and what would be the sign of his Coming and the end of the age.

So altogether we have both dreams and visions that overlap each other. They speak of the time in which Daniel lived, the captivity in Babylon, as well as the resurrection of the dead and the final day of judgment. Since these are parallel dreams and visions, we need to put them side by side to get a better understanding of Daniel. This is similar to detectives doing an investigation. They listen to multiple witnesses describing the same sequence of events, and then put the testimonies together to better form a picture of what really happened.

Daniel's interpretations of dreams and visions extended from his own time living in Babylon to the final Kingdom of Messiah which destroys all other kingdoms. Jesus quoted directly from Daniel; and the book of Revelation uses imagery seen only in Daniel. We need to understand Daniel to understand Revelation. We next turn our attention to looking at these parallel descriptions of events that Daniel was shown through dreams and visions.

> Daniel's interpretations of dreams and visions extended from his own time living in Babylon to the final Kingdom of Messiah which destroys all other kingdoms. Jesus quoted directly from Daniel; and the book of Revelation uses imagery seen only in Daniel. We need to understand Daniel to understand Revelation.

A PROGRESSION OF SPECIFIC KINGDOMS

In the various dreams and visions of Daniel there are references to many different kingdoms. For example, in Nebuchadnezzar's dream of the statue, or in Daniel's vision of the four beasts. Are these actual kingdoms Daniel is speaking of, or merely an allegorical reference to all kingdoms opposed to God throughout history?

Was Daniel speaking of specific kingdoms? This is a key interpretive question. Some church traditions take an allegorical view of Apocalyptic literature, like Revelation and Daniel, and say when the scriptures use symbols that represent kingdoms, they are referring to all kingdoms opposed to Christ throughout history. The power of Satan works through anti-Christian governments, rulers, false religions, and false philosophies throughout every generation. And that is a general statement that is typically true throughout history. Those who oppose Christ, well, they oppose Christ. However, is Daniel speaking of specific kingdoms or is he alluding to all kingdoms throughout history? We will use our Sola Scriptura approach to look at what the scriptures actually say.

A really big question for those holding the allegorical view of Apocalyptic literature is: Since Christ will return and rule all nations with an iron scepter (Dan 2:44, Rev 2:27, 12:5, 19:15, Ps 2:9, 110:2), then does the Bible have anything to say about the final kingdom(s) before his return? If you believe Apocalyptic literature refers to multiple kingdoms throughout history, that it refers to all antichristian governments, then you must believe there will be a final one (whatever the last one standing is when Christ returns). So again, the big question is: does the Bible have anything to say about the final worldly kingdom(s)? What is so bad about the final kingdom(s) that it is (they are) the last one(s)? Why does God decide to end the world as we know it? Why does Christ return on the clouds in glory to judge the living and the dead at that time? Why that particular moment in history? Does the eschatological time clock simply run out, or is there something else going on?

> Why does God decide to end the world as we know it? Why does Christ return on the clouds in glory to judge the living and the dead at that time? Why that particular moment in history? Does the eschatological time clock simply run out, or is there something else going on?

For one of the most important moments in religion, the Second Coming of Christ and the resurrection of the dead to final judgment, what is happening on earth when that time comes? Again, is it something so bad that God finally says "enough"? Or does it just happen in the fullness of time? And if something dreadful is going on, then is the Bible silent about that time of great distress? Does the Bible warn us? Though Jesus returns like a thief in the night when no one is expecting him, and though only the Father in Heaven knows the day and the hour of the Second Coming, does the Bible give any warnings of the state of the world leading up to it?

This is a critical theological point. For some traditions teach that the world will continually get better and better, more and more Christlike until his Second Coming. Other traditions teach that the world will get worse, and the people of God will be oppressed up until his Second Coming. What does the Bible really say?

We should turn once again to the scriptures. We should take our Sola Scriptura approach and see what the scriptures say. We should put our various traditions on hold for a moment and examine the scriptures together. Once we agree on the plain meaning of the text, then we can begin interpretation.

Our first observation is that Daniel says directly that there are four kingdoms from the time of Nebuchadnezzar to the Messianic Kingdom, and that Babylon is the first one. This is seen in Nebuchadnezzar's dream of the statue, where parts of the statue refer to specific kingdoms. This is seen in Daniel's dream of the beasts, where Daniel tells us directly that they represent kings. This is seen in Daniel's vision of the Ram and the Goat where Medo-Persia and Greece are specifically named.

Symbolism	Reference	Scripture (NIV), emphasis added
Nebuchadnezzar is the statue's head of gold	Dan 2:38	in your hands he has placed all mankind and the beasts of the field and the birds in the sky. Wherever they live, he has made you ruler over them all. *You are that head of gold.*
More kingdoms follow Babylon	Dan 2:39	After you, *another kingdom will arise*, inferior to yours. Next, *a third kingdom, one of bronze, will rule over the whole earth.*
The beasts represent kings	Dan 7:17	The *four great beasts* are *four kings* that will rise from the earth.
The horns represent kingdoms	Dan 8:19-22	19 He said: "I am going to tell you what will happen later in the time of wrath, because the vision concerns the appointed time of the end. 20 *The two-horned ram that you saw represents the kings of Media and Persia.* 21 *The shaggy goat is the king of Greece*, and the large horn between its eyes is the first king. 22 The four horns that replaced the one that was broken off *represent four kingdoms that will emerge from his nation* but will not have the same power.
A final kingdom will crush the earlier ones	Dan 2:44	In the time of those kings, *the God of heaven will set up a kingdom that will never be destroyed*, nor will it be left to another people. It will crush all those kingdoms and bring them to an end, but it will itself endure forever.

We see that Daniel speaks of specific kingdoms, and directly names Babylon, Medo-Persia, and Greece. Daniel is told there will be a final kingdom that will never be destroyed. That final kingdom will bring all the former ones to an end. Babylon, Medo-Persia, and Greece are named explicitly by the Bible as specific kingdoms. The Bible nowhere says that the dreams and visions refer to all kingdoms opposed to

Christ throughout history. Let's look at the parallel dreams and visions in Daniel to more clearly see this.

Symbolism	Reference	Scripture (NIV)
Babylon is the first kingdom	Dan 2:38	in your hands he has placed all mankind and the beasts of the field and the birds in the sky. Wherever they live, he has made you ruler over them all. *You are that head of gold.*
	Dan 7:4	*The first was like a lion, and it had the wings of an eagle.* I watched until its wings were torn off and it was lifted from the ground so that it stood on two feet like a human being, and the mind of a human was given to it.
The second kingdom is inferior	Dan 2:39a	After you, *another kingdom will arise*, inferior to yours.
The second kingdom is Medo–Persia	Dan 7:5	And there before me was a *second beast, which looked like a bear*. It was raised up on one of its sides, and it had three ribs in its mouth between its teeth. It was told, 'Get up and eat your fill of flesh!'
	Dan 8:19-20	19 He said: "I am going to tell you what will happen later in the time of wrath, because the vision concerns the appointed time of the end. 20 *The two-horned ram that you saw represents the kings of Media and Persia.*
The third kingdom will rule over the whole earth	Dan 2:39b	Next, *a third kingdom, one of bronze, will rule over the whole earth.*
The third kingdom is Greece	Dan 7:6	After that, I looked, and there before me was *another beast, one that looked like a leopard.* And on its back it had four wings like those of a bird. This beast had four heads, and it was given authority to rule.
	Dan 8:21	21 *The shaggy goat is the king of Greece*, and the large horn between its eyes is the first king. 22 The four horns that replaced the one that was broken off represent four kingdoms that will emerge from his nation but will not have the same power.

While interpreters love to try to explain these symbols, such as the lion with the wings of an eagle, or try to find modern explanations like the second beast looking like a bear meaning the Russian bear, we don't need to look any further than the Bible itself. Daniel is explicitly told that the symbols mean Babylon (Dan 2:38), Media and Persia (Dan 8:19-20), and Greece (Dan 8:21).

> Daniel is explicitly told that the symbols mean Babylon (Dan 2:38), Media and Persia (Dan 8:19-20), and Greece (Dan 8:21).

There is a fourth kingdom that comes after Greece which is not named. Historically Daniel lived before the Roman Empire was established (after the earlier Roman Republic) and so the Roman Empire was unknown to Daniel in his time and was not mentioned by name. This fourth kingdom will be divided into ten, from which a ruler will arise by overtaking three of the ten. It is this ruler who will wage war against the holy people until the Day of Judgment.

Symbolism	Reference	Scripture (NIV)
The fourth kingdom will be divided. The people (the ten toes) will be a mixture.	Dan 2:40–43	40 Finally, there will be *a fourth kingdom*, strong as iron—for iron breaks and smashes everything—and as iron breaks things to pieces, so it will crush and break all the others. 41 Just as you saw that the feet and toes were *partly of baked clay and partly of iron, so this will be a divided kingdom*; yet it will have some of the strength of iron in it, even as you saw iron mixed with clay. 42 As the toes were partly iron and partly clay, so this kingdom will be partly strong and partly brittle. 43 And just as you saw the iron mixed with baked clay, so *the people will be a mixture and will not remain united*, any more than iron mixes with clay.
The fourth kingdom has ten horns.	Dan 7:7	After that, in my vision at night I looked, and there before me was *a fourth beast*—terrifying and frightening and very powerful. It had *large iron teeth; it crushed and devoured its victims and trampled underfoot whatever was left*. It was different from all the former beasts, and *it had ten horns*.
Ten kings will come from the fourth kingdom. Then another king will come and subdue three of the earlier ones. He will oppress the holy people.	Dan 7:23–25	23 "He gave me this explanation: '*The fourth beast is a fourth kingdom* that will appear on earth. It will be different from all the other kingdoms and will devour the whole earth, trampling it down and crushing it. 24 *The ten horns are ten kings who will come from this kingdom*. After them *another king will arise, different from the earlier ones; he will subdue three kings*. 25 He will speak against the Most High and oppress his holy people and try to change the set times and the laws. *The holy people will be delivered into his hands for a time, times and half a time.*
A boastful horn uproots three of the ten horns.	Dan 7:8	While I was thinking about the horns, there before me was *another horn, a little one*, which came up among them; and *three of the first horns were uprooted before it*. This horn had eyes like the eyes of a human being and a *mouth that spoke boastfully*.

Symbolism	Reference	Scripture (NIV)
The boastful horn wages war against the holy people until the Ancient of Days comes in judgment.	Dan 7:19–22	19 Then I wanted to know *the meaning of the fourth beast,* which was different from all the others and most terrifying, with its iron teeth and bronze claws—the beast that crushed and devoured its victims and trampled underfoot whatever was left. 20 I also wanted to know about *the ten horns on its head and about the other horn that came up,* before which three of them fell—the horn that looked more imposing than the others and that had eyes and a mouth that spoke boastfully. 21 As I watched, *this horn was waging war against the holy people and defeating them,* 22 *until the Ancient of Days came and pronounced judgment in favor of the holy people of the Most High, and the time came when they possessed the kingdom.*
A fierce king will arise, oppress the holy people, and stand against the Prince of Princes.	Dan 8:21–25	21 The shaggy goat is the king of Greece, and the large horn between its eyes is the first king. 22 The four horns that replaced the one that was broken off represent *four kingdoms that will emerge from his nation but will not have the same power.* 23 In the latter part of their reign, when rebels have become completely wicked, *a fierce-looking king, a master of intrigue, will arise.* 24 He will become very strong, but not by his own power. He will cause astounding devastation and will succeed in whatever he does. *He will destroy those who are mighty, the holy people.* 25 He will cause deceit to prosper, and he will consider himself superior. When they feel secure, *he will destroy many and take his stand against the Prince of princes. Yet he will be destroyed, but not by human power.*
The King of the North will boast against God and invade Israel.	Dan 11:36, 40–45	36 *The king will do as he pleases. He will exalt and magnify himself above every god and will say unheard-of things against the God of gods. He will be successful until the time of wrath is completed,* for what has been determined must take place. 40 *At the time of the end* the king of the South will engage him in battle, and the king of the North will storm out against him with chariots and cavalry and a great fleet of ships. He will invade many countries and sweep through them like a flood. 41 *He will also invade the Beautiful Land.* Many countries will fall, but Edom, Moab and the leaders of Ammon will be delivered from his hand. 42 He will extend his power over many countries; Egypt will not escape. 43 He will gain control of the treasures of gold and silver and all the riches of Egypt, with the Libyans and Cushites in submission. 44 But reports from the east and the north will alarm him, and he will set out in a great rage to destroy and annihilate many. 45 *He will pitch his royal tents between the seas at the beautiful holy mountain. Yet he will come to his end, and no one will help him.*

Symbolism	Reference	Scripture (NIV)
The beast is an eighth king. Ten kings will support the beast and wage war against the Lamb.	Rev 17:11–14	11 *The beast who once was, and now is not, is an eighth king. He belongs to the seven and is going to his destruction.* 12 *"The ten horns you saw are ten kings who have not yet received a kingdom, but who for one hour will receive authority as kings along with the beast.* 13 *They have one purpose and will give their power and authority to the beast.* 14 *They will wage war against the Lamb, but the Lamb will triumph* over them because he is Lord of lords and King of kings—and with him will be his called, chosen and faithful followers."

Finally, the Messiah will defeat this little horn, the 8th king that leads the ten kings against him. And God will establish his Eternal Messianic Kingdom.

Symbolism	Reference	Scripture (NIV)
The Messianic Kingdom will be set up in the time of the ten kings.	Dan 2:44–45	44 *"In the time of those kings, the God of heaven will set up a kingdom that will never be destroyed, nor will it be left to another people. It will crush all those kingdoms and bring them to an end, but it will itself endure forever.* 45 *This is the meaning of the vision of the rock cut out of a mountain, but not by human hands—a rock that broke the iron, the bronze, the clay, the silver and the gold to pieces.*
The boastful horn wages war against the holy people until the Ancient of Days comes in judgment.	Dan 7:21–22	21 As I watched, this horn was waging war against the holy people and defeating them, 22 *until the Ancient of Days came and pronounced judgment in favor of the holy people of the Most High, and the time came when they possessed the kingdom.*
The boastful horn loses power and God establishes his Messianic Kingdom.	Dan 7:26–27	26 But the court will sit, and *his power will be taken away and completely destroyed forever.* 27 Then the sovereignty, power and greatness of *all the kingdoms under heaven will be handed over to the holy people of the Most High. His kingdom will be an everlasting kingdom, and all rulers will worship and obey him.*
The beast and the ten kings lose the war against Christ.	Rev 19:19–20	19 Then I saw *the beast and the kings of the earth and their armies gathered together to wage war against the rider on the horse and his army.* 20 But the beast was captured, and with it the false prophet who had performed the signs on its behalf. With these signs he had deluded those who had received the mark of the beast and worshiped its image. *The two of them were thrown alive into the fiery lake of burning sulfur.*

Symbolism	Reference	Scripture (NIV)
Satan will attack Israel and be defeated.	Rev 20:7–10	7 When the thousand years are over, *Satan will be released from his prison* 8 *and will go out to deceive the nations in the four corners of the earth—Gog and Magog—and to gather them for battle. In number they are like the sand on the seashore.* 9 They marched across the breadth of the earth and *surrounded the camp of God's people, the city he loves.* But fire came down from heaven and devoured them. 10 And *the devil, who deceived them, was thrown into the lake of burning sulfur*, where the beast and the false prophet had been thrown. They will be tormented day and night for ever and ever.

Again, Daniel is speaking about specific kingdoms leading up to the final and eternal Messianic kingdom. The kingdoms known at the time of Daniel are specifically named (Babylon, Medo–Persia, and Greece). Then an unnamed fourth kingdom is mentioned that itself breaks apart into ten other kingdoms. Daniel is not speaking about an allegory to all kingdoms throughout all time, all governments opposed to God. Daniel is speaking of specific kingdoms, names those that were known at his time, and gives specific details of the kingdoms which will come after. Daniel speaks of a specific progression of kingdoms, from the time of Babylon up until the final and eternal Messianic Kingdom.

> Daniel speaks of a specific progression of kingdoms, from the time of Babylon up until the final and eternal Messianic Kingdom.

ALL NATIONS WILL SERVE THE MESSIAH

The specific progression of kingdoms that Daniel mentions culminates in a final powerful one that oppresses the people of God. The leader of that kingdom which opposes God is finally judged. As we see the judgment of the one who oppresses the people of God in Daniel chapter 7, the one who is thrown into the lake of fire, there also appears one like a Son of Man who will reign in the Eternal Kingdom of God.

> "13 In my vision at night I looked, and there before me was one like a son of man, coming with the clouds of heaven. He approached the Ancient of Days and was led into his presence. 14 He was given authority, glory and sovereign power; all nations and peoples of every language worshiped him. His dominion is an everlasting dominion that will not pass away, and his kingdom is one that will never be destroyed." (Dan 7:13–14, NIV)

A "son of man" is an ancient Hebrew expression for a human being, as opposed to someone divine. In verse 13 Daniel says the one before him was *kavar enash* (כְּבַר

אֱנָשׁ). Literally "like" or "as" a son of man. This one before him is not exactly a son of man, but one like a son of man.

Daniel clearly says this Messianic figure will reign, have dominion, over an everlasting kingdom. His kingdom will never be destroyed. And all nations and peoples of every language will serve him. The word for "serve" or "worship" is a conjugation of *pelach* (פְּלַח), an Aramaic word used to describe reverence and service to a deity.

> This one like a Son of Man reigns over an eternal kingdom, and all nations will revere, serve, and worship him. Most Christians take this part of the passage literally.

This one like a Son of Man reigns over an eternal kingdom, and all nations will revere, serve, and worship him. Most Christians take this part of the passage literally. We believe that Jesus will have a literal eternal Messianic kingdom, not an allegorical temporary and nebulous kingdom. All nations and peoples of every language will worship him, and his kingdom will never be destroyed.

THE ANOINTED ONE WILL BE PUT TO DEATH

As Daniel was studying the book of Jeremiah, he longed to see his people released from their captivity in Babylon as predicted. Jeremiah prophesied the captivity would last for seventy years.

> "8 Therefore the Lord Almighty says this: 'Because you have not listened to my words, 9 I will summon all the peoples of the north and my servant Nebuchadnezzar king of Babylon,' declares the Lord, 'and I will bring them against this land and its inhabitants and against all the surrounding nations. I will completely destroy them and make them an object of horror and scorn, and an everlasting ruin. 10 I will banish from them the sounds of joy and gladness, the voices of bride and bridegroom, the sound of millstones and the light of the lamp. 11 This whole country will become a desolate wasteland, and these nations will serve the king of Babylon seventy years.'" (Jer 25:8–11, NIV)

> "10 This is what the Lord says: 'When seventy years are completed for Babylon, I will come to you and fulfill my good promise to bring you back to this place. 11 For I know the plans I have for you,' declares the Lord, 'plans to prosper you and not to harm you, plans to give you hope and a future.'" (Jer 29:10–11, NIV)

In Daniel we see that God not only confirms that the captivity would end after the seventy years are completed, but three time periods would follow it as we will see below. The result of these periods given in chapter 9 is to bring in everlasting righteousness and put an end to sin. How amazing and wonderful that God promises to bring in everlasting righteousness.

> "Seventy 'sevens' are decreed for your people and your holy city to finish transgression, to put an end to sin, to atone for wickedness, to bring in everlasting righteousness, to seal up vision and prophecy and to anoint the Most Holy Place." (Dan 9:24, NIV)
>
> Daniel clearly speaks of the end of the Babylonian Captivity, and God also promises an end to sin, everlasting righteousness.

Daniel clearly speaks of the end of the Babylonian Captivity, and God also promises an end to sin, everlasting righteousness. This would take place after "seventy sevens." The Hebrew word used here is the plural of *shabua* (שָׁבוּעַ), meaning seven or week (a week has seven days). So this vision is to take place over seventy time periods. Most commentaries will take prophecies like Ezekiel 4:4 or Numbers 14:34 to show that God's punishment was a year for each day. Thus the "seventy sevens" means seventy weeks, or seventy times seven which is four hundred and ninety days. Using a year for a day brings us to four hundred and ninety years to complete this particular vision. From this point one can arrive at the time of Jesus and the destruction of Jerusalem from the decree of Artaxerxes to Nehemiah in 445 BC (considering the Hebrew lunar calendar, along with adjustments for their leap months). But as fun as calendar math is, we should not miss the point that the vision speaks of the end of sin, bringing in everlasting righteousness. As Jesus was crucified, died, and rose again, he achieved atonement for the sins of the world and so brought in everlasting righteousness.

As interesting and edifying as calendar math is, our Sola Scriptura approach forces us to stay with the text only. The passage in Daniel itself does not mention the "year for a day" principle. However, we do see that the total time period has been decreed to bring in everlasting righteousness over "seventy sevens." This total time period is broken down into three periods: a first seven, then sixty-two sevens, and a final seven. There are clear events that happen in each of these three time periods. The first period regards the rebuilding of Jerusalem after the Babylonian captivity ends.

> "Know and understand this: From the time the word goes out to restore and rebuild Jerusalem until the Anointed One, the ruler, comes, there will be seven 'sevens,' and sixty-two 'sevens.' It will be rebuilt with streets and a trench, but in times of trouble." (Dan 9:25, NIV)
>
> Daniel is told the seventy weeks break down into smaller time periods. And he is told they relate to rebuilding Jerusalem after the Babylonian Captivity and the appearance of the Anointed One.

Daniel is told the seventy weeks break down into smaller time periods. And he is told they relate to rebuilding Jerusalem after the Babylonian Captivity and the appearance of the Anointed One. The first period is from the time of the decree to restore and rebuild Jerusalem until the Anointed One comes. It is interesting to see how different translations handle this "Anointed One" (*Mashiach Nagid*, מָשִׁיחַ נָגִיד):

- NIV: the Anointed One, the ruler (New International Version)
- KJV: the Messiah the Prince (King James Version)
- JPS: one anointed, a prince (Jewish Publication Society)
- Chabad: the anointed king (Orthodox Jewish Version)
- NLT: a ruler—the Anointed One (New Living Translation)
- LXX: Christ the prince (Brenton Septuagint Translation)
- GNT: God's chosen leader (Good News Translation)
- ISV: the Anointed Commander (International Standard Version)
- DRB: Christ the prince (Douay-Rheims Bible)
- Peshitta: The Messiah The King (Syriac Aramaic Version)
- CEV: the Chosen Leader (Contemporary English Version)

There is something going on here with these translations. Normally one does not find such a variety of expressions across different translations. We can choose many ways to say the same thing, and translators follow a set of principles about how literally they will translate source text, as well as what equivalent words they will use. They work extremely hard, knowing that God will hold them accountable, and yet the options for expression can be difficult to choose from. If you have ever struggled with how to best say something important, then you can relate to our friends the translators.

Translations are themselves interpretations. For controversial verses we must look beyond English. This specific text in Daniel does look like it points directly to the Messiah, and there are implications to that because this Anointed One comes before the destruction of the Second Temple. If you are looking for Jesus, you might choose particular words in the translated language. If you are not wanting to see Jesus, you might choose other words. Check the Christian versus Jewish translations shown above again. Our emotions may lead us, with our rationalization following afterward to justify our choice. Not surprisingly, the scholarly debates over these translations fill the shelves of theological libraries. Instead, we should look at the actual Hebrew itself, taken from the Masoretic Text (Westminster Leningrad Codex), the definitive Hebrew text accepted by both Christians and the Jewish People.

> Translations are themselves interpretations. For controversial verses we must look beyond English.

The Hebrew words that Daniel uses for "Anointed One" (*Mashiach Nagid*, מָשִׁיחַ נָגִיד), which linguistically means a Messiah (noun) who is Princely (adjective). It is not the reverse, a prince (noun) who is anointed (adjective). Here in the Hebrew the adjective comes after the substantive, it modifies it.[2] The emphasis is on the *Mashiach* and not the *Nagid*. It is not a prince who is anointed (as in the JPS version of the Hebrew Bible), but rather the Anointed who is Princely. Additionally, the Hebrew Masoretic Trope markings (*Teʼamim*, טעמים) use the strongest conjunctive accent found in the non–poetic books, a *Munach* (מֻנַּח), under the word *Mashiach*. These Rabbinic rules of interpretation indicate that the word Messiah is connected to Prince, not separated as some translations show with a comma ("the Anointed One, the ruler" as found in the NIV). Thus, the KJV is the best of the above translations, "the Messiah the Prince."

The Septuagint (LXX), written before the time of Christ, is also a great translation of the original Hebrew. As you can see above, the LXX uses "Christ the prince." In other words, this Anointed One is primarily the *Mashiach*, the Messiah. He is a religious figure. He is also a governmental figure, like a prince or king. As Christians we know this to be the Prince of Peace that Isaiah prophesied would come.

> "For to us a child is born, to us a son is given, and the government will be on his shoulders. And he will be called Wonderful Counselor, Mighty God, Everlasting Father, Prince of Peace." (Isa 9:6, NIV)

This is the long-expected Messiah who would be both High Priest and King, which has never before happened in Judaism to this day. He is the child who was born whom Isaiah says will be called God, the Mighty God, the Prince of Peace, the Everlasting Father, and Wonderful Counselor. He will be the one whom Zechariah described as the Branch, who is both Priest and King (Zech 6:13). Psalm 110 speaks of the Messiah, and in it God declares that the Messiah will be different from past religious rulers. He will not be like the Levitical priests who were never kings, but rather like Melchizedek who was both the King of Salem (King of Peace) and the Priest of the Most High God (Gen 14:18).

> "1 This Melchizedek was king of Salem and priest of God Most High. He met Abraham returning from the defeat of the kings and blessed him, 2 and Abraham gave him a tenth of everything. First, the name Melchizedek means 'king of righteousness'; then also, 'king of Salem' means 'king of peace.' 3 Without father or mother, without genealogy, without beginning of days or end of life, resembling the Son of God, he remains a priest forever." (Heb 7:1–3, NIV)

> Daniel is told his people will be freed from the Babylonian Captivity. They will return to the land of Israel, rebuild Jerusalem and the Temple, and then the Messiah will appear.

Daniel is told his people will be freed from the Babylonian Captivity. They will return to the land of Israel, rebuild Jerusalem and the Temple, and then the Messiah will appear. What happens next? After the second time period, the sixty-two "sevens,"

---

2. Keil and Delitzsch, *Commentary*, Dan 9:25.

we see something shocking. Up to this point those held captive have been freed. They have rebuilt the Temple and the city. Then the Messiah comes. What would you expect to happen next? Worldwide rule from Mount Zion? Everlasting righteousness for the nation of Israel? All nations to submit to the Messiah and be under his rule?

> "After the sixty-two 'sevens,' the Anointed One will be put to death and will have nothing." (Dan 9:26a, NIV)

The *Maschiach Nagid* is put to death. What a surprise! That doesn't sound like what we would have expected. Wouldn't the Messiah, the Prince of Peace, come to rule the world? Daniel says after the Messiah appears he will be put to death. This is during the time of the Second Temple. Some translators desperately do not want to see Daniel speaking about the Messiah and want to say Daniel was not a prophet – relegating his book to another part of the Bible entirely. If the Messiah was to come after the Second Temple was rebuilt and then be put to death, that greatly limits the possibilities of who could fulfill this prophecy.

> Some translators desperately do not want to see Daniel speaking about the Messiah and want to say Daniel was not a prophet – relegating his book to another part of the Bible entirely. If the Messiah was to come after the Second Temple was rebuilt and then be put to death, that greatly limits the possibilities of who could fulfill this prophecy.

After these events, a "ruler who will come" destroys the city and the sanctuary. Think about what Daniel is saying. His people would be set free from captivity and return to the Promised Land. They will rebuild and restore the city and the sanctuary. The Messiah will come. And then the Messiah will be put to death, and the city and the sanctuary will be destroyed. What an immense disaster.

> "The people of the ruler who will come will destroy the city and the sanctuary. The end will come like a flood: War will continue until the end, and desolations have been decreed." (Dan 9:26b, NIV)

Here are the key events that Daniel is seeing in this vision of "seventy sevens":

1. The Judeans are set free from Babylon and return to the land of Israel.
2. Jerusalem is rebuilt and the Second Temple is stood up.
3. An "Anointed One" (*Mashiach Nagid*) appears and is put to death.
4. The city and the sanctuary (the Second Temple) are destroyed.

Daniel is clearly saying the *Mashiach Nagid* will appear after the return from Babylon and before the Second Temple is destroyed. As Christians we see this as a clear prophecy of the time of the appearance of the Messiah. Although the New Testament never directly quotes this passage as a proof text of Jesus fulfilling prophecies about the Messiah, Jesus does quote this passage directly in the Olivet Discourse when speaking about the destruction of the Second Temple and the signs of the times (Matt 24:15). Jesus also warns of false messiahs yet to come (Matt 24:23–24). Whether you regard this passage as Messianic or not, depending on your translation, the people at the time of Jesus were clearly expecting the arrival of the Messiah. And Jesus clearly quoted from this passage of Daniel.

Although the early church was filled with Jewish believers in Jesus, even those who rejected Jesus still expected the Messiah. A later messianic figure, Simon Ben Kosevah (a.k.a. "Bar Kokhba"), tried to push the Romans out after the Second Temple was destroyed. The Jewish people who rejected Jesus accepted Bar Kokhba as their messiah. They wanted a messiah who would push out the Romans. Rabbi Akiva was the spiritual leader at that time and declared that Bar Kokhba was the long-expected Messiah. Rabbi Akiva, considered the "Chief of the Sages" and a major contributor to the Mishna (early teachings) of the Talmud, was clearly wrong about Bar Kokhba being the Messiah. Bar Kokhba was defeated, and the Romans expelled the Jewish people from the land of Israel. Not only did they lose the Second Temple, but they lost the land of Israel itself.

> People who rejected Jesus accepted Simon Bar Kokhba as their messiah. The Chief of the Sages of the Talmud announced the Messiah had finally come. Everyone believed the time of Jesus was the right time for the appearance of the Messiah. But Bar Kokhba was a failed messiah, the Romans defeated him and expelled the Jewish people from the land.

People who rejected Jesus accepted Simon Bar Kokhba as their messiah. The Chief of the Sages of the Talmud announced the Messiah had finally come. Everyone believed the time of Jesus was the right time for the appearance of the Messiah. But Bar Kokhba was a failed messiah, the Romans defeated him and expelled the Jewish people from the land. It is clear from several prophecies, including Dan 9:24–27, that the time of Jesus was the right time for the Messiah.

> "1 After Jesus had finished instructing his twelve disciples, he went on from there to teach and preach in the towns of Galilee. 2 When John, who was in prison, heard about the deeds of the Messiah, he sent his disciples 3 to ask him, 'Are you the one who is to come, or should we expect someone else?' 4 Jesus replied, 'Go back and report to John what you hear and see: 5 The blind receive sight, the lame walk, those who have leprosy are cleansed, the deaf hear, the dead are raised, and the good news is proclaimed to the poor. 6 Blessed is anyone who does not stumble on account of me.'" (Matt 11:1–6, NIV)

The true Messiah was rejected and put to death, just as the prophets had predicted. Daniel's prediction of the death of the Messiah and the destruction of the Second Temple came to pass. We should take Daniel seriously, and not reinterpret parts of his visions we don't like, or worse, say he is no prophet and ignore his writings.

WHAT DID WE LEARN FROM DANIEL?

As we look at what the book of Daniel says, in the plain sense of what the scriptures say, we see that he speaks of the future: both his own as well as God's plan for the whole world. He speaks of the resurrection of the dead, eternal judgment, and a progression of specific kingdoms from the time of Babylon through Medo-Persia and Greece, and then to a succession of ten kingdoms that culminate in a war against the Messiah.

#	Truth Claim	Primary Support	Secondary Support
4.1	Daniel has not been fulfilled yet because he speaks of the resurrection of the dead.	Dan 12:2-3	Matt 13:43, 19:28, 25:46, John 4:36, 5:28-29, 11:24, Acts 24:15, 1 Cor 15:42, Rev 14:13, Isa 26:19, 53:11, 57:2, 66:24, Job 19:25-27, Ezek 37:12
4.2	Daniel has not been fulfilled yet because he speaks of the Eternal Kingdom of Messiah which destroys all other kingdoms.	Dan 2:44	Luke 1:33, 1 Cor 15:24, Rev 11:15, Isa 2:4, 9:6, Ezek 37:25
4.3	Daniel speaks of specific kingdoms from Babylon to the Messianic Kingdom.	Dan 2:38-45, 7:4-8,17-27, 8:19-25, 11:36-45	Rev 17:11-14, 19:19-20, 20:7-10
4.4	Daniel foretells the death of the Messiah.	Dan 9:24-26	Matt 10:4, 24:30, 26:31, 27:3-10, John 16:32, 19:31-37, Mark 14:27, Rev 1:7-8, Isa 53, Ps 2:2, 22, 110:1, Ps 118:22, Zech 11:8-13, 12:10, 13:7
4.5	A boastful leader will lead the nations against Jerusalem and God.	Dan 7:20-25, 9:26-27	Rev 13:5-8, 16:14, 17:12-14, Joel 3:2, 2 Thess 2:1-12, Zech 12:3,9, 14:2,3,13
4.6	The Messiah will reign over an Eternal Kingdom that destroys all other kingdoms.	Dan 7:13-14, 27	Rev 22:5, Ps 2:9, 22:27, 110:2, Isa 2:1-4, 9:7, Acts 4:18-31, 13:26-41, Heb 1:1-5, 5:1-10, Matt 22:41-46

Without turning to any specific denominational interpretation, the Sola Scriptura approach leads us to conclude that the prophecies of Daniel have not yet been completely fulfilled. There will be a progression of specific kingdoms from the time of Babylon to a final war against the Messiah. The Messiah will defeat and destroy all those other kingdoms. The dead will be raised and judged, some to everlasting life, and others to shame and everlasting contempt. Keep all of these things in mind as background context for the book of Revelation.

It is interesting to compare our Sola Scriptura conclusions to an Orthodox Jewish view of the book of Daniel. Orthodox Judaism teaches that Daniel is about specific

The Sola Scriptura Challenge

kingdoms, not an allegory to all kingdoms opposed to God throughout history. Rashi, who lived after the time of Jesus, names Babylon (Nebuchadnezzar), Persia (Darius), Greece (Antiochus Epiphanes), and Rome (Titus) as specific kingdoms Daniel speaks of in his commentary on the Hebrew Bible.[3] The Talmud clearly states that the fourth kingdom of Daniel is Rome (Avodah Zarah 2b:2, Shevuot 6b:13).[4] In looking at just the plain sense of the text, the Orthodox Jewish view agrees with Sola Scriptura that Daniel speaks of a progression of specific kingdoms leading up to the final eternal Messianic Kingdom.

However, the Sola Scriptura approach disagrees with modern Judaism about if Daniel predicted the Messiah would be put to death. Instead, Sola Scriptura agrees with the earlier Rabbis of the Talmud that, indeed, a Messiah would die. Also, in agreement with the scribes of the Masoretic Text as well as the Septuagint which predates Jesus, the Sola Scriptura approaches sees Daniel clearly speaking of the Messiah being put to death before the destruction of the Second Temple. If we stick with what the text actually says, then we will see Jesus as well as a progression of specific kingdoms. To say that Daniel did not speak about the Messiah or that he spoke of all kingdoms opposed to God throughout history is not in line with the scriptures, not in line with the scribes of the Masoretic text, not in line with the Rabbis at the time of Jesus as recorded in the Talmud, not in line with the expectations of the people at the time of Jesus as recorded in the New Testament, and frankly, not supported by the actual scriptures both before and after the time of Jesus. It is only after the time of Jesus that the understanding of these passages changed, both within Judaism as well as within Christianity. Most of Judaism evolved away from Jesus, with some movements even evolving away from the idea of a literal Messiah at all. Some splits in Christianity evolved away from the teachings of the first Christian school in Antioch and instead took up the Greek philosophical approach of allegorizing (spiritualizing) the text looking for hidden secret teachings.

---

3. Rashi, *Commentary of Tanach*, Dan 8:9, 9:23–25.
4. Ashi and Ravina, *Babylonian Talmud*, Avodah Zarah 2b:2, Shevuot 6b:13.

5

Zechariah
Two Messiahs and a Final Battle

"It goes well according to him who explains that the cause is the slaying of Messiah the son of Joseph, as it is written, 'And they shall look upon me because they have thrust him through, and they shall mourn for him as one mourns for his only son'"—Talmud Sukkah 52a:10

WE FIND IN THE opening chapter of the book of Revelation a direct reference to Zechariah (Rev 1:7). From the very beginning of the book of Revelation John references the Hebrew prophets like Daniel and Zechariah. We must understand these books and their message. John tells us about the coming of the Messiah on the clouds (Dan 7:13) who will be seen by all. Every eye will see him, even those who pierced him, and all the peoples on earth will mourn (Zech 12:10).

> "'Look, he is coming with the clouds,' and 'every eye will see him, even those who pierced him'; and all peoples on earth 'will mourn because of him.' So shall it be! Amen." (Rev 1:7, NIV)

> "And I will pour out on the house of David and the inhabitants of Jerusalem a spirit of grace and supplication. They will look on me, the one they have pierced, and they will mourn for him as one mourns for an only child, and grieve bitterly for him as one grieves for a firstborn son." (Zech 12:10, NIV)

Since Revelation opens with references to Daniel and Zechariah, it is important for us to understand them first. In the last section we explored Daniel. In this section we will explore key apocalyptic passages in Zechariah. These form part of the background context for the book of Revelation. When the original audience of Revelation, who were the seven churches in Asia Minor (Rev 1:4), received the Revelation from John, they already knew the Hebrew Bible prophecies as those were in their set of scriptures at the time. The prophecies from Daniel, Zechariah, and the other Hebrew prophets formed their expectations about the Messiah and what was to come. John's message in Revelation directly references these prophecies from the beginning.

> From the very beginning of the book of Revelation John references the Hebrew prophets like Daniel and Zechariah. We must understand these books and their message.

CONTEXT OF THE BOOK OF ZECHARIAH

In the time of King Solomon and the earlier prophets, God warned the Israelites that their kingdom would be split into two, and then each part (the Northern Kingdom referred to as Israel and the Southern Kingdom referred to as Judah) would be taken into captivity by Assyria and Babylon, respectively. Earlier we explored the prophecies of Daniel who grew up in the beginning of the Babylonian captivity. He studied the earlier prophets like Jeremiah and asked God when their captivity would end. We now turn our attention to Zechariah who lived just after that, in the time when the predicted end of the Babylonian captivity came to pass.

Zechariah was a prophet who lived after the Judeans returned to Israel from captivity in Babylon. Some scholars believe he was born in Babylon and left for Israel as a youth in that first group of returning exiles.[1] His prophecies come near the end of the time of the Hebrew prophets. Whereas Malachi was the last prophet (and is the last book of the Hebrew Bible), Zechariah is next to last. Together with his contemporaries Haggai and Malachi, the three were the last prophets to Israel. Zechariah saw the end of the Babylonian Captivity and is one of the last prophets who spoke to Israel before the appearance of Christ.

> Zechariah saw the end of the Babylonian Captivity and is one of the last prophets who spoke to Israel before the appearance of Christ.

Zechariah's name literally means "God has remembered" (*zekaryah*, זְכַרְיָה). This is certainly a fitting name, for in the book we find that God remembers his promises to the earlier prophets. God promised the Judeans would return to the land of Israel, and the city and the sanctuary would be rebuilt. And that is exactly what happened. These promises form the context of the book of Zechariah, who was a firsthand witness to those things. After the time of Zechariah came the rule of Israel by the Seleucids (Greeks), followed by Rome, leading up to the time of Jesus.

---

1. Smith, *Bible Dictionary*, Entry for Zechariah.

Knowing when a prophet lived is important as it helps us put their prophecies into the proper context. When Zechariah prophesies of rebuilding the Jerusalem Temple, the context is after the First Temple had been destroyed by the Babylonians and before the Second Temple had been built. When Zechariah tells the people to come out of Babylon, the context is the actual kingdom of Babylon that the Judeans had been taken captive into. This is different than when God tells his people to come out of Babylon in Revelation 18:4, as Babylon was long gone before the time of writing of Revelation.

The book of Zechariah is not a single continuous story, progressing chronologically from chapter 1 to 14. Three times he tells us "the Word of the Lord that came to Zechariah" (1:1, 7:1, and 8:1) which introduce new sections. And the last two sections of the book are introduced as new prophecies (9:1 and 12:1). So from a context perspective we should understand that the prophecies of later chapters can be parallel to those in earlier chapters, and not necessarily taking place at a later time. We will explore these parallels below, and their importance as background context for the book of Revelation.

HAS ZECHARIAH BEEN FULFILLED YET?

A key question for interpretation is to ask if the book has been completely fulfilled or not. Regarding Zechariah some denominations say yes, others say no, and some say both yes and no. Some Christian denominations teach a view that all Hebrew Bible prophecies have been fulfilled, and all things are fulfilled already in Christ. Other denominations teach that there are still some prophecies yet to be fulfilled. And still others teach that although some have been fulfilled already, they will be fulfilled again in the future. This is a key question because if everything is already fulfilled then there is nothing remaining in the future for Christians. If the prophecies have been partially or not yet fulfilled, then there is still something about the future the prophet has to say for us today. To explore this ourselves let's look at a specific prophecy regarding the future of Jerusalem.

> A key question for interpretation is to ask if the book has been completely fulfilled or not. Regarding Zechariah some denominations say yes, others say no, and some say both yes and no.

In the book of Zechariah, we see that Jerusalem will be raised up and never destroyed again (Zech 14:10–11). This happens right after a worldwide coalition, a group of kings from many nations, comes to fight against Jerusalem (Zech 12:1–9, 14:1–2). God himself saves Israel. We even see that he stands on the Mount of Olives and splits it into two thus forming a great valley through which his people escape the worldwide attack on the city (Zech 14:3–5). This is the same Mount of Olives where Jesus sat and taught his Disciples about prophecy (Matt 24). And afterward God will be the only God known in the world and he will be King over the whole earth (Zech 14:9).

The plain sense of the meaning of the text in Zechariah is that God will save the people of Jerusalem. He will save his people from the attack and the Mount of Olives will be split into two. After the defeat of the nations that attack Jerusalem, the city will be raised back up and never again be destroyed. And afterward God will be the only God known in the world.

> "11 It will be inhabited; never again will it be destroyed. Jerusalem will be secure. 12 This is the plague with which the Lord will strike all the nations that fought against Jerusalem: Their flesh will rot while they are still standing on their feet, their eyes will rot in their sockets, and their tongues will rot in their mouths." (Zech 14:11–12, NIV)

Did this happen already? Perhaps one could envision the Greek invasion of Jerusalem led by Antiochus Epiphanes as the whole known world attacking. This happened after the time of Zechariah. One could go further and see the Jewish Maccabees' success in throwing off Greece as an act of God to save Jerusalem. But did that last forever as Zechariah prophesied (Zech 14:11)? Certainly not. The Maccabees did not remain in power. Later the Romans, led by Titus, conquered the Greeks and ultimately took control of Jerusalem. Then still later the Romans destroyed Jerusalem in 70 AD. So either Zechariah was wrong and not a true prophet of God, or else Zechariah was not fulfilled in the time of the Maccabees and Antiochus Epiphanes.

Perhaps one could envision the Roman Empire's attack on Jerusalem in 70 AD as the whole known world coming to attack her, but did God step in and save Jerusalem? No, it was destroyed. In fact, Israel remained destroyed for almost two millennia until the United Nations declared it a nation once again in 1948 AD. Also, the Mount of Olives is still a single mountain to this day, standing beside the Temple Mount in Jerusalem. It was not split into a valley in the time of Antiochus nor of Titus. And God is clearly not the only god worshiped across the whole world.

> A straightforward interpretation of Zechariah, that Jerusalem would be attacked by many nations, God would step in to save her and split the Mount of Olives in two, Jerusalem would never again be destroyed, and God would be the only god worshiped across the whole world, just does not fit any historical time period to this day.

A straightforward interpretation of Zechariah, that Jerusalem would be attacked by many nations, God would step in to save her and split the Mount of Olives in two, Jerusalem would never again be destroyed, and God would be the only god worshiped across the whole world, just does not fit any historical time period to this day. For those reasons a Sola Scriptura approach which takes the Bible for what it directly says does not see the book of Zechariah as being completely fulfilled yet. It still holds something for the future, and at the time of the writing of the book of Revelation it held as yet unfulfilled prophecies that Revelation would come to address.

ZECHARIAH IN THE NEW TESTAMENT

In the New Testament we see plenty of references to Zechariah. References to the Four Horsemen, the Messiah who is the Branch, the arrival of the Messiah on a donkey, the New and Eternal Jerusalem, the Ingathering of Israel, the rejection of the Shepherd of God, and the thirty pieces of silver found in Zechariah are found referenced across the New Testament. There are both allusions to, as well as direct quotes of, Zechariah. It is clear that Jesus and the Apostles regarded Zechariah as scripture.

Below we will explore the references that are most relevant to the book of Revelation. We will begin by looking at the prophecies about the rejection of the Messiah. Then we will explore prophecies about the invasion of Israel and the coming of the Messianic kingdom. And finally, we will look at the various groups of four: The Four Horsemen, The Four Craftsmen, and The Four Chariots.

THE ONE WHO WAS PIERCED

To understand the reference in the opening of Revelation to a Messiah who was pierced (Rev 1:7), we need to understand how he was pierced to begin with. We will look at several places in Zechariah where he speaks about the rejection of the Messiah, such as the announcement of a time when they look upon the one who was pierced, in the vision of the Two Shepherds, and in a call for the striking of the Shepherd.

In the last vision recorded in Zechariah (chs. 12–14) we see many prophecies Christians hold dear, such as people looking upon the one who was pierced (the crucified Messiah) and a fountain opened up to cleanse from sin (the work of Jesus on the cross). But in this vision there are lesser known prophecies such as the nations of the world attacking Jerusalem but God saving them – never again to be destroyed, as well as a sword being brought against the Messiah. We will explore this worldwide attack on Jerusalem further below, but in this section we want to focus on the piercing of the Messiah and the sword being brought against the Shepherd of the Lord. Keep in mind that all these things are in the same vision, so the way in which we interpret one part of the vision (literal or allegorical) is the same way we should interpret the other parts of this same passage and same vision. This is the same way we interpret the Parables of Jesus, the Sermon on the Mount, the Psalms, the Proverbs, and the Epistles (in other words, the rest of the Bible). The way we interpret specific verses is the same way we should interpret other verses in the same passage. We can't pick and choose our method of interpretation for each verse because we do or don't like what it says.

The way we interpret specific verses is the same way we should interpret other verses in the same passage. We can't pick and choose our method of interpretation for each verse because we do or don't like what it says.

The last vision of Zechariah begins as a prophecy concerning Israel. Specifically, Jerusalem and Judah, who are besieged by the surrounding nations.

> "1 A prophecy: The word of the Lord concerning Israel. The Lord, who stretches out the heavens, who lays the foundation of the earth, and who forms the human spirit within a person, declares: 2 'I am going to make Jerusalem a cup that sends all the surrounding peoples reeling. Judah will be besieged as well as Jerusalem. 3 On that day, when all the nations of the earth are gathered against her, I will make Jerusalem an immovable rock for all the nations. All who try to move it will injure themselves.'" (Zech 12:1–3, NIV)

Within this vision of an attack by surrounding nations on Jerusalem and Judah, God declares the House of David and the inhabitants of Jerusalem will look upon the pierced Messiah and mourn for him.

> "And I will pour out on the house of David and the inhabitants of Jerusalem a spirit of grace and supplication. They will look on me, the one they have pierced, and they will mourn for him as one mourns for an only child, and grieve bitterly for him as one grieves for a firstborn son." (Zech 12:10, NIV)

This is the reference we get at the opening of the book of Revelation (Rev 1:7). We see an allusion to this by Jesus (Matt 24:30) as well as a direct reference in the Gospel of John (John 19:37).

> "'Look, he is coming with the clouds,' and 'every eye will see him, even those who pierced him'; and all peoples on earth 'will mourn because of him.' So shall it be! Amen." (Rev 1:7, NIV)

> "Then will appear the sign of the Son of Man in heaven. And then all the peoples of the earth will mourn when they see the Son of Man coming on the clouds of heaven, with power and great glory." (Matt 24:30, NIV)

> "31 Now it was the day of Preparation, and the next day was to be a special Sabbath. Because the Jewish leaders did not want the bodies left on the crosses during the Sabbath, they asked Pilate to have the legs broken and the bodies taken down. 32 The soldiers therefore came and broke the legs of the first man who had been crucified with Jesus, and then those of the other. 33 But when they came to Jesus and found that he was already dead, they did not break his legs. 34 Instead, one of the soldiers pierced Jesus' side with a spear, bringing a sudden flow of blood and water. 35 The man who saw it has given testimony, and his testimony is true. He knows that he tells the truth, and he testifies so that you also may believe. 36 These things happened so that the scripture would be fulfilled: 'Not one of his bones will be broken,' 37 and, as another

scripture says, 'They will look on the one they have pierced.'" (John 19:31–37, NIV)

Around the time of Jesus, the Jewish sages taught that this piercing was a reference to the piercing of the Messiah, who will be put to death. We see this in the Talmud as well as in notable Jewish commentaries.

> "It goes well according to him who explains that the cause is the slaying of Messiah the son of Joseph, as it is written, 'And they shall look upon me because they have thrust him through, and they shall mourn for him as one mourns for his only son'" (Talmud: Sukkah 52a:10)

> "I will pour – pour the Spirit of grace and supplication on the inhabitants of Jerusalem, before it will move them at first narrow, that Mashiach ben Yosef will be killed, then be angry with God and destroy all the nations following on Jerusalem, and that is to look at me– so they will look at all the nations to me to see what I will do to those who pierced messiah Ben Yosef."[2] (Ibn Ezra on Zech 12:10)

> Jesus and the New Testament viewed Zechariah as literally describing the death of the Messiah. So did the Rabbis who lived around the time of Jesus, as recorded in the Talmud.

Jesus and the New Testament viewed Zechariah as literally describing the death of the Messiah. So did the Rabbis who lived around the time of Jesus, as recorded in the Talmud. Later Jewish theologians began to question that interpretation, however. Afterall, Christianity was spreading, and it used the Jewish prophecies of the Messiah to prove that Jesus was the Messiah.

You can see later Jewish interpretations develop that say the piercing of the Messiah actually refers to either the martyrdom of those who hold true to Torah (the Law of Moses), or the slaying of our inner inclination to do bad things, or both.

> "What is the cause for the above mentioned mourning? R. Dosa and the Rabbis differ: One gives the reason that it [the mourning] is for the Messiah, the son of Joseph, who is to be killed; and the other gives the reason that it is for the evil inclination, which is to be killed. It is quite comprehensible according to the one who holds that it will be for the Messiah, the son of Joseph, as is said (Zech. 12:10)" (Midrash: Ein Yaakov (Glick Edition), Sukkah 5:5)

> "they shall look to me because of those who have been thrust through: Jonathan renders: And they shall supplicate me because of their wanderings. And they shall look to me to complain about those of them whom the nations thrust through and slew during their exile. And they shall mourn over it: over that slaughter." (Rashi on Zech 12:10)

---

2. Ezra, *Commentary of Tanakh*, Zech 12:10.

The same change in interpretation happens with other prophecies about the death of the Messiah such as Isa 53 or Ps 22, key passages used by Christians to show that Jesus is the Messiah. The death of the Messiah, seen by the early Jewish sages as Messianic, is later allegorically reinterpreted after the time of Christ to mean the nation of Israel, the martyrs of Judaism, or the evil desires within each of us. For our purposes here in studying Revelation we only want to establish that the "one who was pierced" referred to by Zechariah, in the book of Revelation, and the Gospels of both Matthew and John all refer to the Messiah, to Jesus. As Christians we take this part of Zechariah literally, not allegorically. Jesus was literally pierced by the sword of the Roman in fulfillment of this prophecy, as we read in the Gospel of John above. This is not a prophecy that is an allegory to something else, like the slaying of our inner desire to do wrong, the martyrdom of Torah-observant Jewish people, or anti-Semitism against the entire nation of Israel. Christians take this part of the vision of Zechariah literally, just like the Gospel of John does.

Since the New Testament takes the passage literally regarding the death of the Messiah, should we take the rest of the same passage literally? We should look at the entire vision in the same way unless the vision itself tells us otherwise. We cannot interpret one sentence in a paragraph literally because we like it, and then interpret another sentence allegorically because we do not like it. Many Christians simply do not like the idea that the Jewish people might have an end-time destiny. The most extreme Christian views hold that the Jewish people have been divorced by God and replaced by Christians, and the Bible has nothing more to say about them. We come face to face with this issue in how we interpret the Hebrew prophecies about the Messiah, his coming eternal Messianic Kingdom, and Jerusalem and Israel in the end times. Honestly ask yourself: if God still has a plan for the Jewish people, then does that bother you? Remember the parable of the Prodigal Son. We are all children of Abraham. Antisemitism is one of the greatest sins of Christians throughout history, and we often don't even recognize it. Sadly, I have seen discussion of this topic trigger anger in many Christians.

> We cannot interpret one sentence in a paragraph literally because we like it, and then interpret another sentence allegorically because we do not like it. Many Christians simply do not like the idea that the Jewish people might have an end-time destiny.
>
> "5 The Lord saw how great the wickedness of the human race had become on the earth, and that every inclination of the thoughts of the human heart was only evil all the time. 6 The Lord regretted that he had made human beings on the earth, and his heart was deeply troubled." (Gen 6:5-6, NIV)

ZECHARIAH

STRIKE THE SHEPHERD AND THE SHEEP WILL BE SCATTERED

As we saw above, the last vision of Zechariah in chapters 12–14 says that the House of David and the inhabitants of Jerusalem will look upon the one who was pierced and mourn for him as if for an only son. In this same vision we will also see that God calls for his Shepherd to be struck and for his sheep to be scattered.

> "7 'Awake, sword, against my shepherd, against the man who is close to me!' declares the Lord Almighty. 'Strike the shepherd, and the sheep will be scattered, and I will turn my hand against the little ones. 8 In the whole land,' declares the Lord, 'two-thirds will be struck down and perish; yet one-third will be left in it. 9 This third I will put into the fire; I will refine them like silver and test them like gold. They will call on my name and I will answer them; I will say, 'They are my people,' and they will say, 'The Lord is our God.'"" (Zech 13:7–9, NIV)

Jesus himself quotes this passage after the Last Supper. Did Jesus take Zechariah literally or allegorically? Did he literally believe he would be killed and his sheep would be scattered?

> "30 When they had sung a hymn, they went out to the Mount of Olives. 31 Then Jesus told them, 'This very night you will all fall away on account of me, for it is written: 'I will strike the shepherd, and the sheep of the flock will be scattered.' 32 But after I have risen, I will go ahead of you into Galilee.'" (Matt 26:30–32, NIV)

Jesus knew he was going to be killed. He willingly offered his soul, his Nephesh (נֶפֶשׁ, the lifeforce in the blood that makes atonement, Lev 17:11) as an offering for our sins. And not for ours only, but for the sins of the whole world, just as predicted by Isaiah, Daniel, Zechariah, and the Psalms. We see in this last vision of Zechariah the piercing of the Messiah, the striking of God's Shepherd, and the scattering of his sheep. Jesus took Zechariah literally, and it was literally fulfilled in his Crucifixion.

> We see in this last vision of Zechariah the piercing of the Messiah, the striking of God's Shepherd, and the scattering of his sheep. Jesus took Zechariah literally, and it was literally fulfilled in his Crucifixion.

AN ATTACK ON JERUSALEM

As we saw previously, Zech 12:10 speaks of the House of David and the inhabitants of Jerusalem looking upon the one who was pierced, and Zech 13:7–9 (quoted by Jesus himself) shows the striking of God's Shepherd. This one who was pierced was held by the Jewish Sages around the time of Jesus to refer to the Messiah, though later majority Jewish opinion changed. The New Testament clearly views this one who was pierced and struck as the Messiah, in agreement with the early Jewish sages. What else happens in that passage, the last vision recorded in Zechariah? We need only to look at the previous sentence to find out.

> "9 On that day I will set out to destroy all the nations that attack Jerusalem. 10 And I will pour out on the house of David and the inhabitants of Jerusalem a spirit of grace and supplication. They will look on me, the one they have pierced, and they will mourn for him as one mourns for an only child, and grieve bitterly for him as one grieves for a firstborn son." (Zech 12:9–10, NIV)

The day that they are looking upon the pierced Messiah is the day that God sets out to destroy all the nations that attack Jerusalem. In other words, on the day when the Messiah appears on the clouds in glory, there is a group of nations that are attacking Jerusalem. It is worth pausing here for a moment to reflect on this. For allegorical interpretations do not accept this in any way. But we should look at what the scriptures actually say. All Christians agree that the one who was pierced is the Messiah, because Jesus, John, and Matthew say so as shown above. Even the Jewish interpretations around the time of Jesus believed this, as we can see from the teachings memorialized in the Talmud. All Christians agree that Zechariah is speaking of Jesus when the last vision (chapters 12–14) speaks of the striking of the Shepherd and the scattering of his sheep, because Jesus himself quotes Zechariah in this way (Matt 26:30–32).

> Though all Christians take these verses (Zech 12:10, 13:7) literally, because Jesus, John, and Matthew did, the denominations disagree if the prior verse (Zech 12:9) is literal or allegorical.

Though all Christians take these verses (Zech 12:10, 13:7) literally, because Jesus, John, and Matthew did, the denominations disagree if the prior verse (Zech 12:9) is literal or allegorical. For example, John Wesley writes in his commentary on Zech 9:9–17 that the attack on Jerusalem refers to the protection of the Apostles from their persecution, and the attacks on the church in general. Allegorical interpretations tend to hold that all references to an attack on Israel are to be interpreted as attacks on the church throughout history. We will see this again and again, as we did earlier with interpretations of Daniel, as we see here in Zechariah, and so we will see again in other prophecies as well as with Revelation. But here in Zechariah, as seen earlier in Daniel (7:19–25, 8:21–25, and 11:36–45), Jerusalem is invaded and the Holy People of God are oppressed right before the Eternal Messianic Kingdom is established.

The Sola Scriptura approach asks us to only consider what the scriptures actually say. If we take Zech 12:10 literally, that the Messiah is literally pierced, then we must take the sentence right before it (Zech 12:9) literally, that Jerusalem is attacked. To say that the one pierced is literally the Messiah, but Jerusalem is allegorically the church is mixing the method of interpretation with no reason for that given by the text itself. This is the same thing that later Rabbis did after the spread of Christianity. They say the verses about the suffering and death of the Messiah refer to the suffering of the nation of Israel. They also say the attack on Jerusalem represents the battle within your heart to do good or to do evil. You can see how an allegorical interpretation can lead in many different directions, even away from Jesus as the Messiah and the atoning work of his Crucifixion.

> The Sola Scriptura approach asks us to only consider what the scriptures actually say. If we take Zech 12:10 literally, that the Messiah is literally pierced, then we must take the sentence right before it (Zech 12:9) literally, that Jerusalem is attacked.

Taking the entire paragraph literally, we see that people are looking at the Messiah who was pierced, and that Jerusalem is attacked. You may recall that Jerusalem has been attacked many times in history. Can we get specific as to which attack Zechariah is talking about? Could he have foreseen the coming of Jesus on Palm Sunday riding on a donkey, followed by Rome's attack on Jerusalem? Let's look at how this vision of Zechariah ends.

> "11 It will be inhabited; never again will it be destroyed. Jerusalem will be secure. 12 This is the plague with which the Lord will strike all the nations that fought against Jerusalem: Their flesh will rot while they are still standing on their feet, their eyes will rot in their sockets, and their tongues will rot in their mouths." (Zech 14:11-12, NIV)

After this specific attack on Jerusalem, it will never again be destroyed (Zech 14:11). Never again. Clearly that did not happen shortly after the time of Jesus, because Jerusalem was destroyed by Rome in 70 AD. So this attack that Zechariah is seeing is a final attack on Jerusalem. One that results in her never again being destroyed. Zechariah clearly sees a final battle between the nations of the world and God before the Eternal Messianic Kingdom is established. The last prophecy in Zechariah, chapters 12-14, describe the nations of the world attacking Jerusalem before God steps in and saves them. And then Jerusalem will be raised up and never destroyed again. This plain meaning of the text is in direct conflict with theologians who teach that the passage allegorically refers to the triumph of Christianity and has nothing to do with Jerusalem.

> "On that day, when all the nations of the earth are gathered against her, I will make Jerusalem an immovable rock for all the nations. All who try to move it will injure themselves." (Zech 12:3, NIV)

> "7 The Lord will save the dwellings of Judah first, so that the honor of the house of David and of Jerusalem's inhabitants may not be greater than that of Judah. 8 On that day the Lord will shield those who live in Jerusalem, so that the feeblest among them will be like David, and the house of David will be like God, like the angel of the Lord going before them. 9 On that day I will set out

to destroy all the nations that attack Jerusalem. 10 And I will pour out on the house of David and the inhabitants of Jerusalem a spirit of grace and supplication. They will look on me, the one they have pierced, and they will mourn for him as one mourns for an only child, and grieve bitterly for him as one grieves for a firstborn son." (Zech 12:7–10, NIV)

We clearly see that this day Zechariah is speaking of is a day when the nations of the world attack Jerusalem. And on that day God will save the inhabitants of the city, pour out on them his Spirit, and they will look upon the one they have pierced. Sola Scriptura takes the scriptures for what they plainly say. In the same way we believe that Jesus will return to judge the living and the dead, he will return in the same way he left – on the clouds in glory. And in the very same passage that speaks of his return and people looking upon him who was pierced and mourning (Zech 12:10) it also says that God saves Jerusalem from an attack of the nations. As Christians we cannot believe in a literal return of Christ, a literal time of people looking upon him who was pierced and mourning, and then say the prior verse about the attack on Israel is purely allegorical. We cannot interpret different verses of the same passage in different ways. We cannot say one verse is allegorical and the next literal, especially when the text nowhere says that and all interpretations of the passage from the New Testament itself are literal. We cannot change the plain meaning of the text to suit our individual theological doctrines.

> As Christians we cannot believe in a literal return of Christ, a literal time of people looking upon him who was pierced and mourning, and then say the prior verse about the attack on Israel is purely allegorical. We cannot interpret different verses of the same passage in different ways. We cannot say one verse is allegorical and the next literal, especially when the text nowhere says that and all interpretations of the passage from the New Testament itself are literal.

In this passage we can clearly see that the appearance of the Messiah is connected to God saving Jerusalem from an attack by the nations of the world. Look at what else Zechariah also has to say about it:

> "1 A day of the Lord is coming, Jerusalem, when your possessions will be plundered and divided up within your very walls. 2 I will gather all the nations to Jerusalem to fight against it; the city will be captured, the houses ransacked, and the women raped. Half of the city will go into exile, but the rest of the people will not be taken from the city. 3 Then the Lord will go out and fight against those nations, as he fights on a day of battle. 4 On that day his feet will stand on the Mount of Olives, east of Jerusalem, and the Mount of Olives will be split in two from east to west, forming a great valley, with half of the mountain moving north and half moving south. 5 You will flee by my mountain valley, for it will extend to Azel. You will flee as you fled from the earthquake in the days of Uzziah king of Judah. Then the Lord my God will come, and all

the holy ones with him. 6 On that day there will be neither sunlight nor cold, frosty darkness. 7 It will be a unique day—a day known only to the Lord—with no distinction between day and night. When evening comes, there will be light. 8 On that day living water will flow out from Jerusalem, half of it east to the Dead Sea and half of it west to the Mediterranean Sea, in summer and in winter. 9 The Lord will be king over the whole earth. On that day there will be one Lord, and his name the only name." (Zech 14:1–9, NIV)

Read verse 9 again. Is the Lord now the King over the whole earth? Is God the only god worshiped today? Is his name the only name? Certainly not, and so this passage has not yet been fulfilled and this final battle of the nations of the world against Jerusalem has not yet happened. Is this something we see in other parts of the Bible? Yes. Consider these related passages:

Symbolism	Reference	Scripture (NIV)
The kings of the world will gather together in Armageddon to fight against God.	Rev 16:14–16	14 They are demonic spirits that perform signs, and they go out to the kings of the whole world, to gather them for the battle on the great day of God Almighty. 15 "Look, I come like a thief! Blessed is the one who stays awake and remains clothed, so as not to go naked and be shamefully exposed." 16 *Then they gathered the kings together to the place that in Hebrew is called Armageddon.*
The beast is an 8th king. Ten kings will support the beast and wage war against the Lamb.	Rev 17:11–14	11 The beast who once was, and now is not, is an eighth king. He belongs to the seven and is going to his destruction. 12 "The ten horns you saw are ten kings who have not yet received a kingdom, but who for one hour will receive authority as kings along with the beast. 13 They have one purpose and will give their power and authority to the beast. 14 *They will wage war against the Lamb,* but the Lamb will triumph over them because he is Lord of lords and King of kings—and with him will be his called, chosen and faithful followers."
The beast is defeated.	Rev 19:19–20	19 Then I saw *the beast and the kings of the earth and their armies gathered together to wage war against the rider on the horse and his army.* 20 But the beast was captured, and with it the false prophet who had performed the signs on its behalf. With these signs he had deluded those who had received the mark of the beast and worshiped its image. The two of them were thrown alive into the fiery lake of burning sulfur.

Symbolism	Reference	Scripture (NIV)
The boastful horn wages war against the holy people until the Ancient of Days comes in judgment.	Dan 7:19-22	19 Then I wanted to know the meaning of the fourth beast, which was different from all the others and most terrifying, with its iron teeth and bronze claws—the beast that crushed and devoured its victims and trampled underfoot whatever was left. 20 I also wanted to know about the ten horns on its head and about the other horn that came up, before which three of them fell—the horn that looked more imposing than the others and that had eyes and a mouth that spoke boastfully. 21 As I watched, *this horn was waging war against the holy people and defeating them, 22 until the Ancient of Days came and pronounced judgment in favor of the holy people of the Most High, and the time came when they possessed the kingdom.*
The blasphemous king will oppress the holy people.	Dan 7:23-25	23 "He gave me this explanation: '*The fourth beast is a fourth kingdom* that will appear on earth. It will be different from all the other kingdoms and will devour the whole earth, trampling it down and crushing it. 24 *The ten horns are ten kings* who will come from this kingdom. After them *another king will arise,* different from the earlier ones; he will subdue three kings. 25 *He will speak against the Most High and oppress his holy people and try to change the set times and the laws. The holy people will be delivered into his hands for a time, times and half a time.*
The King of the North will boast against God and invade Israel.	Dan 11:36, 40-45	36 The king will do as he pleases. He will exalt and magnify himself above every god and will say unheard-of things against the God of gods. He will be successful until the time of wrath is completed, for what has been determined must take place. 40 *At the time of the end the king of the South will engage him in battle*, and the king of the North will storm out against him with chariots and cavalry and a great fleet of ships. He will invade many countries and sweep through them like a flood. 41 *He will also invade the Beautiful Land.* Many countries will fall, but Edom, Moab and the leaders of Ammon will be delivered from his hand. 42 He will extend his power over many countries; Egypt will not escape. 43 He will gain control of the treasures of gold and silver and all the riches of Egypt, with the Libyans and Cushites in submission. 44 But reports from the east and the north will alarm him, and he will set out in a great rage to destroy and annihilate many. 45 *He will pitch his royal tents between the seas at the beautiful holy mountain.* Yet he will come to his end, and no one will help him.

Symbolism	Reference	Scripture (NIV)
A fierce king will arise, oppress the holy people, and stand against the Prince of Princes.	Dan 8:21–25	21 The shaggy goat is the king of Greece, and the large horn between its eyes is the first king. 22 The four horns that replaced the one that was broken off represent four kingdoms that will emerge from his nation but will not have the same power. 23 In the latter part of their reign, when rebels have become completely wicked, a fierce-looking king, a master of intrigue, will arise. 24 He will become very strong, but not by his own power. He will cause astounding devastation and will succeed in whatever he does. *He will destroy those who are mighty, the holy people.* 25 He will cause deceit to prosper, and he will consider himself superior. When they feel secure, *he will destroy many and take his stand against the Prince of princes.* Yet he will be destroyed, but not by human power.
The holy people will be broken during this time period.	Dan 12:7	The man clothed in linen, who was above the waters of the river, lifted his right hand and his left hand toward heaven, and I heard him swear by him who lives forever, saying, *"It will be for a time, times and half a time. When the power of the holy people has been finally broken, all these things will be completed."*
The Day of the Lord comes when a large army is invading Israel.	Joel 2:1–3	1 Blow the trumpet in Zion; sound the alarm on my holy hill. Let all who live in the land tremble, *for the day of the Lord is coming.* It is close at hand— 2 a day of darkness and gloom, a day of clouds and blackness. *Like dawn spreading across the mountains a large and mighty army comes, such as never was in ancient times nor ever will be in ages to come.*
God will save his people and drive out the Northern Horde.	Joel 2:18–20	18 Then the Lord was jealous for his land and took pity on his people. 19 The Lord replied to them: "I am sending you grain, new wine and olive oil, enough to satisfy you fully; *never again will I make you an object of scorn to the nations.* 20 *I will drive the northern horde far from you,* pushing it into a parched and barren land; its eastern ranks will drown in the Dead Sea and its western ranks in the Mediterranean Sea. And its stench will go up; its smell will rise." Surely he has done great things!
God will restore Israel and judge the nations who attack her.	Joel 3:1–2	1 In those days and at that time, when I restore the fortunes of Judah and Jerusalem, 2 *I will gather all nations and bring them down to the Valley of Jehoshaphat. There I will put them on trial for what they did to my inheritance, my people Israel,* because they scattered my people among the nations and divided up my land.

Symbolism	Reference	Scripture (NIV)
The nations will gather and be judged, while Israel is protected by God. Never again will she be invaded.	Joel 3:14–16	14 *Multitudes, multitudes in the valley of decision! For the day of the Lord is near in the valley of decision.* 15 The sun and moon will be darkened, and the stars no longer shine. 16 The Lord will roar from Zion and thunder from Jerusalem; the earth and the heavens will tremble. *But the Lord will be a refuge for his people, a stronghold for the people of Israel.* 17 Then you will know that I, the Lord your God, dwell in Zion, my holy hill. Jerusalem will be holy; *never again will foreigners invade her.*
Satan will attack Israel and be defeated.	Rev 20:7–10	7 When the thousand years are over, Satan will be released from his prison 8 and will go out to deceive the nations in the four corners of the earth—*Gog and Magog*—*and to gather them for battle. In number they are like the sand on the seashore.* 9 They marched across the breadth of the earth and *surrounded the camp of God's people, the city he loves.* But fire came down from heaven and devoured them. 10 And the devil, who deceived them, was thrown into the lake of burning sulfur, where the beast and the false prophet had been thrown. They will be tormented day and night for ever and ever.
Gog will lead many nations against Israel.	Ezek 38:7–9	7 Get ready; be prepared, *you and all the hordes gathered about you*, and take command of them. 8 After many days you will be called to arms. *In future years you will invade a land that has recovered from war, whose people were gathered from many nations to the mountains of Israel, which had long been desolate.* They had been brought out from the nations, and now all of them live in safety. 9 *You and all your troops and the many nations with you will go up, advancing like a storm; you will be like a cloud covering the land.*
Gog is the leader that the prophets spoke of, who will come to invade Israel.	Ezek 38:14–18	14 Therefore, son of man, prophesy and say to Gog: 'This is what the Sovereign Lord says: In that day, when my people Israel are living in safety, will you not take notice of it? 15 *You will come from your place in the far north, you and many nations with you, all of them riding on horses, a great horde, a mighty army.* 16 *You will advance against my people Israel like a cloud that covers the land.* In days to come, Gog, I will bring you against my land, so that the nations may know me when I am proved holy through you before their eyes. 17 This is what the Sovereign Lord says: *You are the one I spoke of in former days by my servants the prophets of Israel.* At that time they prophesied for years that I would bring you against them. 18 This is what will happen in that day: *When Gog attacks the land of Israel*, my hot anger will be aroused, declares the Sovereign Lord.

Symbolism	Reference	Scripture (NIV)
God will destroy Gog and the nations that follow him in attacking Israel.	Ezek 39:1–5	1 Son of man, prophesy against Gog and say: 'This is what the Sovereign Lord says: I am against you, Gog, chief prince of Meshek and Tubal. 2 I will turn you around and drag you along. *I will bring you from the far north and send you against the mountains of Israel.* 3 Then I will strike your bow from your left hand and make your arrows drop from your right hand. 4 *On the mountains of Israel you will fall, you and all your troops and the nations with you.* I will give you as food to all kinds of carrion birds and to the wild animals. 5 You will fall in the open field, for I have spoken, declares the Sovereign Lord.
God will no longer allow his Holy Name to be profaned after Gog is destroyed.	Ezek 39:7–8	7 I will make known my holy name among my people Israel. *I will no longer let my holy name be profaned, and the nations will know that I the Lord am the Holy One in Israel.* 8 It is coming! It will surely take place, declares the Sovereign Lord. *This is the day I have spoken of.*
The dead will be so many that God calls the birds and wild animals to feast on them.	Ezek 39:17–19	17 Son of man, this is what the Sovereign Lord says: *Call out to every kind of bird and all the wild animals: 'Assemble and come together from all around to the sacrifice I am preparing for you, the great sacrifice on the mountains of Israel.* There you will eat flesh and drink blood. 18 *You will eat the flesh of mighty men and drink the blood of the princes of the earth* as if they were rams and lambs, goats and bulls—all of them fattened animals from Bashan. 19 At the sacrifice I am preparing for you, you will eat fat till you are glutted and drink blood till you are drunk.
When the nations wage war against Christ, there will be so many dead that the birds will gather for a great feast.	Rev 19:16–19	16 On his robe and on his thigh he has this name written: KING OF KINGS AND LORD OF LORDS. 17 And I saw an angel standing in the sun, *who cried in a loud voice to all the birds flying in midair, "Come, gather together for the great supper of God, 18 so that you may eat the flesh of kings, generals, and the mighty, of horses and their riders, and the flesh of all people, free and slave, great and small."* 19 Then I saw the beast and the kings of the earth and their armies gathered together to wage war against the rider on the horse and his army.
The nations will be gathered together and punished by God.	Zeph 3:8	8 Therefore wait for me," declares the Lord, "for the day I will stand up to testify. *I have decided to assemble the nations, to gather the kingdoms and to pour out my wrath on them*—all my fierce anger. *The whole world* will be consumed by the fire of my jealous anger.
God will save a remnant in Israel.	Zeph 3:11–12	11 On that day you, Jerusalem, will not be put to shame for all the wrongs you have done to me, because I will remove from you your arrogant boasters. *Never again will you be haughty on my holy hill.* 12 But I will leave within you the meek and humble. *The remnant of Israel will trust in the name of the Lord.*

Symbolism	Reference	Scripture (NIV)
God will turn back Jerusalem's enemies. Never again will they fear any harm.	Zeph 3:15–17	15 *The Lord has taken away your punishment, he has turned back your enemy. The Lord, the King of Israel, is with you; never again will you fear any harm.* 16 On that day they will say to *Jerusalem, "Do not fear, Zion;* do not let your hands hang limp. 17 The Lord your God is with you, the Mighty Warrior who saves. He will take great delight in you; in his love he *will no longer rebuke you,* but will rejoice over you with singing."

As you can see from the numerous passages above, the Bible clearly and directly speaks of an attack of Israel by the nations of the world. God will save Jerusalem and destroy those nations. And then God's Holy Name will never again be profaned, Jerusalem will never again be invaded by foreigners, and the one True God will be the only God known over the whole world. If you look at our world today you can clearly see this has not yet happened. God's Name is continually profaned. Jerusalem has a foreign temple, the Al-Aqsa Mosque, as well as the Dome of the Rock sitting on the Temple Mount complex today. And we must ask: has God poured out his Holy Spirit on the House of David and the inhabitants of Jerusalem as promised? Have they looked upon the Messiah who was pierced and mourned for him? All these things have not happened according to a literal and plain reading of the scriptures. And not just the scripture of a single verse taken out of context, but several verses. The literal interpretation of Zechariah's vision is supported by numerous verses in several passages, in several books of the Bible, in both the Old and New Testaments.

> The literal interpretation of Zechariah's vision is supported by numerous versus in several passages, in several books of the Bible, in both the Old and New Testaments.

Here is where the allegorical interpretations sharply disagree with those that are literal. If the prophets were literally speaking of an attack on Jerusalem, then the land of Israel and the Jewish people have an end-time destiny and God is not done with them. On the other hand, when theologians replace the Jewish people with Christians, when "Spiritual" Israel replaces "Ethnic" Israel, then the attack on Jerusalem is reinterpreted as an attack on Christianity. The nations that come together to attack Jerusalem are reinterpreted to mean all antichristian governments throughout history. But re-read the twenty-two passages quoted above and take them seriously. The final vision of Zechariah plainly speaks of an attack on Jerusalem, just like it plainly speaks of the Messiah as the one who was pierced, the Shepherd who was struck, and his sheep scattered. Jesus and the Gospels plainly and literally interpreted these passages. If someone tells you something different than Jesus did, even if it comes from an angel, do not believe it.

THE TWO ARRIVALS OF THE MESSIAH

As we looked at the last vision recorded in the book of Zechariah, we saw that the Messiah appears as one who was pierced (struck), and great mourning as if for an only son takes place. We also see in that same vision that the day of his appearance is the day when God sets out to destroy all the nations that attack Jerusalem. God will defend Jerusalem and never again will it be destroyed. These amazing prophecies are fundamental background context for Revelation.

Just before this final vision Zechariah gives us another related vision about the Messiah. Chapters 9–11 are the next to last vision in the book of Zechariah. In them we see that the Messiah arrives lowly, riding on a donkey.

> "Rejoice greatly, Daughter Zion! Shout, Daughter Jerusalem! See, your king comes to you, righteous and victorious, lowly and riding on a donkey, on a colt, the foal of a donkey." (Zech 9:9, NIV)

But we saw earlier in Daniel that he predicted something different about the appearance of the Messiah. He predicted that the Messiah would appear on the clouds in glory, not riding lowly on a donkey.

> "In my vision at night I looked, and there before me was one like a son of man, coming with the clouds of heaven. He approached the Ancient of Days and was led into his presence." (Dan 7:13, NIV)

In Revelation John seems to combine these two appearances, one from Zechariah (great mourning for the one who was pierced, who arrives lowly and riding on a donkey) and one from Daniel (one like a Son of Man coming with the clouds of Heaven).

> "'Look, he is coming with the clouds,' and 'every eye will see him, even those who pierced him'; and all peoples on earth 'will mourn because of him.' So shall it be! Amen." (Rev 1:7, NIV)

What is going on here? Does the Messiah appear riding on a donkey in humility (Zech 9:9) or on the clouds in glory (Dan 7:13)? Christians understand this seeming contradiction as two different appearances of the Messiah. A First Coming where he was rejected and died for the sins of others after riding into Jerusalem on a donkey on Palm Sunday, and a Second Coming where he will appear in the clouds in glory and come to judge the living and the dead.

> Does the Messiah appear riding on a donkey in humility (Zech 9:9) or on the clouds in glory (Dan 7:13)? Christians understand this seeming contradiction as two different appearances of the Messiah.

What do Jewish theologians think and teach about this apparent contradiction? Modern Orthodox Rabbis teach there will be only one appearance of the Messiah.

They teach that the Messiah will appear only one way or the other, depending on if the Jewish People deserve redemption or not. In other words, if the Jewish people do enough good in repairing our broken world, then the Messiah will appear on the clouds as a reward. Otherwise, he will appear in humility to their shame. We can see this view most clearly in the Talmud.

> "Rabbi Alexandri says: Rabbi Yehoshua ben Levi raises a contradiction between two depictions of the coming of the Messiah. It is written: 'There came with the clouds of heaven, one like unto a son of man . . . and there was given him dominion and glory and a kingdom . . . his dominion is an everlasting dominion' (Daniel 7:13–14). And it is written: 'Behold, your king will come to you; he is just and victorious; lowly and riding upon a donkey and upon a colt, the foal of a donkey' (Zechariah 9:9). Rabbi Alexandri explains: If the Jewish people merit redemption, the Messiah will come in a miraculous manner with the clouds of heaven. If they do not merit redemption, the Messiah will come lowly and riding upon a donkey." (Talmud Sanhedrin 98a:13)

To better understand how to resolve this apparent contradiction, for which Christians see two comings of Christ and Rabbis see only one (with an assumed choice in how he will appear based on if the people deserve reward or shame), we need to look more closely at Zechariah's entire vision in which the Messiah appears lowly and riding on a donkey. Elsewhere in that same vision (Zech 9–11) we will see that there are actually two shepherds described. The first one is sent by God and rejected. The second one turns out to be worthless.

THE TWO SHEPHERDS

As we explored above in the next to last vision recorded in Zechariah (Zech 9–11) the Messiah appears riding lowly on a donkey. If we look further in this same vision, we will find out that the Messiah is rejected and paid a worthless price of thirty pieces of silver. A second shepherd is then sent who ends up rejecting the flock. The flock rejects the first Shepherd and considers him worthless (only the small sum of thirty pieces of silver), but ironically the second shepherd ends up rejecting the flock and is himself worthless.

> "4 This is what the Lord my God says: 'Shepherd the flock marked for slaughter. 5 Their buyers slaughter them and go unpunished. Those who sell them say, 'Praise the Lord, I am rich!' Their own shepherds do not spare them.'"
> (Zech 11:4–5, NIV)

Zechariah is told to prophetically show what will happen. The leaders of his people don't care about their flock, and they go unpunished. They oppress their people and get rich off of them, without caring for them. God calls Zechariah to prophetically shepherd them. Yet they reject the shepherd and pay him little value.

"7 So I shepherded the flock marked for slaughter, particularly the oppressed of the flock. Then I took two staffs and called one Favor and the other Union, and I shepherded the flock. 8 In one month I got rid of the three shepherds. The flock detested me, and I grew weary of them 9 and said, 'I will not be your shepherd. Let the dying die, and the perishing perish. Let those who are left eat one another's flesh.' 10 Then I took my staff called Favor and broke it, revoking the covenant I had made with all the nations. 11 It was revoked on that day, and so the oppressed of the flock who were watching me knew it was the word of the Lord. 12 I told them, 'If you think it best, give me my pay; but if not, keep it.' So they paid me thirty pieces of silver. 13 And the Lord said to me, 'Throw it to the potter'—the handsome price at which they valued me! So I took the thirty pieces of silver and threw them to the potter at the house of the Lord." (Zech 11:7-13, NIV)

The leaders are oppressing the flock, so God sends them a first Shepherd. But the flock detests this Shepherd and considers him worthless, paying only a small sum of thirty pieces of silver.

The leaders are oppressing the flock, so God sends them a first Shepherd. But the flock detests this Shepherd and considers him worthless, paying only a small sum of thirty pieces of silver. As Christians we see this prophecy of the first shepherd who was rejected as speaking about Jesus, along with related passages in the book of Jeremiah (Jer 19:1-13; 32:6-9).

"1 Early in the morning, all the chief priests and the elders of the people made their plans how to have Jesus executed. 2 So they bound him, led him away and handed him over to Pilate the governor. 3 When Judas, who had betrayed him, saw that Jesus was condemned, he was seized with remorse and returned the thirty pieces of silver to the chief priests and the elders. 4 'I have sinned,' he said, 'for I have betrayed innocent blood.' 'What is that to us?' they replied. 'That's your responsibility.' 5 So Judas threw the money into the temple and left. Then he went away and hanged himself. 6 The chief priests picked up the coins and said, 'It is against the law to put this into the treasury, since it is blood money.' 7 So they decided to use the money to buy the potter's field as a burial place for foreigners." (Matt 27:1-7, NIV)

There are a lot of interpretations of the details of this passage in Zechariah and how it relates to Jesus, but following the Sola Scriptura approach we will look only at what the scriptures directly say. This first shepherd that Zechariah is prophesying about is rejected. In fact, he is detested. In the vision a second shepherd then comes along who turns out to be worthless.

"15 Then the Lord said to me, 'Take again the equipment of a foolish shepherd. 16 For I am going to raise up a shepherd over the land who will not care for the lost, or seek the young, or heal the injured, or feed the healthy, but will eat the meat of the choice sheep, tearing off their hooves. 17 'Woe to the worthless shepherd, who deserts the flock! May the sword strike his arm and his right eye! May his arm be completely withered, his right eye totally blinded!'" (Zech 11:15-17, NIV)

And so ends the vision. Remember that this vision (Zech 9–11) begins with the Messiah arriving lowly on a donkey. The leaders oppress their people and so God sends them a Shepherd. The people reject that Shepherd considering him worthless. Then God sends a second shepherd who doesn't care about the flock. The second one ultimately deserts the flock and is cursed.

> The leaders oppress their people and so God sends them a Shepherd. The people reject that Shepherd considering him worthless. Then God sends a second shepherd who doesn't care about the flock. The second one ultimately deserts the flock and is cursed.

Explanations for this vision vary greatly. A traditional Jewish interpretation given by Rashi in his commentary on Zechariah says these events refer to the time of the Second Temple and its destruction. Christians should take notice because that is the time of Jesus. Not only do Christians believe Zechariah prophesied about the end of the Second Temple period, but so did one of the most famous Jewish theologians. Rashi holds that the leaders at the time of the Second Temple were bad people and oppressed the people of God. While he says he cannot explain the meaning of the thirty pieces of silver, he says these events culminated in the destruction of the Second Temple in 70 AD. We know from history that after the rejection of Jesus, the Jewish leadership soon accepted another person as the Messiah. That man, Simon Bar Kokhba, led a revolt against Rome that ended with Rome's harsh punishment of the Jewish people and their expulsion from the land of Israel. They remained exiled from the time of Jesus until modern times when Israel was once again made a nation in 1948 AD.

Other interpretations identify the foolish shepherd as Barabbas, who was a prisoner chosen to be released instead of Jesus (Luke 23:18). Still other theologians say the foolish shepherd is the coming Antichrist who will again oppress the inhabitants of Jerusalem. You can also find theologians who say the foolish shepherd represents the Pharisees who led the people away from Jesus and ultimately to their expulsion from Israel.

> Though explanations for the second shepherd range from Bar Kokhba, to Barabbas, to the Antichrist, to the Pharisees, Zechariah never actually tells us.

Though explanations for the second shepherd range from Bar Kokhba, to Barabbas, to the Antichrist, to the Pharisees, Zechariah never actually tells us. We are not told who the foolish shepherd is or what is the end of him. Some theologians see a possible match in a reference to the wounding of the Antichrist in Revelation. In

Zechariah the second shepherd is cursed to have a withered arm and a blinded eye from an attack with a sword (Zech 11:17). In Revelation the beast has a fatal wound to the head from a sword, but he survives (Rev 13:3,12-14). Though a possible match, the Sola Scriptura approach will hold us to only what the scriptures directly say. God provided his Shepherd, but the people detested and rejected him, considering him only worth an insulting small price of thirty pieces of silver. And then a foolish shepherd comes who oppresses the people and turns out to be worthless.

If we look at the whole vision Zechariah gives us in chapters 9-11, we can see something really interesting. Near the beginning of the vision the Messiah appears riding lowly on a donkey (Zech 9:9). And the end of that vision shows that the Shepherd of God is detested, rejected, and considered worthless (thirty pieces of silver). Then a second shepherd comes who is the one who actually turns out to be worthless. Now if we consider the last vision of Zechariah in chapters 12-14, we can see when the Messiah appears the people will see that he has been pierced and mourn for him as if for an only son. There are clearly two different arrivals of the Messiah. The first time he comes in humility riding on a donkey and is detested and rejected. A second shepherd comes who turns out to be worthless and abandons the people. Then later the Messiah appears again, but this time on the clouds in glory to save his people from the attack on Jerusalem. At this second appearance they see that he was pierced, and they mourn greatly.

> There are clearly two different arrivals of the Messiah. The first time he comes in humility riding on a donkey and is detested and rejected. A second shepherd comes who turns out to be worthless and abandons the people. Then later the Messiah appears again, but this time on the clouds in glory to save his people from the attack on Jerusalem. At this second appearance they see that he was pierced, and they mourn greatly.

Read again what John has to say in the opening of the Book Revelation:

> "'Look, he is coming with the clouds,' and 'every eye will see him, even those who pierced him'; and all peoples on earth 'will mourn because of him.' So shall it be! Amen." (Rev 1:7, NIV)

When John wrote these words Jesus had already come into the world. On Palm Sunday he rode on a donkey into Jerusalem. The last visions of Zechariah that foretold of the rejection and piercing of God's Shepherd were about to be fulfilled within the following week by Easter Sunday. By the time John wrote Revelation the parts of Zechariah referring to the rejection and piercing of the Messiah had already occurred. The remaining prophecies about the final attack on Jerusalem had not yet been fulfilled. The Pharisees still lived in Jerusalem and the Temple still stood for several years after the Crucifixion of Jesus. Roughly forty years later the Romans destroyed the Second Temple (70 AD). Afterward a Jewish revolt against the Romans, led by one they thought was the messiah (Bar Kokhba), was put down and the Jewish people were exiled from the Promised Land (134 AD). The remainder of Zechariah and Daniel wait for an appointed time, and it will not fail to come to pass. At that time the Messiah will appear on the clouds and every eye will see him, even those who pierced him. And all peoples on earth will mourn at his appearance. Some will rise to everlasting life and others to everlasting contempt. So shall it be. Amen.

THE BRANCH WHO WILL COME

Thus far in our study of Zechariah we have seen that the Messiah would appear riding lowly on a donkey, be detested, and rejected. Another foolish shepherd would then arise who turns out to be worthless. And in the last vision of Zechariah many nations will gather together to attack Jerusalem one last time, but God will step in to save her. In that day the Messiah will appear on the clouds, and everyone will see him, the one who was pierced and struck, and mourn greatly. These are all great prophecies in Zechariah to keep in mind as we seek to better understand the book of Revelation.

After studying the last two visions we now go back toward the beginning of Zechariah to see what else he prophesied about. One of the earliest prophecies we have is about the Messiah himself. Zechariah calls him "the Branch" and says he will build the temple of the Lord. Zechariah says he will be both king and priest and will take away the sin of the land of Israel. These things are all shown symbolically through a vision of the High Priest (Joshua) at the time of Zechariah being crowned king.

> "8 'Listen, High Priest Joshua, you and your associates seated before you, who are men symbolic of things to come: I am going to bring my servant, the Branch. 9 See, the stone I have set in front of Joshua! There are seven eyes on that one stone, and I will engrave an inscription on it,' says the Lord Almighty, 'and I will remove the sin of this land in a single day.'" (Zech 3:8–9, NIV)

> "12 Tell him this is what the Lord Almighty says: 'Here is the man whose name is the Branch, and he will branch out from his place and build the temple of the Lord. 13 It is he who will build the temple of the Lord, and he will be clothed with majesty and will sit and rule on his throne. And he will be a priest on his throne. And there will be harmony between the two.'" (Zech 6:12–13, NIV)

In this vision revealed at the beginning of the book of Zechariah we are clearly told the events taking place are symbolic. The Sola Scriptura method has us take this for what it plainly says, the vision is symbolic of things to come (Zech 3:8). Though Joshua is the High Priest and Zerubbabel the governor, and though they will oversee the building of the Second Temple, they are symbolic of things to come. But what is to come? Zechariah prophesies of "The Branch" to come, which is symbolic for the Messiah. He will branch out from his place and build the temple of the Lord. He will be both a ruler and a priest.

Zechariah prophesies of "The Branch" to come, which is symbolic for the Messiah. He will branch out from his place and build the temple of the Lord. He will be both a ruler and a priest.

This vision of the Branch is regarded in both Judaism and Christianity as prophetic of the Messiah. However, the prophecy of the building of the Temple is understood in many different ways across both religions. In Judaism there is a range of beliefs from the Messiah building the Third Temple in the End Times, to the Reformed Jewish view of there being no need for a future Third Temple. In Christianity we generally take our belief from Revelation that says there is no temple in the New Jerusalem because we Christians are symbolically the temple that Jesus built (a spiritual temple). As Christians we arrive at that conclusion by looking at the book of Revelation, the Gospels, and the Epistles.

> "The one who is victorious I will make a pillar in the temple of my God. Never again will they leave it. I will write on them the name of my God and the name of the city of my God, the new Jerusalem, which is coming down out of heaven from my God; and I will also write on them my new name." (Rev 3:12, NIV)

> "2 I saw the Holy City, the new Jerusalem, coming down out of heaven from God, prepared as a bride beautifully dressed for her husband. 3 And I heard a loud voice from the throne saying, 'Look! God's dwelling place is now among the people, and he will dwell with them. They will be his people, and God himself will be with them and be their God.' 22 I did not see a temple in the city, because the Lord God Almighty and the Lamb are its temple." (Rev 21:2-3,22, NIV)

> "4 As you come to him, the living Stone—rejected by humans but chosen by God and precious to him— 5 you also, like living stones, are being built into a spiritual house to be a holy priesthood, offering spiritual sacrifices acceptable to God through Jesus Christ." (1 Pet 2:4-5, NIV)

> "Don't you know that you yourselves are God's temple and that God's Spirit dwells in your midst?" (1 Cor 3:16, NIV)

> "Do you not know that your bodies are temples of the Holy Spirit, who is in you, whom you have received from God? You are not your own" (1 Cor 6:19, NIV)

> "19 Consequently, you are no longer foreigners and strangers, but fellow citizens with God's people and also members of his household, 20 built on the foundation of the apostles and prophets, with Christ Jesus himself as the chief cornerstone. 21 In him the whole building is joined together and rises to become a holy temple in the Lord. 22 And in him you too are being built together to become a dwelling in which God lives by his Spirit." (Eph 2:19-22, NIV)

> "Jesus said, 'My kingdom is not of this world. If it were, my servants would fight to prevent my arrest by the Jewish leaders. But now my kingdom is from another place.'" (John 18:36, NIV)

> "19 Jesus answered them, 'Destroy this temple, and I will raise it again in three days.' 20 They replied, 'It has taken forty-six years to build this temple, and you are going to raise it in three days?' 21 But the temple he had spoken of was his body. 22 After he was raised from the dead, his disciples recalled what he had said. Then they believed the scripture and the words that Jesus had spoken." (John 2:19-22, NIV)

As Christians we believe that after the judgment there will be a New Heaven and a New Earth, and in the New Jerusalem that comes down from Heaven there will be no temple because God himself is the temple. We, as living stones, will be pillars in the temple of God, never again to be removed. Just as Zechariah is literally told the vision of the Branch is symbolic of things to come, so too we take a symbolic meaning to the temple which the Branch was prophesied to build. As we take a look at Ezekiel in the next section we will see more about this idea of a future temple.

Recall from our previous study of Daniel that he was shown a vision of a worldwide leader that oppresses the people of God and sets up the abomination of desolation in the temple. We need to be careful about symbols and their use across different books and different authors. We would be guilty of conflation, combining and equating things that are otherwise unrelated, if we viewed the future temple as the same in every reference. For example, above we see that Jesus refers to his body as the temple which is raised in three days. In Revelation it says there is no temple in the New Jerusalem. Paul refers to the believers in Christ as each one being a temple wherein the Holy Spirit dwells, and elsewhere as each being a part of the body of Christ (1 Cor 12:27). In Daniel the future temple is a place where the abomination is set up (Dan 8:11, 9:27, 11:31, 12:11) and in Ezekiel you will see there is a massive future temple in his final vision of the future (Ezek 40–48).

> We need to be careful about symbols and their use across different books and different authors. We would be guilty of conflation, combining and equating things that are otherwise unrelated, if we viewed the future temple as the same in every reference.

As you can see, we could combine references to a future temple from different books in the Bible and come up with a variety of explanations. And that is exactly what happens in various commentaries. However, staying just within the book of Zechariah which is our current focus, we see that Joshua the High Priest and Zerubbabel the governor will lead the building of the Second Temple after the Judeans return from the Babylonian Captivity. And they are symbolic of things to come. There is much to say about the Messiah being the Branch, especially when you look at similar references in

Isaiah, Jeremiah, and the New Testament, but less to say about the role of the temple in the end times and how that applies to the book of Revelation.

Christians are not alone in wanting to explain how the symbolism of the building of the Second Temple may apply to the future. When Zechariah is told this is symbolic of things to come, we get excited and want to offer an explanation. Since the Second Temple was still standing at the time of Jesus, Christians cannot look to Jesus building a physical temple, as some Jewish theologians say the Messiah will do when he appears. As we saw above Christians view the literal symbolism as speaking of a spiritual temple, the spiritual body of Christ, us as Christians wherein the Holy Spirit dwells, for there is no temple in the future New Jerusalem to come.

In Judaism there is a different expectation in some movements. Some Jewish movements look to build the Third Temple to prepare for the Messiah, some look for the Messiah himself to build it, and others have no expectation of a new temple. Orthodox Jewish teachings are that the Messiah will appear and there will be a physical Third Temple. It is a great debate whether the Messiah actually builds the Third Temple, or whether he arrives after the Third Temple is built. This extends to modern day efforts to prepare for building the Third Temple on the Temple Mount in Jerusalem. Some look to build the temple as soon as possible to usher in the appearance of the Messiah and the Messianic Age. Others want to wait for the Messiah first and let him build the temple. And still yet in other Jewish movements such as Reform Judaism the idea of a Third Temple is no longer a focus, and even the prayers for the building of it have been removed from their liturgy, the *Siddur* (סִדּוּר).[3]

> Some Jewish movements look to build the Third Temple to prepare for the Messiah, some look for the Messiah himself to build it, and others have no expectation of a new temple.

Similarly, some Christians look for a physical Third Temple to be built, in which the Antichrist will set himself up claiming to be God and then desecrate the temple as seen in Daniel. While others do not look for a Third Temple and only to that future time where there is no temple after Christ returns as seen at the end of Revelation, because the Lord God Almighty and the Lamb are its temple (Rev 21:22).

The Sola Scriptura approach only holds that the New Jerusalem will not have a temple, for God himself dwells among his people. And since we saw in Daniel that all of his prophecies have not yet been fulfilled, the worldwide leader who will one day attack Jerusalem for the last time (as also seen above in Zechariah) will go into a physical temple in Jerusalem claiming to be God. This last view is a claim we make from Daniel, not Zechariah. Here in Zechariah the temple seen was the Second Temple built after the Babylonian Captivity. Though the vision of the Branch is symbolic of things to come, Zechariah does not directly say how the symbolism regarding the temple works itself out and it may only apply to the Second Temple in Zechariah's

---

3. Frishman, *Reform Siddur*.

vision. While the view of Christians as the body of Christ, each in whom the Holy Spirit dwells, is scriptural and held by Sola Scriptura, it is not a claim made specifically from the book of Zechariah (though it is fully compatible with his vision).

> Though the vision of the Branch is symbolic of things to come, Zechariah does not directly say how the symbolism regarding the temple works itself out and it may only apply to the Second Temple in Zechariah's vision. While the view of Christians as the body of Christ, each in whom the Holy Spirit dwells, is scriptural and held by Sola Scriptura, it is not a claim made specifically from the book of Zechariah (though it is fully compatible with his vision).

Zechariah is just not clear about the symbolism of the temple in the vision, and theories about his meaning necessarily pull in references from other books to make assumptions. However, notice in verse 13 that the symbolism of things to come says that the Messiah will be both king and priest.

> "12 Tell him this is what the Lord Almighty says: 'Here is the man whose name is the Branch, and he will branch out from his place and build the temple of the Lord. 13 It is he who will build the temple of the Lord, and he will be clothed with majesty and will sit and rule on his throne. And he will be a priest on his throne. And there will be harmony between the two.'" (Zech 6:12–13, NIV)

This prophecy of a king of Israel who also is the High Priest has never been fulfilled. As Christians we see that Jesus is both the King of Israel and our High Priest. This should remind us of the prophecy about the Mashiach Nagid we saw earlier in Daniel. He was the prophesied Messiah and Prince who would come, be rejected, and put to death. Here again we have a prophecy in Zechariah about the coming of one who is both the head of the government and of religion. In the time of Zechariah, this was not fulfilled. Neither Joshua the High Priest nor Zerubbabel were both High Priest and King. They were only symbolic of things to come.

THE TWO WITNESSES

As we went back to the first vision of Zechariah in the previous section we saw an amazing prophecy about the Messiah, called "the Branch," who would build the temple and be both king and priest. This first vision of Zechariah spans chapters 1 through 6. Chapters 1 and 2 show Four Horsemen, Four Craftsmen, and the rebuilding of Jerusalem and the Temple before we get to the Branch in chapter 3 that we just explored above. We will discuss the various groups of four below in another section. For now, we want to move forward from the Branch in chapter 3 to chapter 4, because this passage is directly referenced by Revelation.

> "Then there was given me a measuring rod like a staff; and someone said, 'Get up and measure the temple of God and the altar, and those who worship in it.

> 2 Leave out the court which is outside the temple and do not measure it, for it has been given to the nations; and they will tread under foot the holy city for forty-two months. 3 And I will grant authority to my two witnesses, and they will prophesy for twelve hundred and sixty days, clothed in sackcloth.' 4 These are the two olive trees and the two lampstands that stand before the Lord of the earth." (Rev 11:1–4, NASB)

Revelation chapter 11 speaks of a time when the world is not following the ways of God. There have been seven seals opened, followed by six trumpets. Right before the seventh trumpet is blown John sees a vision of Two Witnesses that God sends to witness the truth to the world. A Beast comes up from the Abyss and then kills the Two Witnesses while the world rejoices. Then God resurrects the Two Witnesses and takes them up into Heaven.

> "7 When they have finished their testimony, the beast that comes up out of the abyss will make war with them, and overcome them and kill them. 8 And their dead bodies will lie in the street of the great city which mystically is called Sodom and Egypt, where also their Lord was crucified. 9 Those from the peoples and tribes and tongues and nations will look at their dead bodies for three and a half days, and will not permit their dead bodies to be laid in a tomb. 10 And those who dwell on the earth will rejoice over them and celebrate; and they will send gifts to one another, because these two prophets tormented those who dwell on the earth. 11 But after the three and a half days, the breath of life from God came into them, and they stood on their feet; and great fear fell upon those who were watching them. 12 And they heard a loud voice from heaven saying to them, 'Come up here.' Then they went up into heaven in the cloud, and their enemies watched them." (Rev 11:7–12, NASB)

You will see from verse four above that this is a direct reference to Zechariah's first vision that we have been looking at. These Two Witnesses are "the two olive trees" and the two lampstands, and "they stand before the Lord of the earth."

> "2 He said to me, 'What do you see?' And I said, 'I see, and behold, a lampstand all of gold with its bowl on the top of it, and its seven lamps on it with seven spouts belonging to each of the lamps which are on the top of it; 3 also two olive trees by it, one on the right side of the bowl and the other on its left side.' 4 Then I said to the angel who was speaking with me saying, 'What are these, my lord?' 5 So the angel who was speaking with me answered and said to me, 'Do you not know what these are?' And I said, 'No, my lord.' 11 Then I said to him, 'What are these two olive trees on the right of the lampstand and on its left?' 12 And I answered the second time and said to him, 'What are the two olive branches which are beside the two golden pipes, which empty the golden oil from themselves?' 13 So he answered me, saying, 'Do you not know what these are?' And I said, 'No, my lord.' 14 Then he said, 'These are the

two anointed ones who are standing by the Lord of the whole earth.'" (Zech 4: 2–5,11–14, NASB)

You might recall that John received his vision from Jesus and told us in the first chapter what he saw as he turned around to see who was speaking to him.

> "12 Then I turned to see the voice that was speaking with me. And having turned I saw seven golden lampstands; 13 and in the middle of the lampstands I saw one like a son of man, clothed in a robe reaching to the feet, and girded across His chest with a golden sash." (Rev 1:12–13, NASB)

John clearly has Zechariah in mind, so understanding the book of Zechariah is critical to understanding the book of Revelation. We are told that the Two Witnesses we see in Revelation 11 are the same two we symbolically see in Zechariah's first vision. Zechariah had just seen that Joshua the High Priest and Zerubbabel were symbolic of things to come, that the Messiah would be both a King and a Priest. These two anointed ones are witnesses to God's truth in a world that rejects him. Zechariah only tells us that they are anointed to serve the Lord of all the earth. John tells us they serve the Lord by being his two witnesses right before the final seventh trumpet is blown, and the Day of Judgment arrives.

Remember, Zechariah is told that he is seeing things which are symbolic of what is to come. And the Branch, the Messiah, will be both a king and priest. In Revelation John tells us these two are the last to witness about Jesus to an unbelieving world before the seventh trumpet is blown on the Day of Judgment.

> "And the nations were enraged, and Your wrath came, and the time came for the dead to be judged, and the time to reward Your bond-servants the prophets and the saints and those who fear Your name, the small and the great, and to destroy those who destroy the earth.'" (Rev 11:18, NASB)

As you have likely now come to expect, interpretations of these Two Witnesses, the Two Olive Trees, vary greatly. Here is a sample of the many possibilities theologians have claimed:

- Christ and the Holy Spirit
- Christ as King and Christ as High Priest
- Moses and Elijah
- Moses and Aaron
- Ezekiel and Daniel
- God's representatives who parallel the Beast and the False Prophet of Revelation
- Two who will preach the Gospel to the World just before Jesus returns
- Jewish scholars in Israel and Babylonia

- The law and the prophets
- The Hebrew Bible and the New Testament
- The good inclination within us and the complementary evil inclination
- The church and the Word
- All civil and religious powers throughout history that testify of Jesus
- Grace and sanctification

Theologians who make a claim go to great lengths to prove their claim using multiple verses, books, reason, and even emotion. But the Sola Scriptura approach only looks at what the scriptures plainly say. Neither Zechariah nor John actually name the Two Olive Trees, the Two Witnesses, therefore Sola Scriptura does not take a position. But Revelation clearly references the prophecies of Zechariah. Zechariah clearly prophesies that the Messiah will be both King and Priest, the Messiah will be struck and pierced, and there will be a final attack on Jerusalem at the time of the arrival of the Messiah. All of this is background context for Revelation and agrees with the visions of the other prophets.

> Theologians who make a claim go to great lengths to prove their claim using multiple verses, books, reason, and even emotion. But the Sola Scriptura approach only looks at what the scriptures plainly say. Neither Zechariah nor John actually name the Two Olive Trees, the Two Witnesses, therefore Sola Scriptura does not take a position.

THE INGATHERING OF ISRAEL

Earlier we looked at the next to last vision recorded in Zechariah, chapters 9–11. In the beginning of that vision the Messiah appears riding lowly on a donkey. We saw that the Messiah was rejected and paid a worthless price of thirty pieces of silver. At the end of that vision, we saw a second shepherd was then sent who ended up rejecting the flock and being worthless. This vision speaks of the Messiah who comes riding lowly on a donkey being rejected, and another who comes after that is worthless.

In the middle of this amazing vision there is an interesting prophecy regarding the nation of Israel. At the time when Zechariah had this vision the Judeans were just coming out of the Babylonian Captivity and returning to the land of Israel. Zechariah's prophecies spoke of the immediate restoration of the land and the building of the Second Temple, and they were also symbolic of things to come as God told Zechariah. The prophesied Branch who would come is the Messiah. And in the visions regarding his Coming there are also prophecies about the restoration of Israel. Notice that the restoration follows the coming of the Cornerstone. As Christians we know that Jesus is the Cornerstone that the builders rejected (Ps 118:22, Matt 21:42, Mark 12:10–11,

Luke 20:17, Acts 4:11, Eph 2:20, 1 Pet 2:7), so we should look more closely at the associated prophecies regarding the restoration of Israel.

> "4 'From them will come the cornerstone, from them the tent peg, from them the bow of battle, from them every ruler, all of them together. 5 'They will be as mighty men, treading down the enemy in the mire of the streets in battle; and they will fight, for the Lord will be with them; and the riders on horses will be put to shame. 6 'I will strengthen the house of Judah, and I will save the house of Joseph, and I will bring them back, because I have had compassion on them; and they will be as though I had not rejected them, for I am the Lord their God and I will answer them. 7 'Ephraim will be like a mighty man, and their heart will be glad as if from wine; indeed, their children will see it and be glad, their heart will rejoice in the Lord. 8 'I will whistle for them to gather them together, for I have redeemed them; and they will be as numerous as they were before. 9 'When I scatter them among the peoples, they will remember Me in far countries, and they with their children will live and come back. 10 'I will bring them back from the land of Egypt and gather them from Assyria; and I will bring them into the land of Gilead and Lebanon until no room can be found for them. 11 'And they will pass through the sea of distress and He will strike the waves in the sea, so that all the depths of the Nile will dry up; and the pride of Assyria will be brought down and the scepter of Egypt will depart. 12 'And I will strengthen them in the Lord, and in His name they will walk,' declares the Lord." (Zech 10:4–12, NASB)

We see in this vision of Zechariah that the Israelites will be gathered back into their land and the Messiah will come from Judah (a descendant of the House of Judah). The Messiah, the Cornerstone, will be the leader when Israel's enemies are defeated, and Israel will be restored. The Messiah will lead the fight against the enemies of Israel and Israel will be restored. They will be regathered into their land from all the places they were scattered.

> The Messiah will lead the fight against the enemies of Israel and Israel will be restored. They will be regathered into their land from all the places they were scattered.

Historically we haven't seen the full ingathering of Israel yet. Although the Judeans taken into the Babylonian Captivity did return around the time of Zechariah, those Israelites who were taken captivity into Assyria have not returned to this day. They are generally referred to as "The Lost Tribes" who were dispersed across the Assyrian Empire. What is interesting about this entire vision of Zechariah is that the Messiah, the Cornerstone, comes and is rejected. Then a second shepherd shows up whom the people accept, but he turns out to be worthless. And in the middle of this vision we have the ingathering of Israel. Although historically Jesus rode on a donkey

ZECHARIAH

into Jerusalem on Palm Sunday and was rejected, the ingathering of Israel has not happened yet. Confused?

What do theologians think about this prophecy? Many different things, as you might expect. Some theologians hold that while Jesus literally came riding on a donkey, the associated prophecy about the ingathering and restoration of Israel is an allegory about the church. Some hold they are both literal events events and Zechariah was wrong. Some hold they are both literal and Zechariah saw a future ingathering before the Second Coming of Jesus.

> Some theologians hold that while Jesus literally came riding on a donkey, the associated prophecy about the ingathering and restoration of Israel is an allegory about the church. Some hold they are both literal events and Zechariah was wrong. Some hold they are both literal and Zechariah saw a future ingathering before the Second Coming of Jesus.

Christian theologians who take an allegorical interpretation of Zechariah see a literal fulfillment in him arriving on a donkey, but a spiritualized fulfillment of the ingathering of Israel. They see the ingathering as God bringing in the Gentiles into his kingdom, making a new creation where Christians replace Jewish people: "spiritual" Israel replaces "ethnic" Israel. So while there is a literal fulfillment of the part of the vision about riding on a donkey, there is instead an allegorical fulfillment of the part about the ingathering of Israel.

Other theologians see the ingathering as referring only to the return of the Judeans from Babylonian Captivity around the time of Zechariah. Since this happened well before the time of Christ, and the ingathering wasn't all of Israel but only the Judeans, they see Zechariah as being wrong. Of course, that would mean he wasn't a real prophet of God, and we cannot trust his book.

Still other theologians see the entire vision as literal. The Messiah would come riding on a donkey, be rejected, be paid the worthless price of thirty pieces of silver, and Israel would be gathered together again in their own land never again to be removed. They look to the events of Palm Sunday as the literal fulfillment of the First Coming of the Messiah, and to a future time when Israel will be gathered in again to her land and then attacked, when the Messiah will appear for the second time. Since Israel is now once again a nation after nearly two thousand years of dispersion, they look to events in today's headlines for signs of the times of the Second Coming.

Interestingly, Orthodox Jewish theologians such as Rashi see this passage of Zechariah as also referring to the ingathering of Israel in the time of the end, something yet to come in the future. There is great debate within the Jewish religious circles over whether the current modern state of Israel is the legitimate ingathering Zechariah spoke of or not. One does not have to look very far into the news headlines to see that the nation today struggles greatly within and without and does not appear to yet be in the final state God has envisioned for Zion. Clearly the nations have not yet beaten their swords into plowshares nor look to Zion for leadership.

The Sola Scriptura approach will only look at what the scriptures say. It will not make an allegorical reinterpretation nor try to force fit the prophecies to historical events. The context of the vision is that the Messiah appears riding lowly on a donkey. There is an ingathering of Israel. And following that prophecy is the rejection of the Messiah followed by a second worthless shepherd. At a minimum we should see the rejection of Jesus, who entered Jerusalem riding on a donkey on Palm Sunday. Sola Scriptura allows from this passage both the ingathering of Judeans during the time of Zechariah as well as a potential future ingathering before the Second Coming. This passage does not directly and plainly say which things were in Zechariah's time and which were symbolic of things to come. And although it does say those returning to Israel will live securely, this passage does not have any singularities such as saying "never again will they be removed." Since Zechariah is told things that would happen in his time, as well as things symbolic of the future, a plain reading of his next to last vision is not able to pin down the timing of the ingathering of Israel. However the Cornerstone, the Messiah, is the one who leads the battle against Israel's enemies.

> Since Zechariah is told things that would happen in his time, as well as things symbolic of the future, a plain reading of his next to last vision is not able to pin down the timing of the ingathering of Israel. However the Cornerstone, the Messiah, is the one who leads the battle against Israel's enemies.

Think about the Messiah, the Cornerstone, leading the battle against the enemies of Israel. This could fit with an allegorical interpretation where Jesus leads his flock spiritually against the enemies of the church over time. It can also be seen literally as in the final attack on Jerusalem as seen in other prophecies where God steps in to save Israel. Do the other visions of Zechariah help us better understand? How about other prophecies about the future of Israel? In a related, but different vision, Zechariah speaks of an ingathering of Israel as a singularity, never to be removed again.

> "10 All the land will be changed into a plain from Geba to Rimmon south of Jerusalem; but Jerusalem will rise and remain on its site from Benjamin's Gate as far as the place of the First Gate to the Corner Gate, and from the Tower of Hananel to the king's wine presses. 11 People will live in it, and there will no longer be a curse, for Jerusalem will dwell in security." (Zech 14:10–11, NASB)

Several other prophets also speak about an ingathering of Israel connected to the coming of the Messiah.

> "3 'Then I Myself will gather the remnant of My flock out of all the countries where I have driven them and bring them back to their pasture, and they will be fruitful and multiply. 4 I will also raise up shepherds over them and they will tend them; and they will not be afraid any longer, nor be terrified, nor will

any be missing,' declares the Lord. 5 'Behold, the days are coming,' declares the Lord, 'When I will raise up for David a righteous Branch; and He will reign as king and act wisely and do justice and righteousness in the land. 6 'In His days Judah will be saved, And Israel will dwell securely; And this is His name by which He will be called, 'The Lord our righteousness.'" (Jer 23:3-6, NASB)

In Amos we also hear of an ingathering of Israel, never again to be uprooted.

"13 'Behold, days are coming,' declares the Lord, 'When the plowman will overtake the reaper and the treader of grapes him who sows seed; when the mountains will drip sweet wine and all the hills will be dissolved. 14 'Also I will restore the captivity of My people Israel, and they will rebuild the ruined cities and live in them; they will also plant vineyards and drink their wine, and make gardens and eat their fruit. 15 'I will also plant them on their land, and they will not again be rooted out from their land which I have given them,' says the Lord your God." (Amos 9:13-15, NASB)

Daniel had earlier seen that when the Messiah comes then the people of God will receive the kingdom and never again be removed.

"13 'I kept looking in the night visions, and behold, with the clouds of heaven one like a Son of Man was coming, and He came up to the Ancient of Days and was presented before Him. 14 'And to Him was given dominion, glory and a kingdom, that all the peoples, nations and men of every language might serve Him. His dominion is an everlasting dominion which will not pass away; and His kingdom is one which will not be destroyed. 15 'As for me, Daniel, my spirit was distressed within me, and the visions in my mind kept alarming me. 16 I approached one of those who were standing by and began asking him the exact meaning of all this. So he told me and made known to me the interpretation of these things: 17 'These great beasts, which are four in number, are four kings who will arise from the earth. 18 But the saints of the Highest One will receive the kingdom and possess the kingdom forever, for all ages to come.'" (Dan 7:13-18, NASB)

Isaiah saw a time when the nations of the earth would look to Jerusalem for everlasting leadership.

"1 The word which Isaiah the son of Amoz saw concerning Judah and Jerusalem. 2 Now it will come about that in the last days the mountain of the house of the Lord will be established as the chief of the mountains, and will be raised above the hills; and all the nations will stream to it. 3 And many peoples will come and say, 'Come, let us go up to the mountain of the Lord, to the house of the God of Jacob; that He may teach us concerning His ways and that we may walk in His paths.' for the law will go forth from Zion and the word of the Lord from Jerusalem. 4 And He will judge between the nations, and will render decisions for many peoples; and they will hammer their swords into plowshares and their spears into pruning hooks. Nation will not lift up sword against nation, and never again will they learn war." (Isa 2:1–4, NASB)

Joel saw a future restored Judah and Jerusalem in the days of the end times.

> "31 'The sun will be turned into darkness and the moon into blood before the great and awesome day of the Lord comes. 32 'And it will come about that whoever calls on the name of the Lord will be delivered; for on Mount Zion and in Jerusalem there will be those who escape, as the Lord has said, even among the survivors whom the Lord calls. 'For behold, in those days and at that time, when I restore the fortunes of Judah and Jerusalem, 2 I will gather all the nations and bring them down to the valley of Jehoshaphat. Then I will enter into judgment with them there on behalf of My people and My inheritance, Israel, whom they have scattered among the nations; and they have divided up My land." (Joel 2:31–3:2, NASB)

Ezekiel also speaks of an ingathering of Israel, never again to be removed. Ezekiel's final vision in chapters 40–48 also discusses in great detail the future state of Israel. We will explore the book of Ezekiel in detail next.

> "24 My servant David will be king over them, and they will all have one shepherd; and they will walk in My ordinances and keep My statutes and observe them. 25 They will live on the land that I gave to Jacob My servant, in which your fathers lived; and they will live on it, they, and their sons and their sons' sons, forever; and David My servant will be their prince forever. 26 I will make a covenant of peace with them; it will be an everlasting covenant with them. And I will place them and multiply them, and will set My sanctuary in their midst forever. 27 My dwelling place also will be with them; and I will be their God, and they will be My people. 28 And the nations will know that I am the Lord who sanctifies Israel, when My sanctuary is in their midst forever." (Ezek 37:24–28, NASB)

> Zechariah, Jeremiah, Amos, Daniel, Isaiah, Joel, and Ezekiel all spoke about the restoration of Israel: an ingathering where they will never again be removed from the land.

Zechariah, Jeremiah, Amos, Daniel, Isaiah, Joel, and Ezekiel all spoke about the restoration of Israel: an ingathering where they will never again be removed from the land. Yet for the specific vision of Zechariah we are looking at, chapters 9–11, we see an ingathering of Israel but it could be interpreted in many different ways to fit different historical circumstances (past and/or future). We cannot take a position based on this passage alone. However, when you look at the other visions Zechariah had as well as the greater testimony of the prophets as shown above, you can see a clear prophecy about a literal ingathering of God's people to the land of Israel, where Jerusalem will be established as providing worldwide leadership that brings worldwide peace. Israel will dwell securely, never again to be removed.

Remember these prophecies as background context as you study the book of Revelation. And be aware of how theologians handle this expectation of the future state of Israel: whether Jewish people have an end-time destiny, or if everything is taken allegorically and reinterpreted to focus exclusively on Christians alone. Then consider if your beliefs require some sentences to be taken literally (like the arrival of the Messiah riding on a donkey, being rejected, being considered a worthless sum of only thirty pieces of silver) while other sentences in the very same passages are taken allegorically (like the attack on Jerusalem or the ingathering of Israel). John Calvin, a famous Protestant theologian and founder of the Presbyterian and Reformed churches, once said we should only base our doctrinal beliefs on the plain sense of scripture. While allegorical interpretations may turn out to be true, they are interpretations and not what the text says directly and so should not be taught as doctrine. Also remember that an allegorical interpretation is used by Rabbis to teach against Jesus being the Messiah.

> John Calvin, a famous Protestant theologian and founder of the Presbyterian and Reformed churches, once said we should only base our doctrinal beliefs on the plain sense of scripture. While allegorical interpretations may turn out to be true, they are interpretations and not what the text says directly and so should not be taught as doctrine. Also remember that an allegorical interpretation is used by Rabbis to teach against Jesus being the Messiah.

ALLUSIONS AND GROUPS OF FOUR

In the book of Revelation we see similarities to other imagery in Zechariah such as the Four Horsemen (Zech 1:7–11), the Four Horns (Zech 1:18–21), the Four Craftsmen (Zech 1:20–21), the Four Chariots (Zech 6:1–8), a wicked woman taken to Babylon (Zech 5:5–11), and the rebuilding of Jerusalem and the Temple (Zech 8:1–23). But Revelation does not quote Zechariah directly in these places. While we can guess that Revelation had these images in mind, the context of the passages in their original setting in Zechariah does not exclusively place them in the end times. In other words, while Zechariah sees the power of God being expressed symbolically with these images, it is not clear from a plain reading of the text if they are only about the time of Israel's return from the Babylonian captivity, or if they may also (or only) refer to the end times. For example, we see a direct reference to the end of the seventy years of Babylonian Captivity that occurred in the time of Zechariah, as well as a reference to God dwelling among his people which is typically viewed as the Messianic Age of worldwide peace yet to come.

> "12 Then the angel of the Lord said, 'O Lord of hosts, how long will You have no compassion for Jerusalem and the cities of Judah, with which You have been indignant these seventy years?' 13 The Lord answered the angel who was

speaking with me with gracious words, comforting words." (Zech 1:12–13, NASB)

"10 Sing for joy and be glad, O daughter of Zion; for behold I am coming and I will dwell in your midst,' declares the Lord. 11 'Many nations will join themselves to the Lord in that day and will become My people. Then I will dwell in your midst, and you will know that the Lord of hosts has sent Me to you. 12 The Lord will possess Judah as His portion in the holy land, and will again choose Jerusalem." (Zech 2:10–12, NASB)

Theologians go many different ways in trying to explain each of these groups of four things (horsemen, horns, craftsmen, chariots) and other allusions. Some images in Zechariah appear to be in Revelation, but it does not quote Zechariah in those places, nor does it match those images exactly. Such images as the Four Horsemen, the Four Craftsmen, or the rebuilding of the Temple in Jerusalem are interesting, but not directly and plainly referenced. They also aren't explicitly set by Zechariah in the end times.

> Some images in Zechariah appear to be in Revelation, but it does not quote Zechariah in those places, nor does it match those images exactly. Such images as the Four Horsemen, the Four Craftsmen, or the rebuilding of the Temple in Jerusalem are interesting, but not directly and plainly referenced. They also aren't explicitly set by Zechariah in the end times.

The Sola Scriptura approach looks at only what the scriptures directly and plainly say. We look for anchor points in time such as "never again," "from that day forward and forever," "everlasting," or other words that indicate a permanent change or unending situation. As none of these accompany the allusions mentioned above, our method will not conjecture about their meaning. In other words, these allusions are interesting, but unprovable. Until, of course, our Messiah returns and explains all things. However, many, many things are directly and plainly stated in Zechariah that do give us a clearer picture of God's revelation as we will summarize next.

WHAT DID WE LEARN FROM ZECHARIAH?

As we reflect back over the book of Zechariah and what it means for the book of Revelation, we can see some major themes. First, we see that Zechariah has not yet been completely fulfilled, if for no other reason than God is not the only god worshiped across the whole world yet. In Zechariah we see prophecies that were for his time as well as symbolic of the future. The Judeans returned to Israel after the Babylonian Captivity and rebuilt Jerusalem and the Temple (the Second Temple). But Zechariah also spoke of a future ingathering of all the tribes of Israel, a worldwide attack on Jerusalem, God stepping in to save Jerusalem and it never again being destroyed, and then the God of Israel being the only one worshiped by the whole world. Clearly that has never happened. One need only look at the Al Aqsa Mosque sitting on the Temple Mount in Jerusalem today to know the truth. To the original audience of the book of Revelation, sitting in Asia Minor outside a Jerusalem controlled by Rome, they would have been waiting for this ultimate fulfillment of the Eternal Messianic Kingdom ruling over the whole world, where the one True God is the only one worshiped. Every knee will bow, and every tongue will confess that Jesus Christ is Lord. They, and we, do not live in such a time.

Yet Zechariah also spoke of the Messiah, the Servant, the Branch, the Shepherd, the Cornerstone, who would come riding lowly on a donkey and be pierced and rejected. This Messiah in Zechariah would remove sin but be considered worthless by the people. As Christians we clearly see Jesus as fulfilling these prophecies literally during his First Coming. Ironically, Zechariah also spoke about a false shepherd who comes after the Messiah, who instead of helping the people turns out to be the truly worthless one.

As we look forward to the Second Coming where Jesus will rule over the entire world, we should keep in mind that Zechariah spoke of a final battle of the world against Jerusalem before the end. If we are to take Jesus as the one who literally fulfilled Zechariah's prophecies about the rejected and pierced Messiah, then we must also take literally Zechariah's prophecies about the final attack on Jerusalem where God steps in to defend her before the Eternal Messianic Kingdom is established. We should not read one sentence allegorically (Zech 12:9) and the next one literally (Zech 12:10) because we don't like the implication of a literal meaning. This narrative of a final battle of a world opposed to God fighting against him in Jerusalem is the same one we see in other prophets. Zechariah is not the only prophet to speak about this. We also see this final battle in Daniel (Dan 7:21-25, 8:21-25, 11:36-45), Joel (Joel 2:1-3, 3:2), Ezekiel (Ezek 38:7-9,14-18), as well as in the New Testament (Rev 16:14-16, 17:11-14, 19:19, 20:8-9, 1 Tim 4:1). And Good News: the Messiah will defeat all these kingdoms and establish his Everlasting Messianic Kingdom. The kingdoms of this world will become the Kingdom of Our Lord, and God will wipe every tear. There will be no more death, mourning, crying, or pain. This narrative forms the background context for the book of Revelation.

Those who received the Apocalypse from John would have been expecting all of Zechariah to be fulfilled. It would have been hard to think about the prophecies of the worldwide kingdom of Messiah and yet see Jesus crucified and die. Even the disciples walking on the road to Emmaus from Jerusalem after the Crucifixion were downcast and confused (Luke 24:13-27). How could Jesus be the Messiah who will rule the world, when he was just crucified and died? Fortunately, Jesus met them on that road that day, and beginning with Moses and all the Prophets he explained everything to them. Sadly, the Rabbis of the time refused such explanations and instead believed there would be two messiahs, one who would die for the sins of others and the other

The Sola Scriptura Challenge

who would be victorious over the world (as we explored in an earlier section of this book).

Keep this prophecy of a final battle in mind as you read about the Battle of Armageddon in the book of Revelation (Rev 16:14–16, 17:11–14, 19:19, 20:8–9). Remember the prophecy of a second worthless shepherd who comes after the Good Shepherd is rejected for thirty pieces of silver (Zech 11:7–17). And keep the prophecies about the future Messianic Kingdom in mind, as they form part of the background context of Revelation.

#	Truth Claim	Primary Support	Secondary Support
5.1	Zechariah has not been fulfilled yet because he speaks of Jerusalem never again being destroyed.	Zech 14:11–12	Rev 22:3, Joel 2:19, Jer 16:15, 23:1–8, 30:3, 25:30–31, 31:12,40, Ezek 34:22–31, 36:12–15, 37, 38, Hos 2:16–20, Isa 2:3–4, 11, 34:1–17, 43:5–6, 52, 60:18, 66:6, Amos 9, Hos 3, Zeph 1:14, 3:9–20, Zech 9:8, 12, 14, Mic 4
5.2	Zechariah has not been fulfilled yet because he speaks of the splitting of the Mount of Olives.	Zech 14:4–5	Ezek 38:20, 47:1, Mic 1:3–4
5.3	Zechariah has not been fulfilled yet because he speaks of living water flowing out from Jerusalem to the surrounding regions.	Zech 14:8	Ezek 47:1, Joel 3:18, Rev 22:1–2, Ps 46:4, Isa 12:3, 35:6–7, 44:3, 55:1, Jer 2:13
5.4	Zechariah has not been fulfilled yet because he speaks of God being king over the whole earth, the only one worshiped.	Zech 14:9	Ps 22:28, Isa 2:2, 45:23, Rom 14:11, Philp 2:10
5.5	God's Spirit will accomplish his will, his plan will not unfold because of the power of mankind.	Zech 4:6	Gen 41:16, 1 Sam 14:6, 1 Sam 17:47, 2 Chron 32:7–8, Ezra 5:2, Dan 2:34, Hos 1:7, Eph 6:17, Heb 4:12, Gal 5:16,24–25, Rom 8:4, 13:4, Php 3:3, 1 Pet 2:11
5.6	The Messiah, The Servant, the Branch, will remove sin.	Zech 3:8–9	Isa 4:2, 11:1, 53:2, Jer 23:5, 33:15, John 15:5, 1 John 1:9, 2:1–2, 3:5, 2 Cor 5:21, Rom 6:23
5.7	The Messiah, the Branch, is both King and Priest	Zech 6:12–13	Ps 110:4, Isa 9:6–7, 11:10, Jer 23:5, 33:15, Heb 5:6–10, 6:19–20, 7:1–17
5.8	The Messiah will arrive lowly riding on a donkey.	Zech 9:9	Matt 21:2–9, Mark 11:1–9, Luke 19:28–36

#	Truth Claim	Primary Support	Secondary Support
5.9	The Messiah, The Cornerstone, will descend from the tribe of Judah.	Zech 10:4	Isa 28:16, Ps 118:22, Matt 21:42, Acts 4:11, Eph 2:20, 2 Pet 2:4-7
5.10	The Messiah, The Shepherd, will be pierced and rejected.	Zech 11:8-13, 12:10, 13:7	Matt 10:4, 24:30, 26:31, 27:3-10, John 16:32, 19:31-37, Mark 14:27, Rev 1:7-8, Dan 9:24-26, Isa 53, Ps 2:2, 22, 110:1, Ps 118:22
5.11	God will regather the tribes of Israel near the end.	Zech 10:8-12	Ezek 36:24-28, 37:24-28, 38:8,12, 39:7,25-29, Amos 9:13-15, Hos 3:5, Isa 11:10-12, 43:5-6, 54:7-8, 60:4-9, Jer 30:3-9, 31:8-10
5.12	All nations will gather against Jerusalem to overthrow it.	Zech 12:3,9, 14:2,3,13	Rev 16:14-16, 17:11-14, 19:19, 20:8-9, 1 Tim 4:1, Dan 7:21-25, 8:21-25, 11:36-45, Joel 2:1-3, 3:2, Ezek 38:7-9,14-18
5.13	God will defeat the nations that attack Israel and establish an everlasting kingdom of peace ruled by the Messiah.	Zech 9:8-10, 14:12-19	Rev 11:15, 19:11-21, 20:7-10, 21:24,26, 22:2, Luke 1:33, 1 Cor 15:24, 2 Thess 2:8, Zech 14:12-19, Ezek 37:25, 39:7-8, Dan 2:44, 7:11-14,18-22,26-27, Isa 2:4, 9:6-7, Joel 2:18-20, 3:1-2,14-16

6

Ezekiel
The Aftermath of Gog

"So I, having entered on the ocean of holy scriptures and mysteries of God shall speak like the labyrinth"—Jerome

JEROME, A FAMOUS LATIN priest and theologian who lived in the fourth century called the book of Ezekiel a labyrinth of the mysteries of God. Jewish tradition holds that no one should read it until they are at least thirty years old. Some Rabbis even have secret teachings about the book of Ezekiel that are only taught to the initiated. And Christian theologians strongly debate the meaning of the end of Ezekiel. Pay close attention to what Ezekiel is saying, and the implications of what that means.

Though Ezekiel is nowhere quoted directly in the New Testament, there are numerous unique visions and references in Revelation that only appear in Ezekiel. The book of Ezekiel forms a major part of the background context for Revelation. It is critical that we understand Ezekiel if we want to really understand Revelation. Ezekiel prophecies both before and after the destruction of Jerusalem by Babylon so there is a lot of discussion about Jerusalem, the temple, and future of Israel. Sometimes Ezekiel references the First Temple which was standing at the time of the beginning of his ministry. And sometimes Ezekiel talks about a future temple which is everlasting in "the latter days."

> It is critical that we understand Ezekiel if we want to really understand Revelation. Ezekiel prophecies both before and after the destruction of Jerusalem by Babylon so there is a lot of discussion about Jerusalem, the temple, and future

of Israel. Sometimes Ezekiel references the First Temple which was standing at the time of the beginning of his ministry. And sometimes Ezekiel talks about a future temple which is everlasting in "the latter days."

Ezekiel has a lot of mysteries in its pages that have caused controversies in Judaism, Christianity, and even modern critical scholarship. The portion of his book that speaks about the time in which he lived, the time of the First Temple, seems mostly clear to everyone. Israel's Southern Kingdom was sinful, and as punishment God sent Babylon to take them away into the Babylonian Captivity, just as the Northern Kingdom of Israel had gone in the Assyrian Captivity earlier. Other portions of his book are less clear, such as those describing "the latter days." Ezekiel is actually very clear about what he says will happen. What is not as clear is what that means for both Judaism and Christianity.

In Judaism the controversy over how Ezekiel envisions the latter days almost caused Ezekiel to be dropped from the Jewish Canon of scripture. That may have meant both Jewish and Christian people would have lost the book of Ezekiel from their Bibles, since the early Christian community adopted the Jewish Canon as "the Old Testament." The Rabbis saw different laws for Temple worship in Ezekiel's future temple than was prescribed by Moses in the Torah, as well as conflicts with the Laws of Moses that caused them to debate if Ezekiel was really inspired scripture or not.[1] But ultimately Ezekiel was accepted as divinely inspired. The differences in what Ezekiel says compared to Moses and the other prophets is a source of debate even today in modern critical scholarship.

Judaism also takes an interesting turn with Ezekiel. Having finally accepted it as authoritative, a tradition arose that viewed the opening vision of the throne of God (Ezekiel chapters 1–3) in a mystical way. This mystical way of studying Ezekiel has led to the development of what is known as Kabbalah. Kabbalah is a mystical Jewish practice of entering the Presence of God through specific secret use of the text. However, there are warnings given of the dangers of attempting to approach God in this way, and so the practice is only taught in secret to those whom the Rabbis consider worthy.

In Christianity there is also great controversy over how Ezekiel envisions the latter days. Depending on the different interpretive approach one takes (literal, allegorical, or a mix of the two) you can end up in vastly different places. And at the heart of the Christian debate is what Christians believe about the future destiny of the Jewish People, the land of Israel, the Millennium, and the Eternal Messianic Kingdom.

The Sola Scriptura approach will only look at what the scriptures say directly. We will need to do so bearing in mind that there are controversies within Judaism, Christianity, and even modern critical scholarship. But also bearing in mind that Ezekiel is inspired scripture and has numerous allusions found in the book of Revelation that appear nowhere else in the Bible. Though the New Testament never quotes Ezekiel

---

1. Ashi and Ravina, *Babylonian Talmud*, Sabbath 13b.

directly, his book is clearly in view, and we must understand it so we can better understand Revelation. Below we will explore the major prophecies in Ezekiel that are alluded to in Revelation. But first we will look at the context of the book itself.

CONTEXT OF THE BOOK OF EZEKIEL

We know from the Bible that Ezekiel was a priest who was taken away from Jerusalem into the Babylonian Captivity (Ezek 1:1–3). Like Daniel, he experienced the harsh realities of God's punishment of the Israelites. Just as God had warned Israel through the earlier prophets like Isaiah and Jeremiah, they were taken away from the Promised Land because of their sins. But like a great parent, God always promises restoration after the punishment. God strengthens his people through the words of the prophets, and Ezekiel's name literally bears out his role in life, for it literally means "God will strengthen" from the Hebrew *yechezak* (יְחֶזְק) and *El* (אֵל).

As the conquest of the Southern Kingdom of Judah began, Nebuchadnezzar got closer and closer to Jerusalem. Inside Jerusalem there were false prophets telling the leader of Jerusalem (King Zedekiah) that the king of Babylon (Nebuchadnezzar) would not attack Jerusalem. These false prophets spoke against the clear warnings that Jeremiah was giving about the coming invasion of Jerusalem and so they sought to kill him. They put him into the deep pit of a cistern which had only mud and Jeremiah sank down into the miry clay. They hoped that he would starve to death (Jer 38:1–9).

The first part of the book of Ezekiel (chapters 1–24) describes God's reasons for punishing Israel and warns them that Jerusalem will fall to Babylon. Ezekiel is shown the sins of the people, and even secret idolatry going on at the Temple (Ezek 8:1–18). God shows Ezekiel all the detestable things that were going on at the Temple and then shows the Glory of God, his Presence, leaving the Temple (Ezek 10:1–11:25). As Ezekiel sat in exile in Babylon by the Kebar River, he saw this vision of God leaving the Temple in Jerusalem because of their blatant idolatry and sins. Just as Jeremiah had warned from within Jerusalem, Ezekiel also warned from the land of exile: Jerusalem was going to fall to Babylon.

In this first vision recorded in Ezekiel there is a vision of the throne of God (Ezek 1:1–28, 10:1–22, 11:22–25). He sees an immense cloud with four living creatures inside. Each creature had four faces: a human, lion, ox, and eagle. Each had wings and looked like fire. This is the same vision John has in Revelation (Rev 4:2–11). This vision of the four living creatures in Revelation is found nowhere else in the Bible except in Ezekiel. Although Ezekiel is never directly quoted in the New Testament, we will see there are numerous unique allusions that can only be from Ezekiel, for they are found nowhere else in scripture.

> This vision of the four living creatures in Revelation is found nowhere else in the Bible except in Ezekiel. Although Ezekiel is never directly quoted in the

New Testament, we will see there are numerous unique allusions that can only be from Ezekiel, for they are found nowhere else in scripture.

As with other prophets, Ezekiel also promises a future restoration. Though God is punishing Israel for their sins, he will allow a remnant to survive. This remnant would return to the land of Israel and one day rebuild Jerusalem. Among these promises of restoration in Ezekiel are famous visions like the Valley of Dry Bones (Ezek 37:1-14), a New Covenant (Ezek 37:15-28), and the Good Shepherd (Ezek 34:1-31).

But before all these wonderful things can take place there is also a prophecy of another attack on Jerusalem, one that takes place in the latter days. A leader called Gog leads many nations against the restored Israel. He sees their restoration, their life of prosperity, and their feeling of living in safety all around them. So he sets his heart against them and leads many nations to attack. God steps in and prevents Gog from overtaking Jerusalem, and then never again will Israel be attacked. This final attack on Jerusalem by Gog is described in the book of Ezekiel in chapters 38 and 39. Revelation chapter 20 directly mentions Gog leading many nations in a final attack on Jerusalem (Rev 20:7-10). Again, we have an allusion in the book of Revelation that is found nowhere else but in the book of Ezekiel.

> This final attack on Jerusalem by Gog is described in the book of Ezekiel in chapters 38 and 39. Revelation chapter 20 directly mentions Gog leading many nations in a final attack on Jerusalem (Rev 20:7-10). Again, we have an allusion in the book of Revelation that is found nowhere else but in the book of Ezekiel.

Ezekiel closes with a final vision from chapters 40 through 48 that shows a new Temple in a new Jerusalem that gets a new name. God's glory returns to the Temple, and he will live there forever. The priesthood is restored and the land of Israel surrounding the Temple is divided up among the 12 tribes once again. A river flows from under the Temple which goes out providing Living Water to the surrounding region. On the banks of the river are trees which give fruit for food and leaves for healing. This is another allusion in Revelation that is only found in Ezekiel.

> "Then he showed me a river of the water of life, clear as crystal, coming from the throne of God and of the Lamb, 2 in the middle of its street. On either side of the river was the tree of life, bearing twelve kinds of fruit, yielding its fruit every month; and the leaves of the tree were for the healing of the nations. 3 There will no longer be any curse; and the throne of God and of the Lamb will be in it, and His bond-servants will serve Him; 4 they will see His face, and His name will be on their foreheads. 5 And there will no longer be any night; and they will not have need of the light of a lamp nor the light of the sun, because the Lord God will illumine them; and they will reign forever and ever." (Rev 22:1-5, NASB)

It's clear that Ezekiel is important to understand if we really want to understand Revelation. We will look at the major prophecies that are alluded to, each in detail below. But one of the big questions we must always ask of any book of prophecy is: have all these prophecies been fulfilled already? This is an important question because some Christian denominations teach that all Hebrew Bible prophecies have already been fulfilled. Everything has already been fulfilled in Christ. There is nothing in the Hebrew Bible for Christians to know and we should just ignore it. It is finished and all things have been completed. The Sola Scriptura approach will look at what the scriptures directly say and ask if that is really true. Have all these things really come to pass?

HAS EZEKIEL BEEN FULFILLED YET?

One of the things we always look for are time markers that show us a permanent change in things. Words like "never again," "forever," or "everlasting" are keys to our understanding. Consider the current Temple Mount in Jerusalem on which no Jewish Temple stands today, but instead the Muslim Dome of the Rock and Al Aqsa Mosque beside it. If the Bible says there will be a physical Temple in Jerusalem where God dwells forever, then seeing an Islamic Mosque standing there means either that the time has not yet come to pass, or the Bible is not to be taken literally and we must explain it in some other way. And if we explain it in some way that is different from what the text plainly says then do we sound credible? Or are we just rationalizing and spiritualizing to make the Jewish scriptures sound the way Christians want them to? And since we can explain things spiritually in several different ways, who says which version is the right one?

One of the first things we should look at is the river mentioned above. Ezekiel says the Temple in the latter days will have a river flowing out from under it (Ezek 47:1–12). This river will have trees on either side that bear fruit and have leaves for healing. In the book of Revelation John also says there is a river flowing out from the Throne of God (Rev 22:1–2). The river will have the tree of life on each side of the river, and it will bear fruit and have leaves for the healing of the nations.

Ezekiel speaks of a river flowing out from the Temple Mount and so does Revelation. But there has never been one. Some theologians will point to an allegorical explanation giving an alternative meaning. Other theologians point to a future fulfillment. And some say Ezekiel was idealistic but just wrong. Though there are underground springs nearby which you can walk in, there has never been a river. Either Ezekiel has not been fulfilled yet, or you must spiritualize it to mean that God pours out his Spirit of Living Water like a river flowing out from the Temple. Orthodox Jews and some Protestant Christians hold that there will be a future Temple with an actual river flowing from under it. Other Jewish movements and Christian denominations see this allegorically only. They do not believe in a physical future Temple. In this one example you can see how mysterious Ezekiel is and where the debates begin. We will explore some possibilities for the river in detail below.

> Ezekiel speaks of a river flowing out from the Temple Mount and so does Revelation. But there has never been one. Some theologians will point to an allegorical explanation giving an alternative meaning. Other theologians point to a future fulfillment. And some say Ezekiel was idealistic but just wrong.

We should now turn our attention to the Temple itself. While most Christians are familiar with Ezekiel's vision of the Valley of Dry Bones, many do not know the very next vision Ezekiel sees. In that vision he is told to take two sticks and join them together as one. This is a sign that the Northern Kingdom of Israel and the Southern Kingdom of Judah will one day be reunited together under a single king. Taken together, God can raise up the dead bones of Israel and reunite them together under a single king. As Ezekiel sat by the Kebar River in the land of Babylon, he would have understood God's promise to bring restoration to all of Israel and not just the Southern Kingdom of Judah where he was taken from.

> "20 The sticks on which you write will be in your hand before their eyes. 21 Say to them, 'Thus says the Lord God, 'Behold, I will take the sons of Israel from among the nations where they have gone, and I will gather them from every side and bring them into their own land; 22 and I will make them one nation in the land, on the mountains of Israel; and one king will be king for all of them; and they will no longer be two nations and no longer be divided into two kingdoms. 23 They will no longer defile themselves with their idols, or with their detestable things, or with any of their transgressions; but I will deliver them from all their dwelling places in which they have sinned, and will cleanse them. And they will be My people, and I will be their God. 24 My servant David will be king over them, and they will all have one shepherd; and they will walk in My ordinances and keep My statutes and observe them. 25 They will live on the land that I gave to Jacob My servant, in which your fathers lived; and they will live on it, they, and their sons and their sons' sons, forever; and David My servant will be their prince forever. 26 I will make a covenant of peace with them; it will be an everlasting covenant with them. And I will place them and multiply them, and will set My sanctuary in their midst forever. 27 My dwelling place also will be with them; and I will be their God, and they will be My people. 28 And the nations will know that I am the Lord who sanctifies Israel, when My sanctuary is in their midst forever.''" (Ezek 37:20–28, NASB)

Notice that God says all the Israelites will return to their own land (verse 20). They are made one nation in the land (verse 22), on the mountains of Israel (verse 22). They will live in the land where their ancestors lived (verse 25). They and their descendants will live there forever (verse 25). God will make an everlasting covenant with them and put his sanctuary among them forever (verse 26). God's sanctuary will be among them forever (verse 28). Note that Ezekiel then describes this everlasting Temple in the last nine chapters of his book, something we will explore in detail below.

Ezekiel says five times that the Israelites will live in the land, the land where their ancestors lived. He describes an ingathering where they are brought back from all the surrounding nations. And then they will live in the land forever. God will make an everlasting covenant with them. God will place his sanctuary among them forever. And David will be their prince forever. Forever, forever, forever, and everlasting. That is a permanent change which doesn't match the reality of the land of Israel today.

The scriptures are plainly speaking of a return of the Jewish people to the land of Israel where they will never again be taken away. They and their descendants will live there forever, God's servant David will be king over them. They will be a united nation living under one king. Then the nations around Israel will know that God is with her when his sanctuary is among them forever.

> The scriptures are plainly speaking of a return of the Jewish people to the land of Israel where they will never again be taken away. They and their descendants will live there forever, God's servant David will be king over them. They will be a united nation living under one king. Then the nations around Israel will know that God is with her when his sanctuary is among them forever.

Have all of these things happened? Has Ezekiel been completely fulfilled? In a literal sense no. The Jewish people have not all returned from across the world to the land of their ancestors, though many have. There is not a united nation of Israel with a single King David over them. And God's sanctuary is not there, instead the Al Aqsa mosque and the Dome of the Rock sit on the Temple Mount today. There is also no river flowing out from the Temple Mount either. We cannot say that Ezekiel has been fulfilled in a literal sense.

Some theologians will explain that Ezekiel has been fulfilled in an allegorical spiritual sense. They say that God has brought together Christians from all over the world into the Kingdom of Christ. While the spiritual statement that Gentiles all over the world are united under a single King Christ is true, to say this is what Ezekiel meant simply ignores the plain sense of what Ezekiel is saying. He says five times the Israelites will return to the land of their ancestors. That makes no sense if allegorically we are talking about Christians. Christians do not have anything to return to, having come from pagan practices and heathen lands to begin with. Ezekiel says the two kingdoms are joined together again and united. Again, that makes no allegorical sense. Where are these two kingdoms of Christians? Or if it represents Judaism and Christianity then how is Judaism today united with Christianity under the rule of King Jesus? And saying that God's sanctuary is among the Christians already and forever ignores what Revelation has to say. For Revelation describes a future time when there is a new Heaven, a new Earth, and new Jerusalem where there is no temple because God himself is there. Revelation does not say the sanctuary of God is already now among Christians and will remain there forever. It says something quite different.

> "Then I saw a new heaven and a new earth; for the first heaven and the first earth passed away, and there is no longer any sea. 2 And I saw the holy city, new Jerusalem, coming down out of heaven from God, made ready as a bride adorned for her husband. 3 And I heard a loud voice from the throne, saying, 'Behold, the tabernacle of God is among men, and He will dwell among them, and they shall be His people, and God Himself will be among them, 4 and He will wipe away every tear from their eyes; and there will no longer be any death; there will no longer be any mourning, or crying, or pain; the first things have passed away.'" (Rev 21:1–4, NASB)

Has God wiped away every tear already? Is there no more death already? Or mourning, or crying, or pain? No, the old older of things has not yet passed away. The new Heaven and new Earth have not yet come. The new Jerusalem has not yet come down from Heaven where God will dwell among his people forever. God is not dwelling among his people forever now. Ezekiel's vision of the united Israel living together in the land with the sanctuary of God forever has not happened yet.

We cannot say Ezekiel has been literally fulfilled. The Jewish people have not been gathered back into their own land, united under a single King David, with God's sanctuary among them forever. To say Ezekiel has been fulfilled spiritually in an allegorical sense ignores repeated references to the physical land of Israel, nine chapters describing the future Temple (Ezek 40–48), and a united Israel living under King David whom the Jewish people today do not accept as Jesus. You can see why Jerome called this book "a labyrinth of the mysteries of God" and why Christian theologians argue over its meaning. On top of this even the Rabbis wanted to exclude Ezekiel from the canon because of the differences in Temple worship and other laws found in the Mosaic Covenant of the Torah.

Neither a literal nor an allegorical interpretation can claim Ezekiel has been completely fulfilled. Thus, the Hebrew Bible still has something relevant for Christians to understand today. We cannot set Ezekiel aside saying, "all things are fulfilled in Christ . . . so let us ignore Ezekiel."

> Neither a literal nor an allegorical interpretation can claim Ezekiel has been completely fulfilled. Thus, the Hebrew Bible still has something relevant for Christians to understand today. We cannot set Ezekiel aside saying, "all things are fulfilled in Christ . . . so let us ignore Ezekiel."

To close out the argument against Ezekiel being completely fulfilled, here is one last point to consider. At the end of the book Ezekiel describes the Temple in great detail over the course of nine chapters. In the last chapter he describes how the physical land around the Temple is to be divided among the 12 tribes (Ezek 48:1–29). And the very last thing Ezekiel says is that Jerusalem will receive a new name.

"35 The city shall be 18,000 cubits round about; and the name of the city from that day shall be, 'The Lord is there.'" (Ezek 48:35, NASB)

That is not what anyone calls Jerusalem today. In fact, Orthodox Jews would not say this phrase at all because it is against Rabbinic teaching to pronounce the first part of the phrase, the ineffable name of God (יהוה). They would likely choose *Adonai* ("master") or *HaShem* ("the Name") as a substitute word. And across Christianity this name is pronounced and written in a variety of ways (Yahweh, Yehowah, Jehovah, Lord, LORD), indicating that we do not all agree on how to pronounce God's name, nor the name of this New Jerusalem which John says will come down out of Heaven (Rev 21:2). Jerusalem is not known all over the world today, neither literally nor allegorically, as the place called "The LORD is there." And to say his sanctuary dwells there, we must realize we are looking at the Islamic Dome of the Rock and the Al Aqsa Mosque. No, Ezekiel has not been completely fulfilled yet.

EZEKIEL IN THE NEW TESTAMENT

As mentioned earlier, Ezekiel is not directly quoted anywhere in the New Testament. However, there are numerous allusions to it. Below we will explore the allusions in the book of Revelation to Ezekiel's visions of the throne of God, the Valley of Dry Bones, the two sticks, the attack of Gog and Magog, the Temple, and the river of the water of life flowing from under the Temple whose leaves are for healing. Before we do that, it is important to think about how we are going to interpret all of these visions. And we should also ask: has God ever said how we are to interpret these specific prophecies?

DOES GOD TAKE THE PROPHETS LITERALLY?

Before we jump into specific visions that Ezekiel showed us it is important to ask if God takes the prophets literally. If God said that he told the prophets things that would literally happen, then we should take notice. Especially if we are tempted to provide a spiritual re-interpretation that is different from what the prophets literally and plainly said.

God tells Ezekiel that a leader named Gog will arise and lead many nations to attack Israel. Christians with a literal interpretation believe that there will be (or was) a leader of many nations that will literally attack (or attacked) Israel. If it happened in the past, they suggest it was Antiochus Epiphanes, or perhaps Titus. If in the future, then perhaps some worldwide leader from a country to the north of Israel like Russia, Turkey, or Syria will lead the attack on Israel.

Christians who hold an allegorical interpretation say there is no actual Gog, and it represents all nations and governments throughout history that are opposed to Christ. Alternatively, they may say it represents the battle within your own heart to either follow Christ or not. Everywhere a Hebrew prophet speaks of an attack on Jerusalem they interpret the plain meaning of what the prophets said to hold this alternative spiritual meaning.

But how does God actually interpret what the prophets had to say about this attack on Israel? Did God tell us how to interpret the attack by Gog? Did God say it was an allegory to all evil kingdoms opposed to Christ throughout history? Did God say it was an allegory to an inner battle within your heart? Did God say it was a literal attack with a real person leading many nations? While there is definitely an inner battle in our hearts going on, is that what God intended with the prophecies? While there are clearly kingdoms opposed to Christ throughout history, is that what God really meant when the prophets speak of this attack by Gog on Israel?

> Did God tell us how to interpret the attack by Gog? Did God say it was an allegory to all evil kingdoms opposed to Christ throughout history? Did God say it was an allegory to an inner battle within your heart? Did God say it was a literal attack with a real person leading many nations?

God directly addresses this in speaking to Ezekiel about Gog, the worldwide leader who will lead many nations to attack Israel in the latter days. God directly speaks to Gog.

> "17 'Thus says the Lord God, 'Are you the one of whom I spoke in former days through My servants the prophets of Israel, who prophesied in those days for many years that I would bring you against them? 18 It will come about on that day, when Gog comes against the land of Israel,' declares the Lord God, 'that My fury will mount up in My anger.'" (Ezek 38:17-18, NASB)

This is what the Sovereign Lord said to Ezekiel: Gog is the one he spoke of in the earlier prophets. God says the earlier prophets spoke of this leader who would come against Israel. God is saying those earlier prophets were speaking of a literal person, Gog. God is not saying the earlier prophets were speaking of a constant battle in your heart to choose to follow his Will. God is not saying antichristian governments, powers, and principalities throughout history will battle against the Gospel. Instead, God states that the earlier prophets prophesied for years that Gog would arise and come against Israel. The Sovereign Lord told us that what he said to the prophets was a literal event to take place.

God says his Word means what it plainly says. And that he said it time and again through multiple prophets. Gog is the one that God "spoke of in former days by [his] servants the prophets of Israel." They spoke of a day that would come "when Gog attacks the land of Israel." You can see this clearly and plainly predicted in both the Old and New Testaments (Zech 12:3,9, 14:2,3,13, Dan 7:21-25, 8:21-25, 11:36-45, Joel 2:1-3, 3:2, Ezek 38:7-9,14-18, Rev 16:14-16, 17:11-14, 19:19, 20:8-9, 1 Tim 4:1).

To suggest that the prophets were saying something different, something allegorical, something spiritualized, is to go directly against what the scriptures themselves plainly say, against what God himself tells Ezekiel. We must let scripture interpret scripture. God clearly tells Ezekiel that the earlier prophets spoke of a specific leader who would attack Israel. Gog is a specific leader, not an inner battle with your heart, not a symbol for all antichristian governments, philosophies, religions, and ideologies throughout history. This is key for understanding Revelation which directly mentions Gog.

> We must let scripture interpret scripture. God clearly tells Ezekiel that the earlier prophets spoke of a specific leader who would attack Israel. Gog is a specific leader, not an inner battle with your heart, not a symbol for all antichristian governments, philosophies, religions, and ideologies throughout history. This is key for understanding Revelation which directly mentions Gog.

A VISION OF GOD'S THRONE

The book of Ezekiel opens with a unique vision of the Throne of God. Nowhere else in the Bible do we see this much detail except in the vision John has in the book of Revelation.

> "4 As I looked, behold, a storm wind was coming from the north, a great cloud with fire flashing forth continually and a bright light around it, and in its midst something like glowing metal in the midst of the fire. 5 Within it there were figures resembling four living beings. And this was their appearance: they had human form. 6 Each of them had four faces and four wings. 7 Their legs were straight and their feet were like a calf's hoof, and they gleamed like burnished bronze. 8 Under their wings on their four sides were human hands. As for the faces and wings of the four of them, 9 their wings touched one another; their faces did not turn when they moved, each went straight forward. 10 As for the form of their faces, each had the face of a man; all four had the face of a lion on the right and the face of a bull on the left, and all four had the face of an eagle. 11 Such were their faces. Their wings were spread out above; each had two touching another being, and two covering their bodies. 15 Now as I looked at the living beings, behold, there was one wheel on the earth beside the living beings, for each of the four of them. 16 The appearance of the wheels and their workmanship was like sparkling beryl, and all four of them had the same form, their appearance and workmanship being as if one wheel were within another. 17 Whenever they moved, they moved in any of their four directions without turning as they moved. 18 As for their rims they were lofty and awesome, and the rims of all four of them were full of eyes round about." (Ezek 1:4–11, 15–18, NASB)

"After these things I looked, and behold, a door standing open in heaven, and the first voice which I had heard, like the sound of a trumpet speaking with me, said, 'Come up here, and I will show you what must take place after these things.' 2 Immediately I was in the Spirit; and behold, a throne was standing in heaven, and one sitting on the throne. 3 And He who was sitting was like a jasper stone and a sardius in appearance; and there was a rainbow around the throne, like an emerald in appearance. 4 Around the throne were twenty-four thrones; and upon the thrones I saw twenty-four elders sitting, clothed in white garments, and golden crowns on their heads. 5 Out from the throne come flashes of lightning and sounds and peals of thunder. And there were seven lamps of fire burning before the throne, which are the seven Spirits of God; 6 and before the throne there was something like a sea of glass, like crystal; and in the center and around the throne, four living creatures full of eyes in front and behind. 7 The first creature was like a lion, and the second creature like a calf, and the third creature had a face like that of a man, and the fourth creature was like a flying eagle. 8 And the four living creatures, each one of them having six wings, are full of eyes around and within; and day and night they do not cease to say, 'Holy, holy, holy is the Lord God, the Almighty, who was and who is and who is to come.'" (Rev 4:1–8, NASB)

Ezekiel and John both saw the Throne of God in Heaven. In both visions there are four living creatures with multiple wings, multiple eyes, and faces like a human, lion, ox, and eagle. Although Revelation does not quote Ezekiel directly, it is clearly an allusion to this unique vision only found in the book of Ezekiel.

The most important part of this vision is who Ezekiel saw sitting on the throne of God. Above these four living creatures was a vault on which the throne sat. If you were a Judean living thousands of years ago sitting in the Babylonian Captivity, and you saw a vision of God's throne, what do you think you would see sitting on the throne?

"25 And there came a voice from above the expanse that was over their heads; whenever they stood still, they dropped their wings. 26 Now above the expanse that was over their heads there was something resembling a throne, like lapis lazuli in appearance; and on that which resembled a throne, high up, was a figure with the appearance of a man. 27 Then I noticed from the appearance of His loins and upward something like glowing metal that looked like fire all around within it, and from the appearance of His loins and downward I saw something like fire; and there was a radiance around Him. 28 As the appearance of the rainbow in the clouds on a rainy day, so was the appearance of the surrounding radiance. Such was the appearance of the likeness of the glory of the Lord. And when I saw it, I fell on my face and heard a voice speaking." (Ezek 1:25–28, NASB)

On the throne Ezekiel saw a figure like that of a man. It was not a man exactly, but a figure like that of a man. Recall from earlier that Daniel also saw this mysterious figure like a man.

> "13 'I kept looking in the night visions, and behold, with the clouds of heaven one like a Son of Man was coming, and He came up to the Ancient of Days and was presented before Him. 14 'And to Him was given dominion, glory and a kingdom, that all the peoples, nations and men of every language might serve Him. his dominion is an everlasting dominion which will not pass away; and His kingdom is one which will not be destroyed." (Dan 7:13-14, NASB)

This one sitting on the Throne who looks like "the figure" of a man in Ezekiel, the one who Daniel saw that was "like" a Son of Man, was given authority, glory, and sovereign power. All nations and peoples of every language worship him. His dominion is everlasting. As Christians we know this one who is like a man is Christ. God himself incarnated as a human. Most Christians take Ezekiel, Daniel, and John literally about a figure like a man sitting on the throne of God. Most see Jesus. Jesus is the figure who was like the figure of a man, the Son of Man, the one who appears at the throne of God over and above the four living creatures. That's clearly how John saw it too.

> "13 And every created thing which is in heaven and on the earth and under the earth and on the sea, and all things in them, I heard saying, 'To Him who sits on the throne, and to the Lamb, be blessing and honor and glory and dominion forever and ever.' 14 And the four living creatures kept saying, 'Amen.' And the elders fell down and worshiped." (Rev 5:13-14, NASB)
>
> Though Christians generally see the Son of Man as a literal figure who is Christ appearing on Earth as a man, they differ greatly on the rest of the same passages in Ezekiel and Daniel.

Though Christians generally see the Son of Man as a literal figure who is Christ appearing on Earth as a man, they differ greatly on the rest of the same passages in Ezekiel and Daniel. Ezekiel does not explain the four living creatures and neither does John. Yet theologians have offered many explanations, as we explored in the opening part of this book. Theologians have said the four living creatures represent:

- The Four Gospels (Matthew, Mark, Luke, John)
- The Four Great Apostles (Peter, James, Matthew, Paul)
- The Four Principal Angels (Gabriel, Michael, Raphael, Uriel)
- The Four Patriarchal Churches (Alexandria, Jerusalem, Antioch, Constantinople)
- The Four Doctors of the church (Augustine, Pope Gregory I, Jerome, Ambrose)
- The Four Ancient Elements (Earth, Air, Fire, Water)
- Four Motive Powers of the Soul (Reason, Anger, Desire, Conscience)

- Four Orders (Pastor, Deacon, Doctor, Contemplative)
- Four Attributes of Divinity (wisdom, power, omniscience, creation)
- Four Orders of life (human, ox/domesticated animals, lion/wild animals, eagle/birds)
- And even more.

The allegorical approach with spiritualized explanations varies greatly as you can see above. Yet the Bible itself does not explain what (or who) these four living creatures are. So, the Sola Scriptura approach will also not offer an explanation. It must be enough for us to see the amazing and bewildering vision as the power of God that is beyond our understanding. And we must hold to the strictly literal interpretation that the one who appears like the figure of a man, the Son of Man, is Christ.

If we take an allegorical view and say the four living creatures represent reason, anger, desire, and conscience, then we must also offer an alternative to the Son of Man sitting on the throne as well. An allegorical view might even be inclined to suggest that if the four living creatures are reason, anger, desire, and conscience, then the figure of the man represents what psychoanalyst Carl Jung called the universal collective subconsciousness. This is called the "Cosmic Christ Consciousness" in the gnostic New Age movement which teaches that Jesus is really a god of Hinduism (an emanation of Brahman). No, Jesus is not a lesser god of Hinduism. No, we cannot take part of a passage allegorically and another literally. The one, who is like a man, is Jesus, who was literally incarnated as a man.

> "14 And the Word became flesh, and dwelt among us, and we saw His glory, glory as of the only begotten from the Father, full of grace and truth." (John 1:14, NASB)

We should humbly stay within the bounds of scripture and not add anything that is not already there. We should neither turn to the left nor to the right. We should stay on the straight path, for broad is the path that leads to destruction and only a few find the narrow path that leads to everlasting life.

> We should humbly stay within the bounds of scripture and not add anything that is not already there.

We must also see that although Revelation does not quote Ezekiel directly, it is clearly alluding to it. The vision John has of the throne of God is highly unique and only appears elsewhere in the Bible in the book of Ezekiel. Thus, we must understand Ezekiel if we want to better understand Revelation. Perhaps we can respond to these bewildering visions in the same way Ezekiel and Daniel did?

> "And when I saw it, I fell on my face" (Ezek 1:28b, NASB)

"15 'As for me, Daniel, my spirit was distressed within me, and the visions in my mind kept alarming me." (Dan 7:15, NASB)

Though we may be disturbed by these confusing visions that are not explained in scripture, we should humbly fall facedown at the Presence of God who declared from the beginning, who literally revealed through the prophets, that it is one like a Son of Man who will be worshiped by all nations and peoples of every language. His dominion is everlasting, and his kingdom will never be destroyed.

THE GOOD SHEPHERD AT THE CENTER OF THE THRONE

As Christians, one of the things we cherish about Ezekiel is the promises God made to be the Shepherd over his people, to heal the brokenhearted, and to search for the lost. This is a primary motivation for many ministries and serves a wonderful purpose in God's Kingdom to bring healing and direction in the world. This image of Jesus as the Good Shepherd who came to release the brokenhearted and search for the lost is found in Ezekiel, Isaiah, Jeremiah, the Psalms, the Gospels, and in Revelation. In Ezekiel we hear God say that he will bring his people back to the land of Israel and take care of them himself.

> "11 For thus says the Lord God, 'Behold, I Myself will search for My sheep and seek them out. 12 As a shepherd cares for his herd in the day when he is among his scattered sheep, so I will care for My sheep and will deliver them from all the places to which they were scattered on a cloudy and gloomy day. 13 I will bring them out from the peoples and gather them from the countries and bring them to their own land; and I will feed them on the mountains of Israel, by the streams, and in all the inhabited places of the land. 14 I will feed them in a good pasture, and their grazing ground will be on the mountain heights of Israel. There they will lie down on good grazing ground and feed in rich pasture on the mountains of Israel. 15 I will feed My flock and I will lead them to rest,' declares the Lord God. 16 'I will seek the lost, bring back the scattered, bind up the broken and strengthen the sick;" (Ezek 34:11–16a, NASB)

We see this image of God in Isaiah as well.

> "10 Behold, the Lord God will come with might, with His arm ruling for Him. behold, His reward is with Him and His recompense before Him. 11 Like a shepherd He will tend His flock, in His arm He will gather the lambs and carry them in His bosom; he will gently lead the nursing ewes." (Isa 40:10–11, NASB)

And it is this very image of Jesus as the Good Shepherd that we see at the center of the throne of God in the book of Revelation.

> "17 for the Lamb in the center of the throne will be their shepherd, and will guide them to springs of the water of life; and God will wipe every tear from their eyes." (Rev 7:17, NASB)

This beautiful image of God wiping every tear and caring for his people follows from the Hebrew prophets' visions of God caring for his flock, binding up the brokenhearted, proclaiming freedom for the captives, and releasing prisoners from the darkness.

> "15 I will feed My flock and I will lead them to rest,' declares the Lord God. 16 'I will seek the lost, bring back the scattered, bind up the broken and strengthen the sick; but the fat and the strong I will destroy. I will feed them with judgment." (Ezek 34:15–16, NASB)

> "The Spirit of the Lord God is upon me, because the Lord has anointed me to bring good news to the afflicted; he has sent me to bind up the brokenhearted, to proclaim liberty to captives and freedom to prisoners; 2 To proclaim the favorable year of the Lord" (Isa 61:1–2a, NASB)

When Jesus read from the scroll of Isaiah on a Sabbath Day in Nazareth, he proclaimed that he was the Messiah who was the Good Shepherd come into the world to save the lost.

> "18 'The Spirit of the Lord is upon Me, because He anointed Me to preach the gospel to the poor. He has sent Me to proclaim release to the captives, and recovery of sight to the blind, to set free those who are oppressed, 19 To proclaim the favorable year of the Lord.' 20 And He closed the book, gave it back to the attendant and sat down; and the eyes of all in the synagogue were fixed on Him. 21 And He began to say to them, 'Today this Scripture has been fulfilled in your hearing.'" (Luke 4:18–21, NASB)

This one who Ezekiel saw like the figure of a man on the throne of God was on a mission: to seek and save the lost like a Good Shepherd.

> This one who Ezekiel saw like the figure of a man on the throne of God was on a mission: to seek and save the lost like a Good Shepherd.

> "9 And Jesus said to him, 'Today salvation has come to this house, because he, too, is a son of Abraham. 10 For the Son of Man has come to seek and to save that which was lost.'" (Luke 19:9–10, NASB)

> "11 'I am the good shepherd; the good shepherd lays down His life for the sheep. 12 He who is a hired hand, and not a shepherd, who is not the owner of the sheep, sees the wolf coming, and leaves the sheep and flees, and the wolf snatches them and scatters them. 13 He flees because he is a hired hand and is not concerned about the sheep." (John 10:11–13, NASB)

Another key thing we learn from the book of Ezekiel that forms the background context for the book of Revelation as well as the entire New Testament is that although God is the Shepherd of his people, and although Jesus is the Good Shepherd who came to seek and save the lost, there will be a time of judgment. Those who do wrong will not always rule the world. In Ezekiel God is not happy with the leaders of Israel and so he judges them and sets up his servant David to be their Shepherd, their Prince.

> "16 'I will seek the lost, bring back the scattered, bind up the broken and strengthen the sick; but the fat and the strong I will destroy. I will feed them with judgment. 17 'As for you, My flock, thus says the Lord God, 'Behold, I will judge between one sheep and another, between the rams and the male goats. 18 Is it too slight a thing for you that you should feed in the good pasture, that you must tread down with your feet the rest of your pastures? Or that you should drink of the clear waters, that you must foul the rest with your feet? 19 As for My flock, they must eat what you tread down with your feet and drink what you foul with your feet!" 20 Therefore, thus says the Lord God to them, 'Behold, I, even I, will judge between the fat sheep and the lean sheep. 21 Because you push with side and with shoulder, and thrust at all the weak with your horns until you have scattered them abroad, 22 therefore, I will deliver My flock, and they will no longer be a prey; and I will judge between one sheep and another. 23 'Then I will set over them one shepherd, My servant David, and he will feed them; he will feed them himself and be their shepherd. 24 And I, the Lord, will be their God, and My servant David will be prince among them; I the Lord have spoken." (Ezek 34:16–24, NASB)
>
> Knowing that the Messiah is one who comes to shepherd the flock in justice, and that the leaders of Israel at that time were prophesied to be bad and selfish people, how could the leaders of Israel at the time of Jesus accept him? They would only be pointing the finger at themselves as the bad leaders that Ezekiel had predicted.

Knowing that the Messiah is one who comes to shepherd the flock in justice, and that the leaders of Israel at that time were prophesied to be bad and selfish people, how could the leaders of Israel at the time of Jesus accept him? They would only be pointing the finger at themselves as the bad leaders that Ezekiel had predicted. Not only were they jealous of the following Jesus had, not only were they jealous of the miracles God did through Jesus and the Apostles, not only were they afraid of the Roman powers and their fragile position within the government hierarchy, but they knew that the scriptures predicted the leaders of Israel were so bad that God himself would judge them and replace them with his Servant David, the Good Shepherd. They knew they were the ones who were drinking the clear water upstream and muddying it downstream for others. They were doing the opposite of caring for the flock and searching for the lost.

> "Then the word of the Lord came to me saying, 2 'Son of man, prophesy against the shepherds of Israel. Prophesy and say to those shepherds, 'Thus says the Lord God, 'Woe, shepherds of Israel who have been feeding themselves! Should not the shepherds feed the flock? 3 You eat the fat and clothe yourselves with the wool, you slaughter the fat sheep without feeding the flock. 4 Those who are sickly you have not strengthened, the diseased you have not healed, the broken you have not bound up, the scattered you have not brought back, nor have you sought for the lost; but with force and with severity you have dominated them. 5 They were scattered for lack of a shepherd, and they became food for every beast of the field and were scattered. 6 My flock wandered through all the mountains and on every high hill; My flock was scattered over all the surface of the earth, and there was no one to search or seek for them.'" 7 Therefore, you shepherds, hear the word of the Lord: 8 'As I live,' declares the Lord God, 'surely because My flock has become a prey, My flock has even become food for all the beasts of the field for lack of a shepherd, and My shepherds did not search for My flock, but rather the shepherds fed themselves and did not feed My flock; 9 therefore, you shepherds, hear the word of the Lord: 10 'Thus says the Lord God, 'Behold, I am against the shepherds, and I will demand My sheep from them and make them cease from feeding sheep. So the shepherds will not feed themselves anymore, but I will deliver My flock from their mouth, so that they will not be food for them.''''
> (Ezek 34:1–10, NASB)

Even the Jewish Talmud records that the leaders of Israel at the time of Jesus were bad people who desecrated the Temple sacrifices, clubbed and beat people, spread false rumors about their enemies, and kept their power by keeping control of the Temple treasuries only within their immediate families.[2] Hear what Jeremiah predicted about the leaders of Israel at the time of the Messiah.

> "'Woe to the shepherds who are destroying and scattering the sheep of My pasture!' declares the Lord. 2 Therefore thus says the Lord God of Israel concerning the shepherds who are tending My people: 'You have scattered My flock and driven them away, and have not attended to them; behold, I am about to attend to you for the evil of your deeds,' declares the Lord. 3 'Then I Myself will gather the remnant of My flock out of all the countries where I have driven them and bring them back to their pasture, and they will be fruitful and multiply. 4 I will also raise up shepherds over them and they will tend them; and they will not be afraid any longer, nor be terrified, nor will any be missing,' declares the Lord. 5 'Behold, the days are coming,' declares the Lord, 'When I will raise up for David a righteous Branch; and He will reign as king and act wisely and do justice and righteousness in the land.'" (Jer 23:1–5, NASB)

---

2. Ashi and Ravina, *Babylonian Talmud*, Pesachim 57a.

This promise of the ingathering of the remnant of Israel, their bad leaders being replaced by a single King, a descendant of David, a Righteous Branch, is fundamental to the background context of the book of Revelation. And since the return to Israel after the Babylonian Captivity did not result in Israel living in peace forever under King David, then Jeremiah and Ezekiel have not been completely fulfilled. Though the Judeans returned from Babylon, not all those who went north into Assyria returned. Though Persia overthrew Babylon and set the Judeans free to return, they remained under Persian control and then Greek, and finally Roman control until the time of Jesus. And then just after the rejection of Christ they were dispersed from the Promised Land for nearly two thousand years until their "return" (*aliyah*, עֲלִיָּה) began in the nineteenth century. Today they still have no king but are instead a parliamentary democracy.

THE VALLEY OF DRY BONES

The vision of the Valley of Dry Bones is familiar to most Christians. We typically learn about this vision as a child growing up in the church, and the moral of the story that is taught is usually that God can revive any dead bones, including yours, your church, or your nation. God is able to put his Spirit into any person or group of people and revive them from a spiritual death. While it is certainly true that God is able to do that, is that what the vision is really about? Is the Valley of Dry Bones really about Christians? Is it really about your own heart? Does it align with the book of Revelation?

> Is the Valley of Dry Bones really about Christians? Is it really about your own heart? Does it align with the book of Revelation?

Recall that Ezekiel lived in the Babylonian Captivity and the biggest question on the minds of people just taken into slavery is how long until they will be free again? Chapters 33 to 37 of Ezekiel describe the punishment of Israel for their sins as well as their eventual restoration. God promises to restore the people back to their own land, forgive them, cleanse them, give them a new heart, and put a new spirit into them: his Spirit. And then God showed Ezekiel this vision of the Valley of Dry Bones (Ezek 37:1–14). Ezekiel is taken to the middle of a valley and is shown a great number of dry bones on the floor of the valley. God asks Ezekiel if the bones can live again and then shows him a prophecy that they will indeed live again. But does God say who the bones are? Are they really Christians who are living sinful lives that hear the Gospel and become born again, as some interpretations hold?

> "11 Then He said to me, 'Son of man, these bones are the whole house of Israel; behold, they say, 'Our bones are dried up and our hope has perished. We are completely cut off.' 12 Therefore prophesy and say to them, 'Thus says the Lord God, 'Behold, I will open your graves and cause you to come up out of your graves, My people; and I will bring you into the land of Israel. 13 Then

you will know that I am the Lord, when I have opened your graves and caused you to come up out of your graves, My people. 14 I will put My Spirit within you and you will come to life, and I will place you on your own land. Then you will know that I, the Lord, have spoken and done it,' declares the Lord.'" (Ezek 37:11–14, NASB)

The Bible plainly says the bones are the people of Israel (Ezek 37:11). God also says they will be brought back to the land of Israel. Recall that this vision to Ezekiel was when he sat in the Babylonian Captivity, when the Judeans had just lost the Promised Land. While the general principle is true that God is able to revive and restore any person or nation, that is not what this specific text actually says. The text refers to the land of Israel directly multiple times. Ezekiel was shown a vision of Israel being restored after the Babylonian Captivity. We know from history that the Judeans were released and did return to the land. And that is the background context for the Gospels and the book of Revelation.

There is a teaching in some Christian denominations that says Christians have replaced the Jewish people as God's people, and anywhere there is an unfulfilled promise in the Hebrew Bible then it now applies to Christians only. That teaching, known as Replacement Theology, holds that this passage in Ezekiel is about a "spiritual Israel" (the church) taking possession of a "Heavenly Canaan." The views of Replacement Theology were popular until suddenly Israel was made a nation again after two millennia. Prophecies about a return to the Promised Land suddenly seemed to be coming true. We should note that many people hold this view, called Supersessionism, to be Anti-Semitic.

> The views of Replacement Theology were popular until suddenly Israel was made a nation again after two millennia. Prophecies about a return to the Promised Land suddenly seemed to be coming true.

Another interesting interpretation is that of some Rabbis as found in their writings. They hold that when Ezekiel sees the people of Israel brought out of their graves back to the land of Israel (Ezek 37:13–14) that they will be literally resurrected and sent back to Israel through underground tunnels that God will create specifically for that purpose. It is better to be buried in the land of Israel and not have to undergo the painful underground journey back to the land at the time of the resurrection of the dead (Midrash Tanchuma Buber, Vayechi 6:1).

The Sola Scriptura approach will hold to only what the text directly says. The vision of the Valley of Dry Bones is set in the context of the Babylonian Captivity where God promises to Ezekiel that there will be a restoration of the people of Israel back to their land. God will put his Spirit in them, and they will settle in their own land. This is both a spiritual and a physical restoration. Though some theologians see this spiritual restoration as a mass conversion of Jewish people to Christianity in the end times, the text does not directly say that, and subsequent chapters of the book of

Ezekiel regarding the temple worship system bring that interpretation into question as we will see below. The physical restoration to their own land is the context for the next vision of the two sticks, as well as the next two chapters (Ezek 38–39) which describe Gog and Magog coming to attack a restored Israel. We will explore both below, as well as the implications for the book of Revelation.

THE TWO STICKS

Although most Christians are familiar with the vision of the Valley of Dry Bones, the very next part of the very same chapter is rarely discussed. All over Christianity people love the vision of the Valley of Dry Bones, even making pictures and T-shirts from it. But the following vision of the two sticks in the very same chapter is relatively unknown. As you will see in the remainder of chapter 37 Ezekiel again describes a restored Israel and an ideal permanent future state where there is one king, David, over a united Israel in the land of Israel, forever. This idea of a permanently restored and reunited Israel under a single king forever is interpreted in many different ways in Christianity as well as in Judaism, as we will explore below.

In this vision where the Word of the Lord came to Ezekiel, he is told to take two sticks representing the two nations of Israel (the Northern and Southern Kingdoms in the time of Ezekiel) and join them together as a symbolic prophecy.

> "15 The word of the Lord came again to me saying, 16 'And you, son of man, take for yourself one stick and write on it, 'For Judah and for the sons of Israel, his companions'; then take another stick and write on it, 'For Joseph, the stick of Ephraim and all the house of Israel, his companions.' 17 Then join them for yourself one to another into one stick, that they may become one in your hand." (Ezek 37:15–17, NASB)

When the people ask Ezekiel what it means, God provides the explanation. Note here again that the Bible itself provides the interpretation of the symbolism.

> "20 The sticks on which you write will be in your hand before their eyes. 21 Say to them, 'Thus says the Lord God, 'Behold, I will take the sons of Israel from among the nations where they have gone, and I will gather them from every side and bring them into their own land; 22 and I will make them one nation in the land, on the mountains of Israel; and one king will be king for all of them; and they will no longer be two nations and no longer be divided into two kingdoms." (Ezek 37:20–22, NASB)

If the Bible explains directly what a symbol means then we should not listen to theologians who give an alternative explanation. Even if an angel gives us another meaning different from what the scriptures have said, we should be wary.

Any interpretation that says the sticks mean something other than the Israelites being regathered as one nation, no longer two, into the land of Israel, on the mountains of Israel, is an interpretation that disagrees with what God said. Yet that doesn't stop theologians from doing just that. If the Bible explains directly what a symbol means, then we should not listen to theologians who give an alternative explanation. Even if an angel gives us another meaning different from what the scriptures have said, we should be wary.

Did God really say the two sticks mean Israel? Did God really say you can't eat from the Tree of the Knowledge of Good and Evil? Does God really say he forgives our sins? Maybe he meant something else. Here are some of the interpretations offered by theologians. As you read these, remember that God already told Ezekiel that the sticks referred to the scattered Israelites being regathered into the Promised Land for a final time (Ezek 37:20–22).

Some Christian theologians say the sticks refer to:

- The future ingathering of Israel to the Christian church, Jews and Gentiles united under Christ.
- A prediction of the coming of the book of Mormon, being joined to the Bible.
- The restoration of the Jewish people to the land of Israel.

Some Jewish theologians say the sticks refer to:

- The restoration of the Jewish people to the land of Israel, the Full Redemption.
- Two different Messiahs, one who dies (*Ben Yosef*) and one who reigns (*Ben David*).

Again, let scripture interpret scripture. God clearly says what the two sticks mean. And that explanation given by God fits perfectly within the context of Ezekiel sitting in the Babylonian Captivity. It fits perfectly within the narrative of the restoration of Israel after their punishment in Babylon. And it fits perfectly with the preceding vision of the Valley of Dry Bones. The people are promised to be brought back and settled in the Promised Land. In addition, God says the reunited and regathered people of Israel will live under the rule of one king.

> "24 'My servant David will be king over them, and they will all have one shepherd; and they will walk in My ordinances and keep My statutes and observe them. 25 They will live on the land that I gave to Jacob My servant, in which your fathers lived; and they will live on it, they, and their sons and their sons' sons, forever; and David My servant will be their prince forever. 26 I will make a covenant of peace with them; it will be an everlasting covenant with them. And I will place them and multiply them, and will set My sanctuary in their midst forever." (Ezek 37:24–26, NASB)

Notice a few things about these verses. First, we again see the references to a return to the land of Israel, the land God gave to his servant Jacob, the land where their ancestors lived. The land is referred to in many different ways, which emphasizes a literal and not an allegorical interpretation. If the return to the land was an allegorical reference to your heart or to a "Heavenly Canaan," then how would you explain all the different land references? The mountains of Israel, the land given to Jacob, the land where the ancestors lived? The Bible is clearly, plainly, and directly referring to physical land, the land of Promise, the Promised Land.

Next notice that there is one king, David, the one Shepherd. He is their Prince forever. And notice that God will make an everlasting covenant of peace with them. This is a permanent change, a new covenant, an unending and everlasting condition that clearly doesn't exist today. None of the potential explanations for the regathering have been fulfilled yet. Neither the literal nor the allegorical. Jews are not joined with Christians under the rule of Christ today. Not all of the dispersed tribes of Israel have returned to the modern land of Israel. And there have not been two proven messiahs accepted by the Jewish people. This prophecy of the restoration of the tribes of Israel to the Promised Land under one king David waits for another day. This prophecy of a covenant of peace for those living in the land of Israel also clearly waits for another day, as is evident by the ongoing tensions in the Middle East.

Interestingly, some interpretations in both Christianity and Judaism see the reference to King David as not the Messiah but a second-in-command leader who operates under the authority of the Messiah. This is a surprising development in Christianity, which so often holds Christ to be the promised descendant of David who is the Branch and the Good Shepherd. This is also a surprising development in Judaism but found within the Talmud (Sanhedrin 98b:16) and has been disputed among Jewish theologians.

The Sola Scriptura approach holds only to what the scriptures themselves say. In this passage God says the two sticks represent a reunited Israel which has been regathered into the land of Israel under one king, the one Shepherd, and this is an unending, everlasting, and permanent change forever. The following two chapters of Ezekiel which describe an attack by Gog and Magog is an attack on this reunited Israel. And we will see that the attack will fail, and the people will remain in the land forever.

> In this passage God says the two sticks represent a reunited Israel which has been regathered into the land of Israel under one king, the one Shepherd, and this is an unending, everlasting, and permanent change forever.

GOG AND MAGOG

Although the New Testament never directly quotes from the book of Ezekiel, we have a clear reference to it in the book of Revelation. Revelation specifically mentions Gog and Magog which is otherwise only found in the book of Ezekiel. In Ezekiel it is a prophecy about a final attack on the reunited people of Israel after they have been regathered a final time into the Promised Land. Gog leads many nations to attack Jerusalem, but God will defeat Gog. And then the devil who deceived them will be defeated for ever and ever.

> "7 When the thousand years are completed, Satan will be released from his prison, 8 and will come out to deceive the nations which are in the four corners of the earth, Gog and Magog, to gather them together for the war; the number of them is like the sand of the seashore. 9 And they came up on the broad plain of the earth and surrounded the camp of the saints and the beloved city, and fire came down from heaven and devoured them. 10 And the devil who deceived them was thrown into the lake of fire and brimstone, where the beast and the false prophet are also; and they will be tormented day and night forever and ever." (Rev 20:7–10, NASB)
>
> Gog leads many nations to attack Jerusalem, but God will defeat Gog. And then the devil who deceived them will be defeated for ever and ever.

If the Rabbis who argued over including the book of Ezekiel in the Jewish canon had decided against it, then we would have an obscure reference in the New Testament to something outside Jewish canon. Yet the Rabbis did ultimately decide to include it, and the Christians inherited the book along with the overall Hebrew Bible which we refer to as the Old Testament. And as we have seen from exploring passages in Ezekiel so far, we have a rich trove of background materials to better understand the book of Revelation. We have the vision of the Throne of God with the four living creatures, as seen in Revelation. We have the Good Shepherd of Ezekiel at the center of the throne of God in Revelation. And we have the idea of a restored Israel under one king as a permanent future state, as the Valley of Dry Bones and the symbolism of the two sticks shows us in Ezekiel.

We now will add to our background knowledge this king called Gog who leads the nation of Magog together with other nations in a final attack on Jerusalem. We know it is a final attack because the people regathered into the reunited Israel live there forever, under an everlasting covenant of peace that God makes with them. They will live in the Promised Land, the land given to Jacob, the land where their ancestors lived, on the mountains of Israel. And it is precisely there where they will be attacked by Gog. Rashi, one of the most famous Jewish Theologians, says that in the last days Israel will be ingathered back into the Promised Land, and shortly after Gog will attack. As we look at this prophecy in chapters 38 and 39, we see God telling Ezekiel to prophesy against Gog, telling him:

> "7 'Be prepared, and prepare yourself, you and all your companies that are assembled about you, and be a guard for them. 8 After many days you will be summoned; in the latter years you will come into the land that is restored

from the sword, whose inhabitants have been gathered from many nations to the mountains of Israel which had been a continual waste; but its people were brought out from the nations, and they are living securely, all of them. 9 You will go up, you will come like a storm; you will be like a cloud covering the land, you and all your troops, and many peoples with you.'" (Ezek 38:7–9, NASB)

Some interpreters have tried to identify who Gog is because he is otherwise unknown in history, and the people he leads were not historically enemies of Israel. It is a mystery who this person of Gog is, as well as these unknown enemies of Israel. Though allegorical interpretations say Gog represents all kingdoms throughout history that ever opposed the people of God (Jewish people in pre-Christian times or Christians in modern times), the language of the scriptures themselves speaks of a specific man, not a generalization of multiple kingdoms throughout history. Allegorical interpretations hold that Gog represents all evil powers throughout history that are opposed to Christ. Yet the scriptures plainly speak of Gog as a specific man who leads many nations in a final battle against Jerusalem.

> Allegorical interpretations hold that Gog represents all evil powers throughout history that are opposed to Christ. Yet the scriptures plainly speak of Gog as a specific man who leads many nations in a final battle against Jerusalem.
>
> "2 'Son of man, set your face toward Gog of the land of Magog, the chief prince of Meshech and Tubal, and prophesy against him 3 and say, 'Thus says the Lord God, 'Behold, I am against you, O Gog, chief prince of Meshech and Tubal.'" (Ezek 38:2–3, NASB)

Gog is the chief prince of Meshek and Tubal. These were peoples living to the north of Israel and have historically never been enemies of Israel like Egypt, Assyria, or Babylon. Some theologians see the title "chief prince" as chief of *rosh* because the Hebrew word for chief or head leader is *rosh* (רֹאשׁ). In this way they see a similarity in the sounds of *rosh* with Russia, *Meshek* with Moscow, and *Tubal* with Tobolsk (a Russian city). The similarity of the sounds of the words is interesting, but the Bible has been specific about city names in the past, such as the Messiah will be born in "Bethlehem," the Messiah will come to "Jerusalem," and the River of the Water of Life will flow to the "Arabah." Moreover, the word *rosh* means "chief" and is part of the title of Gog as is used twice in verses Ezek 38:2 and 3.

To get very technical in the Hebrew language, the Masoretic Text also indicates by a *Tifcha* (טִפְחָא) under both occurrences of *rosh* that the word is connected with "prince" and not connected to *Meshek* and *Tubal* as a listing of locations. The KJV, NIV, NLT, ISV, ESV, NASB, GNT, Berean as well as the Jewish version (JPS) translate *rosh* as the "chief prince." In other words, Gog is a "chief prince," and not the prince of some unknown place called *rosh*.

However, the Septuagint translates the verse as "ruler of Rosh, Meshech, and Tubal" (ἄρχοντα Ρως Μοσόχ και Θουβάλ).[3] The NKJV and older NASB versions translate it as "the prince of Rosh, Mesheck, and Tubal." Therefore, if your translation follows the Masoretic text, you will understand *rosh* to be "chief" and not a place called *rosh*. Otherwise, if your translation follows the older Septuagint, you will understand *rosh* to be a place. Even the KJV differs from the NKJV on this point.

Instead of identifying the final antichrist as a future leader of Russia, the Sola Scriptura approach will only hold that a future leader will lead many nations to attack Israel, after she has been ingathered with none left behind. God will defeat this leader and his armies. This context of Gog and Magog forms a critical part of the background context of the book of Revelation.

THE AFTERMATH

As we explored before, God told Ezekiel that the earlier prophets had spoken of one who would come to attack Israel. They were literally prophesying of an attack by the nations on Israel and so we can read those earlier prophets in that way. This great attack which ends in Gog's defeat is something that the world will see as an act of God.

> "22 And the house of Israel will know that I am the Lord their God from that day onward. 23 The nations will know that the house of Israel went into exile for their iniquity because they acted treacherously against Me, and I hid My face from them; so I gave them into the hand of their adversaries, and all of them fell by the sword." (Ezek 39:22–23, NASB)

After the people of Israel are gathered back into their land and Gog attacks, Israel will have a spiritual awakening and the world will know that God has done this. This will be a permanent change because God will pour out his Spirit on them and no longer hide his face from them.

> "27 When I bring them back from the peoples and gather them from the lands of their enemies, then I shall be sanctified through them in the sight of the many nations. 28 Then they will know that I am the Lord their God because I made them go into exile among the nations, and then gathered them again to their own land; and I will leave none of them there any longer. 29 I will not hide My face from them any longer, for I will have poured out My Spirit on the house of Israel,' declares the Lord God." (Ezek 39:27–29, NASB)

> After the people of Israel are gathered back into their land and Gog attacks, Israel will have a spiritual awakening and the world will know that God has done this. This will be a permanent change because God will pour out his Spirit on them and no longer hide his face from them.

---

3. Nestle, *Diatheke*, Ezek 38:2.

Allegorical interpretations that see these prophecies as representing all kingdoms throughout history which are opposed to Christianity also see "Israel" as a "spiritual Israel," meaning Christians. However, look again at what is happening in the scriptures. Above you can see that God is bringing back the Israelites from the nations where they had been scattered to. God brings them back from exile among the nations. Christians were never sent by God into exile among the nations. To say that Christians are gathered back into their land makes no sense, because Christians did not have a land to begin with. Christians have not been exiled from a specific land. Oftentimes allegorical interpretations will also say that "land" refers to the "Heavenly Canaan," the future place where Christians where live. And again, that does not line up with the scriptures and does not make sense. Allegorical interpretations that claim the "ingathering" refers to Christians being regathered into a "Heavenly Canaan" after exile makes no sense. God did not scatter Christians away from any land, as the Israelites clearly were. The ingathering and restoration of ethnic Israel is clearly spoken of by the prophets, not a restoration of Christians as a "spiritual Israel" returning to a "Heavenly Canaan."

> Allegorical interpretations that claim the "ingathering" refers to Christians being regathered into a "Heavenly Canaan" after exile makes no sense. God did not scatter Christians away from any land, as the Israelites clearly were. The ingathering and restoration of ethnic Israel is clearly spoken of by the prophets, not a restoration of Christians as a "spiritual Israel" returning to a "Heavenly Canaan."

Also notice in Ezekiel that none of the people of Israel are left behind. Verse 28 clearly shows a full restoration of Israel which did not happen after the Babylonian Exile and has not happened to this day. This spiritual awakening of all Israel should remind us of Paul's letter to the Romans. Note that Paul distinguishes between Israel and the Gentiles and does not speak of a "spiritual" Israel. He says that "all" Israel will be saved, and God will make a covenant with them when he takes away their sins.

> "25 For I do not want you, brethren, to be uninformed of this mystery—so that you will not be wise in your own estimation—that a partial hardening has happened to Israel until the fullness of the Gentiles has come in; 26 and so all Israel will be saved; just as it is written, 'The Deliverer will come from Zion, he will remove ungodliness from Jacob.' 27 'This is My covenant with them, when I take away their sins.'" (Rom 11:25–27, NASB)

Paul speaks of both Israel and the Gentiles, not one united "spiritual Israel" and not one single group of people. Paul also says Gentiles should not be conceited, because Israel has experienced a hardening in part until the full number of the Gentiles has come in. The deliverer "will come" from Zion, not "the deliverer has already come." But the deliverer will come from Zion, and he will turn godlessness away from Jacob, he will take away their sins. Paul speaks of a future coming of the deliverer from Zion who will turn ethnic Israel back toward God and will take away their sins. Replacement Theology, where Christians have replaced Israel to form a new "spiritual Israel" is not compatible with what Paul says, nor with what the prophets have declared.

> Replacement Theology, where Christians have replaced Israel to form a new "spiritual Israel" is not compatible with what Paul says, nor with what the prophets have declared.

At the defeat of Gog, Ezekiel tells us that God will call out to every kind of bird and animal to a great sacrifice on the mountains of Israel. This is similar language that we see in the book of Revelation.

> "17 'As for you, son of man, thus says the Lord God, 'Speak to every kind of bird and to every beast of the field, 'Assemble and come, gather from every side to My sacrifice which I am going to sacrifice for you, as a great sacrifice on the mountains of Israel, that you may eat flesh and drink blood. 18 You will eat the flesh of mighty men and drink the blood of the princes of the earth, as though they were rams, lambs, goats and bulls, all of them fatlings of Bashan. 19 So you will eat fat until you are glutted, and drink blood until you are drunk, from My sacrifice which I have sacrificed for you." (Ezek 39:17–19, NASB)

> "17 Then I saw an angel standing in the sun, and he cried out with a loud voice, saying to all the birds which fly in midheaven, 'Come, assemble for the great supper of God, 18 so that you may eat the flesh of kings and the flesh of commanders and the flesh of mighty men and the flesh of horses and of those who sit on them and the flesh of all men, both free men and slaves, and small and great.' 19 And I saw the beast and the kings of the earth and their armies assembled to make war against Him who sat on the horse and against His army. 20 And the beast was seized, and with him the false prophet who performed the signs in his presence, by which he deceived those who had received the mark of the beast and those who worshiped his image; these two were thrown alive into the lake of fire which burns with brimstone. 21 And the rest were killed with the sword which came from the mouth of Him who sat on the horse, and all the birds were filled with their flesh." (Rev 19:17–21, NASB)

Ezekiel says that "the great supper of God" will be after the defeat of Gog at the final attack on Jerusalem. The birds will gather together to eat the flesh of kings, generals, mighty people, and all those opposed to God. This attack will end in the defeat of Gog and his armies. Israel will be saved and experience a spiritual awakening. Never again will God turn away from her, and the nations will know that God has done this.

> Ezekiel says that "the great supper of God" will be after the defeat of Gog at the final attack on Jerusalem. The birds will gather together to eat the flesh of kings, generals, mighty people, and all those opposed to God. This attack will end in the defeat of Gog and his armies. Israel will be saved and experience a

spiritual awakening. Never again will God turn away from her, and the nations will know that God has done this.

Compare the future state that Ezekiel sees after Gog is defeated with the future state John describes in Revelation after the beast and Gog have been defeated:

> "Then I saw a new heaven and a new earth; for the first heaven and the first earth passed away, and there is no longer any sea. 2 And I saw the holy city, new Jerusalem, coming down out of heaven from God, made ready as a bride adorned for her husband. 3 And I heard a loud voice from the throne, saying, 'Behold, the tabernacle of God is among men, and He will dwell among them, and they shall be His people, and God Himself will be among them, 4 and He will wipe away every tear from their eyes; and there will no longer be any death; there will no longer be any mourning, or crying, or pain; the first things have passed away.'" (Rev 21:1-4, NASB)
>
> The aftermath of the defeat of Gog, in both Ezekiel as well as in the book of Revelation, is a beautiful future state where the enemies of God have been utterly defeated and the people of God will forever live in peace.

The aftermath of the defeat of Gog, in both Ezekiel as well as in the book of Revelation, is a beautiful future state where the enemies of God have been utterly defeated and the people of God will forever live in peace. In Ezekiel the people of Israel will have a spiritual awakening and live under a new everlasting covenant of peace. In Revelation the people of God will live in a new heaven and a new earth and live in a new order of things where there is only peace. The rest of the book of Ezekiel describes the vision of the future state, which includes a river flowing out from under the sanctuary (Ezek 47:1) just like we see a river flowing out from under the Throne of God in Revelation (Rev 22:1). Along the banks of the river grow trees that provide fruit as well as leaves for healing (Ezek 47:12, Rev 22:2). We will explore these fascinating chapters next.

THE TEMPLE OF EZEKIEL

What we have learned so far in Ezekiel has been great background context for the book of Revelation. But the closing portion of Ezekiel, chapters 40-48, presents the most difficulty to Christians who hold a literal interpretation. That is because we find therein a detailed description of a temple, sacrificial worship, and duties of "the Prince." The last nine chapters of Ezekiel are difficult for Christians because they describe a future temple where there are animal sacrifices. Because the blood of Jesus was the last and perfect offering for sins, there is no need for animal sacrifices. A future temple where the people of God are offering animal sacrifices, as described in Ezekiel, causes some theological issues that need to be worked out for Christians.

The last nine chapters of Ezekiel are difficult for Christians because they describe a future temple where there are animal sacrifices. Because the blood of Jesus was the last and perfect offering for sins, there is no need for animal sacrifices.

It would be convenient to dismiss the future temple Ezekiel saw in some way. At least three approaches have been tried by theologians: Ezekiel had a failed vision, the vision refers to the Second Temple, or an allegorical dismissal of a literal temple.

Did Ezekiel have a failed vision? Some theologians argue that Ezekiel saw a possible future for the Jewish people, but because they rejected Christ then the vision of the future temple would not come to pass. Yet this explanation ignores the clear promises of what is to come. If a prophet says things that do not come to pass, then he is not a prophet. If one says that the Jewish people failed and the prophecies of Ezekiel are now invalid, then who is to decide which prophecies are right and which are canceled? And if God was all-knowing, then he would know what would happen and would not have sent a prophecy that would fail. Besides, God already sent prophecies about the rejection and death of the Messiah so that is already part of prophecy before Ezekiel even began his work. The rejection of the Messiah by his own people was already foretold and is a fact we can all observe. So we cannot dismiss Ezekiel as failed prophecy.

Did Ezekiel see the Second Temple? Some theologians say that Ezekiel had a grand vision of the Second Temple, but the people were unable to completely fulfill it. Because the Second Temple did not have the grandeur described by Ezekiel, because they built a more limited temple, then the vision of eternal peace for the Jewish people did not come to pass. Yet this does not accord with scripture either. The Second Temple was destroyed, yet Ezekiel said God would live forever in the temple.

> "6 Then I heard one speaking to me from the house, while a man was standing beside me. 7 He said to me, 'Son of man, this is the place of My throne and the place of the soles of My feet, where I will dwell among the sons of Israel forever. And the house of Israel will not again defile My holy name, neither they nor their kings, by their harlotry and by the corpses of their kings when they die," (Ezek 43:6–7, NASB)

Since God says the temple that Ezekiel saw is where he will live among the Israelites forever, and the Second Temple was destroyed, then either Ezekiel saw another temple, or his prophecy failed. As with the previous explanation, we cannot accept Ezekiel had a failed prophecy, so he could not have been describing the Second Temple.

Did Ezekiel see an allegory of some deeper underlying truth? Some theologians think that the future temple described by Ezekiel is purely symbolic. They claim it refers to the Christian church. Because the Judeans living in the Babylonian Captivity would not have understood Christianity, God chose to reveal the truth in a manner they would understand: that of a future temple with animal sacrifices. However, standing against this interpretation other theologians point out that there are nine chapters of detail about the worship practices and the temple dimensions. God did not provide chapters and chapters of detail just to be swept away as if it meant nothing. It was nine chapters, after all, compared to the number of verses describing the death of the Messiah and its significance for humanity.

> We would probably like to allegorically cancel out a verse or command here or there, at least the ones we keep breaking. But nine whole chapters? That's audacious.

We would probably like to allegorically cancel out a verse or command here or there, at least the ones we keep breaking. But nine whole chapters? That's audacious. Additionally, God was very clear about the death of the Messiah and the Messiah's soul being a sacrificial offering for sin. That was something the Judeans would not have understood either, yet God revealed those truths directly without allegory, so God is able to use the direct language of truth and has no need to cast future visions in very different and confusing terms.

While it would be convenient for Christians to dismiss the vision of Ezekiel's temple, we simply cannot do so. The book of Revelation clearly has Ezekiel's vision in mind when it speaks of the Living Water running from under the Throne of God out into the surrounding regions. Revelation speaks of trees bearing fruit along the banks and their leaves being used for healing.

> "Then he brought me back to the door of the house; and behold, water was flowing from under the threshold of the house toward the east, for the house faced east. And the water was flowing down from under, from the right side of the house, from south of the altar." (Ezek 47:1, NASB)

> "By the river on its bank, on one side and on the other, will grow all kinds of trees for food. Their leaves will not wither and their fruit will not fail. They will bear every month because their water flows from the sanctuary, and their fruit will be for food and their leaves for healing.'" (Ezek 47:12, NASB)

This is directly referenced in Revelation in the vision of the future state after the beast is destroyed, and after Satan is defeated, in the New Heaven and the New Earth.

> "Then he showed me a river of the water of life, clear as crystal, coming from the throne of God and of the Lamb, 2 in the middle of its street. On either side of the river was the tree of life, bearing twelve kinds of fruit, yielding its fruit every month; and the leaves of the tree were for the healing of the nations." (Rev 22:1–2, NASB)

Since John's vision of the future has this very unique river of the water of life flowing from Jerusalem, with trees along the banks for food and healing of the nations, and since that only otherwise appears in Ezekiel's future vision, we cannot dismiss Ezekiel. Since John uses the unique language of Ezekiel's temple in Revelation we cannot dismiss Ezekiel as a failed prophecy, and we cannot dismiss it as the Second Temple. We also cannot say nine whole chapters of the book merely represent the Christian church and the details are irrelevant. No, we must see Ezekiel's temple as something yet unfulfilled, something in the future.

> Since John uses the unique language of Ezekiel's temple in Revelation we cannot dismiss Ezekiel as a failed prophecy, and we cannot dismiss it as the Second Temple. We also cannot say nine whole chapters of the book merely represent the Christian church and the details are irrelevant. No, we must see Ezekiel's temple as something yet unfulfilled, something in the future.

This is perhaps the only part of the Bible that is the most challenging to the literal view and is perhaps the best argument for an allegorical interpretation. Jesus said that he came to provide Living Water (John 4:11,14) and it would flow from within each of us out toward others (John 7:38). If we are the temple of God, then the water flowing out from us should be living water to those around us. Living out our lives as Christians in a broken world, drawing from God's Holy Spirit working in and among us, brings sustenance for others and healing across the nations of the world. However, this argument only goes so far since there are nine chapters of great detail that cannot be dismissed and cannot be explained by allegorical generalization. For example, the prince who rules the people and comes to the temple also performs animal sacrifices in the future.

> "17 It shall be the prince's part to provide the burnt offerings, the grain offerings and the drink offerings, at the feasts, on the new moons and on the sabbaths, at all the appointed feasts of the house of Israel; he shall provide the sin offering, the grain offering, the burnt offering and the peace offerings, to make atonement for the house of Israel.' 18 'Thus says the Lord God, 'In the first month, on the first of the month, you shall take a young bull without blemish and cleanse the sanctuary. 19 The priest shall take some of the blood from the sin offering and put it on the door posts of the house, on the four corners of the ledge of the altar and on the posts of the gate of the inner court. 20 Thus you shall do on the seventh day of the month for everyone who goes astray or is naive; so you shall make atonement for the house." (Ezek 45:17-20, NASB)

> An allegorical interpretation holds that the prince who rules is Jesus. Yet why does Ezekiel say the prince provides animals for sacrifices to make atonement? Why would Jesus provide animals to sacrifice? Wasn't the blood of Jesus enough for all sin? And who is the priest that takes the animals from the prince and sacrifices them? Isn't Jesus our High Priest (Heb 8:1)? We cannot dismiss nine chapters of detail because it doesn't fit our theology.

An allegorical interpretation holds that the prince who rules is Jesus. Yet why does Ezekiel say the prince provides animals for sacrifices to make atonement? Why would Jesus provide animals to sacrifice? Wasn't the blood of Jesus enough for all sin? And who is the priest that takes the animals from the prince and sacrifices them? Isn't Jesus our High Priest (Heb 8:1)? We cannot dismiss nine chapters of detail because it doesn't fit our theology.

> "8 After saying above, 'Sacrifices and offerings and whole burnt offerings and sacrifices for sin You have not desired, nor have You taken pleasure in them' (which are offered according to the Law), 9 then He said, 'Behold, I have come to do Your will.' He takes away the first in order to establish the second. 10 By this will we have been sanctified through the offering of the body of Jesus Christ once for all." (Heb 10:8–10, NASB)

So how do we explain this future temple of Ezekiel, one where there are sacrifices of bulls to make atonement? It would be most expedient to dismiss this vision somehow, but yet we see the direct reference in Revelation and so we must accept it. While the allegorical interpretation that it means something other than what it says is most convenient, it just does not line up with the nine chapters of detail that Ezekiel sees. God had already told the prophets about the Messiah who would die, offering his soul as a sacrifice for the sins of others, so God had already used the language of Christianity and didn't need to use the language of bulls for Ezekiel to understand through allegory.

Matthew Henry, one of the most famous commentaries widely used today, says this is the most difficult part of the whole Bible and we must wait for God to explain it.[4] John Wesley, co-founder of the Methodists, surprisingly says that the sacrifices allegorically represent the gifts and offices of the church.[5] Some academics shockingly say Ezekiel was using the ancient pagan myth of the "cosmic mountain" to encourage those held in the Babylonian Captivity to not lose hope, but it's basically a lie.

Theologians with a literal interpretation offer different possibilities as well. One explanation is that Ezekiel's temple refers to a future temple to be built during the one-thousand-year Millennial reign of Christ. This interpretation holds that the Jewish people will rebuild the temple and restart the sacrifices. Other literal interpretations say these sacrifices will be memorial sacrifices and only remind the Jewish people (who are by then already converted to Christianity) of the sacrifice of Jesus. Just like Christians celebrate Communion today, a reminder and memorial of Christ's sacrifice, so too will future Jewish believers in Christ offer animal sacrifices as a reminder and memorial of Christ's sacrifice. Some of these literal interpretations also say the Prince spoken of by Ezekiel is a future leader of Israel, a future David to come, who is under the direction of Jesus, but not Jesus himself. To complicate the situation even more we also must recognize that in the book of Revelation there is no temple in the New Jerusalem.

---

4. Henry, *Concise Commentary*, Ezek 40:1.
5. Wesley, *Explanatory Notes*, Ezek 40:19.

"I saw no temple in it, for the Lord God the Almighty and the Lamb are its temple." (Rev 21:22, NASB)

If there is no temple in the New Jerusalem, because God and the Lamb are its temple, then Ezekiel's vision of a future temple where God dwells forever adds to the confusion because the river of the water of life and the trees for food and for healing of the nations appear in both prophecies. It's no wonder Jerome called the book of Ezekiel a "labyrinth of the mysteries of God."

Do other prophets speak of a future temple in the End Times? Yes, they do. In one of the most famous passages of Isaiah where he predicts the nations will beat their swords into plowshares, we also see a future temple.

> "2 Now it will come about that in the last days the mountain of the house of the Lord will be established as the chief of the mountains, and will be raised above the hills; and all the nations will stream to it. 3 And many peoples will come and say, 'Come, let us go up to the mountain of the Lord, to the house of the God of Jacob; that He may teach us concerning His ways and that we may walk in His paths.' for the law will go forth from Zion and the word of the Lord from Jerusalem. 4 And He will judge between the nations, and will render decisions for many peoples; and they will hammer their swords into plowshares and their spears into pruning hooks. nation will not lift up sword against nation, and never again will they learn war." (Isa 2:2-4, NASB)

Isaiah says in the last days the nations will stream to the Lord's temple, which is established on the highest of the mountains. It will be a time of unending worldwide peace without war. Clearly that time has not yet come to pass. Isaiah also sees that the future temple will be rebuilt by foreigners and never again be closed.

> "10 'Foreigners will build up your walls, and their kings will minister to you; for in My wrath I struck you, and in My favor I have had compassion on you. 11 'Your gates will be open continually; they will not be closed day or night, so that men may bring to you the wealth of the nations, with their kings led in procession." (Isa 60:10-11, NASB)

And in this future temple there will be animal sacrifices.

> "All the flocks of Kedar will be gathered together to you, the rams of Nebaioth will minister to you; they will go up with acceptance on My altar, and I shall glorify My glorious house." (Isa 60:7, NASB)

The prophet Micah, a contemporary of Isaiah, also confirms the vision of a future temple in the last days.

> "And it will come about in the last days that the mountain of the house of the Lord will be established as the chief of the mountains. it will be raised above the hills, and the peoples will stream to it. 2 Many nations will come

and say, 'Come and let us go up to the mountain of the Lord and to the house of the God of Jacob, that He may teach us about His ways and that we may walk in His paths.' For from Zion will go forth the law, even the word of the Lord from Jerusalem. 3 And He will judge between many peoples and render decisions for mighty, distant nations. then they will hammer their swords into plowshares and their spears into pruning hooks; nation will not lift up sword against nation, and never again will they train for war." (Mic 4:1–3, NASB)

Jeremiah also says that the Branch who will sprout from David's line will come. In those days Jerusalem will be saved and given a new name. And there will be unending sacrifices in the temple.

"14 'Behold, days are coming,' declares the Lord, 'when I will fulfill the good word which I have spoken concerning the house of Israel and the house of Judah. 15 In those days and at that time I will cause a righteous Branch of David to spring forth; and He shall execute justice and righteousness on the earth. 16 In those days Judah will be saved and Jerusalem will dwell in safety; and this is the name by which she will be called: the Lord is our righteousness.' 17 For thus says the Lord, 'David shall never lack a man to sit on the throne of the house of Israel; 18 and the Levitical priests shall never lack a man before Me to offer burnt offerings, to burn grain offerings and to prepare sacrifices continually.'" (Jer 33:14–18, NASB)

The prophet Joel also speaks of a future temple where a fountain flows out of it to the surrounding region. This is in the future state when Jerusalem is never again invaded, an unending permanent condition. As an aside, this happens after the defeat of the nations that attack Jerusalem for a final time.

"17 Then you will know that I am the Lord your God, dwelling in Zion, My holy mountain. So Jerusalem will be holy, and strangers will pass through it no more. 18 And in that day the mountains will drip with sweet wine, and the hills will flow with milk, and all the brooks of Judah will flow with water; and a spring will go out from the house of the Lord to water the valley of Shittim." (Joel 3:17–18, NASB)

Last, but certainly not least, you may recall from our earlier section on Zechariah that the Messiah is prophesied to build the temple, and the nations that participate in the final attack on Jerusalem will go up to offer sacrifices (Zech 6:12).

There are many other references to a temple that hasn't existed on earth before as well. For example, we see that Moses made the Tabernacle to be a copy of what he saw in Heaven (Exod 25:40, Heb 8:5). Jesus entered the Heavenly Temple where he now intercedes for us (Heb 9:24). The Psalmist describes God in his heavenly temple (Ps 11:4). And last but not least, the temple of God in heaven appears in the book of Revelation (Rev 11:19, 14:16–21, 15:5–8, 16:1,17) at the time of judgment when the seventh trumpet is sounded.

We also see Jesus refer to his body which was to be crucified as the Temple that would be raised in three days (John 2:19–22). Paul says our own bodies are temples of the Holy Spirit (1 Cor 3:16, 6:19, 2 Cor 6:16). Paul elsewhere says all believers are the temple (Eph 2:21,22) and Revelation says believers will be pillars in the temple of God (Rev 3:12). Revelation also says there is no temple in the New Jerusalem because God is the temple (Rev 21:22). In the book of Revelation alone "temple" is used in three different ways: 1) the temple in Heaven where the Ark of the Covenant is, 2) believers who are pillars of the temple, and 3) God himself.

> Across the Bible we have many different symbolic uses of "temple": the temple in Heaven, the physical body of Christ, believers in Christ, our own physical body, and God himself. In the book of Revelation "temple" is used in three very different ways. We cannot choose one of these explanations which best matches our theology and say that is what Ezekiel saw.

Across the Bible we have many different symbolic uses of "temple": the temple in Heaven, the physical body of Christ, believers in Christ, our own physical body, and God himself. In the book of Revelation "temple" is used in three very different ways. We cannot choose one of these explanations which best matches our theology and say that is what Ezekiel saw. That would be taking verses from other books (or other parts of the same book) out of context.

To illustrate the problems you run into, consider if we say the temple seen by John is symbolic of believers, then when John says there isn't a temple in the New Jerusalem you would be saying there are no Christians in the New Jerusalem. If you replied that John said there was no temple because God was the temple, you would be saying that Christians (the temple) are God (the temple). Clearly Christians are not God. In the same way, we can't take the meaning of the temple in one vision of a different book and say that it is Ezekiel's temple. If we did, which use of temple would we pick and who is to say we picked the right one?

While it is difficult for Christians to understand a future temple where sacrifices are being made, since Christ is our sacrifice for sins, we do see this described by Ezekiel, Isaiah, Jeremiah, Joel, Micah, and Zechariah. The Sola Scriptura approach holds only to what the scriptures directly say. It is clear from numerous passages in six different prophets that in the last days there will be a temple in Jerusalem and sacrifices will be offered there. Even though it is unsatisfying to not explain how this works, doing so would be to step outside of what is directly and plainly said in the scriptures. Remember that all things have not been revealed through scripture yet, and not even John understood everything he saw in the book of Revelation. John was even told to not write certain things down (Rev 10:4). It is God's will that not all things are yet revealed. There is still much room for faith. Let us close this unsatisfying analysis looking once again at Paul's words to the Romans regarding the Jewish people who appear in the last days offering sacrifices in a future temple.

> "25 For I do not want you, brethren, to be uninformed of this mystery—so that you will not be wise in your own estimation—that a partial hardening has happened to Israel until the fullness of the Gentiles has come in; 26 and so all Israel will be saved; just as it is written, 'The Deliverer will come from Zion, he will remove ungodliness from Jacob.' 27 'This is My covenant with them, when I take away their sins.' 28 From the standpoint of the gospel they are enemies for your sake, but from the standpoint of God's choice they are beloved for the sake of the fathers; 29 for the gifts and the calling of God are irrevocable." (Rom 11:25–29, NASB)

God loves the Jewish people. God's call is irrevocable. When the Deliverer comes from Zion there will be a spiritual awakening. All Israel will be saved.

WHAT DID WE LEARN FROM EZEKIEL?

The book of Ezekiel provides important context for understanding the book of Revelation. Although Ezekiel is never quoted in Revelation or the entire New Testament, we see many allusions to his unique visions. One important allusion is to the throne of God. Ezekiel sees four living creatures unlike anywhere else in the Hebrew Bible. They looked like a lion, an ox, a human, and an eagle, and they moved on wheels with rims that were covered with eyes (Ezek 1:4–18). In Revelation John also sees these four living creatures at the throne of God, found nowhere else but in Ezekiel (Rev 4:1–8a). And mysteriously Ezekiel sees the figure of a man sitting on the throne of God (Ezek 1:25–28), just like Daniel saw (Dan 7:13–14). As Christians we know this one like the figure of a man, like a Son of Man, but not merely a man, is King Jesus, to whom all authority, glory, and sovereign power was given.

Another important allusion is the mention of Gog and Magog in Rev 20:7–10. A final attack on Jerusalem by the nations of the world appears in the writings of many prophets (Daniel, Zechariah, Joel, Zephaniah, Ezekiel), but nowhere is directly named Gog and Magog except in Revelation and Ezekiel. Other key allusions to Ezekiel are found in the Good Shepherd at the center of the throne of God, the restoration of Israel (the valley of dry bones, the two sticks joined together), the aftermath of the attack by Gog, and the river of the water of life flowing from under the temple whose leaves are for food and the healing of the nations.

We know that Ezekiel has not been completely fulfilled because the city of Jerusalem today is not known all over the world as the place where God dwells. Buddhists, Hindus, Muslims, and many others around the world would disagree that the God of Israel is the God of the whole world. Moreover, there has never been an actual river that flows out from the Temple Mount to the surrounding regions as described in Ezekiel (and in Revelation), and there have been no trees along its banks that provide for food and healing. Ezekiel also prophesied of a re-united people of Israel (all twelve tribes) living in the Promised Land under one king. Even though in modern times

Israel has been born again as a nation, not all of the tribes have returned and there is not a single king over them. Today they do not have a monarchy. Even in any allegorical sense the vision isn't fulfilled yet because only Christians are under the rule of King Jesus today, and not all Christians obey our Lord. Since the prophecies in Ezekiel have not been fulfilled yet and Revelation directly mentions a final attack on Jerusalem led by Gog, as also mentioned by several other prophets and declared by God as a literal event (Ezek 38:17–18), we still await this final event before the Great Day of the LORD.

The Sola Scriptura approach holds that Ezekiel has not been completely fulfilled, one day a powerful leader will bring many nations against a restored and reunited Israel, and God will defend Jerusalem. The Sola Scriptura approach holds that the one seated on the throne of God is King Jesus, just as seen in other prophets. He is the Good Shepherd who cares for the flock and searches for the lost. He is the one who will be King over the entire world after the final attack on Jerusalem, and every knee will bow, and every tongue will confess that Jesus is Lord. The Sola Scriptura approach holds that the river of the water of life will flow from under the throne of God, and trees will grow along its banks that will provide food and healing for the nations.

#	Truth Claim	Primary Support	Secondary Support
6.1	Ezekiel has not been fulfilled yet because he speaks of a river flowing out from the sanctuary which has never been the case.	Ezek 47:1–12	Joel 3:18, Zech 14:8, Rev 22:1–2, Ps 46:4, Isa 12:3, 35:6–7, 44:3, 55:1, Jer 2:13
6.2	Ezekiel has not been fulfilled yet because he speaks of a re-united Israel (the twelve tribes) living under the rule of a single king.	Ezek 37:20–28	Ezek 11:17–20, 20:40–44, 34:20–31, 36:23–38, 37:1–14,20–28, 38:8, 39:25–29, 40–48, Joel 2:27–29, Isa 11:1, 32:14–18, 55:3–4, Jer 24:7, 30:8–33:26, 50:4–5, Zeph 3:8–20, Hos 3:5, John 10:16, Luke 1:69, Matt 2:2, Acts 2:30, 13:23, Heb 13:20
6.3	Ezekiel has not been fulfilled yet because the New Jerusalem will be known all over the world as the place where God dwells, and this has not yet come to pass. This will be a permanent change.	Ezek 48:35	Ezek 37:27–28, 43:7,9, Isa 7:14, John 1:14, Rev 21:1–4,22, Col 1:19, 2:9, Luke 3:22
6.4	God declares that the attack on Jerusalem by Gog is a literal event to take place.	Ezek 38:17–18	Zech 12:3,9, 14:2,3,13, Dan 7:21–25, 8:21–25, 11:36–45, Joel 2:1–3, 3:2, Ezek 38:1–18, 39:1–11, Rev 16:14–16, 17:11–14, 19:19, 20:8–9, 1 Tim 4:1

#	Truth Claim	Primary Support	Secondary Support
6.5	God will defeat the nations that attack Israel and establish an everlasting kingdom of peace ruled by the Messiah.	Ezek 39:17–21	Ezek 38:16, 39:7–8,17–21, Zech 14:12–19, Dan 7:11–14,18–22,26–27, Isa 9:6–7, Joel 2:18–20, 3:1–2.14–16, Rev 19:11–21, 20:7–10, 2 Thess 2:8
6.6	A figure like that of a man sits on the throne of God.	Ezek 1:25–28	Dan 7:13–14, Rev 5:13–14, John 1:14, Isa 9:6–7, Rev 1:13, 4:2, Mark 2:10,28,14:21, Matt 11:19,16:27,24:30,26:2
6.7	God himself is the Good Shepherd.	Ezek 34:11–24	Isa 40:10–11, 53:6, 61:1–2, Jer 23:1–5, Ps 23:1–2, Luke 4:18–21, 19:9–10, John 10:11–13, Rev 7:17
6.8	God heals the brokenhearted and searches for the lost.	Ezek 34:16	Ps 147:2–3, Isa 61:1–3, Luke 4:18–21, Matt 18:12
6.9	The leaders at the time of the Messiah are like bad shepherds.	Ezek 34:1–10, 18–19	Jer 23:1–5, John 10:8, Matt 21:23,30–31,38–39,45
6.10	God will judge between the rams and the goats.	Ezek 34:17, 20	Mal 4:1, Zech 10:3, Matt 25:31–36, John 10:22–30

7

Joel
The Valley of Decision

"[The northern horde] can be interpreted as referring to the host of locusts, upon which the expression, 'and I will drive him to a land barren and desolate,' fits aptly. Another explanation: The people that come from the north, viz., the kings of Assyria. And our Sages (Talmud Sukkah 52a) state: This is the temptation, which is hidden in a person's heart."—Rashi

CONTEXT OF THE BOOK OF JOEL

THE PROPHET JOEL LIVED in the southern kingdom of Judah before the time of the Babylonian Captivity, while the First Temple was still standing.[1] His name is a declaration of who the True God is, as opposed to the false gods of the surrounding nations. "Joel" (*yowel*, יוֹאֵל) is a combination of words that mean "Yahweh" (*Yah*, יְהוָה) is "God" (*El*, אֵל).

Like many debates among the early Protestant Reformers, theologians debated if Joel had been fulfilled or not. Joel spoke of the nations of the world coming together against Israel in the Valley of Decision. There, God judges the nations and forever after dwells in his Eternal Kingdom of Zion. As a contemporary of Amos and Isaiah he warned the Judeans of the impending judgment of God (Joel 1:1–2:11). He tells them of the coming Day of the Lord and pleads with them to repent (Joel 2:12–17). Their reward for penance and turning back toward God will lead to both physical restoration

---

1. Easton, *Bible Dictionary*, Entry for Joel.

as well as an outpouring of the Spirit of God (Joel 2:18–32). This outpouring of the Holy Spirit predicted by Joel was referred to by Peter on the Day of Pentecost (Acts 2:14–21). Afterward the nations are gathered together in the Valley of Decision to be judged by God for what they did to his people Israel (Joel 3:1–16). Thereafter God dwells forever in Zion and never again will foreigners invade her (Joel 3:17–21). In the prophecies of Joel we have three major themes that form part of the background context for the book of Revelation: 1) the nations of the world gather together against Israel, 2) the repentance and restoration of Israel, and 3) God's eternal kingdom of Zion where his people receive an outpouring of his spirit and thereafter dwell in safety with God forever.

> Like many debates among the early Protestant Reformers, theologians debated if Joel had been fulfilled or not. Joel spoke of the nations of the world coming together against Israel in the Valley of Decision. There, God judges the nations and forever after dwells in his Eternal Kingdom of Zion.

John Calvin, in his preface to the book of Joel, says that this last part of Joel's prophecy refers to the Kingdom of Christ.[2] God had not forgotten the covenant he made with the fathers and so Christ would come to gather the scattered remnants and restore his people. Calvin saw the prophecies of the Hebrew Bible as already having been fulfilled up to the time of Christ. This Preterist view was different from that of the early church as well as other early Reformers, as shown in the first part of this book, but would have a lasting impact on the development of Christian theology down to modern times.

Opposed to Calvin was another theologian named Jacobus Hermanszoon (Arminius). Their disagreements over the scriptures evolved into the Calvinism and Arminianism movements within the Protestant Reformation. Presbyterian, Anglican, and Reformed churches generally hold to Calvinist interpretations of scripture. Early English Baptists as well as John Wesley and his Methodists held to Arminian views especially as it relates to predestination and salvation, but also in their arguments about eschatology and the meaning of the book of Revelation and Hebrew prophets like Joel. Below we will explore the prophecies of Joel in detail and consider if they have really been fulfilled or not. These prophecies have a huge bearing on our understanding of Revelation. If all things were already fulfilled, then what does that mean for the book of Revelation? Likewise, if there is yet a future fulfillment spoken of by Joel, then what does that mean for our understanding? And if Joel's prophecies are still in the future, then do they refer to the ethnic people of Israel (Jewish people) or an allegorical Israel which secretly means all Christians?

---

2. Calvin, *Preface to Joel*, 1.

HAS JOEL BEEN FULFILLED YET?

The first question we come to in our understanding of Joel is if his prophecies have been fulfilled or not. Like other prophets Joel uses language that unmistakably describes a permanent change, an everlasting and unending condition. This singularity only happens one time, and forever after things are different. If Joel has already been fulfilled, then we would see this permanent situation he describes existing today (and forever after). Or else what the prophet said did not come to pass and therefore he was not a real prophet of God, according to the Law of Moses (Deut 18:22). And if he was not a prophet then the Bible has scriptures which are not truly the Word of God. We should think carefully about what we say about Joel. We begin with his own words.

> "14 Multitudes, multitudes in the valley of decision! For the day of the Lord is near in the valley of decision. 15 The sun and moon grow dark and the stars lose their brightness. 16 The Lord roars from Zion and utters His voice from Jerusalem, and the heavens and the earth tremble. But the Lord is a refuge for His people and a stronghold to the sons of Israel. 17 Then you will know that I am the Lord your God, dwelling in Zion, My holy mountain. So Jerusalem will be holy, and strangers will pass through it no more. 18 And in that day the mountains will drip with sweet wine, and the hills will flow with milk, and all the brooks of Judah will flow with water; and a spring will go out from the house of the Lord to water the valley of Shittim. 19 Egypt will become a waste, and Edom will become a desolate wilderness, because of the violence done to the sons of Judah, in whose land they have shed innocent blood. 20 But Judah will be inhabited forever and Jerusalem for all generations. 21 And I will avenge their blood which I have not avenged, for the Lord dwells in Zion." (Joel 3:14–21, NASB)

Notice that God speaks of a day when the nations will be gathered together in the valley of decision, the Day of the Lord. God will defend his people and never again will foreigners invade Jerusalem. Never again, which is a permanent change of state for Jerusalem. Judah and Jerusalem will be inhabited forever, and God will dwell in Zion. Also notice the fountain flowing out from the sanctuary.

> These two permanent changes: Jerusalem never again being invaded, and a fountain of water flowing out from under the sanctuary, have not taken place. We cannot say Joel has been fulfilled.

These two permanent changes: Jerusalem never again being invaded, and a fountain of water flowing out from under the sanctuary, have not taken place. We cannot say Joel has been fulfilled. We have seen other prophets speak of these things as well (Zech 14:8, Rev 22:1–2, Ps 46:4, Isa 12:3, 35:6–7, 44:3, 55:1, Jer 2:13). After Jerusalem was destroyed by the Romans in 70 AD it was later inhabited and rebuilt, only to be invaded yet again later in history. And never in history has there been a fountain of water or a river flowing out from under the Temple Mount to the surrounding region. As we saw earlier in other prophets, these things have not yet come to pass.

A Preterist view that holds all these things happened in the past is easily shown to be false, because of the repeated invasion of Jerusalem by foreigners since the time of Christ, as well as no fountain of water flowing out to the surrounding regions (only a small underground spring that trickles through the nearby hills which you can visit today, known as Hezekiah's Tunnel). Seeing that these things have not been literally fulfilled, an allegorical view holds that the vision instead refers to the ultimate victory of Christianity over the world, and the Holy Spirit pouring out through the church throughout the ages like a fountain of water flowing from God himself.

The Sola Scriptura approach holds only to what the scriptures plainly say. One day the nations will be gathered together in the Valley of Decision to be judged. Afterward Jerusalem will live peacefully and never again be invaded by foreigners, and a fountain will flow out from underneath the sanctuary and water the surrounding region. This interpretation is in line with what other prophets have declared and also lines up with the book of Revelation, the coming Day of the Lord when the beast, his armies, Gog and Magog, and Satan are judged and defeated, and the river of the water of life will flow out from under the throne of God in the New Jerusalem. Along its banks will be trees that provide food and leaves for the healing of the nations. God will wipe away every tear and there will be no more death, mourning, crying, or pain. There is a beautiful day that awaits us upon the return of Christ.

JOEL IN THE NEW TESTAMENT

As mentioned above, Peter refers to the book of Joel (Joel 2:28–32) on the Day of Pentecost.

> "14 But Peter, taking his stand with the eleven, raised his voice and declared to them: 'Men of Judea and all you who live in Jerusalem, let this be known to you and give heed to my words. 15 For these men are not drunk, as you suppose, for it is only the third hour of the day; 16 but this is what was spoken of through the prophet Joel: 17 'And it shall be in the last days,' God says, 'That I will pour forth of My Spirit on all mankind; and your sons and your daughters shall prophesy, and your young men shall see visions, and your old men shall dream dreams; 18 Even on My bondslaves, both men and women, I will in those days pour forth of My Spirit and they shall prophesy. 19 'And I will grant wonders in the sky above and signs on the earth below, blood, and fire, and vapor of smoke. 20 'The sun will be turned into darkness and the moon into blood, before the great and glorious day of the Lord shall come. 21 'And it shall be that everyone who calls on the name of the Lord will be saved.'" (Acts 2:14–21, NASB)

As Christians we see the outpouring of the Holy Spirit on the Day of Pentecost as the miracle of the Gospel being preached in many tongues to the Gentiles. This outpouring has continued to spread the Gospel across most of the world, with only a few places still left today that have not yet heard the Gospel.

The context of the part of Joel that Peter quotes comes after God saves Israel from an invasion of a large army of locusts that brings great destruction. This northern horde is driven out by God and the land of Judah is saved. This is a final attack on Israel, according to Joel:

> "18 Then the Lord will be zealous for His land and will have pity on His people. 19 The Lord will answer and say to His people, 'Behold, I am going to send you grain, new wine and oil, and you will be satisfied in full with them; and I will never again make you a reproach among the nations. 20 'But I will remove the northern army far from you, and I will drive it into a parched and desolate land, and its vanguard into the eastern sea, and its rear guard into the western sea. And its stench will arise and its foul smell will come up, for it has done great things.'" (Joel 2:18–20, NASB)

Since God says the Promised Land, the land of Judah, will never again be an object of scorn to the nations we know that this has not yet been fulfilled. All the ongoing conflict in the Middle East over the land of Israel makes this evident. Even in an allegorical sense, referring to the progress of the Gospel across the world, we see continuing religious conflict around the world. We also see the language of an invading army of locusts in Revelation (Rev 9:1–11) as we will explore further below.

After God drives out the northern horde, Joel tells us that "afterward" God will pour out his Holy Spirit on all flesh. This is different from how the Holy Spirit worked in the past, when God sent his spirit on specific people only (like Moses and other leaders). Joel also tells us this happens after the restoration of Israel, when God repays what the locusts had destroyed. And never again will his People be shamed. All this is still before the dreadful Day of the Lord.

> "25 'Then I will make up to you for the years that the swarming locust has eaten, the creeping locust, the stripping locust and the gnawing locust, my great army which I sent among you. 26 'You will have plenty to eat and be satisfied and praise the name of the Lord your God, who has dealt wondrously with you; then My people will never be put to shame. 27 'Thus you will know that I am in the midst of Israel, and that I am the Lord your God, and there is no other; and My people will never be put to shame. 28 'It will come about after this that I will pour out My Spirit on all mankind; and your sons and daughters will prophesy, your old men will dream dreams, your young men will see visions. 29 'Even on the male and female servants I will pour out My Spirit in those days." (Joel 2:25–29, NASB)

The context of Joel shows that at the time of Peter the people were still expecting Joel to be fulfilled. They were still expecting this final attack on Jerusalem to be rebuffed and for Israel to be restored. And afterward for God to pour out his Spirit on all people. Never again would his people be shamed. A permanent change, another singularity which changes things forever.

Does this mean that Peter viewed the Romans as the locusts, and that God was just about to throw them out and set Israel free from their cruelty? From history we know that things did not happen that way. Israel was further oppressed by Rome, the Second Temple was destroyed, and the Judeans were scattered once again. That's certainly not an unending permanent change where God's people are no longer shamed, and the land is never again an object of scorn to the nations. The centuries of conquest of Israel that came afterward show that to be false. You can see why this causes theologians to debate the meaning of Joel, and Revelation.

> Since Joel has not been literally fulfilled, yet Peter quotes from Joel on the Day of Pentecost, theologians have wondered and argued about the meaning of the book. Allegorical explanations take the arguments away from the literal meaning which has obviously not been fulfilled.

Since Joel has not been literally fulfilled, yet Peter quotes from Joel on the Day of Pentecost, theologians have wondered and argued about the meaning of the book. Allegorical explanations take the arguments away from the literal meaning which has obviously not been fulfilled. One popular allegorical interpretation says instead of a literal attack on the nation of Israel, Joel refers to a future spiritual attack on Christians. Another popular allegorical interpretation says instead of a literal attack, Joel is referring to a spiritual attack on our souls, and especially those who devote themselves to studying scripture.

> One popular allegorical interpretation says instead of a literal attack on the nation of Israel, Joel refers to a future spiritual attack on Christians. Another popular allegorical interpretation says instead of a literal attack, Joel is referring to a spiritual attack on our souls, and especially those who devote themselves to studying scripture.

Some theologians with an allegorical view reinterpret this final attack on Israel as an ongoing attack on Christianity throughout history. The northern horde is seen to represent all governments and powers through history that oppose Christ, defeated again and again by God throughout history. Some reinterpret the restoration of Israel and outpouring of God's Spirit as the birth of the church and the advent of Christianity since the Day of Pentecost.

Jewish theologians that take an allegorical view reinterpret the northern horde as the "evil inclination" (*yetzer hara*, יֵצֶר הָרַע) within each of us that leads us into sin.[3]

---

3. Ashi and Ravina, *Babylonian Talmud*, Sukkah 52a:9.

Moreover it is this evil inclination within the enemies of the Jewish people which led to their oppression and the destruction of both their temples. This evil inclination which we all fight against works even stronger against Torah scholars to bring them down.

> And what damage does the evil inclination cause? 'With its face toward the eastern [hakadmoni] sea' (Joel 2:20), as it set its eyes on the First [mukdam] Temple and destroyed it, and killed the Torah scholars that were in it; 'and its end toward the western [ha'aḥaron] sea' (Joel 2:20), as it set its eyes on the Second [aḥaron] Temple and destroyed it, and killed the Torah scholars that were in it; 'its foulness may come up, and its ill odor may come up' (Joel 2:20), as it forsakes the nations of the world and incites the enemies of the Jewish people: In this context, the term the nations is a euphemism for the Jewish people. The evil inclination seeks to corrupt the Jews more than it does the members of any other nation. 'Because it has done greatly' (Joel 2:20): Abaye said: And it provokes Torah scholars more than it provokes everyone else."
> (Talmud Sukkah 52a:10)

Both allegorical interpretations are built on some underlying principles which are true. There are governments and powers throughout history that have opposed Christianity. Eventually God will defeat all evil. There is also an inclination within humanity to sin, and perhaps it is strongest in those who should know better, those who study the scriptures. But are either of these what Joel was really saying? Would Joel or his audience have understood the prophecy about an attack on Israel as a repeated future spiritual attack on Christianity, or an internal battle within your soul? Would Peter have thought either of those on the Day of Pentecost? From the context of Joel, the people at the time of Joel would not have come up with either of those explanations. They would look for an actual attack and for God to actually save his people. And afterward to pour out his spirit on everyone, not just the select few leaders. What about Peter? Would he have come up with either of these interpretations? When he saw the Holy Spirit descend and the speaking in tongues on that Day of Pentecost, did he interpret the book of Joel as speaking of events that repeat throughout history? Would he have thought of either the anti-Christian governments that rise and fall throughout history, or the evil inclination within the hearts of people throughout history?

> Would Joel or his audience have understood the prophecy about an attack on Israel as a repeated future spiritual attack on Christianity, or an internal battle within your soul? Would Peter have thought either of those on the Day of Pentecost?

The Sola Scriptura approach holds only to what the scriptures say. There will be an invasion of the land of Judah by a great army coming from the north that covers it like a swarm of locusts. God will save Israel and afterward pour out his Holy Spirit on all people (which would include all Jewish people, a spiritual restoration). Never again will his people be shamed, and never again will the land be an object of scorn to the nations.

THE LOCUST INVASION

As we looked above at the expectations about the outpouring of the Holy Spirit, we saw that it occurs after the invasion of the land of Judah. We need to look closer at this invasion seen like locusts coming up from the Abyss, because there is a very similar passage in Revelation.

As you saw above, the allegorical interpretations hold that the armies that come against Judah are either all anti-Christian governments and powers throughout history, or the evil inclination within your heart. Those theologians say it is not a specific army. But notice something interesting that God says to his people through Joel.

> "25 'Then I will make up to you for the years that the swarming locust has eaten, the creeping locust, the stripping locust and the gnawing locust, my great army which I sent among you." (Joel 2:25, NASB)

God says this locust invasion is a great army that he himself sent. The Bible directly says that the locusts in the vision are symbolic of an actual army, one sent by God. To say that the locusts represent all armies throughout history that are opposed to God is directly against what scripture says. Nowhere does the Bible ever say these locusts are multiple armies over multiple generations. Moreover, to say that the locusts represent an inner battle between doing good things or bad things is also directly against what scripture says. Nowhere in the Bible does it ever say these locusts are an inner experience. Let scripture interpret scripture, especially when it directly tells us what it means. God is leading this army and it comes on the great Day of the Lord.

> The Bible directly says that the locusts in the vision are symbolic of an actual army, one sent by God. To say that the locusts represent all armies throughout history that are opposed to God is directly against what scripture says. Nowhere does the Bible ever say these locusts are multiple armies over multiple generations. Moreover, to say that the locusts represent an inner battle between doing good things or bad things is also directly against what scripture says. Nowhere in the Bible does it ever say these locusts are an inner experience.
>
> "11 The Lord utters His voice before His army; surely His camp is very great, for strong is he who carries out His word. The day of the Lord is indeed great and very awesome, and who can endure it?" (Joel 2:11, NASB)

In the opening chapter of Joel, we are told that a great army will invade Israel, unlike anything that has ever happened before. They will be like locusts swarming over the land. They are a mighty army without number.

> "The word of the Lord that came to Joel, the son of Pethuel: 2 Hear this, O elders, and listen, all inhabitants of the land. Has anything like this happened in your days or in your fathers' days? 3 Tell your sons about it, and let your sons tell their sons, and their sons the next generation. 4 What the gnawing locust has left, the swarming locust has eaten; and what the swarming locust has left, the creeping locust has eaten; and what the creeping locust has left, the stripping locust has eaten. 5 Awake, drunkards, and weep; and wail, all you wine drinkers, on account of the sweet wine that is cut off from your mouth. 6 For a nation has invaded my land, mighty and without number; its teeth are the teeth of a lion, and it has the fangs of a lioness." (Joel 1:1–6, NASB)

> "4 Their appearance is like the appearance of horses; and like war horses, so they run. 5 With a noise as of chariots they leap on the tops of the mountains, like the crackling of a flame of fire consuming the stubble, like a mighty people arranged for battle." (Joel 2:4–5, NASB)

God tells Joel that the people should warn future generations about this. The imagery of swarming locusts pouring over land is well known to farmers, especially in the region of Israel where they cover the land, at times like rain pouring down. Notice that in verse 6 Joel says again they are a mighty army from an invading nation. This is a single event, not something repeated throughout every generation, not an allegory of all governments opposed to Christ throughout history, and not the evil inclination within your heart. Also notice the imagery of these locusts: a mighty army with teeth like a lion, the appearance of horses, and a great noise like chariots drawn up for battle. Compare this imagery to the locusts seen in Revelation. After the fifth trumpet is blown an army of locusts is sent by God to torture those who don't have the seal of God.

> "Then the fifth angel sounded, and I saw a star from heaven which had fallen to the earth; and the key of the bottomless pit was given to him. 2 He opened the bottomless pit, and smoke went up out of the pit, like the smoke of a great furnace; and the sun and the air were darkened by the smoke of the pit. 3 Then out of the smoke came locusts upon the earth, and power was given them, as the scorpions of the earth have power. 4 They were told not to hurt the grass of the earth, nor any green thing, nor any tree, but only the men who do not have the seal of God on their foreheads." (Rev 9:1–4, NASB)

> "7 The appearance of the locusts was like horses prepared for battle; and on their heads appeared to be crowns like gold, and their faces were like the faces of men. 8 They had hair like the hair of women, and their teeth were like the teeth of lions. 9 They had breastplates like breastplates of iron; and the sound of their wings was like the sound of chariots, of many horses rushing to battle." (Rev 9:7–9, NASB)

The Bible elsewhere uses the imagery of locusts as an invading army, such as in Amos 4:9, but in the case of Joel this is a final invasion as we have shown above. Because after this attack is defeated by God, the people of Judah will never again be shamed, and a foreigner will never again invade Jerusalem (Joel 3:17–20). The Sola Scriptura approach holds only to what the scriptures actually say. A great army will come against the land of Israel, unlike anything ever before. God will defeat this army and never again will Jerusalem be invaded by a foreigner.

> The Sola Scriptura approach holds only to what the scriptures actually say. A great army will come against the land of Israel, unlike anything ever before. God will defeat this army and never again will Jerusalem be invaded by a foreigner.

Do other prophets support the idea of a final invasion of Jerusalem? Of course, as we have already seen earlier in Daniel, Zechariah, and Ezekiel as well as in the New Testament (Dan 7:21–25, 8:21–25, 11:36–45, Zech 12:3,9, 14:2,3,13, Ezek 38:1–18, 39:1–11, Rev 16:14–16, 17:11–14, 19:19, 20:8–9, 1 Tim 4:1).

Do other prophets support the idea of God defeating this last invasion of Jerusalem and setting up his Eternal Messianic Kingdom? Yes, as we have also seen earlier (Dan 7:11–14,18–22,26–27, Zech 14:12–19, Ezek 38:16, 39:7–8,17–21, Isa 9:6–7, Rev 19:11–21, 20:7–10, 2 Thess 2:8).

WHY AN INVASION OF JERUSALEM?

As you have seen in several of the prophets including Joel, as well as in the New Testament, the idea of a final invasion of the land of Judah before the establishment of the eternal Messianic Kingdom is well attested to. But what is the reason for this invasion according to Joel?

The macro structure of Joel is that he first warns of the coming invasion of Israel (Joel 1:1–2:11). Next God pleads with his people to repent and turn back toward him (Joel 2:12–17). Then God takes pity on those living in Zion and turns back the invasion of the northern horde (Joel 2:18–20). The land is restored, the people of God are blessed with an outpouring of God's Spirit, and never again will foreigners invade her (Joel 2:21–3:21). This big picture overview shows that God sends the northern horde to invade Israel because of her sins. It is a punishment because they don't follow God. And they are encouraged to repent to turn away wrath.

> "12 'Yet even now,' declares the Lord, 'Return to Me with all your heart, and with fasting, weeping and mourning; 13 And rend your heart and not your garments.' now return to the Lord your God, for He is gracious and compassionate, slow to anger, abounding in lovingkindness and relenting of evil. 14 Who knows whether He will not turn and relent and leave a blessing behind Him, even a grain offering and a drink offering for the Lord your God? 15 Blow

> a trumpet in Zion, consecrate a fast, proclaim a solemn assembly, 16 Gather the people, sanctify the congregation, assemble the elders, gather the children and the nursing infants. Let the bridegroom come out of his room and the bride out of her bridal chamber. 17 Let the priests, the Lord's ministers, weep between the porch and the altar, and let them say, 'Spare Your people, O Lord, and do not make Your inheritance a reproach, a byword among the nations. Why should they among the peoples say, 'Where is their God?'"" (Joel 2:12–17, NASB)

This is not unlike so many other times that God calls his people to repent (Deut 4:29, 1 Sam 7:3, Jer 4:1, Ezek 33:11, Hos 12:6, Exod 34:6, Ps 34:18, 86:5, 103:8, Isa 57:15). However, after they repent and God turns back the northern horde, there is a permanent change of state. This permanent change indicates that this is a final act, so the invasion of the northern horde is a final invasion. In God's reply to their repentance, we see that never again will God make them an object of scorn to the nations.

> "18 Then the Lord will be zealous for His land and will have pity on His people. 19 The Lord will answer and say to His people, 'Behold, I am going to send you grain, new wine and oil, and you will be satisfied in full with them; and I will never again make you a reproach among the nations. 20 'But I will remove the northern army far from you, and I will drive it into a parched and desolate land, and its vanguard into the eastern sea, and its rear guard into the western sea. And its stench will arise and its foul smell will come up, for it has done great things.'" (Joel 2:18–20, NASB)

Israel's turning back toward God, rewarded by the northern horde being driven back, is accompanied by an outpouring of his Holy Spirit. Never again will God's people be shamed.

> "27 Thus you will know that I am in the midst of Israel, and that I am the Lord your God, and there is no other; and My people will never be put to shame. 28 It will come about after this that I will pour out My Spirit on all mankind; and your sons and daughters will prophesy, your old men will dream dreams, your young men will see visions. 29 Even on the male and female servants I will pour out My Spirit in those days." (Joel 2:27–29, NASB)

The scriptures plainly say that this final invasion of Israel is because of their sins. And like other times before, God calls them to repent. However, this is a final repentance which leads to both a physical and spiritual restoration of the people of Judah and Jerusalem. After the nation of Israel repents, God is jealous for his land and takes pity on his people. The land will be restored, and the invading army driven out. Never again will his people be an object of scorn to the nations. Never again will they be shamed. Is this true for either the Jewish people or Christians today? The Jewish people are still shamed today by the surrounding Anti-Semitic nations that hate them. Even allegorically speaking, Christians are shamed in the world today by antichristian governments, leaders, and unbelievers.

> After the nation of Israel repents God is jealous for his land and takes pity on his people. The land will be restored, and the invading army driven out. Never again will his people be an object of scorn to the nations. Never again will they be shamed. Is this true for either the Jewish people or Christians today?

If we compare this final invasion to that spoken of by Ezekiel and referenced in the last part of the book of Revelation, we can see that this northern horde led by Gog also had their own selfish interests in invading. They were not invading because they were righteous and carrying out God's commands to punish Israel for their sins. The northern horde invades because they think Israel is living in peace and prosperity, and they want to invade when they think they can easily plunder her wealth.

> "7 'Be prepared, and prepare yourself, you and all your companies that are assembled about you, and be a guard for them. 8 After many days you will be summoned; in the latter years you will come into the land that is restored from the sword, whose inhabitants have been gathered from many nations to the mountains of Israel which had been a continual waste; but its people were brought out from the nations, and they are living securely, all of them. 9 You will go up, you will come like a storm; you will be like a cloud covering the land, you and all your troops, and many peoples with you.' 10 'Thus says the Lord God, 'It will come about on that day, that thoughts will come into your mind and you will devise an evil plan, 11 and you will say, 'I will go up against the land of unwalled villages. I will go against those who are at rest, that live securely, all of them living without walls and having no bars or gates'" (Ezek 38:7–11, NASB)

Notice that the hordes invade thinking Israel lives in peace. A land without walls, gates, and bars. This is after Israel has been gathered back together from the many nations she was dispersed to. The hordes that come cover the land like a cloud, like a swarm of locusts.

> "14 'Therefore prophesy, son of man, and say to Gog, 'Thus says the Lord God, 'On that day when My people Israel are living securely, will you not know it? 15 You will come from your place out of the remote parts of the north, you and many peoples with you, all of them riding on horses, a great assembly and a mighty army; 16 and you will come up against My people Israel like a cloud to cover the land. It shall come about in the last days that I will bring you against My land, so that the nations may know Me when I am sanctified through you before their eyes, O Gog.' 17 'Thus says the Lord God, 'Are you the one of whom I spoke in former days through My servants the prophets of Israel, who prophesied in those days for many years that I would bring you against them?'" (Ezek 38:14–17, NASB)

We see in Joel that God has sent this final northern horde to invade because of Israel's sins. They are told to repent. And we see in Ezekiel that this final northern horde is self-motivated to plunder a land they see as prosperous and living in peace. They think it will be easy to plunder them. At the last, God turns back this northern horde and they are not successful. Afterward, never again will foreigners invade the land, and never again will his people be shamed. They will receive an outpouring of the Holy Spirit.

An allegorical interpretation holds that Joel is talking about every particular judgment in history. The Day of the Lord repeats again and again, any time there is judgment on the enemies of God. However, the plain sense of the text is that Joel speaks of a single final invasion. And he speaks of God turning back the northern horde and forever after living in Zion with his people. Never again will foreigners invade. Never again will his people be shamed. The words "never again" completely refute the idea of something that repeats. "Never again" is not the same thing as "again and again," it is the opposite.

A Preterist interpretation holds that Joel was speaking of a (now past) invasion by Assyria. There are important Jewish and Christian theologians such as Rashi and John Calvin who held to this Preterist view. John Wesley also held to this as an event in the past but identifies the Babylonians and not the Assyrians as the invading army Joel spoke of. If this was an event in the past, however, why did Peter quote Joel on the Day of Pentecost (Acts 2:16-21) as something that was happening right then? If the locusts represent the Assyrians, then the much later invasion of the land by Babylon would make Joel wrong about the northern horde being driven back and forever after the people living in peace with God dwelling among them in Zion. If the locusts were the Babylonians, then the much later Arabic invasions and Christian Crusades also would show Joel to have been wrong, not to mention the warfare and struggle that occurs in modern Israel today.

> If the locusts represent the Assyrians, then the much later invasion of the land by Babylon would make Joel wrong about the northern horde being driven back and forever after the people living in peace with God dwelling among them in Zion. If the locusts were the Babylonians, then the much later Arabic invasions and Christian Crusades also would show Joel to have been wrong, not to mention the warfare and struggle that occurs in modern Israel today.

The Sola Scriptura approach holds only to what the scriptures themselves say. Joel speaks of a single event, a final invasion by a northern horde. This invading army is like locusts swarming across the land, but Israel repents, and God turns the invading army back. Afterward God pours out his Holy Spirit and dwells forever in Zion. This is a singular event that has not happened yet because we haven't seen the permanent change take place. It was not the Assyrians, Babylonians, Greek Seleucids, Philistines, nor Phoenicians, as Peter and history bear witness to. It was not the Romans nor the

Arabs, as history bears witness to after the time of Peter. The struggle in the land of Israel continues to this day. The shaming of the Jewish people by Anti-Semitic nations continues to this day. The shaming of Christians by unbelievers also continues to this day. Joel has not been completely fulfilled yet, neither literally nor allegorically.

How then should we respond to this amazing prophecy? Perhaps we should just take Peter's advice after he quoted from the book of Joel and other Hebrew scriptures on the Day of Pentecost.

> "37 Now when they heard this, they were pierced to the heart, and said to Peter and the rest of the apostles, 'Brethren, what shall we do?' 38 Peter said to them, 'Repent, and each of you be baptized in the name of Jesus Christ for the forgiveness of your sins; and you will receive the gift of the Holy Spirit. 39 For the promise is for you and your children and for all who are far off, as many as the Lord our God will call to Himself.'" (Acts 2:37–39, NASB)

The promise of the outpouring of the Holy Spirit is for us, our children, and for all who are far off, for all whom the Lord our God will call.

THE VALLEY OF DECISION

We have seen above and in other prophets that there will be a literal final invasion of the land of Israel. This invasion will not be successful, and God will permanently change the course of history thereafter. Israel will never again be invaded by a foreigner, and God's people will receive an outpouring of the Holy Spirit and never again be shamed.

After the northern horde shows up to invade Israel, the people of Israel repent, and God then turns back the invaders. The invaders are brought together in a specific place.

> "'For behold, in those days and at that time, when I restore the fortunes of Judah and Jerusalem, 2 I will gather all the nations and bring them down to the valley of Jehoshaphat. Then I will enter into judgment with them there on behalf of My people and My inheritance, Israel, whom they have scattered among the nations; and they have divided up My land.'" (Joel 3:1–2, NASB)

This Valley of Jehoshaphat was already famous at the time of Joel for having been the place of God's deliverance. God delivered his people from the Moabites, Ammonites, and Edomites under King Jehoshaphat's reign (2 Chron 20:1–30). Interestingly, the name of King "Jehoshaphat" (*yehoshaphat*, יְהוֹשָׁפָט) in Hebrew literally means "God/Yahweh" (*Yah*, יְהוֹ) has "judged" (*shaphat*, שָׁפַט). This valley represents the judgment of God on the nations which attack his people. In the book of Joel this is the place where the nations which come against Israel in the final invasion are gathered together for judgment.

> "12 Let the nations be aroused and come up to the valley of Jehoshaphat, for there I will sit to judge all the surrounding nations. 13 Put in the sickle, for the harvest is ripe. Come, tread, for the wine press is full; the vats overflow, for their wickedness is great. 14 Multitudes, multitudes in the valley of decision! For the day of the Lord is near in the valley of decision. 15 The sun and moon grow dark and the stars lose their brightness. 16 The Lord roars from Zion and utters His voice from Jerusalem, and the heavens and the earth tremble. But the Lord is a refuge for His people and a stronghold to the sons of Israel. 17 Then you will know that I am the Lord your God, dwelling in Zion, My holy mountain. So Jerusalem will be holy, and strangers will pass through it no more. 18 And in that day the mountains will drip with sweet wine, and the hills will flow with milk, and all the brooks of Judah will flow with water; and a spring will go out from the house of the Lord to water the valley of Shittim." (Joel 3:12–18, NASB)
>
> Joel sees the nations of the world that come to attack Israel gathered together in the Valley of Jehoshaphat, the Valley of Decision. There God will defend the people of Israel and never again will foreigners invade Jerusalem. Never again. Never.

Joel sees the nations of the world that come to attack Israel gathered together in the Valley of Jehoshaphat, the Valley of Decision. There God will defend the people of Israel and never again will foreigners invade Jerusalem. Never again. Never. This is a permanent change that we have not seen yet in history. And a fountain will flow out from the Lord's house and water the surrounding region, also something that has never before happened. Compare this gathering of the nations opposed to Israel into a valley with what we see in the prophet Zephaniah.

> "8 'Therefore wait for Me,' declares the Lord, 'For the day when I rise up as a witness. Indeed, My decision is to gather nations, to assemble kingdoms, to pour out on them My indignation, all My burning anger; for all the earth will be devoured by the fire of My zeal. 9 'For then I will give to the peoples purified lips, that all of them may call on the name of the Lord, to serve Him shoulder to shoulder. 10 'From beyond the rivers of Ethiopia my worshipers, My dispersed ones, will bring My offerings. 11 'In that day you will feel no shame because of all your deeds by which you have rebelled against Me; for then I will remove from your midst your proud, exulting ones, and you will never again be haughty on My holy mountain." (Zeph 3:8–11, NASB)
>
> Zephaniah also saw that God would one day gather the nations, the whole world, to punish them in his righteous anger. On that day Jerusalem will be saved and never again will there be haughtiness. Never again.

Zephaniah also saw that God would one day gather the nations, the whole world, to punish them in his righteous anger. On that day Jerusalem will be saved and never again will there be haughtiness. Never again. Zephaniah, a contemporary of Jeremiah that served as a prophet in the southern kingdom of Judah during the reign of King Josiah and before the Babylonian Captivity, speaks at length in his writings about the coming Day of the Lord. It is a great day of terror (Zeph 1:15) that is a judgment on the whole world for sin (Zeph 1:17). It falls upon all creation (Zeph 1:2–3, 2:4–15, 3:8). As we can see above in verse 3:8, God decided to assemble the nations of the world together to pour out his wrath on them. On that day Jerusalem will not be put to shame for her sins because her arrogant people will be removed forever. Never again will there be haughtiness (גַּבְה, or prideful people who lift themselves up) on God's holy hill. Notice that it is these prideful, haughty people that are leading Israel to sin. They are removed along with the sinners of the world and then Israel is made holy again. Interestingly, the Hebrew word for haughtiness that Zephaniah uses can also be translated in other contexts as "locust." Zephaniah says that God will judge the whole world. They will be gathered together. You may recall from earlier that Zechariah also speaks about the Day of the Lord when the nations are gathered together against Jerusalem, but God steps in.

> "Behold, a day is coming for the Lord when the spoil taken from you will be divided among you. 2 For I will gather all the nations against Jerusalem to battle, and the city will be captured, the houses plundered, the women ravished and half of the city exiled, but the rest of the people will not be cut off from the city. 3 Then the Lord will go forth and fight against those nations, as when He fights on a day of battle. 4 In that day His feet will stand on the Mount of Olives, which is in front of Jerusalem on the east; and the Mount of Olives will be split in its middle from east to west by a very large valley, so that half of the mountain will move toward the north and the other half toward the south." (Zech 14:1–4, NASB)

Together we can see that part of the background context for the book of Revelation is that the nations are gathered together against Israel in the Valley of Jehoshaphat, the Valley of Decision. As this final invasion of Israel progresses God steps in and saves the remnant of Israel. Never again will she be invaded by a foreigner. Never again will she be shamed. Never again will arrogant people stand on the Holy Hill. Compare this background context in the minds of the seven churches to whom John sent the letter we know as the book of Revelation with what John tells us. Right before the sounding of the seventh and last trumpet of Revelation we see that the nations of the world are gathered together in the Valley of Armageddon.

> "12 The sixth angel poured out his bowl on the great river, the Euphrates; and its water was dried up, so that the way would be prepared for the kings from the east. 13 And I saw coming out of the mouth of the dragon and out of the mouth of the beast and out of the mouth of the false prophet, three unclean spirits like frogs; 14 for they are spirits of demons, performing signs, which go

out to the kings of the whole world, to gather them together for the war of the great day of God, the Almighty. 15 ('Behold, I am coming like a thief. Blessed is the one who stays awake and keeps his clothes, so that he will not walk about naked and men will not see his shame.') 16 And they gathered them together to the place which in Hebrew is called Har-Magedon. 17 Then the seventh angel poured out his bowl upon the air, and a loud voice came out of the temple from the throne, saying, 'It is done.'" (Rev 16:12–17, NASB)

Jesus will come again. But in the Second Coming he will come like a thief in the night. In other words, he will return when we least expect it. This final battle takes place where the nations of the world, driven by demonic forces that influence world leaders, gather together in the Valley of Armageddon. This is the valley where the nations will be judged. In Joel, Ezekiel, Zephaniah, and Zechariah we can see this gathering of the nations as God's impending judgment of Israel for their sins by bringing a northern horde to attack Israel. We also see that the nations are gathering together to invade because they see that Israel dwells in safety and they want to plunder her prosperity.

Clearly a world that gathers together to attack Jerusalem is not expecting God to defend her. Clearly a group of nations that attack Jerusalem do not fear the God of Israel. And clearly these people do not expect to see Jesus appearing on the clouds in glory. In Joel in particular we see that Israel repents and God steps in to turn back the invasion by the northern hordes. Thereafter, forever more, Israel will no longer be attacked nor shamed. It will never happen again.

> Clearly a world that gathers together to attack Jerusalem is not expecting God to defend her. Clearly a group of nations that attack Jerusalem do not fear the God of Israel. And clearly these people do not expect to see Jesus appearing on the clouds in glory!

Some theologians hold the book of Joel to refer to a future restoration of the Jewish people and the Day of Judgment where hardened sinners are cut off on the day of wrath. The nations which come together against Israel are an antichristian confederacy that respects neither Judaism nor Christianity. Those world powers only seek to take away the wealth of Israel. Driven by greed and presumed swift victory, they gather together in a valley thought to be just outside the Old City of Jerusalem (the Valley of Armageddon, the Valley of Decision, the Valley of Jehoshaphat). And there they will meet the God of Israel face to face and suffer utter defeat.

An allegorical interpretation views Joel as speaking of the deliverance of Christians throughout history and the destruction of all those opposed to Christianity. That view holds Joel as being symbolic of events that repeat again and again throughout history. However, the language of Joel, Ezekiel, Zephaniah, and Zechariah is very clear about a singular event. You would be hard pressed to read any of the above passages as different than a single occurrence. These passages provide many details of a final battle, such as the gathering of the nations in the Valley of Jehoshaphat where God judges the world. Numerous prophets describe it as a single end-time event. Nowhere does the Bible say it happens again and again throughout history.

> The language of Joel, Ezekiel, Zephaniah, and Zechariah is very clear about a singular event. You would be hard pressed to read any of the above passages as different than a single occurrence. These passages provide many details of a final battle, such as the gathering of the nations in the Valley of Jehoshaphat where God judges the world. Numerous prophets describe it as a single end-time event. Nowhere does the Bible say it happens again and again throughout history.

The allegorical interpretation also holds that the promises in the Hebrew Bible which are still unfulfilled now refer only to Christians, as they have replaced the Jewish people as the "people of God." As we look at Joel we see promises of the restoration of Judah and Jerusalem, numerous references directly to the land, and a distinction between Israel and the nations of the world that envy her. The language of Joel is unmistakably about the physical land of Israel and the people of Joel who dwell there. To say Joel has nothing to do with ethnic Israel and the physical land is to ignore most of Joel. Recall that the nations of the world gather together against Israel. If the nations of the world believed Israel was nothing and not supported by God as an allegorical view holds, then they would have no fear of invading her. To do away with the promises of God to the Jewish people is to ironically set the stage for the very end-time scenario the Hebrew prophets foretold. The only way nations would invade Israel is if they no longer believed God would protect her. The allegorical view sadly teaches this very thing. The nations will attack because they have no fear of reprisal. They see a prosperous people living in the land at ease and believe they can easily conquer them, just like the prophets said would happen.

> To do away with the promises of God to the Jewish people is to ironically set the stage for the very end-time scenario the Hebrew prophets foretold. The only way nations would invade Israel is if they no longer believed God would protect her. The allegorical view sadly teaches this very thing.

Some Christians hold to the Apostle's Creed, which is outside of scripture and therefore not considered with the Sola Scriptura approach. But in the Apostle's Creed it is stated that Christ "will come again to judge the living and the dead." In the Hebrew prophets like Joel, we see this language of the nations of the world coming against God and God judging them. This Day of Judgment is a judgment of the whole world. Either you take the non-literal approach that the judgment occurs again and again throughout history, repeated in the lives of all believers, or you take the literal approach that there will be a singular Day of Judgment where the whole world will be judged. Jesus is seated at the right hand of the Father and will come again to judge the living and the dead.

The Sola Scriptura approach holds only to what the scriptures plainly say, without regard to a particular religious tradition that developed later. The book of Joel tells us plainly that the nations of the world which are gathered together at the last to invade Israel, are gathered together in the Valley of Decision. Multitudes are gathered there together, and God will be a refuge for his people, a stronghold for the people of Israel. The nations will be driven back and defeated. Afterward Jerusalem will never again be invaded, and God's people will never again be shamed. This is important background context for understanding Revelation. The last thing Joel said was:

> "20 But Judah will be inhabited forever and Jerusalem for all generations. 21 And I will avenge their blood which I have not avenged, for the Lord dwells in Zion." (Joel 3:20–21, NASB)

WHAT DID WE LEARN FROM JOEL?

Joel is a fascinating book and one we cannot ignore. Peter quotes from Joel on the Day of Pentecost, so clearly we must understand it to better understand Revelation. Since Peter quotes from Joel (and other Hebrew Bible passages) to explain what is going on during Pentecost, interpretations which view Joel as having been fulfilled before the time of Christ are mistaken. Historical facts also demonstrate that Joel had not been fulfilled by the time Christ. History also shows that Joel has not yet been fulfilled to this day.

The narrative of Joel begins with an invasion of Jerusalem by a northern horde. This giant army is bigger than anything else that ever comes against Jerusalem. This invasion is sent by God as his punishment of the unfaithful in Israel. God calls the people to repent, and afterward we see him halting the invasion. God steps in and drives the northern horde back. Afterward God pours out his spirit on Israel and declares that never again will a foreigner invade Jerusalem, and never again would his people be shamed.

History since the time of Christ has shown that Jerusalem has been repeatedly invaded, and this vision Joel had of a never-ending time of peace for Israel has not yet happened. Within the book of Joel, we see there is a point in time where God gathers together all the nations that are opposed to Israel. Multitudes, multitudes are gathered together in the Valley of Decision where God will judge them and decide their fate. The enemies of God will lose and be driven back. And afterward God will pour out his Spirit on his people and a fountain will be opened up in Jerusalem that will water the surrounding region.

Compare the image of the invading northern hordes, like locusts spreading across the land, to that seen at the fifth trumpet in Revelation (Rev 9:1–9). Compare the gathering of the armies opposed to God in a valley where they are defeated with that gathering in the Valley of Armageddon (Rev 16:12–17). And compare the ultimate victory of God where his people live peacefully in a Jerusalem where water flows out to the surrounding regions with that found at the end of Revelation where the river of the water of life flows out from the New Jerusalem (Rev 22:1–2). Joel unmistakably describes a final attack on Jerusalem by the nations of the world, their defeat, and God's ultimate reward for his people. Together with the other Hebrew prophets, this is crucial background information to understand the book of Revelation.

#	Truth Claim	Primary Support	Secondary Support
7.1	Joel has not been fulfilled because he predicted a time when Jerusalem would never again be invaded by foreigners.	Joel 2:19, 3:17	Jer 31:12, Ezek 34:22–31, 36:12–15, 37, 38, Hos 2:16–20, Isa 2:3–4, 34:1–17, Amos 9, Hos 3
7.2	Joel has not been fulfilled because he predicted a time when a fountain would flow out of the Lord's house and water the surrounding region.	Joel 3:18	Ezek 47:1, Zech 14:8, Rev 22:1–2, Ps 46:4, Isa 12:3, 35:6–7, 44:3, 55:1, Jer 2:13
7.3	There will be an invasion of the land of Judah by a great army coming from the north. The attack of these northern hordes will be the last attack on Jerusalem.	Joel 1:1–2:11	Dan 7:21–25, 8:21–25, 11:36–45, Zech 12:3,9, 14:2,3,13, Ezek 38:1–18, 39:1–11, Rev 16:14–16, 17:11–14, 19:19, 20:8–9, 1 Tim 4:1
7.4	Before the Day of the Lord multitudes will be gathered together in the Valley of Jehoshaphat. The nations which are opposed to Israel will be judged by God.	Joel 3:1–2, 12–21	Dan 7:11–14,18–22,26–27, Zech 14:12–19, Ezek 38:16, 39:7–8,17–21, Isa 9:6–7, Rev 19:11–21, 20:7–10, 2 Thess 2:8
7.5	After God defeats the invasion of Jerusalem, his people will never again be shamed and he will pour out his Spirit on his servants.	Joel 2:21–29	Jer 16:15, 23:1–8, 30:3, 25:30–31, 31:12,40, Ezek 34:22–31, 36:12–15, 37, 38, Hos 2:16–20, Isa 2:3–4, 11, 34:1–17, 43:5–6, 52, 66:6, Amos 9, Hos 3, Zeph 1:14, 3:9–20, Zech 12,14, Mic 4, Acts 1:4–5, 2:16–18,33, John 7:39, 14:16–17,26, 16:7–8, Ps 68:18, Luke 24:49

8

The Background Context of Revelation

"The Scriptures of God are my only foundation and substance in all matters of weight and importance."—John Knox

AT THE TIME THE book of Revelation was written its audience did not yet have the New Testament. Their scriptures were the Hebrew Bible. They knew the writings of the prophets and were waiting for those promises to be fulfilled. The seven churches of Asia Minor, to whom Revelation is addressed, lived in persecution from both the Roman government outside the church, as well as splits within the church from unbelieving Jewish people in the synagogues where Christianity started. The seven churches also faced internal controversies from people who mixed pagan religions with Christianity or claimed to have secret knowledge and teachings. We see all of these struggles within the writings of the New Testament as the Apostles set out to correct and encourage the true faith. And in making these corrections the Apostles readily quoted from the scriptures, such as the prophets. This is all part of the background context for the book of Revelation. We need to clearly understand what the Hebrew prophets said in order to understand what the audience of the book of Revelation was expecting. Understanding who wrote a letter and to whom and how it would be understood, is key to keeping things in context. Otherwise you run the risk of taking things out of context.

NOT EVERYTHING HAS BEEN FULFILLED

One of the biggest things we learn from the prophets is that their prophecies have not been completely fulfilled yet. Although some Christian denominations hold to a Preterist view that teaches all prophecies have been fulfilled already, a study of the prophecies themselves shows this to be untrue. Here are some of the many reasons we explored above that show the prophecies have not all be fulfilled:

1. Daniel spoke of:
    - the resurrection of the dead (Dan 12:2-3)
    - the Kingdom of Messiah destroying all other kingdoms (Dan 2:44)

2. Zechariah spoke of:
    - Jerusalem never again being destroyed (Zech 14:11-12)
    - the splitting of the Mount of Olives (Zech 14:4-5)
    - Living Water flowing out from Jerusalem to the surrounding regions (Zech 14:8)
    - God is the only god worshiped in the whole earth (Zech 14:9)

3. Ezekiel spoke of:
    - a river flowing out from the sanctuary (Ezek 47:1-12)
    - a re-united Israel (the Twelve Tribes) living under the rule of a single king (Ezek 37:20-28)
    - the New Jerusalem known all over the world as the place God dwells (Ezek 48:35)

4. Joel spoke of:
    - a time when Jerusalem is never again invaded by foreigners (Joel 2:19, 3:17)
    - a fountain will flow out from the Lord's house and water the region (Joel 3:18)

Given that the dead are still buried, there are still numerous kingdoms which oppose Christianity today, God is not the only god worshiped across the world, Jerusalem does not live in peace, and no river has ever flowed out from Jerusalem or the Temple Mount, we cannot say the prophecies have been fulfilled. They await a future fulfillment, a future great Day of the Lord. We wait for these things to happen, just like those living at the time of the writing of Revelation. We wait for the Second Coming.

THE COMING JUDGMENT OF THE WORLD

Another huge learning from the prophecies in the Hebrew Bible is that there will be a final judgment of the whole world. This is seen as the destruction of the kingdoms opposed to God and the establishment of the Eternal Messianic Kingdom.

Daniel sees the Messiah reigning over an Eternal Kingdom which destroys all other kingdoms (Dan 2:44, 7:13-14,27). Zechariah sees that Jerusalem is never again destroyed (Zech 14:11-12) and the nations that attack her are defeated before God sets up his Everlasting Kingdom (Zech 9:8-10, 14:12-19). Ezekiel also sees this judgment and defeat of the nations of the world (Ezek 39:17-21). Ezekiel describes this judgment like God separating the rams and goats (Ezek 34:17, 20). Joel too describes this judgment of the multitudes from the nations gathered together in the Valley of Decision (Joel 3:1-2,12-21). Micah also describes this judgment of the nations (Mic 4:1-3) as does Zephaniah (Zeph 1:2-17, 2:4-15, 3:8-11). This coming judgment before the Eternal Messianic Kingdom is a key part of the background context of the book of Revelation.

EXPECTATIONS FOR THE MESSIAH

In the Hebrew Bible there are numerous prophecies of the Messiah. Expectations about what the Messiah will do and how he will appear show up repeatedly in the Hebrew Bible. These expectations form the background context for the entire New Testament. We see numerous references to them throughout the writing of the Apostles. And Christians generally take these prophecies literally. The Messiah would be born in Bethlehem. The Messiah would be a descendent of David. The Messiah would be rejected by his own people. The leaders of Israel at the time of the Messiah will not care about their flock, and the Messiah will be a Good Shepherd who does care for them. The Messiah would die for the sins of others. The Messiah would offer his own soul as a sacrifice. The Messiah would be resurrected and be glad for the souls he saves. The Messiah would come two times: riding on a donkey and also appearing on the clouds in Heaven. The teachings of the Messiah would spread across the entire world, and the Gentiles will look to him. The Messiah will come a second time to judge the living and the dead. The Messiah will reign from Zion in an Everlasting Messianic Kingdom. All nations will serve the Messiah. Every knee will bow, and every tongue will confess, that there is one True God over the whole world, and his name alone will be worshiped. All glory, power, dominion, and authority will be given to the Messiah and all peoples will worship him.

Amazingly, Christians do not have so many different ways of interpreting the expectations about the Messiah. There is not an allegorical interpretation that says the Messiah will not actually die, giving his soul as an offering for sacrifice. The Blood of Jesus poured out for the sins of others is fundamental to all mainstream beliefs in Christ. There is not a Preterist interpretation that says all things are fulfilled already and Jesus is not coming back. The Second Coming of Christ is fundamental to all mainstream Christian denominations. Yet mainstream theologians will argue about how to interpret the other verses in the very same passages. Yes, the verses about the Messiah are to be taken literally, but what about those other verses?

From our earlier look at the Hebrew prophecies here are ones about the Messiah for you to consider. Do you take these literally, allegorically, and possibly already fulfilled? Ask yourself if you are consistent with how you interpret passages of scripture, at least regarding the verses that speak about the Messiah.

1. The Messiah will remove sin (Zech 3:8–9).
   - Isa 4:2, 11:1, 53:2, Jer 23:5, 33:15, John 15:5, 1 John 1:9, 2:1–2, 3:5, 2 Cor 5:21, Rom 6:23

2. The Messiah will be both King and Priest (Zech 6:12–13)
   - Ps 110:4, Isa 9:6–7, 11:10, Jer 23:5, 33:15, Heb 5:6–10, 6:19–20, 7:1–17

3. The Messiah will arrive lowly riding on a donkey (Zech 9:9)
   - Matt 21:2–9, Mark 11:1–9, Luke 19:28–36

4. The Messiah will come on the clouds in glory (Dan 7:13)
   - Ezek 1:26, Matt 24:30, 26:64, Mark 13:26, 14:62, Luke 21:27

5. The Messiah will be a descendant of the tribe of Judah (Zech 10:4)
   - Isa 28:16, Ps 118:22, Matt 21:42, Acts 4:11, Eph 2:20, 2 Pet 2:4–7

6. The Messiah will be pierced and rejected (Zech 11:8–13, 12:10, 13:7)
   - Dan 9:24–26, Isa 53, Ps 2:2, 22, 110:1, Ps 118:22, Matt 10:4, 24:30, 26:31, 27:3–10, John 16:32, 19:31–37, Mark 14:27, Rev 1:7–8

7. The Messiah will be put to death (Dan 9:24–26)
   - Isa 53, Ps 2:2, 22, 110:1, Ps 118:22, Zech 11:8–13, 12:10, 13:7, Matt 10:4, 24:30, 26:31, 27:3–10, John 16:32, 19:31–37, Mark 14:27, Rev 1:7–8

8. God will establish an Everlasting Kingdom ruled by Messiah (Zech 9:8–10, 14:12–19, Ezek 39:17–21)
   - Ezek 37:25, 39:7–8, Dan 2:44, 7:11–14,18–22,26–27, Isa 2:4, 9:6–7, Joel 2:18–20, 3:1–2,14–16, Rev 11:15, 19:11–21, 20:7–10, 21:24,26, 22:2, Luke 1:33, 1 Cor 15:24, 2 Thess 2:8

9. The Kingdom of Messiah will destroy all other kingdoms (Dan 2:44, 7:13–14, 27)
   - Isa 2:4, 9:6, Ezek 37:25, Luke 1:33, 1 Cor 15:24, Rev 11:15

10. The Son of Man sits on the throne of God (Ezek 1:25–28, Dan 7:13–14)
    - Isa 9:6–7, Rev 5:13–14, John 1:14, Rev 1:13, 4:2, Mark 2:10,28,14:21, Matt 11:19,16:27,24:30,26:2

11. Israel will be reunited under a single king (Ezek 37:20–28)
    - Ezek 11:17–20, 20:40–44, 34:20–31, 36:23–38, 37:1–14,20–28, 38:8, 39:25–29, 40–48, Joel 2:27–29, Isa 11:1, 32:14–18, 55:3–4, Jer 24:7, 30:8–33:26, 50:4–5,

Zeph 3:8-20, Hos 3:5, John 10:16, Luke 1:69, Matt 2:2, Acts 2:30, 13:23, Heb 13:20

12. God himself is the Good Shepherd (Ezek 34:11-24)

    - Isa 40:10-11, 53:6, 61:1-2, Jer 23:1-5, Ps 23:1-2, Luke 4:18-21, 19:9-10, John 10:11-13, Rev 7:17

13. God heals the brokenhearted and searches for the lost (Ezek 34:16)

    - Ps 147:2-3, Isa 61:1-3, Luke 4:18-21, Matt 18:12

14. The leaders of Israel at the time of the Messiah are like bad shepherds (Ezek 34:1-10, 18-19)

    - Jer 23:1-5, John 10:8, Matt 21:23,30-31,38-39,45

The Sola Scriptura approach takes these verses literally, as do most denominations of Christianity and their theologians. Consider in your heart if you are confused about the above literal assertions for the Messiah. And if you hold a non-literal view of the other verses in these same passages ask yourself why, or more importantly: on whose authority do you interpret some sentences differently in the same paragraphs? Does the Bible itself tell you to do that? Did Jesus ever do that? Even if you still cling to a non-literal interpretation of select passages, you should at least be able to understand what a literal Sola Scriptura approach concludes. And though you may not hold it, you should understand why others do and not be quick to dismiss their views. For literalists take the Bible for what it plainly says, if there are no accompanying commands or explanations from the same passage to do otherwise.

AN ATTACK ON JERUSALEM

We see in the Hebrew prophets a time when the nations of the world will gather together against Jerusalem to attack her. In Daniel we see that a boastful leader arises who is opposed to Israel and to God himself. Through many visions and dreams we see that this final boastful leader is defeated by God and then the Messiah will reign over an Eternal Kingdom that destroys all other kingdoms. This boastful leader is seen in Daniel, Joel, Zechariah, 2 Thessalonians, and Revelation (Rev 13:5-8, 16:14, 17:12-14, Joel 3:2, 2 Thess 2:1-12, Zech 12:3,9, 14:2,3,13, Dan 7:20-25, 9:26-27). Though there are many antichrists, this final one that Paul calls the "man of lawlessness," that Ezekiel and the book of Revelation call "Gog," is the one that God literally spoke of through the prophets. This final antichrist will attack Israel.

> "17 'Thus says the Lord God, 'Are you the one of whom I spoke in former days through My servants the prophets of Israel, who prophesied in those days for many years that I would bring you against them? 18 It will come about on that

day, when Gog comes against the land of Israel,' declares the Lord God, 'that My fury will mount up in My anger." (Ezek 38:17–18, NASB)

"7 When the thousand years are completed, Satan will be released from his prison, 8 and will come out to deceive the nations which are in the four corners of the earth, Gog and Magog, to gather them together for the war; the number of them is like the sand of the seashore. 9 And they came up on the broad plain of the earth and surrounded the camp of the saints and the beloved city, and fire came down from heaven and devoured them." (Rev 20:7–9, NASB)

THE INGATHERING OF ISRAEL

Having established that the Hebrew prophets speak of a final attack on Jerusalem, we can see the necessity for Israel to be a restored land that would be attacked. In other words, before the nations of the world attack Israel, Israel will be a restored land where the tribes are regathered. It is this regathered and restored people that live in prosperity that the nations of the world see as living in ease and easy prey to be plundered. We learn from the prophets that this is actually the case. God does promise a restoration of Israel before the events of the final attack which leads to the decisive battle in the Valley of Decision and the establishment of the Eternal Messianic Kingdom.

"2 'Son of man, set your face toward Gog of the land of Magog, the chief prince of Meshech and Tubal, and prophesy against him 3 and say, 'Thus says the Lord God, 'Behold, I am against you, O Gog, chief prince of Meshech and Tubal.'" (Ezek 38:2–3, NASB)

"7 'Be prepared, and prepare yourself, you and all your companies that are assembled about you, and be a guard for them. 8 After many days you will be summoned; in the latter years you will come into the land that is restored from the sword, whose inhabitants have been gathered from many nations to the mountains of Israel which had been a continual waste; but its people were brought out from the nations, and they are living securely, all of them. 9 You will go up, you will come like a storm; you will be like a cloud covering the land, you and all your troops, and many peoples with you.'" (Ezek 38:7–9, NASB)

"27 When I bring them back from the peoples and gather them from the lands of their enemies, then I shall be sanctified through them in the sight of the many nations. 28 Then they will know that I am the Lord their God because I made them go into exile among the nations, and then gathered them again to their own land; and I will leave none of them there any longer. 29 I will not hide My face from them any longer, for I will have poured out My Spirit on the house of Israel,' declares the Lord God." (Ezek 39:27–29, NASB)

This ingathering is something that is promised throughout the Hebrew prophets, it is not a single verse from one book being taken out of context. We see this ingathering of Israel in Ezekiel, Zechariah, Amos, Hosea, Isaiah, and Jeremiah (Ezek 36:24-28, 37:24-28, 38:8,12, 39:7,25-29, Amos 9:13-15, Hos 3:5, Isa 11:10-12, 43:5-6, 54:7-8, 60:4-9, Jer 30:3-9, 31:8-10). Among the many references one sees that this is a final ingathering, after which Jerusalem will never again be uprooted.

> "13 'Behold, days are coming,' declares the Lord, 'When the plowman will overtake the reaper and the treader of grapes him who sows seed; when the mountains will drip sweet wine and all the hills will be dissolved. 14 'Also I will restore the captivity of My people Israel, and they will rebuild the ruined cities and live in them; they will also plant vineyards and drink their wine, and make gardens and eat their fruit. 15 'I will also plant them on their land, and they will not again be rooted out from their land which I have given them,' says the Lord your God." (Amos 9:13-15, NASB)

The most famous prophecy of this is probably found in Isaiah.

> "1 The word which Isaiah the son of Amoz saw concerning Judah and Jerusalem. 2 Now it will come about that in the last days the mountain of the house of the Lord will be established as the chief of the mountains, and will be raised above the hills; and all the nations will stream to it. 3 And many peoples will come and say, 'Come, let us go up to the mountain of the Lord, to the house of the God of Jacob; that He may teach us concerning His ways and that we may walk in His paths.' for the law will go forth from Zion and the word of the Lord from Jerusalem. 4 And He will judge between the nations, and will render decisions for many peoples; and they will hammer their swords into plowshares and their spears into pruning hooks. Nation will not lift up sword against nation, and never again will they learn war." (Isa 2:1-4, NASB)

THE COMING OF THE KINGDOM OF ZION

Daniel sees the Messiah reigning over an Eternal Kingdom which destroys all other kingdoms (Dan 2:44, 7:13-14,27). Zechariah also sees God establishing an everlasting kingdom of peace ruled by the Messiah (Zech 9:8-10, 14:12-19). Ezekiel sees the Twelve Tribes of Israel living together in peace under the rule of a single king (Ezek 37:20-28).

> "13 'I kept looking in the night visions, and behold, with the clouds of heaven one like a Son of Man was coming, and He came up to the Ancient of Days and was presented before Him. 14 'And to Him was given dominion, glory and a kingdom, that all the peoples, nations and men of every language might serve Him. His dominion is an everlasting dominion which will not pass away; and His kingdom is one which will not be destroyed." (Dan 7:13-14, NASB)

> "8 But I will camp around My house because of an army, because of him who passes by and returns; and no oppressor will pass over them anymore, for now I have seen with My eyes. 9 Rejoice greatly, O daughter of Zion! shout in triumph, O daughter of Jerusalem! behold, your king is coming to you; he is just and endowed with salvation, humble, and mounted on a donkey, even on a colt, the foal of a donkey. 10 I will cut off the chariot from Ephraim and the horse from Jerusalem; and the bow of war will be cut off. and He will speak peace to the nations; and His dominion will be from sea to sea, and from the River to the ends of the earth." (Zech 9:8–10, NASB)

> "16 Then it will come about that any who are left of all the nations that went against Jerusalem will go up from year to year to worship the King, the Lord of hosts, and to celebrate the Feast of Booths." (Zech 14:16, NASB)

> "20 The sticks on which you write will be in your hand before their eyes. 21 Say to them, 'Thus says the Lord God, 'Behold, I will take the sons of Israel from among the nations where they have gone, and I will gather them from every side and bring them into their own land; 22 and I will make them one nation in the land, on the mountains of Israel; and one king will be king for all of them; and they will no longer be two nations and no longer be divided into two kingdoms. 23 They will no longer defile themselves with their idols, or with their detestable things, or with any of their transgressions; but I will deliver them from all their dwelling places in which they have sinned, and will cleanse them. And they will be My people, and I will be their God. 24 'My servant David will be king over them, and they will all have one shepherd; and they will walk in My ordinances and keep My statutes and observe them. 25 They will live on the land that I gave to Jacob My servant, in which your fathers lived; and they will live on it, they, and their sons and their sons' sons, forever; and David My servant will be their prince forever. 26 I will make a covenant of peace with them; it will be an everlasting covenant with them. And I will place them and multiply them, and will set My sanctuary in their midst forever." (Ezek 37:20–26, NASB)

The children of Israel will live forever in the Promised Land. They will live under one king forever. God will make an everlasting (lasts forever) covenant of peace with them. The survivors from the nations that attacked Jerusalem will go up year after year to worship the King, the Lord Almighty. Never again will an oppressor overrun God's people. The rule of the Messiah will extend to the ends of the Earth. All nations and peoples of every language will worship him, and his kingdom is one that will never be destroyed. This vision of the eternal kingdom of Messiah is what the Disciples of Jesus were expecting to happen, as we can clearly see in the New Testament. But when is the coming of the Kingdom of Zion?

> "6 So when they had come together, they were asking Him, saying, 'Lord, is it at this time You are restoring the kingdom to Israel?' 7 He said to them, 'It is

not for you to know times or epochs which the Father has fixed by His own authority; 8 but you will receive power when the Holy Spirit has come upon you; and you shall be My witnesses both in Jerusalem, and in all Judea and Samaria, and even to the remotest part of the earth.' 9 And after He had said these things, He was lifted up while they were looking on, and a cloud received Him out of their sight. 10 And as they were gazing intently into the sky while He was going, behold, two men in white clothing stood beside them. 11 They also said, 'Men of Galilee, why do you stand looking into the sky? This Jesus, who has been taken up from you into heaven, will come in just the same way as you have watched Him go into heaven.'" (Acts 1:6–11, NASB)

It is worth pausing and reflecting deeply on what happened here. When the disciples asked Jesus if the time was right for God to restore the kingdom to Israel, how did Jesus respond? The Disciples asked directly about the fulfillment of the prophecies to restore the kingdom to Israel. Preterists hold those prophecies to have been fulfilled in the past. Allegorical views hold them to mean a spiritual and not a physical kingdom, where Christians replace Jewish people as recipients of the promises of God. When the disciples asked Jesus about the restoration of Israel, did Jesus respond as a Preterist, Allegorist, or Literalist?

> When the disciples asked Jesus about the restoration of Israel, did Jesus respond as a Preterist, Allegorist, or Literalist?

Did Jesus reply that Christians will replace Jewish people, and the Hebrew prophets spoke in allegory? Did Jesus say the restoration was actually the rejection of Israel and the establishment of the church? Did Jesus say the restoration was not a literal event? Did Jesus say their idea about a restoration already happened in the past when the Maccabees took control of Jerusalem? No, none of those things.

Jesus said it was not for them to know the time when it would happen. He spoke of it as a literal future event, not a past event, and not an allegory. And then the angels told the disciples that Jesus would return on the clouds in the same way he left. He will literally return, and it will be on the clouds appearing in glory. Everyone will know when it happens, just like when you see lightning flashing across the sky. The Second Coming will be obvious. It won't be a self-declared Messiah that has a big church somewhere. It won't be a Rabbi that performs miracles and has a large following. It won't be a child born with special signs in the heavens or that selects the "right" item among many choices to "indicate" his divinity. And it won't be a charismatic world leader that appears to have brought peace to the Middle East. No, it will be obvious to everyone (even Atheists). Every eye shall see him, everyone will know that he is Lord, and we will mourn because of our sins. Every knee will bow, and every tongue will confess that Jesus is Lord. The Parousia (παρουσία, a Greek word for the Second Coming) will be obvious to everyone and the world will be taken by surprise. People expected it at the time of Christ, but people at the time of the Second Coming will not be expecting it, just like a thief in the night comes when he is least expected.

> "9 And Jesus said to him, 'Today salvation has come to this house, because he, too, is a son of Abraham. 10 For the Son of Man has come to seek and to save that which was lost.' 11 While they were listening to these things, Jesus went on to tell a parable, because He was near Jerusalem, and they supposed that the kingdom of God was going to appear immediately." (Luke 19:9–11, NASB)

> "17 As Jesus was about to go up to Jerusalem, He took the twelve disciples aside by themselves, and on the way He said to them, 18 'Behold, we are going up to Jerusalem; and the Son of Man will be delivered to the chief priests and scribes, and they will condemn Him to death, 19 and will hand Him over to the Gentiles to mock and scourge and crucify Him, and on the third day He will be raised up.' 20 Then the mother of the sons of Zebedee came to Jesus with her sons, bowing down and making a request of Him. 21 And He said to her, 'What do you wish?' She said to Him, 'Command that in Your kingdom these two sons of mine may sit one on Your right and one on Your left.'" (Matt 20:17–21, NASB)

> "20 Now having been questioned by the Pharisees as to when the kingdom of God was coming, He answered them and said, 'The kingdom of God is not coming with signs to be observed; 21 nor will they say, 'Look, here it is!' or, 'There it is!' For behold, the kingdom of God is in your midst.' 22 And He said to the disciples, 'The days will come when you will long to see one of the days of the Son of Man, and you will not see it. 23 They will say to you, 'Look there! Look here!' Do not go away, and do not run after them. 24 For just like the lightning, when it flashes out of one part of the sky, shines to the other part of the sky, so will the Son of Man be in His day. 25 But first He must suffer many things and be rejected by this generation. 26 And just as it happened in the days of Noah, so it will be also in the days of the Son of Man: 27 they were eating, they were drinking, they were marrying, they were being given in marriage, until the day that Noah entered the ark, and the flood came and destroyed them all. 28 It was the same as happened in the days of Lot: they were eating, they were drinking, they were buying, they were selling, they were planting, they were building; 29 but on the day that Lot went out from Sodom it rained fire and brimstone from heaven and destroyed them all. 30 It will be just the same on the day that the Son of Man is revealed. 31 On that day, the one who is on the housetop and whose goods are in the house must not go down to take them out; and likewise the one who is in the field must not turn back. 32 Remember Lot's wife. 33 Whoever seeks to keep his life will lose it, and whoever loses his life will preserve it. 34 I tell you, on that night there will be two in one bed; one will be taken and the other will be left. 35 There will be two women grinding at the same place; one will be taken and the other will be left." (Luke 17:20–35, NASB)

Clearly the Disciples, the Pharisees, and the people at the time of Jesus expected the Kingdom of God spoken of by the prophets to be established right then. However we can see in Jesus' own words that the Kingdom will come when people least expect it. The world will be caught up in its own daily madness and people will be surprised. When it comes, some will be taken immediately and others will be left. It is a literal event coming in the future when Jesus returns on the clouds in glory. And again, the world will not be expecting or looking for Christ.

OVERALL

There is a lot to remember from the Hebrew prophets. As the background context for the book of Revelation it is important to know these scriptures, for they were the set of scriptures the people at the time of Jesus had and form the context for the entire New Testament.

Not everything has been fulfilled in what the prophets spoke of. The Messiah will appear on the clouds in glory and establish his Everlasting Kingdom and all nations of the world will worship the only True God. There will be a resurrection of the dead and a final judgment of all people. The enemies of the people of God will be punished and the followers of God will be rewarded and dwell with God forever in safety. God will wipe away every tear and there will be no more mourning, death, or pain.

The Messiah will be both a King and Priest. He will arrive lowly riding on a donkey, and he will also arrive on the clouds in glory. He will be pierced and rejected, and he will be put to death. He will remove the sins of others. His Kingdom will destroy all other kingdoms and he will sit on the throne of God. He will be the Good Shepherd who cares for his flock, unlike the religious leaders of the time who only care about themselves. He heals the brokenhearted and searches for the lost.

Before the final judgment there will be an attack on Israel. God will defeat the nations of the world that attack Jerusalem and never again will a foreigner oppress her. The people of God will live in the land and never again be uprooted. The nations that attack Israel will be punished. Afterward nations will beat their swords into plowshares and their spears into pruning hooks. They will no longer fight each other, nor will they train for war anymore. A river will flow out from under the sanctuary in Jerusalem and water the surrounding region. Trees will grow along the banks of the river which provide both fruit for food and leaves for the healing of the nations.

Before the final attack on Israel the Twelve Tribes will be gathered together into the land. They will be prosperous and appear to live in peace. This prosperity and appearance of an easy plunder is what leads the nations of the world to attack. They are led by a charismatic leader that the world follows. This beast, a man who boasts against God himself, actually sets himself up to be worshiped in the Temple of Israel, but he is brought down along with the nations that follow him.

Remember to consider all these things in your heart. If you take the prophecies about the Messiah literally, then you should carefully consider the other verses in those very same passages that refer to a final attack on Jerusalem by the nations of the world. If you believe Jesus will return on the clouds in glory and God will wipe away every tear, then consider if the prophets also spoke of the time of the end and the signs of the time. Yet also remember that no one knows the day or hour of Jesus' return and many theologians and cults have incorrectly set dates for his appearance. The coming of the Lord will be when people least expect it. It will be at a time when the world is carrying on in its worldly ways. People will be taken by surprise. The world will not be ready. The nations of the world will even be supportive of, and directly involved in, attacking Jerusalem. Clearly there is no respect of the God of Israel for those circumstances to come about. As those days approach, we should keep the faith, we should never lose hope, and we should boldly proclaim that Jesus is that Messiah who died for the sins of the world. He will come again to judge the living and the dead. Some will rise to everlasting life, and others to everlasting contempt. Until that day, we should be about the business of our father who art in Heaven, hallowed be his name.

9

The Structure of Revelation

"All the Fathers with one heart execrated, and with one mouth protested against, contaminating the word of God with the subtleties of sophists, and involving it in the brawls of dialecticians. Do they keep within these limits when the sole occupation of their lives is to entwine and entangle the simplicity of Scripture with endless disputes, and worse than sophistical jargon? So much so, that were the Fathers to rise from their graves, and listen to the brawling art which bears the name of speculative theology, there is nothing they would suppose it less to be than a discussion of a religious nature."—John Calvin

NOW THAT WE HAVE covered the context of the book of Revelation, both the book itself as well as the secondary sources of the Hebrew prophets, we are ready to move into the book itself. Since you now know the background context of the book as the original audience would have understood it, set in the context of the Hebrew prophets that were the scriptures at the time of the writing of Revelation, you can better understand the messages in the book. Below is an outline of the plain sense of the text. The Sola Scriptura approach does not seek to redefine nor re-explain anything the book says. What follows is a straight-forward reading from the text. You are welcomed and encouraged to make your own outline and compare your results. Be careful not to bring any outside interpretation of the symbols into your work.

The Sola Scriptura Challenge

OUTLINE

Brief Overview

Chapters 1-3: Messages to the Seven Churches

The opening of the book of Revelation contains an amazing vision of Jesus with direct references to the writings of the Hebrew Prophets. In this vision John is given messages addressed to the seven churches in Asia Minor.

Chapters 4-7: The Seven Seals

John sees an amazing vision of God's throne in Heaven. In this vision he sees a scroll which only the Lamb of God is able to open. The scroll has seven seals, and as each seal is opened, we see a sequence of events represented by symbols such as the Four Horsemen, signs in Heaven, signs on Earth, and the sealing on the foreheads of the servants of God.

Chapters 8-11: The Seven Trumpets

As the seventh seal of the scroll is opened John sees and hears seven trumpets. With the first four trumpets comes destruction of a third of the earth, sea and waters, and the heavens. The fifth and sixth trumpets bring a plague of locusts up from an Abyss who target those without the seal of God on their foreheads. A third of mankind is killed by plagues, yet the rest of mankind is still unrepentant. Two Witnesses are sent by God, and they prophesy against mankind for one thousand two hundred and sixty days until a beast from the Abyss kills them. The Two Witnesses are resurrected from the dead and taken up into Heaven, and the seventh trumpet is blown. At the blowing of this trumpet Heaven is opened and the temple in Heaven is seen.

Chapters 12-14: The Woman and Her Son vs. the Dragon and the Beasts

John sees signs in Heaven: a pregnant woman giving birth to the Messiah while Satan stands waiting to destroy the child. The child is caught into Heaven and the woman flees. War breaks out in Heaven and Satan is thrown out with his angels. Satan tries to persecute the woman but she flees so he persecutes her children who follow Jesus.

A beast rises out of the sea, empowered by Satan, and people worship them both. The beast slanders God and attacks his people. A second beast rises out of the earth and forces people to worship the first beast. People are forced to receive the mark of the first beast if they want to buy or sell anything. People are warned by angels not to worship the beast but instead to follow God. The earth is harvested.

Chapters 15-16: The Seven Bowls

Seven angels pour out the seven final plagues, bowls full of the wrath of God. Complete destruction comes to living creatures in the sea and people are punished with malignant sores and scorching heat. The throne of the beast is plunged into darkness while preparations are made for the kings of the East. Evil spirits go out from Satan, the beast, and a false prophet which spur people to battle. Great earthquakes destroy cities, islands, and mountains while a plague of large hailstones rains down.

Chapters 17-19: The Fall of the Prostitute and the Beasts

The mystery of the great prostitute and the beast she sits on is discussed. Her punishment is announced. The powerful people and leaders of the world lament her fall. The beast, false prophet, and kings of the earth wage war against the Messiah and are defeated. The beast and the false prophet are thrown into the fiery lake of burning sulfur.

Chapters 20-22: Judgment of the Dragon, the New Heaven and the New Earth

Satan is thrown into the Abyss for one thousand years while Christ reigns with his followers. After the one thousand years are over Satan is released. Satan builds an army to fight the saints but is defeated and thrown into the lake of fire and sulfur, where the beast and false prophet had been thrown, to be tormented forever and ever.

All people alive and dead are judged, resulting in either eternal life or a second death. God makes all things new, a new Heaven and a new Earth, and a new Jerusalem comes down out of Heaven. Inside the city the river of life flows and God and the Lamb provide its light to all who are given the right to enter in. Revelation closes with a testimony to the authority of the prophecy and a warning not to change it.

Detailed Outline

Chapters 1-3: Messages to the Seven Churches

CHAPTER 1

1-8	Introduction and Greetings to the Seven Churches
9-20	Vision of the Son of Man

CHAPTER 2

1-7	To Ephesus

The Sola Scriptura Challenge

8–11	To Smyrna
12–17	To Pergamum
18–29	To Thyatira

Chapter 3

1–6	To Sardis
7–13	To Philadelphia
14–22	To Laodicea

Chapters 4–7: The Seven Seals

Chapter 4

1–11	Vision of God's Throne in Heaven

Chapter 5

1–4	Challenge to Open the Scroll with Seven Seals
5–14	Only the Lamb is Worthy to Open the Scroll

Chapter 6

1–2	The First Seal: The White Horse – To Overcome and Conquer
3–4	The Second Seal: The Bright Red Horse – War on Earth
5–6	The Third Seal: The Black Horse – Famine
7–8	The Fourth Seal: The Pale Horse – Death
9–11	The Fifth Seal: Voice of the Martyrs
12–17	The Sixth Seal: A Great Earthquake and Signs in the Heavens

Chapter 7

1–8	Interruption of Destruction for Sealing the Servants of God
9–17	Praise of the Followers of the Lamb Who Came out of the Tribulation

Chapters 8–11: The Seven Trumpets

CHAPTER 8

1–6	The Seventh Seal: Seven Trumpets and Casting Down of Fire
7	The First Trumpet: Hail and Fire (Third of Earth Burned Up)
8–9	The Second Trumpet: Great Mountain Thrown Into the Sea
10–11	The Third Trumpet: Star Fell into Waters
12	The Fourth Trumpet: Third of Heavens Struck
13	Warning of the Eagle Flying Overhead

CHAPTER 9

1–2	The Fifth Trumpet: Opening of the Abyss (The First Woe)
3–12	The Plague of The Locusts for Those Without the Seal of God
13–19	The Sixth Trumpet: Third of Mankind Killed by Plagues
20–21	The Rest of Mankind Still Unrepentant

CHAPTER 10

1–7	The Mystery of The Angel with the Small Scroll
8–11	Prophecies of the Small Scroll

CHAPTER 11

1–2	Measurement of the Temple
3–6	Two Witnesses to Prophecy
7–10	The Beast from the Abyss to Kill the Two Witnesses
11–12	The Two Witnesses Are Resurrected
13–14	A Great Earthquake Kills Thousands
15–19	The Seventh Trumpet: The Day of Judgment Has Come

Chapters 12–14: The Woman and Her Son vs. the Dragon and the Beasts

Chapter 12

1–2	A Sign in Heaven: A Pregnant Woman Is Giving Birth
3–4	A Sign in Heaven: A Great Red Dragon Waits to Destroy the Child
5–6	The Child is Born and Caught into Heaven, and the Woman Flees
7–12	War Breaks Out in Heaven and The Satan Is Thrown Out with His Angels
13–16	Satan Tries to Persecute the Woman but She Flees
17	Satan Persecutes the Children of the Woman, Who Follow Jesus

Chapter 13

1–2	A Beast Rose Out of the Sea, Empowered by The Dragon
3–4	People Worshiped the Beast and the Dragon
5–7	The Beast Slanders God and Attacks His People
8–10	Those Destined for Captivity or Destruction
11–15	A Second Beat Rises Out of the Earth
16–18	People Forced to Receive the Mark of the First Beast

Chapter 14

1–5	Singing to the Lamb on Mount Zion
6–11	Three Angels Warn Mankind, Babylon Is Fallen
12–13	Those Who Die in Christ Will Find Rest
14–20	The Earth Is Harvested

Chapters 15–16: The Seven Bowls

Chapter 15

1	Seven Angels with Seven Final Plagues
2–4	Singing of Those Triumphant Over the Beast
5–8	The Temple of Heaven Opened, Seven Angels Given Seven Bowls of Wrath

Chapter 16

1–2	The First Bowl – Poured on the Earth: Loathsome, Malignant Sores
3	The Second Bowl – Poured on the Sea: Every Living Thing in the Sea Died
4–7	The Third Bowl – Poured into Rivers and Springs: They Turned to Blood
8–9	The Fourth Bowl – Poured on the Sun: Scorched People with Intense Heat
10–11	The Fifth Bowl – Poured on the Throne of the Beast
12	The Sixth Bowl – Poured on Euphrates
13–16	Three Unclean Spirits
17	The Seventh Bowl – Poured into the Air: Announcing "It is Done!"
18–19	A Great Earthquake Splits the City into Three Parts
20–21	Islands and Mountains Flee and a Plague of Huge Hailstones Rains Down

Chapters 17–19: The Fall of the Prostitute and the Beasts

Chapter 17

1–13	Mystery of the Great Prostitute and the Beast She Sits On
14	War of the Lamb and His Chosen Against the Beast and His Kings
15–19	Punishment of the Great Prostitute, The Great City That Rules

Chapter 18

1–8	Announcements from Heaven Declare Babylon is Fallen
9–19	Kings, Merchants, Shipmasters, and Others Mourn the Falling of Babylon
20–24	Pronouncement of Judgment Against Babylon

Chapter 19

1–5	Praise in Heaven over Judgment of Babylon
6–10	Marriage of the Lamb to His Bride
11–16	The White Horse with the Rider
17–19	The Beast, False Prophet, and Kings of the Earth Wage War
20–21	The Beast, False Prophet, and the Rest Are Defeated

The Sola Scriptura Challenge

Chapters 20-22: Judgment of the Dragon, the New Heaven and the New Earth

CHAPTER 20

1–3	Satan Is Thrown into The Abyss
4–6	Christ Reigns with His Followers
7–8	Satan Is Released and Builds an Army to Fight the Saints
9–10	The Devil is Thrown into the Lake of Fire and Sulfur
11–15	People Are Judged Resulting in Either Eternal Life or the Second Death

CHAPTER 21

1–4	A New Heaven and a New Earth, with a New Jerusalem
6–8	God Makes All Things New, Eternal Judgment Is Done
9–27	Vision of the New Jerusalem

CHAPTER 22

1–5	Inside the City: The River of Life, God, and the Lamb
6–21	Testimony to The Authority of This Prophecy

A CHIASM OF SINGULARITIES

As you can see above there are a lot of symbols and events described in the book of Revelation. Some of these events seem like a related set of things, like the seven seals, seven trumpets, and seven bowls. When a similar idea is repeated later in a book it is known as a parallelism. Two parallel lines are lines that run next to each other lengthwise and never cross (like two lowercase l's or ll). As similar ideas run through a set of things, like seals, trumpets, or bowls, theologians have seen parallel patterns that lead them to varying conclusions.

For example, some see the events described by the seals, trumpets, and bowls as successive events where each seal, trumpet, and bowl describe a chronological next step in God's plan. Some see them as parallel events, where Revelation is describing the same set of events in three different ways. Others see them as telescoping, where the last in each sequence is subdivided into seven further things (e.g., the seventh seal includes everything in the seven trumpets, and the trumpets provide more detail of the seventh seal). Yet the book of Revelation does not actually tell us. We will explore this in further detail in an upcoming section below. These theological positions are traditions thought up by theologians but not directly stated in the scriptures. Yet the study of parallelisms gives more depth and understanding to the scriptures. One of the best examples of the use of parallelisms is the book of Psalms. Recognizing the parallel structures of Hebrew poetry used in the Psalms helps us to better understand their meaning. When the same idea is repeated a different way, in other words when you use other words to communicate the same idea, it can help us better convey meaning.

A chiasm is a unique parallel arrangement of ideas. It usually has two parts. A forward part where ideas are developed, followed by a second part that reverses that order of ideas. The idea is like the letter X, which in Greek gives us our word chiasm (*chiasma*, χίασμα) which means "crossing" and starts with χ (*chi*, pronounced like "eye" starting with a hard k sound: k–eye). Chiastic structures are found throughout the Bible, and like the use of other parallelisms, help us to better understand the scriptures. However, we should note that chiasms and other parallelisms are something you notice but are not directly stated in the scriptures themselves.

The Bible nowhere says, "here is a parallelism," nor does it say "here is a chiasm." And the identification of chiasms within the Bible is highly subjective and varies by theologian. Many arguments have arisen over identification of these arrangements. Seeing patterns where none may exist, called pareidolia, is common. It is like looking at the clouds and seeing objects that really aren't there. The famous Rorschach Inkblot Test goes further to suggest that what we see are actually projections of our own inner thoughts and not what is really there.

Within the book of Revelation there are significant things we must understand, even if we don't understand all the details. We must understand what Satan is doing in the world. We must understand the warnings about the beast, Babylon, and the judgments of God. Interestingly, we could see these things spoken of in Revelation in a chiastic arrangement across chapters 12–20.

    12 – Satan
        13 – the beast
            14 – Babylon
                15/16 – the 7 bowls of judgment
            17/18 – Babylon defeated
        19 – the beast defeated
    20 – Satan defeated

Typically, a chiasm centers around a single theme on which the whole arrangement turns. In the suggested chiasm above, the turn (χ) occurs on God's judgment. The forward motion of the structure is Satan, the power behind all evil, leading to the rise of the beast and Babylon which lead people away from God. The turn is God's judgment on all these things opposed to God. And then the reverse structure is the defeat of Babylon, the beast, and ultimately Satan. Each of these defeats happens only one time. They are each a single event, a singularity, which helps us connect Revelation with the singularities we saw back in our study of the Hebrew prophets.

For example, when the beast and the false prophet are defeated and thrown into the lake of fire, yet later Satan leads an army to attack Jerusalem and is defeated, we see that he is thrown into the lake of fire where the beast and false prophet had already been thrown. This shows us the attack on Jerusalem led by Satan happens after the beast's attacks. It is not a parallel event or an allegory representing all attacks on Christianity throughout history by evil leaders in every generation. One event follows another, according to the Bible.

Chiasms and other parallelisms have led some theologians to set doctrine about the interpretation of Revelation. But note that Revelation nowhere says certain events are parallel, and instead uses the language of successive events. Given that these theological constructs are outside the Bible itself, vary greatly depending on the interpreter, and may even be a projection of their own inner desires, we need to watch out for those who set doctrine based on perceived, yet unprovable, parallelisms. Although they may give fancy and complicated explanations, one can readily find another theologian who opposes them through other fancy and complicated explanations. Reader beware. It's useful for you to know how some theologians arrive at their conclusions, and what the underpinnings of their work really are based on. You should know if someone is teaching you something the Bible directly says, or instead something a theologian came up with outside the Bible itself. You should also know that different theologians come up with different explanations using different outside constructs.

Our only purpose in using the suggested chiasm of singularities above is to set the organization for the rest of this book. We will discuss the important themes, each in turn, beginning with the ultimate revelation of God around which all things turn: the Messiah, the Christ (*Christos*, Χρίστος). However, the Sola Scriptura approach does not assert any chiasm or parallelism as truth, no matter how useful, as they are theological constructs outside of scripture. It is a useful way to organize our thoughts below, but only that. We will not use any perceived parallelisms within Revelation to form our understanding. We will make no truth claims based on a perceived parallelism. However, we will explain the claims others have come up with using different perceptions. We will examine these important themes: revelations about Jesus, Satan, the beast, Babylon, and eternal judgment.

10

Revelations About Jesus

"In essentials, unity; in differences, liberty; in all things, charity." —Philipp Melanchthon

WHILE MANY INTERPRETATIONS OF Revelation substitute the plain sense of the text with other symbolic possibilities, all Christian traditions clearly agree that the symbols of the Messiah are of Jesus as the conquering warrior who defeats evil. All worldly kingdoms are destroyed and Jesus reigns over them from Zion in his Eternal Messianic Kingdom. This is true for an allegorical view where Jesus reigns today over the hearts of Christians all over the world, a historical view where Jesus defeated the Roman powers by his resurrection, and a futuristic view where Jesus will reign over all souls after the final judgment and/or during a Millennial Period. In all these views of how the Hebrew Bible prophecies work themselves out (allegorically or literally; past, present, and/or future) they all hold that Jesus is literally returning and will literally rule over all. The Second Coming is a literal event. A literal interpretation of Jesus as the returning and victorious Messiah is held by all major denominations. In fact, in most mainstream churches you are very likely to find a picture of Jesus returning on the clouds in glory somewhere in the building. Surely you have seen this picture somewhere in your life experience.

You'll recall the following prophecies (all taken literally) from the Hebrew Bible: the Messiah will be both a king and priest, he will arrive lowly riding on a donkey and also arrive on the clouds in glory, he will be pierced and rejected, he will be put to death, he will remove the sins of others, his kingdom will destroy all other kingdoms, he will sit on the throne of God, and he will be the Good Shepherd who cares for his flock, heals the brokenhearted, and searches for the lost. None of these prophecies are given an alternative allegorical explanation that they mean something other than what the scriptures plainly say.

What does the book of Revelation add to our knowledge of the Messiah? What revelations does it show us? As you will see below, the Revelation to John shows us that Jesus is the Son of Man in fulfillment of the Hebrew prophecies, Jesus will finally defeat Satan and the beast, and there will be a period of trouble leading up to the Eternal Messianic Kingdom.

THE SON OF MAN

The opening of the book of Revelation makes direct references to Hebrew Bible prophecies. Understanding the context of these prophecies and how they were understood at the time of Jesus is key to understanding the book of Revelation. Taking things out of context can lead to many wrong conclusions. If you have not yet read the earlier part of this book regarding the Hebrew prophets like Daniel, Zechariah, Ezekiel, or Joel then I encourage you to read them before continuing here. This is because the first thing we see in the book of Revelation is that John directly quotes from Daniel and Zechariah.

> "Behold, He is coming with the clouds, and every eye will see Him, even those who pierced Him; and all the tribes of the earth will mourn over Him. So it is to be. Amen." (Rev 1:7, NASB)

John opens his letter to the seven churches in verse 4 and says grace and peace to them from God. He then speaks of Jesus and quotes from the Hebrew Bible prophecies about the return of the Messiah. The first quote, from Dan 7:13, is from a vision Daniel has about the Day of Judgment. You'll recall from the earlier part of this book that in this vision Daniel sees the throne of God, and one like a Son of Man comes on the clouds and approaches the Ancient of Days. He is given authority, glory, and sovereign power. All nations and peoples of every language will worship him and his dominion, his kingdom, will never be destroyed.

These promises had been unfulfilled at the time John wrote the letter we know as the book of Revelation. The Messiah had not yet appeared on the clouds at the Day of Judgment. The Day of Judgment had not yet occurred. And all nations and people of every language around the world had not yet worshiped him. As Christians we look for this event to occur in the future. We believe that Jesus will return a Second time, and at his coming he will appear on the clouds in glory. He will return the same way he left on Ascension Sunday. And every knee will bow, and every tongue will confess that Jesus Christ is Lord.

This is a generally accepted literal interpretation of the vision in Daniel. Jesus is the one, the Messiah, that Daniel saw. Jesus will literally return on the clouds as he literally left while the disciples stood and looked up at his ascension into Heaven.

> "9 And after He had said these things, He was lifted up while they were looking on, and a cloud received Him out of their sight. 10 And as they were gazing

intently into the sky while He was going, behold, two men in white clothing stood beside them. 11 They also said, 'Men of Galilee, why do you stand looking into the sky? This Jesus, who has been taken up from you into heaven, will come in just the same way as you have watched Him go into heaven.'" (Acts 1:9-11, NASB)

What else happens in that same vision of Daniel we just took literally? You'll recall from our earlier look that the vision had four great beasts that came up out of the sea. Each beast comes in succession, and Daniel gets more detail about the fourth one, specifically its horns. Daniel is then given the interpretation, so we don't have to decide if it's allegorical, literal, or otherwise. Daniel is told directly what the vision means. The beasts represent kings and their kingdoms which will rise up over time. And Daniel sees a final worldwide kingdom that wages war against the Holy people of God until God pronounces judgment. And it is at this judgment that the Son of Man appears on the clouds in glory and all nations and peoples then will worship him.

> "21 I kept looking, and that horn was waging war with the saints and overpowering them 22 until the Ancient of Days came and judgment was passed in favor of the saints of the Highest One, and the time arrived when the saints took possession of the kingdom. 23 'Thus he said: 'The fourth beast will be a fourth kingdom on the earth, which will be different from all the other kingdoms and will devour the whole earth and tread it down and crush it. 24 As for the ten horns, out of this kingdom ten kings will arise; and another will arise after them, and he will be different from the previous ones and will subdue three kings. 25 He will speak out against the Most High and wear down the saints of the Highest One, and he will intend to make alterations in times and in law; and they will be given into his hand for a time, times, and half a time. 26 But the court will sit for judgment, and his dominion will be taken away, annihilated and destroyed forever. 27 Then the sovereignty, the dominion and the greatness of all the kingdoms under the whole heaven will be given to the people of the saints of the Highest One; His kingdom will be an everlasting kingdom, and all the dominions will serve and obey Him.'" (Dan 7:21-27, NASB)

What we learn from Daniel is that there is a progression of kingdoms up until a final worldwide kingdom. This final worldwide kingdom will set itself against the people of God and oppress them until God steps in and pronounces judgment. And then the Messiah will appear on the clouds in glory and his everlasting kingdom will be established. This is what John wants us to remember. This is what John is pointing at when he quotes Dan 7:13 in the opening of the book of Revelation. For those who know the Hebrew Bible well, John is setting the context for the book of Revelation based on the as-yet unfulfilled prophecies in Daniel. These are prophecies of a progression of powerful kingdoms leading up to a final battle, in which God will defeat all evil and establish his Everlasting Messianic Kingdom.

> For those who know the Hebrew Bible well, John is setting the context for the book of Revelation based on the as–yet unfulfilled prophecies in Daniel. These are prophecies of a progression of powerful kingdoms leading up to a final battle, in which God will defeat all evil and establish his Everlasting Messianic Kingdom.

We cannot say Jesus will literally return on the clouds in glory, but there are no literal kingdoms leading up to a final worldwide kingdom that wages war against the people of God. To do so would be to interpret some verses literally and others allegorically in the very same passage. The passage of Daniel is a narrative of events and Daniel is even given the interpretation. Daniel is not told that the beasts represent all kingdoms opposed to Christ throughout history, one of the Christian allegorical views. Daniel is not told that the beasts represent an internal struggle in your heart between choosing good or evil, one of the Jewish allegorical views. No, Daniel is told the beasts represent specific kingdoms. And Daniel is told of the final battle where God decisively wins, and the Messiah appears on the clouds in glory. This Son of Man is the Son of Promise. He is the one who is promised to come, the one who will be the Eternal King and Priest reigning from Zion.

To hold that Christ reigns now and his Eternal Kingdom is already fully established is to both ignore what Daniel tells us the vision means (as told to him when he received the vision), as well as to ignore reality. One need look no further than the headlines of today's newspaper to see that Jesus is not worshiped by every nation and people. We are not living in the Eternal Messianic Kingdom which destroys all other kingdoms. Other kingdoms rule for now, and you are currently living in one of them. Christ sits at the right hand of the Father while his enemies are being made a footstool. He will come again on the clouds in glory to judge the living and the dead. Of the greatness of his government and peace there will be no end. He will reign on David's throne upholding it with justice and righteousness forever and ever. But we are clearly not there yet.

THE ONE WHO WAS PIERCED

We also see a quote from Zechariah in the opening of Revelation.

> "Behold, He is coming with the clouds, and every eye will see Him, even those who pierced Him; and all the tribes of the earth will mourn over Him. So it is to be. Amen." (Rev 1:7, NASB)

> "10 'I will pour out on the house of David and on the inhabitants of Jerusalem, the Spirit of grace and of supplication, so that they will look on Me whom they have pierced; and they will mourn for Him, as one mourns for an only son, and they will weep bitterly over Him like the bitter weeping over a firstborn." (Zech 12:10, NASB)

REVELATIONS ABOUT JESUS

As we examined earlier, Zechariah received many different prophecies about the future. John quotes from the last vision, which spans Zechariah chapters 12 through 14. In this last vision of Zechariah, he saw the nations of the world attack Jerusalem and God stepping in to save his people. And when God steps in to save his people, they will be surprised because they will look upon the one they pierced.

> "8 In that day the Lord will defend the inhabitants of Jerusalem, and the one who is feeble among them in that day will be like David, and the house of David will be like God, like the angel of the Lord before them. 9 And in that day I will set about to destroy all the nations that come against Jerusalem. 10 'I will pour out on the house of David and on the inhabitants of Jerusalem, the Spirit of grace and of supplication, so that they will look on Me whom they have pierced; and they will mourn for Him, as one mourns for an only son, and they will weep bitterly over Him like the bitter weeping over a firstborn. 11 In that day there will be great mourning in Jerusalem, like the mourning of Hadadrimmon in the plain of Megiddo." (Zech 12:8–11, NASB)
>
> In the opening of Revelation John quotes from Zec 12:10. He is setting the context for the book of Revelation, which is the revelation of how the as–yet unfulfilled prophecies in Zechariah will still come to pass.

In the opening of Revelation John quotes from Zec 12:10. He is setting the context for the book of Revelation, which is the revelation of how the as–yet unfulfilled prophecies in Zechariah will still come to pass. This passage shows God stepping in to save Jerusalem from the nations which are attacking her. And amazingly when God does this, he also gives them a spiritual awakening. God pours out a spirit of grace and supplication on the House of David and the inhabitants of Jerusalem. In this spiritual awakening they will look upon the one they have pierced. And they will mourn greatly. The prophecy of Zechariah is that the nations that attack Jerusalem will be defeated, and on that day God will pour out his spirit on his people. The end result is that that they are both saved as well as recognize the one they have pierced.

You may recall that on the Day of Pentecost Peter refers to Joel about the outpouring of the Holy Spirit. That happened just a few weeks after Christ rose from the dead. When John writes the book of Revelation it is many years later than that first Day of Pentecost. When John quotes from Zech 12:10 about people looking upon the Messiah and mourning for him, he brings in the context of Zech 12 which includes the outpouring of the Holy Spirit on the House of David and the inhabitants of Jerusalem. Since the Day of Pentecost had already passed years before Revelation was written, we see John looking to a future fulfillment of Zechariah.

> Since the Day of Pentecost had already passed years before Revelation was written, we see John looking to a future fulfillment of Zechariah.

Does Zechariah tell us how the one who was pierced was actually pierced? Yes, he does. You'll recall from earlier that Zechariah sees that God sends a Shepherd, but the Shepherd is struck and his sheep are scattered. In fact, the land of Israel itself will suffer and most of the people will be scattered.

> "7 'Awake, O sword, against My Shepherd, and against the man, My Associate,' declares the Lord of hosts. 'Strike the Shepherd that the sheep may be scattered; and I will turn My hand against the little ones. 8 'It will come about in all the land,' declares the Lord, 'That two parts in it will be cut off and perish; but the third will be left in it.'" (Zech 13:7–8, NASB)

After Jesus was crucified, and the Roman soldier pierced him in the side with a sword, the Romans continued their oppression of the Jewish people until they finally destroyed the Second Temple and dispersed most of the Jewish people from their land. They remained exiled until modern times.

In the final vision of Zechariah from chapters 12–14 we see that God's Shepherd is struck, his sheep are scattered, and most of the people of Israel will be forced out of the Promised Land. We also see that one day there will be an ingathering of the people of Israel and the nations of the world will gather together to attack Jerusalem. In this attack God himself will step in to save Israel. And when he does, he will pour out his Spirit on his people. This spiritual awakening will cause them to recognize the one whom they pierced.

> In the final vision of Zechariah from chapters 12–14 we see that God's Shepherd is struck, his sheep are scattered, and most of the people of Israel will be forced out of the Promised Land. We also see that one day there will be an ingathering of the people of Israel and the nations of the world will gather together to attack Jerusalem.

When John quotes from this passage of Zechariah he combines it with the quote from the book of Daniel. Theses promises of the future, that the Messiah will appear on the clouds in glory, and God's people will look upon the one who was pierced, show us that John had in mind the vision of Daniel regarding the final kingdoms leading up the worldwide attack on Jerusalem, as well as the vision of Zechariah regarding the final attack on Jerusalem. Both visions speak of many nations coming together against Jerusalem. Both visions speak of God himself stepping in to save her. And both visions speak of the Messiah who will appear and establish his Eternal Messianic Kingdom. In Daniel's vision the Messiah is the one who appears on the clouds in glory. In Zechariah's vision the Messiah is the one who was pierced, who was struck.

Revelation tells us that God is the one who is, who was, and who is to come (Rev 1:8). God was before all time, the Creator of the Heavens and the Earth. God is, now, present in the world today through his Holy Spirit. And God is the one who is to come. There is yet something God will do. John quotes from Daniel and Zechariah to bring to mind all that God prophesied would yet happen. Promises of an end to the madness of this world. Promises of an everlasting kingdom of peace yet to come. And reminders that God's Shepherd came and was rejected. But he will come again on the clouds in glory and every eye will see him. All peoples on earth will mourn because of him. Even believing Christians. But we will all have our own reasons for mourning. For me it will be because of my own personal sin, because of how I failed to do everything I could do to live a better life, and because of how wretched my innermost thoughts are and how unclean I am on the inside. And at the moment he comes, time will be up to change my ways and do anything to lead a better life, a life worthy of the calling, a life worthy of the price he paid on the cross. How great the mourning will be at his appearance? How great the regret, shame, and sorrow will be. For both those who don't believe, and for those who do believe in him.

> "'I am the Alpha and the Omega,' says the Lord God, 'who is and who was and who is to come, the Almighty.'" (Rev 1:8, NASB)

THE THRONE OF GOD

We saw that the opening of Revelation draws directly from the books of Daniel and Zechariah. John's letter to the seven churches then reveals to each of them a specific message in chapters 2 and 3. After this John is taken up in the Spirit to Heaven where he sees the throne of God.

> "After these things I looked, and behold, a door standing open in heaven, and the first voice which I had heard, like the sound of a trumpet speaking with me, said, 'Come up here, and I will show you what must take place after these things.' 2 Immediately I was in the Spirit; and behold, a throne was standing in heaven, and One sitting on the throne." (Rev 4:1–2, NASB)

In this amazing vision of the throne of God John sees four living creatures. Their faces look like a lion, an ox, a man, and an eagle. These creatures had multiple wings, and day and night they never stopped saying "Holy, holy, holy is the Lord God Almighty, who was, and is, and is to come." You will recall from earlier that this vision of the throne of God with the four unique creatures only appears in one other place in the Bible, in the book of Ezekiel. Even though Revelation does not quote Ezekiel directly, this very unique vision occurs only there.

Refer back to the earlier section of this book regarding Ezekiel for the great variety of interpretations of the meaning of the four creatures. However, in the book of Revelation the vision of the throne of God also has twenty–four elders surrounding it. Similar to the interpretations of the four living creatures, theologians also offer a wide variety of interpretations about these elders.

Some have thought they represent the twelve tribes and the twelve Apostles. Others suggest they represent the great and minor prophets. Yet others suggest they are angels, and specifically a set of higher and more powerful angels. Some theologians think they are the elders of the early church at Jerusalem, or represent Gentiles, or perhaps even the books of the Hebrew Bible (with the four living creatures representing the four Gospels: Matthew, Mark, Luke, and John). John does not say in Revelation who they are, so the Sola Scriptura approach will not take a position. Like the four living creatures themselves, neither the New nor the Old Testaments directly give an explanation. It is enough for us to see that John has a vision of the throne of God and it appears uniquely like that vision that only Ezekiel describes for us.

One of the most mysterious parts of Ezekiel is that above these four living creatures sitting on the throne of God is one who looks like a man. Ezekiel does not say it is a man on the throne of God, but one who appears "like" a man. Daniel tries to explain this mysterious figure also, saying he is one "like" a son of man.

> "25 And there came a voice from above the expanse that was over their heads; whenever they stood still, they dropped their wings. 26 Now above the expanse that was over their heads there was something resembling a throne, like lapis lazuli in appearance; and on that which resembled a throne, high up, was a figure with the appearance of a man." (Ezek 1:25–26, NASB)

> "13 'I kept looking in the night visions, and behold, with the clouds of heaven one like a Son of Man was coming, and He came up to the Ancient of Days and was presented before Him. 14 'And to Him was given dominion, glory and a kingdom, that all the peoples, nations and men of every language might serve Him. His dominion is an everlasting dominion which will not pass away; and His kingdom is one which will not be destroyed." (Dan 7:13–14, NASB)

This Messiah is like the figure of a man, he is one like a son of man. The nature of the humanity and divinity of this one sitting on the throne of God was perplexing to Ezekiel and Daniel. It has been perplexing to the Rabbis. The nature of the humanity and divinity of Jesus is perplexing to theologians today. And for some unbelievers the nature of Jesus as both God and man may be one of the most difficult things to accept and believe. From the prophets of old to your own inner thoughts today, God works in mysterious ways.

> The nature of the humanity and divinity of this one sitting on the Throne of God was perplexing to Ezekiel and Daniel. It has been perplexing to the Rabbis. The nature of the humanity and divinity of Jesus is perplexing to theologians today. And for some unbelievers the nature of Jesus as both God and man may be one of the most difficult things to accept and believe.

In the book of Ezekiel, we also learn that the Messiah is the Good Shepherd who searches for God's lost sheep. He is the one who searches for people who have gone astray from God. He is the one who actually cares about the flock, unlike the untrustworthy leaders. Ezekiel saw this one who looked like the figure of a man sitting on the throne of God. This one comes to seek and save the lost. Though the Messiah is rejected, pierced, and struck, the mission of the Messiah is to bring salvation to the lost. Though the prophecies speak of the everlasting Kingdom of Messiah which destroys all other kingdoms, the focus of the Messiah is on being the Good Shepherd to seek and save the lost. He is not like a Roman Emperor who sends out armies to conquer other lands. He is not like the arrogant one of Daniel who leads many nations. No, the Messiah is different than we might expect. The one who sits on the throne of God is the Good Shepherd and cares for his flock. He even knows the prophecy of his own impending death but continues ahead anyway in his mission to care for others.

> The one who sits on the throne of God is the Good Shepherd and cares for his flock. He even knows the prophecy of his own impending death but continues ahead anyway in his mission to care for others.
>
> "I am the good shepherd; the good shepherd lays down His life for the sheep." (John 10:11, NASB)

When John sees the throne of God and describes the four living creatures to us, we should immediately think of Ezekiel, for it is found nowhere else in the Bible. And we should immediately think of the promises in Ezekiel that the Messiah is the Good Shepherd who cares about his flock. And we should remember that Jesus called himself the Good Shepherd and he sends us out to seek the lost, the oppressed, the forgotten, and to help them. In fact, we could do nothing better right now than to set this book down and go out to serve the poor and needy. While God will work out all things for good, and Jesus will return on the clouds in glory, until then our mission should be to help those in need.

THE LAMB WHO WAS SLAIN

There is a secret within Revelation (among many). There is a scroll which is sealed. John sees this scroll and desires to know what is written on it. But in the vision John sees that there is no one who is worthy to open the scroll. What a terribly sad moment. There John is in Heaven, with the four living creatures and the twenty-four Elders. Yet none of them are worthy to open the scroll. Just imagine being in Heaven, seeing this mysterious scroll, and then realizing that no one, not even these amazing four living creatures, are worthy enough. I think I would just cry and cry.

> "I saw in the right hand of Him who sat on the throne a book written inside and on the back, sealed up with seven seals. 2 And I saw a strong angel proclaiming with a loud voice, 'Who is worthy to open the book and to break its seals?' 3 And no one in heaven or on the earth or under the earth was able to

open the book or to look into it. 4 Then I began to weep greatly because no one was found worthy to open the book or to look into it;" (Rev 5:1–4, NASB)

John wept and wept. That takes time. We tend to gloss over things when we read scripture. It takes only a moment to read that John wept and wept, but think about it. We're talking about the passing of some real time here for John. It's not like he just teared up and one tear fell across his cheek. No, this went on for quite some time. Long enough for John to stand there waiting for someone to appear who was worthy. Long enough to realize that no one on earth was worthy, obviously. Long enough to look at the twenty-four Elders and see that even they weren't worthy. Long enough to look at the four living creatures and see that they weren't worthy either. Long enough for fear, sadness, and sorrow to well up inside enough that it caused John to start to cry. Long enough that those tears came out as real crying. Long enough that it went on and on. Long enough that John wept and wept. Just imagine that. This is one of the saddest moments in the entire Bible. Here John was in the presence of all the host of Heaven, looking at a scroll in the right hand of him who sat on the throne, yet no one was found worthy to open it. And then finally one was found who was worthy. Finally, one appeared who was able to open the scroll. This was such a great moment that the four living creatures and twenty-four Elders broke out in song.

> "9 And they sang a new song, saying, 'Worthy are You to take the book and to break its seals; for You were slain, and purchased for God with Your blood men from every tribe and tongue and people and nation. 10 'You have made them to be a kingdom and priests to our God; and they will reign upon the earth.'" (Rev 5:9–10, NASB)

The Lamb who was slain was worthy to open the scroll. He is worthy because he offered his soul as a sacrifice for the sins of others. With his blood he purchased for God people from every part of the world. Who would believe that the Messiah would die? Who would believe that he would die for the sins of others? And if so, then to whom would God reveal such a plan?

> "1 Who has believed our message? And to whom has the arm of the Lord been revealed? 2 For He grew up before Him like a tender shoot, and like a root out of parched ground; He has no stately form or majesty that we should look upon Him, nor appearance that we should be attracted to Him. 3 He was despised and forsaken of men, a man of sorrows and acquainted with grief; and like one from whom men hide their face he was despised, and we did not esteem Him. 4 Surely our griefs He Himself bore, and our sorrows He carried; yet we ourselves esteemed Him stricken, smitten of God, and afflicted. 5 But He was pierced through for our transgressions, He was crushed for our iniquities; the chastening for our well-being fell upon Him, and by His scourging we are healed. 6 All of us like sheep have gone astray, each of us has turned to his

own way; but the Lord has caused the iniquity of us all to fall on Him." (Isa 53:1–6, NASB)

What had long been prophesied from old, that a Messiah would come and be rejected, struck, and pierced, had finally come to pass. The prophecies that a Messiah would come who would be the Good Shepherd and seek out the lost had come true. The prophecies that a Messiah who would offer his own life, his own *nephesh* (נַפְשׁוֹ), his own soul as an offering for the sins of others came true. God would lay on him the iniquity of others, the transgressions of others, the sin of others. He would be crushed and punished, wounded and pierced, because of the sins of others. We all, like sheep, have gone astray and turned to our own ways. And God has laid on him the iniquity of us all.

For this reason, the Lamb who was slain was worthy to open the mysterious scroll. And at this the four living creatures and twenty-four Elders broke out in song. Surely John stopped weeping then. The words of the song said that the people whom Jesus died for are "to be a kingdom and priests to serve our God, and they will reign on the earth." We learn that the Messiah, the Good Shepherd, who lays his life down for the sheep, who offers his soul as a sacrifice for the sins of others, who is like a Son of Man, rejected and pierced, makes us to be a kingdom and priests to serve God.

> "9 And they sang a new song, saying, 'Worthy are You to take the book and to break its seals; for You were slain, and purchased for God with Your blood men from every tribe and tongue and people and nation. 10 'You have made them to be a kingdom and priests to our God; and they will reign upon the earth.'" (Rev 5:9–10, NASB)

THE DEFEAT OF SATAN

One of the most wonderful prophecies about the Messiah is that he will defeat Satan. The evil power which is behind all opposition to God will be defeated. The tendency we have to hurt ourselves and each other will end; and the source of temptation which leads us astray will be finally destroyed. We see this promise first appear way back in the Garden of Eden. After the serpent deceives Adam and Eve God judges them all. In the punishment of the serpent we see a promise about the Messiah. Look closely and you will see that the seed of a woman (a baby) will ultimately defeat Satan.

> "14 The Lord God said to the serpent, 'Because you have done this, cursed are you more than all cattle, and more than every beast of the field; on your belly you will go, and dust you will eat all the days of your life; 15 And I will put enmity between you and the woman, and between your seed and her seed; he shall bruise you on the head, and you shall bruise him on the heel.'" (Gen 3:14–15, NASB)

The expectation that the Messiah would defeat evil forms the background context of the book of Revelation. We see this clearly in the scriptures. For example, in Paul's closing of his letter to the church at Rome he states:

> "The God of peace will soon crush Satan under your feet. The grace of our Lord Jesus be with you." (Rom 16:20, NASB)

We see discussion of God binding the evil powers for the Day of Judgment in Jude, Isaiah, Peter, and Matthew.

> "And angels who did not keep their own domain, but abandoned their proper abode, He has kept in eternal bonds under darkness for the judgment of the great day," (Jude 1:6, NASB)

> "21 So it will happen in that day, that the Lord will punish the host of heaven on high, and the kings of the earth on earth. 22 They will be gathered together like prisoners in the dungeon, and will be confined in prison; and after many days they will be punished. 23 Then the moon will be abashed and the sun ashamed, for the Lord of hosts will reign on Mount Zion and in Jerusalem, and His glory will be before His elders." (Isa 24:21–23, NASB)

> "4 For if God did not spare angels when they sinned, but cast them into hell and committed them to pits of darkness, reserved for judgment; 9 then the Lord knows how to rescue the godly from temptation, and to keep the unrighteous under punishment for the day of judgment," (2 Pet 2:4,9, NASB)

> "Then He will also say to those on His left, 'Depart from Me, accursed ones, into the eternal fire which has been prepared for the devil and his angels'" (Matt 25:41, NASB)

And we also see this ultimate defeat in the book of Revelation.

> "7 When the thousand years are completed, Satan will be released from his prison, 8 and will come out to deceive the nations which are in the four corners of the earth, Gog and Magog, to gather them together for the war; the number of them is like the sand of the seashore. 9 And they came up on the broad plain of the earth and surrounded the camp of the saints and the beloved city, and fire came down from heaven and devoured them. 10 And the devil who deceived them was thrown into the lake of fire and brimstone, where the beast and the false prophet are also; and they will be tormented day and night forever and ever." (Rev 20:7–10, NASB)

Our adversary, *Satan* (הַשָּׂטָן), who roams the earth looking for people to devour, who shoots the flaming arrows of temptation into our minds and hearts, who is the father of lies and enchants the worldly powers, who was the most beautiful of all the angels but desired to be worshiped instead of God, will be finally defeated. From Genesis through Revelation it is clear that Satan will be defeated. Though we are tempted to sin and constantly led astray by the power of evil in our world today, God will ultimately defeat Satan.

> From Genesis through Revelation it is clear that Satan will be defeated. Though we are tempted to sin and constantly led astray by the power of evil in our world today, God will ultimately defeat Satan.

THE DEFEAT OF THE BEAST

In the promises of the defeat of Satan we see that he is ultimately thrown into the lake of burning sulfur.

> "And the devil who deceived them was thrown into the lake of fire and brimstone, where the beast and the false prophet are also; and they will be tormented day and night forever and ever." (Rev 20:10, NASB)

There are at least two interesting things to note in the scriptures here. The first is that the torment goes on forever, day and night forever and ever. For those theologians who teach that there is no hell and after an appropriate period of purgation everyone eventually goes to heaven, this passage (and others) are problematic. The words "forever and ever," (the ages of the ages, the eternity of eternities, τοὺς αἰῶνας τῶν αἰώνωνin the Greek), mean everlasting and without end. The theology that all people eventually go to Heaven, called Christian Universalism, is just not what we see written in the Bible. A Sola Scriptura approach only supports what the scriptures directly say.

The second thing of interest is that when Satan is defeated, he is thrown into the lake of burning sulfur where the beast and the false prophet had been thrown. The beast and false prophet are already there when Satan is thrown in. This shows that the beast is not the same as Satan. It also shows that the events described in Revelation chapter 20 happen after the defeat of the beast. Revelation 20 is the first place the book of Revelation mentions a one-thousand-year period known as the Millennium. We will discuss this further below but keep in mind that the events in Rev 20 come after the beast and the false prophet have already been defeated. The defeat of Satan in Revelation chapter 20 comes after the defeat of the beast and the false prophet in Revelation chapter 19. Satan is cast into the lake of burning sulfur where the beast and false prophet had already been thrown.

> The defeat of Satan in Revelation chapter 20 comes after the defeat of the beast and the false prophet in Revelation chapter 19. Satan is cast into the lake of burning sulfur where the beast and false prophet had already been thrown.

> "19 And I saw the beast and the kings of the earth and their armies assembled to make war against Him who sat on the horse and against His army. 20 And the beast was seized, and with him the false prophet who performed the signs

in his presence, by which he deceived those who had received the mark of the beast and those who worshiped his image; these two were thrown alive into the lake of fire which burns with brimstone. 21 And the rest were killed with the sword which came from the mouth of Him who sat on the horse, and all the birds were filled with their flesh." (Rev 19:19–21, NASB)

The beast is defeated, along with the nations of the world that come to wage war against the Messiah. The beast and the false prophet are both thrown into the fiery lake of burning sulfur. How do we know that the Messiah is the one who defeats the beast? Because scripture tells us so.

> "11 And I saw heaven opened, and behold, a white horse, and He who sat on it is called Faithful and True, and in righteousness He judges and wages war. 12 His eyes are a flame of fire, and on His head are many diadems; and He has a name written on Him which no one knows except Himself. 13 He is clothed with a robe dipped in blood, and His name is called The Word of God. 14 And the armies which are in heaven, clothed in fine linen, white and clean, were following Him on white horses. 15 From His mouth comes a sharp sword, so that with it He may strike down the nations, and He will rule them with a rod of iron; and He treads the wine press of the fierce wrath of God, the Almighty. 16 And on His robe and on His thigh He has a name written, 'KING OF KINGS, AND LORD OF LORDS.'" (Rev 19:11–16, NASB)

The King of Kings and Lord of Lords leads a heavenly army to defeat the beast and his armies. As we have seen in our past examination of the Hebrew prophets there was an expectation of a great battle against the people of God, a final attack on Jerusalem led by an arrogant and cunning world leader who is opposed to God. We see this expectation fulfilled in the book of Revelation when the beast and the kings of the earth and their armies wage war against the Messiah and his army. The beast is defeated, and he and the false prophet are thrown into the fiery lake of burning sulfur.

> As we have seen in our past examination of the Hebrew prophets there was an expectation of a great battle against the people of God, a final attack on Jerusalem led by an arrogant and cunning world leader who is opposed to God. We see this expectation fulfilled in the book of Revelation when the beast and the kings of the earth and their armies wage war against the Messiah and his army.

Notice also that the Messiah who defeats the beast is the one who "will rule them with an iron scepter." This is a direct reference to the Messianic Psalm number 2.

> "8 'Ask of Me, and I will surely give the nations as Your inheritance, and the very ends of the earth as Your possession. 9 'You shall break them with a rod of iron, You shall shatter them like earthenware.'" (Ps 2:8–9, NASB)

As John describes the defeat of the beast and the armies of the world that wage war against the Messiah, he directly quotes the second Psalm. Psalm 2 is an amazing

Psalm because centuries before Christ there was a prophecy of the Messiah being the Son of God. In fact, Psalm 2 clearly warns people to follow the Son of God or else suffer wrath.

> "6 'But as for Me, I have installed My King upon Zion, My holy mountain.' 7 'I will surely tell of the decree of the Lord: he said to Me, 'You are My Son, today I have begotten You.'" (Ps 2:6-7, NASB)

> "10 Now therefore, O kings, show discernment; take warning, O judges of the earth. 11 Worship the Lord with reverence and rejoice with trembling. 12 Do homage to the Son, that He not become angry, and you perish in the way, for His wrath may soon be kindled. How blessed are all who take refuge in Him!" (Ps 2:10-12, NASB)

> "32 And we preach to you the good news of the promise made to the fathers, 33 that God has fulfilled this promise to our children in that He raised up Jesus, as it is also written in the second Psalm, 'You are My Son; today I have begotten You.'" (Acts 13:32-33, NASB)

Notice that this Psalm is set in the context of the nations of the world plotting together against God.

> "Why are the nations in an uproar and the peoples devising a vain thing? 2 The kings of the earth take their stand and the rulers take counsel together against the Lord and against His Anointed, saying, 3 'Let us tear their fetters apart and cast away their cords from us!'" (Ps 2:1-3, NASB)

The Messiah defeats the beast and his armies, just as Psalm 2 tells us the nations conspire against the Son of God and they are defeated. God installs his King in Zion who will rule the world with an iron scepter. Kings and rulers are warned to follow God's Son or else suffer destruction. And blessed are all those who take refuge in the Son of God.

THE MESSIANIC WOES

As we have seen from the background context of the Hebrew prophets, the nations of the world gather together against God and his Messiah and make a final attack on Jerusalem. We see this narrative also in the book of Revelation with the beast leading the kings of the earth and their armies to wage war against the Messiah. Leading up to this final battle is a great oppression of the people of God. As we saw in Daniel, this oppression led by the boastful horn culminates in this evil figure declaring himself to be a god. This abomination in the temple was specifically mentioned by Jesus when his Disciples asked him about the destruction of the temple and the end of the age. We see this culmination of a final attack of Jerusalem in the prophecies of Zechariah, Ezekiel, and Joel. Ezekiel speaks of many nations being led by an evil ruler referred to as Gog, while Joel uses the imagery of an invasion like locusts (as also does the book of Revelation).

The time period just before the final attack and the victory of the Messiah is generally referred to by theologians as the "Messianic Woes." In both Judaism and Christianity this is seen as a time of trouble, distress, and suffering for the people of God. The world itself closes in on God's people and only God can save them.

> "15 'Therefore when you see the abomination of desolation which was spoken of through Daniel the prophet, standing in the holy place (let the reader understand), 16 then those who are in Judea must flee to the mountains. 17 Whoever is on the housetop must not go down to get the things out that are in his house. 18 Whoever is in the field must not turn back to get his cloak. 19 But woe to those who are pregnant and to those who are nursing babies in those days! 20 But pray that your flight will not be in the winter, or on a Sabbath. 21 For then there will be a great tribulation, such as has not occurred since the beginning of the world until now, nor ever will. 22 Unless those days had been cut short, no life would have been saved; but for the sake of the elect those days will be cut short." (Matt 24:15-22, NASB)

> The time period just before the final attack and the victory of the Messiah is generally referred to by theologians as the "Messianic Woes." In both Judaism and Christianity this is seen as a time of trouble, distress, and suffering for the people of God.

THE MILLENNIUM

The first, last, and only time we hear about a one-thousand-year period in the Bible is in Revelation chapter 20. With only two more chapters to the end of the book it's amazing that so much of the theological divide occurs over a single chapter. As we explored in the first part of this book there are a great variety of views of the Millennium and what it means. And as you might expect, the Sola Scriptura approach will rely only on what the scriptures themselves say and not later traditions which developed over time. For context, recall earlier that when Satan is defeated, he is thrown into the lake of burning sulfur where the beast and false prophet had already been thrown (Rev 20:10). The events of Rev 20 happen after Rev 19 where the beast is defeated.

> "Then I saw an angel coming down from heaven, holding the key of the abyss and a great chain in his hand. 2 And he laid hold of the dragon, the serpent of old, who is the devil and Satan, and bound him for a thousand years; 3 and he threw him into the abyss, and shut it and sealed it over him, so that he would not deceive the nations any longer, until the thousand years were completed; after these things he must be released for a short time." (Rev 20:1-3, NASB)

After the defeat of the beast, the kings of the earth, and their armies that attack Jerusalem and wage war against the Messiah in chapter 19, John then sees Satan being bound and thrown into the Abyss. The scriptures say this is for one thousand years.

> "4 Then I saw thrones, and they sat on them, and judgment was given to them. And I saw the souls of those who had been beheaded because of their testimony of Jesus and because of the word of God, and those who had not worshiped the beast or his image, and had not received the mark on their forehead and on their hand; and they came to life and reigned with Christ for a thousand years. 5 The rest of the dead did not come to life until the thousand years were completed. This is the first resurrection. 6 Blessed and holy is the one who has a part in the first resurrection; over these the second death has no power, but they will be priests of God and of Christ and will reign with Him for a thousand years." (Rev 20:4–6, NASB)

Revelation says that after the beast and the armies that wage war against the Messiah are defeated, the martyrs who suffered under the beast will be resurrected and reign with Christ for one thousand years. The rest of the dead do not come to life until the one thousand years are over.

> Revelation says that after the beast and the armies that wage war against the Messiah are defeated, the martyrs who suffered under the beast will be resurrected and reign with Christ for one thousand years. The rest of the dead do not come to life until the one thousand years are over.

> "7 When the thousand years are completed, Satan will be released from his prison, 8 and will come out to deceive the nations which are in the four corners of the earth, Gog and Magog, to gather them together for the war; the number of them is like the sand of the seashore. 9 And they came up on the broad plain of the earth and surrounded the camp of the saints and the beloved city, and fire came down from heaven and devoured them. 10 And the devil who deceived them was thrown into the lake of fire and brimstone, where the beast and the false prophet are also; and they will be tormented day and night forever and ever." (Rev 20:7–10, NASB)

At the end of the one thousand years Satan is released from the Abyss and convinces the nations, Gog and Magog, to gather together and attack Jerusalem. Note that in the previous chapter, the beast and the kings of the world waged war against the Messiah and lost. But only the beast and the false prophet are thrown in the fiery lake of burning sulfur. The peoples of the world are still there and are put under a one-thousand-year rule by the Messiah and the martyrs as seen above. Recall from verse 20:5 that the rest of the dead do not get resurrected until the end of the one thousand years. Thus, at the end of the one-thousand-year period Satan is released and convinces the peoples of the world to attack Jerusalem. Satan loses and is thrown into the lake of burning sulfur where the beast and the false prophet already are. And at that time, the end of the one-thousand-year period, the rest of the dead are resurrected.

Recall from the earlier part of this book that there are many views of this passage. Some hold that the one thousand years is not really one thousand years but instead refers to all time since the birth of Christianity (Amillennial). Others view the one thousand years as a specific timeframe and next ask when is the Second Coming in relation to the one thousand years? Those who hold that Jesus returns before the one thousand years begins are Pre-Millennial, while those who hold he returns at the end of the one thousand years are Post-Millennial.

The Sola Scriptura approach holds to only what the scriptures say. The scriptures clearly reference a time period of one thousand years and do not offer any allegorical or symbolic interpretation. The scriptures also say the martyrs who did not worship the beast will reign with Christ for one thousand years. The rest of the dead will not be resurrected until the end of the one-thousand years. We also know that in the prior chapter the beast and the armies he commands wage war against the Messiah, hence the Messiah has already returned by this time. In other words, the one-thousand-year period mentioned in Rev 20 comes after the beast has already been defeated in Rev 19 after leading the armies of the world in an attack against Jerusalem. Since the beast wages war against the Messiah and is defeated by the Messiah, the Messiah necessarily returns before the one thousand years. This is a Pre-millennial view and based only on what the scriptures plainly say without relying on any external theological framework.

> The one-thousand-year period mentioned in Rev 20 comes after the beast has already been defeated in Rev 19 after leading the armies of the world in an attack against Jerusalem. Since the beast wages war against the Messiah and is defeated by the Messiah, the Messiah necessarily returns before the one thousand years.

The Amillennial view that the one thousand years refers to all time since the birth of Christianity does not make sense if Christ returns before that time period to defeat the beast. The beast wages war against the Messiah and is then defeated. To say we are living in that time now does not make sense with the one-thousand-year period coming after the defeat of the beast. We cannot be living in the one-thousand-year period now, as held by the Amillennial view, since the one thousand years come after the defeat of the beast. We also cannot be in the time period represented by the one thousand years because Jesus has not returned yet to defeat the beast. It also makes no sense to suggest the beast represents kingdoms waging war against Christianity during this time period because Revelation clearly says the beast is defeated and thrown into the lake of burning sulfur before the one-thousand-year time period. It is after the one thousand years that Satan is released, defeated, and thrown into the lake of burning sulfur where the beast had already been thrown. The details of Revelation just do not line up with the Amillennial view, and we cannot ignore the details. Every part of scripture is profitable for reproof, and not one jot or tittle will be changed until it is fulfilled.

> "17 'Do not think that I came to abolish the Law or the Prophets; I did not come to abolish but to fulfill. 18 For truly I say to you, until heaven and earth pass away, not the smallest letter or stroke shall pass from the Law until all is accomplished.'" (Matt 5:17–18, NASB)

As you saw in an earlier section of this book, the Rabbis of the Talmud also interestingly believed in a literal one-thousand-year period of Messianic rule. They taught that each day of creation represents one thousand years, and thus the seven days of creation correspond to a seven-thousand-year cycle of world history culminating with the one thousand year reign of the Messiah after the war of Gog and Magog.[1]

> "The Sages taught in a baraita: With regard to the seven-year period, i.e., the Sabbatical cycle, during which the Messiah, son of David, comes: During the first year, this verse will be fulfilled: 'And I will cause it to rain upon one city and cause it not to rain upon another city' (Amos 4:7). During the second year of that period, arrows of famine will be shot, indicating that there will be famine only in certain places. During the third year there will be a great famine, and men, women, children, the pious, and men of action will die, and the Torah is forgotten by those who study it. During the fourth year there will be plenty but not great plenty. During the fifth year there will be great plenty and they will eat, and drink, and rejoice, and the Torah will return to those who study it. During the sixth year, heavenly voices will be heard. During the Sabbatical Year, wars, e.g., the war of Gog and Magog, will be waged involving the Jewish people. During the year after the conclusion of the Sabbatical Year, the son of David will come." (Talmud Sanhedrin 97a)

THE ETERNAL MESSIANIC KINGDOM

As we have seen above, the beast and the nations of the world that follow him wage war against the Messiah in Revelation chapter 19. They lose, and the beast and false prophet are thrown into the lake of burning sulfur while birds feast on the dead bodies of the slain. This follows along with Ezekiel's vision of Gog leading the nations of the world to attack Jerusalem, and then God defeating them: ending with a feast of the slain for the birds and wild animals. In the next chapter of Revelation, we see a one-thousand-year period where Satan is bound in the abyss and the martyrs of the beast reign with Christ. At the end of the one-thousand-year period Satan is released and deceives the nations to attack Jerusalem. They are defeated and Satan is thrown into the lake of burning sulfur where the beast and false prophet had already been thrown. After these amazing attacks and defeats we see Revelation speak of the second

---

1. Ashi and Ravina, *Babylonian Talmud*, Sukkah 52a:2.

resurrection, the resurrection of all the dead. These are the rest of the dead that come to life at the end of the one thousand years and face their judgment at the great white throne.

> "11 Then I saw a great white throne and Him who sat upon it, from whose presence earth and heaven fled away, and no place was found for them. 12 And I saw the dead, the great and the small, standing before the throne, and books were opened; and another book was opened, which is the book of life; and the dead were judged from the things which were written in the books, according to their deeds. 13 And the sea gave up the dead which were in it, and death and Hades gave up the dead which were in them; and they were judged, every one of them according to their deeds." (Rev 20:11–13, NASB)

It is after this judgment that John then sees a new heaven and a new earth. In Revelation chapter 21 he sees a new Jerusalem coming down out of heaven. She is the bride prepared for the husband. God will dwell among his people, and he will wipe away every tear. There will be no more death or mourning or crying or pain.

> "Then I saw a new heaven and a new earth; for the first heaven and the first earth passed away, and there is no longer any sea. 2 And I saw the holy city, new Jerusalem, coming down out of heaven from God, made ready as a bride adorned for her husband. 3 And I heard a loud voice from the throne, saying, 'Behold, the tabernacle of God is among men, and He will dwell among them, and they shall be His people, and God Himself will be among them, 4 and He will wipe away every tear from their eyes; and there will no longer be any death; there will no longer be any mourning, or crying, or pain; the first things have passed away.' 5 And He who sits on the throne said, 'Behold, I am making all things new.' And He said, 'Write, for these words are faithful and true.'" (Rev 21:1–5, NASB)

> "17 'For behold, I create new heavens and a new earth; and the former things will not be remembered or come to mind. 18 'But be glad and rejoice forever in what I create; for behold, I create Jerusalem for rejoicing and her people for gladness. 19 'I will also rejoice in Jerusalem and be glad in My people; and there will no longer be heard in her the voice of weeping and the sound of crying." (Isa 65:17–19, NASB)

> "He who overcomes, I will make him a pillar in the temple of My God, and he will not go out from it anymore; and I will write on him the name of My God, and the name of the city of My God, the new Jerusalem, which comes down out of heaven from My God, and My new name." (Rev 3:12, NASB)

> "10 But the day of the Lord will come like a thief, in which the heavens will pass away with a roar and the elements will be destroyed with intense heat, and the earth and its works will be burned up. 11 Since all these things are to be destroyed in this way, what sort of people ought you to be in holy conduct

and godliness, 12 looking for and hastening the coming of the day of God, because of which the heavens will be destroyed by burning, and the elements will melt with intense heat! 13 But according to His promise we are looking for new heavens and a new earth, in which righteousness dwells." (2 Pet 3:10–13, NASB)

This new order of things has not yet come to pass, unlike the Preterist view claims. There is still death, there is still mourning, and there is still much pain in the current world. The Allegorical interpretation that holds that Christ already reigns now and his kingdom is already here now also misses the plain sense of what the scriptures say. The Sola Scriptura approach will hold only what the scriptures directly say, and as you can see there will be a new heaven and a new earth, a new order of things, where there is no more death or mourning or crying or pain.

> There will be a new heaven and a new earth, a new order of things, where there is no more death or mourning or crying or pain.

Going forth from the New Jerusalem will be the river of the water of life. Along the banks of the river will be trees that yield fruit every month and whose leaves are for the healing of the nations. This is an eternal kingdom where God himself dwells among his people, there is no more crying or pain or death, and there is endless food and healing.

> "Then he showed me a river of the water of life, clear as crystal, coming from the throne of God and of the Lamb, 2 in the middle of its street. On either side of the river was the tree of life, bearing twelve kinds of fruit, yielding its fruit every month; and the leaves of the tree were for the healing of the nations. 3 There will no longer be any curse; and the throne of God and of the Lamb will be in it, and His bond-servants will serve Him; 4 they will see His face, and His name will be on their foreheads. 5 And there will no longer be any night; and they will not have need of the light of a lamp nor the light of the sun, because the Lord God will illumine them; and they will reign forever and ever." (Rev 22:1–5, NASB)

This beautiful vision is the fulfillment of the prophecies to Ezekiel about the eternal kingdom to come. In Ezekiel's last vision he sees water flowing out from under the threshold of the temple. This water grows into a river which waters the surrounding region. Joel sees the same thing.

> "By the river on its bank, on one side and on the other, will grow all kinds of trees for food. Their leaves will not wither and their fruit will not fail. They will bear every month because their water flows from the sanctuary, and their fruit will be for food and their leaves for healing.'" (Ezek 47:12, NASB)

> "17 Then you will know that I am the Lord your God, dwelling in Zion, My holy mountain. So Jerusalem will be holy, and strangers will pass through it

no more. 18 And in that day the mountains will drip with sweet wine, and the hills will flow with milk, and all the brooks of Judah will flow with water; and a spring will go out from the house of the Lord to water the valley of Shittim." (Joel 3:17–18, NASB)

God himself will be the light of the New Jerusalem and there will be no more need for the sun or moon, just as the prophets said. A new order of things is coming. Our days of sorrow will end.

"22 I saw no temple in it, for the Lord God the Almighty and the Lamb are its temple. 23 And the city has no need of the sun or of the moon to shine on it, for the glory of God has illumined it, and its lamp is the Lamb." (Rev 21:22–23, NASB)

"3 There will no longer be any curse; and the throne of God and of the Lamb will be in it, and His bond-servants will serve Him; 4 they will see His face, and His name will be on their foreheads. 5 And there will no longer be any night; and they will not have need of the light of a lamp nor the light of the sun, because the Lord God will illumine them; and they will reign forever and ever." (Rev 22:3–5, NASB)

"19 'No longer will you have the sun for light by day, nor for brightness will the moon give you light; but you will have the Lord for an everlasting light, and your God for your glory. 20 'Your sun will no longer set, nor will your moon wane; for you will have the Lord for an everlasting light, and the days of your mourning will be over." (Isa 60:19–20, NASB)

A new order of things is coming. Our days of sorrow will end.

WHAT DID WE LEARN ABOUT JESUS?

The book of Revelation is wonderful in helping us to better understand our Messiah, Jesus Christ. It helps us to understand how the Hebrew prophets spoke of him, and what is still yet to come in human destiny. From the outset Revelation quotes from Daniel and Zechariah directly. And then John sees a vision only otherwise found in the writings of Ezekiel.

The first references to the Hebrew prophets are about the Son of Man seen in Daniel. Jesus himself often referred to himself as the Son of Man. This Son of Man that Daniel saw was the mysterious person that God gives all authority, dominion, and power to. This one is the one like a Son of Man (but not merely a human) that all nations will one day worship. The worship of Jesus as the Son of God is something not only found in the New Testament, but it also has its origin in the Hebrew prophecies themselves. This is the first direct quote of the Hebrew prophecies that we see in the opening chapter of the book of Revelation.

Revelations About Jesus

The second quote is of Zechariah's vision of the Messiah who was pierced. This one who was pierced and rejected by his own people is the one who will come on the clouds in glory at the time of judgment. At his Second Coming Jesus Christ will return on the clouds in glory to judge the living and the dead. This is not a Christian invention but instead comes directly from the Hebrew prophecies about the Messiah, and the book of Revelation brings this to the forefront in its opening chapter. John expected his readers to be familiar with Daniel and Zechariah in particular. We also see in Revelation a vision of the throne of God that is just like the vision Ezekiel had. The vision of the four living creatures is found nowhere else in scripture and clearly is an allusion to those prophecies.

In the prophecies of Daniel, Zechariah, and Ezekiel we see that the Messiah is rejected by his own people and put to death. But at the end of days, he will return on the clouds in glory to defeat the final worldwide kingdom that oppresses the people of God. After the final kingdom and its ruler, Gog, are defeated, then the eternal Messianic Kingdom will be established. Never again will God's people be oppressed; never again will they live in fear. God will wipe away every tear and there will be peace. A new Heaven and a new Earth will be created, and a New Jerusalem will come down from Heaven. The river of the water of life will flow out from Zion and water the surrounding region. Along the banks of the river will be trees that provide year-round food and leaves for healing. These prophecies, all in the Hebrew Bible, form the background context of the book of Revelation. And together with Revelation we see that Jesus will fulfill all the prophecies we still wait for. One day evil will be completely defeated and there will be no more death, mourning, crying, or pain. Every knee will bow, and every tongue will confess that Jesus Christ is Lord. In that day only the one true God will be worshiped across the whole world.

#	Truth Claim	Primary Support	Secondary Support
10.1	The Messiah will return on the clouds in glory.	Rev 1:7	Dan 7:13, Matt 24:30, 25:31, Mark 13:26, 14:62, Luke 21:27, 1 Thess 4:17
10.2	One like a man sits on God's throne. One like a Son of Man will be worshiped.	Rev 5:11-14	Rev 1:13, 4:2, Mark 2:10,28, 14:21, Matt 11:19, 16:27, 24:30, 26:2, Ezek 1:26-28, Dan 7:13-14, Isa 9:6-7
10.3	The Messiah will be rejected.	Rev 1:7	Ps 2:9-10, 110:1-6, Dan 7:14, Isa 2:1-4, 11:4
10.4	The Messiah is slain to atone for the sins of others.	Rev 5:9	Rev 5:3-12, Phlp 2:5-11, Matt 28:18, Eph 1:21, Heb 2:9, Dan 7:14, Isa 11:1-5, 53:1-12, Ps 22

The Sola Scriptura Challenge

#	Truth Claim	Primary Support	Secondary Support
10.5	Every eye will look upon the slain Messiah and be sorry.	Rev 1:7	John 19:37, Matt 24:30, Zech 12:10-14, Dan 9:24-26, Isa 53, Ps 22 [also Ibn Ezra/Zech 12:10, Talmud Sukkah 5:5, 52a:6,10, Ruth Rabbah 2.14, Yom Kippur Siddur Prayer]
10.6	Jesus Christ will return to judge the Living and the Dead.	Rev 20:11-15	Rev 2:11,23, 3:5, 11:18, 14:10, 20:6,11-15, 22:12, John 5:24-29, Jude 1:14-15,23, Luke 10:20, 14:14, 1 Thes 4:16, Matt 16:27, 19:28, 25:41-46, 1 Cor 15:20-57, Rom 2:5-11, Dan 7:9-10, 12:2-3, Isa 26:19-21, 40:10, 62:11, Ps 69:28, Job 34:11, Jer 17:10
10.7	God will defeat the final evil worldwide kingdom and establish an everlasting kingdom of peace ruled by the Messiah.	Rev 19:11-21	Rev 20:7-10, 2 Thess 2:8, Dan 7:11-14,18,22,26-27, Isa 9:6-7
10.8	God will create a new heaven and a new earth, with a new Jerusalem.	Rev 21:1	Rev 3:12, 6:14, 20:11, 21:1,5,10, 22:19, Rom 8:19,21, 2 Pet 3:10-13, Gal 4:26, Heb 11:10,16, 12:22-29, Matt 24:35, Isa 65:17, 66:22, Ezek 48:30-35
10.9	God will wipe away every tear and there will be no more death.	Rev 21:4	Rev 7:17, 20:14, 1 Cor 15:26, Isa 25:8, 30:19, 35:10, 51:11, 60:20, 65:19, Jer 31:12

11

Revelations About Satan

"The Gemara continues its discussion of the river that will in the future come out of the Holy of Holies. Rabbi Yehuda ben Pazi said: Even the Angel of Death does not have permission to pass through it to the other side of this river, and proof of this is in the verse, as it is written here: 'No galley with oars can travel' and as it was written there: 'Then Satan answered the Lord and said: From going to and fro the earth and from walking up and down in it' (Job 1:7). Even Satan, who is also the Angel of Death, cannot cross through this river."—Talmud Yoma 77b:16

THE BOOK OF REVELATION tells us many things about Satan that we don't see elsewhere in the Bible. We are well acquainted with the actions of our "adversary" (*Satan*, הַשָּׂטָן) who seeks his own glory and not God's, who tempts us to disobey God, who lies to us trying to convince us of how self-important and righteous we are, just like the lies he apparently tells himself. He believes he is so wonderful that everyone should worship him, and tempts us to believe we are also so wonderful people should honor us. He believes he is so powerful that he can even wage war against the Messiah, and tempts us to believe we are so powerful we don't need God either. He knows the scriptures, he knows Jesus, and he rejects them both, and tempts us to reject the Word and Jesus also. He has a self-delusion and wants us to be just like him. He is the father of lies and shoots flaming arrows of temptation at our hearts, minds, and souls.

A SEQUENCE OF EVENTS

Just like the Bible reveals more and more about the Messiah over time, it also reveals more and more about Satan over time. From the promise in the Garden of Eden that the head of Satan would be crushed (Gen 3:15), to seeing the actions of the devil roaming the earth tempting and devouring people (Job 1:7,2:2, 1 Pet 5:8), to the revelations of the extent of his power and influence over the world as seen throughout the New Testament, to his final defeat in the book of Revelation, we have an evolving picture of his character throughout history. The culmination of all this is his final defeat, which only occurs in one place in the entire Bible.

> "10 And the devil who deceived them was thrown into the lake of fire and brimstone, where the beast and the false prophet are also; and they will be tormented day and night forever and ever." (Rev 20:10, NASB)

We have numerous references to the defeat of Satan throughout the Bible, but it actually only occurs in one place. This singularity, an event which only occurs one time, marks the shift from the world as we know it to the New Heaven and New Earth which follows in Revelation chapters 21 and 22. Notice that in this single event we also have a distinguishing between Satan and the beast and the false prophet. According to the scriptures, the beast is not Satan. Neither is the false prophet. They get their inspiration and power from Satan, but all the verses which speak of the beast are not referring to Satan himself. Also notice that there is sequence of events in Revelation leading up to the defeat of Satan:

1. War breaks out in heaven after the Messiah is taken up into Heaven (Rev 12:7),
2. Satan loses and is cast out of Heaven (Rev 12:9,12),
3. Satan is then enraged and wages war against the believers of Jesus (Rev 12:17),
4. Satan deceives the nations and is eventually thrown into the Abyss for one thousand years (Rev 20:2–3),
5. after one thousand years Satan is released and once again deceives the nations (Rev 20:7–8),
6. Satan leads a final attack on Jerusalem, leading the armies of the world (Rev 20:8–9),
7. Satan is finally defeated and thrown into the lake of burning sulfur (Rev 20:9–10),
8. Satan will be tormented day and night for ever and ever (Rev 20:10).

> "And there was war in heaven, Michael and his angels waging war with the dragon. The dragon and his angels waged war," (Rev 12:7, NASB)

> "And the great dragon was thrown down, the serpent of old who is called the devil and Satan, who deceives the whole world; he was thrown down to the earth, and his angels were thrown down with him." (Rev 12:9, NASB)

> "For this reason, rejoice, O heavens and you who dwell in them. Woe to the earth and the sea, because the devil has come down to you, having great wrath, knowing that he has only a short time." (Rev 12:12, NASB)

"So the dragon was enraged with the woman, and went off to make war with the rest of her children, who keep the commandments of God and hold to the testimony of Jesus." (Rev 12:17, NASB)

"2 And he laid hold of the dragon, the serpent of old, who is the devil and Satan, and bound him for a thousand years; 3 and he threw him into the abyss, and shut it and sealed it over him, so that he would not deceive the nations any longer, until the thousand years were completed; after these things he must be released for a short time." (Rev 20:2–3, NASB)

"7 When the thousand years are completed, Satan will be released from his prison, 8 and will come out to deceive the nations which are in the four corners of the earth, Gog and Magog, to gather them together for the war; the number of them is like the sand of the seashore. 9 And they came up on the broad plain of the earth and surrounded the camp of the saints and the beloved city, and fire came down from heaven and devoured them. 10 And the devil who deceived them was thrown into the lake of fire and brimstone, where the beast and the false prophet are also; and they will be tormented day and night forever and ever." (Rev 20:7–10, NASB)

THE TIME OF GREATEST DISTRESS

Notice that it is the Archangel Michael who leads the war against Satan in Heaven (Rev 12:7). Michael is only seen fighting in one other place inside scripture, in the book of Daniel.

"Now at that time Michael, the great prince who stands guard over the sons of your people, will arise. And there will be a time of distress such as never occurred since there was a nation until that time; and at that time your people, everyone who is found written in the book, will be rescued. 2 Many of those who sleep in the dust of the ground will awake, these to everlasting life, but the others to disgrace and everlasting contempt. 3 Those who have insight will shine brightly like the brightness of the expanse of heaven, and those who lead the many to righteousness, like the stars forever and ever. 4 But as for you, Daniel, conceal these words and seal up the book until the end of time; many will go back and forth, and knowledge will increase." (Dan 12:1–4, NASB)

Daniel describes a time of great distress for the people of Israel, unlike anything that has happened before. This would be worse than the European Pogroms or the Holocaust. But Michael will protect Israel and then the resurrection of the dead and final judgment will follow. Some will rise to everlasting life, others to shame and everlasting contempt. Daniel sees the time of the end as the worst time of distress for Israel, unlike anything ever seen before in history. This ends with a battle where the

Archangel Michael protects Israel, followed by the resurrection of the dead to final judgment.

In Revelation, after the Messiah is taken up into Heaven John sees war break out there. Michael fights against Satan and Satan is cast out. Satan roams the world deceiving the nations and is eventually bound in the Abyss for one thousand years. Afterward Satan is released and once again deceives the nations. Then Satan leads the nations of the world in a final attack on Jerusalem. John sees Satan finally defeated and thrown into the lake of burning sulfur, followed by the resurrection of the dead to the final judgment.

> Daniel and John both see the Archangel Michael in their visions. They both see a time of the greatest distress for Jerusalem as being followed by the resurrection of the dead and the final judgment. As the resurrection of the dead and the final judgment have not happened yet, neither has this final attack on Jerusalem happened.

Daniel and John both see the Archangel Michael in their visions. They both see a time of the greatest distress for Jerusalem as being followed by the resurrection of the dead and the final judgment. As the resurrection of the dead and the final judgment have not happened yet, neither has this final attack on Jerusalem happened. However, in this final attack, the time of greatest distress for Israel, the Archangel Michael will protect and defend Jerusalem. And then Satan will finally be defeated, followed by the resurrection of the dead and the final judgment.

VIEWS OF THE RAPTURE

When Jesus was questioned by his Disciples about the time of the end, he quoted from the book of Daniel (Mark 13:14). Jesus spoke of a terrible distress, days unequaled to anything that has ever happened before, a time of tribulation unmatched from the beginning of creation.

> "For those days will be a time of tribulation such as has not occurred since the beginning of the creation which God created until now, and never will." (Mark 13:19, NASB)

Following that distress the Messiah will appear. Jesus quotes from Isaiah (Isa 13:10, 34:4) and references Daniel's prophecy that the Messiah will appear on the clouds in glory at the final judgment (Dan 7:9–14).

> "24 'But in those days, after that tribulation, the sun will be darkened and the moon will not give its light, 25 and the stars will be falling from heaven, and the powers that are in the heavens will be shaken. 26 Then they will see the Son of Man coming in clouds with great power and glory. 27 And then He will send forth the angels, and will gather together His elect from the four

winds, from the farthest end of the earth to the farthest end of heaven." (Mark 13:24–27, NASB)

"9 Behold, the day of the Lord is coming, cruel, with fury and burning anger, to make the land a desolation; and He will exterminate its sinners from it. 10 For the stars of heaven and their constellations will not flash forth their light; the sun will be dark when it rises and the moon will not shed its light. 11 Thus I will punish the world for its evil and the wicked for their iniquity; I will also put an end to the arrogance of the proud and abase the haughtiness of the ruthless. 12 I will make mortal man scarcer than pure gold and mankind than the gold of Ophir. 13 Therefore I will make the heavens tremble, and the earth will be shaken from its place at the fury of the Lord of hosts in the day of His burning anger." (Isa 13:9–13, NASB)

"Draw near, O nations, to hear; and listen, O peoples! Let the earth and all it contains hear, and the world and all that springs from it. 2 For the Lord's indignation is against all the nations, and His wrath against all their armies; he has utterly destroyed them, he has given them over to slaughter. 3 So their slain will be thrown out, and their corpses will give off their stench, and the mountains will be drenched with their blood. 4 And all the host of heaven will wear away, and the sky will be rolled up like a scroll; all their hosts will also wither away as a leaf withers from the vine, or as one withers from the fig tree." (Isa 34:1–4, NASB)

The testimony of Daniel, the testimony of John, and most importantly the testimony of Jesus is that there will be a time of great distress for Israel, worse than anything that has happened since the beginning of creation. God is angry at the nations. They have gathered together for a final attack on Jerusalem, and she suffers the greatest distress ever before seen. Jesus says he will return on the clouds in glory after the time of the greatest distress, which has never been seen before on the earth. At his appearance the angels will gather his elect.

> Jesus says he will return on the clouds in glory after the time of the greatest distress, which has never been seen before on the earth. At his appearance the angels will gather his elect.

There are a variety of interpretations about when Jesus returns and how that fits into this overall sequence of events. The timing of the return of Jesus in relation to "the greatest distress" gives different popular theological views: Pre–Trib (before), Mid–Trib (during), or Post–Trib (after). Explanations also vary according to the timing of the millennium. A view which holds that Jesus returns before this time of greatest distress (tribulation) and gathers his elect is called a "Pre-Tribulation Rapture" view. A view that holds Jesus returns after the distress of those days and takes up his followers is a "Post–Tribulation Rapture" view. And a view that a rapture happens somewhere in the middle of the distress (during those days) is a "Mid–Tribulation Rapture" view.

These views of a rapture are also usually associated with the view that Jesus reigns for one thousand years after the beast is defeated, known as a Pre-Millennial view (Jesus returns before the one-thousand-year period begins). The Pre-, Mid-, and Post-Tribulation Rapture views are typically also Pre-Millennial.

> The timing of the return of Jesus in relation to "the greatest distress" gives different popular theological views: Pre-Trib (before), Mid-Trib (during), or Post-Trib (after). Explanations also vary according to the timing of the millennium.

The distress of the beast leading the nations of the world in a final attack on Jerusalem, and setting himself up in the Temple to be worshiped as god, is the moment when it all breaks down. Jesus appears on the clouds in glory and gathers his elect. The beast wages war against the Messiah in the valley of Armageddon and is defeated. And then a period of one thousand years of peaceful rule by Christ with the resurrected martyrs of the beast ensues.

At the heart of interpretation differences is identifying who the elect are which are gathered together with Jesus at his appearance. Are those gathered the ones alive on the earth at the time Jesus returns, the ones who were martyred before his arrival, all believers in Jesus throughout history?

> "26 Then they will see the Son of Man coming in clouds with great power and glory. 27 And then He will send forth the angels, and will gather together His elect from the four winds, from the farthest end of the earth to the farthest end of heaven." (Mark 13:26–27, NASB)

> "13 But we do not want you to be uninformed, brethren, about those who are asleep, so that you will not grieve as do the rest who have no hope. 14 For if we believe that Jesus died and rose again, even so God will bring with Him those who have fallen asleep in Jesus. 15 For this we say to you by the word of the Lord, that we who are alive and remain until the coming of the Lord, will not precede those who have fallen asleep. 16 For the Lord Himself will descend from heaven with a shout, with the voice of the archangel and with the trumpet of God, and the dead in Christ will rise first. 17 Then we who are alive and remain will be caught up together with them in the clouds to meet the Lord in the air, and so we shall always be with the Lord. 18 Therefore comfort one another with these words." (1 Thess 4:13–18, NASB)

Note that in verse 1 Thess 4:17 Paul uses a conjugation of the Greek word *harpazo* (ἁρπάζω), which is translated as "caught up" in most English translations. Paul also uses this word to describe someone he knew who was "caught up to the third heaven" (2 Cor 12:2–4). Luke uses this word to describe how the Holy Spirit suddenly took Philip away after he baptized the Ethiopian official (Acts 8:39). And the word also appears, of course, in the book of Revelation. It is used to describe how the Messiah was snatched up into Heaven (Rev 12:5). The word is used fourteen times in the Greek New Testament in various ways. In the Latin Vulgate Jerome used the Latin word *rapiemur* in his translation of 1 Thess 4:17, from which we get the modern English word "rapture."

> "1 Now we request you, brethren, with regard to the coming of our Lord Jesus Christ and our gathering together to Him, 2 that you not be quickly shaken from your composure or be disturbed either by a spirit or a message or a letter as if from us, to the effect that the day of the Lord has come. 3 Let no one in any way deceive you, for it will not come unless the apostasy comes first, and the man of lawlessness is revealed, the son of destruction, 4 who opposes and exalts himself above every so-called god or object of worship, so that he takes his seat in the temple of God, displaying himself as being God." (2 Thess 2:1–4, NASB)

> "8 Then that lawless one will be revealed whom the Lord will slay with the breath of His mouth and bring to an end by the appearance of His coming; 9 that is, the one whose coming is in accord with the activity of Satan, with all power and signs and false wonders, 10 and with all the deception of wickedness for those who perish, because they did not receive the love of the truth so as to be saved. 11 For this reason God will send upon them a deluding influence so that they will believe what is false, 12 in order that they all may be judged who did not believe the truth, but took pleasure in wickedness." (2 Thess 2:8–12, NASB)

The view that this is a rapture of the church happening when Christ appears to defeat the beast, but before the one-thousand-year period after the beast is defeated, is a Pre-Millennial view. Seeing that the elect are gathered at his appearance begs the question of when the appearance is in relation to the tribulation, the greatest time of distress. In the scriptures he appears "after the distress," but "in those days." So the theological arguments for the timing of the Rapture include Pre-Trib Pre-Millennial (when the Messiah appears, before the beast wages war against the Messiah), Pre-Trib Post-Millennial (before the distress of the attack by Satan after the one thousand years are over), Post-Trib Pre-Millennial (after the distress of the attack by the beast, but before the one thousand years), and many more. This leads to the question of which tribulation, which time of distress are we talking about? The distress of the beast attacking Jerusalem before the one-thousand-year period, or the attack of Jerusalem by Satan after the one thousand period?

Further compounding the argument are Paul's letters to the Thessalonians that describe the resurrection of all the believers in Christ at his appearance. Yet the book of Revelation clearly speaks of two different resurrections. The resurrection of the martyrs of the beast before the one-thousand-year period, and the resurrection of all the dead after the one-thousand-year period (Rev 20:1–5, 12–13). Theologians argue that if the elect are gathered to Christ at his appearance before the one-thousand-year period when he reigns over the earth, then those elect cannot include all believers because the rest of the dead are not resurrected until after the one thousand years. A counter argument is that all believers are resurrected at the first resurrection before the one thousand years and the church reigns with Christ during the Millennium. Only the unbelievers are resurrected after the one thousand years. Again, a counter-counterargument to that is that the scriptures say the first group resurrected are only (and exclusively) martyrs (Rev 20:4-5). Yet Paul makes no distinction between martyred believers and other believers in his letters to the church at Thessalonica, but instead speaks only of a single resurrection of the dead. Given all this, some theologians teach that Jesus returns twice, a Second Coming for the rapture and a Third Coming for the final judgment. You can see just how complex the arguments about the rapture are.

Allegorical interpretations say these are all spiritual references only. Believers are spiritually raised up with Christ when they come to faith. Believers currently reign with Christ now (him above, us below). There is no literal Millennium, no literal rapture, and no literal final attack on Jerusalem. The first resurrection is the regeneration of your soul upon belief in Christ. We are raised to new life through the waters of Baptism. We put away the old person and are born again to new life. The second resurrection is the general and bodily resurrection of all to final judgment. There will be nothing visible on the earth as everything is happening invisibly in Heaven.

The Sola Scriptura approach will hold only to what the scriptures directly say. There will be a time of great distress for Israel, unlike anything ever seen before. The beast will lead the nations to attack Jerusalem. After the distress of those days the Messiah will appear on the clouds in glory and gather his elect. The beast will wage war against Christ and lose. Afterward there will be a period of one thousand years of peaceful rule by Christ. After the one thousand years Satan will lead the nations of the world to attack Jerusalem but he will be defeated. And then the second resurrection will occur, the resurrection of all the dead. Some will rise to everlasting life, and others to everlasting shame and contempt.

WHAT DID WE LEARN ABOUT SATAN?

As we look across the span of the Bible, we see that Satan and his power is revealed more and more over time, from the temptation in the Garden of Eden all the way to leading the nations of the world to fight against God, and ultimately to his final defeat. We see that there is a sequence of events from Satan being cast out of Heaven to ultimately being thrown into the lake of burning sulfur, where he will be tormented day and night forever.

In Revelation we learn of a great battle in Heaven where the Archangel Michael leads angels in battle against Satan and his angels. This happens after the Messiah is taken up into Heaven. After Satan is cast out, he comes down to the earth full of wrath and fury, seeking to punish the followers of the Messiah. In our examination of Daniel, we see that the Archangel Michael protects Israel during a time of great distress. This is the greatest distress Israel ever had since creation. After this greatest time of distress, we see the resurrection of the dead and the final judgment. Likewise in the book of Revelation we see the resurrection of the dead and the final judgment just after Satan is finally defeated after attacking Jerusalem. Since the resurrection of the dead and the final judgment have not happened yet, neither has this final attack on Jerusalem.

Interestingly, after the beast who is inspired by the devil is defeated, Satan is not immediately defeated. Instead, he is thrown into the Abyss for one thousand years while the martyrs of the time of the beast reign with Christ for one thousand years of peace. And then after the one thousand years are over Satan is released and once again deceives the nations of the world. He inspires them to attack Jerusalem but again God delivers the city. Then Satan is ultimately defeated, being thrown into the lake of burning sulfur where the beast and the false prophet had previously been thrown after their defeat.

#	Truth Claim	Primary Support	Secondary Support
11.1	Satan leads the whole world astray.	Rev 12:9	1 Pet 5:8, Matt 4:10, Gen 3:1,13–14
11.2	Satan was cast out of Heaven to the Earth.	Rev 12:7–12	Luke 10:18, Isa 14:12, Ezek 28:12–19
11.3	Satan is the accuser.	Rev 12:10	Rev 13:6, Gen 3:4–5, Job 1:9–11,2:4, Zech 3:1
11.4	Satan will be defeated.	Rev 20:10	Rev 12:10,12, Rom 16:20, Jude 1:6, Matt 25:41–46, Gen 3:15, Isa 24:21–23, Dan 7:26
11.5	We triumph over Satan by the blood of the Lamb and the word of our testimony.	Rev 12:11	Rev 2:10,13, 6:9, 7:14, 15:2, 1 John 2:13
11.6	The time of the devil on earth is short.	Rev 12:12	Rev 3:11, 1 Cor 7:29, Matt 8:29
11.7	The dead will be resurrected and receive eternal judgment.	Rev 20:11–15	Rev 2:11, 3:5, 11:18, 14:10, 20:6, John 5:24–29, Jude 1:14–15,23, Luke 10:20, 14:14, 1 Thes 4:16, Matt 16:27, 19:28, 25:41–46, 1 Cor 15:20–57, Dan 7:9–10, 12:2–3, Isa 26:19–21, Ps 69:28

12

Revelations About the Beast

"At the beginning of the sixth millennium, there will arise the rulership of a controlling, fearful and violent nation, and one that comes closer to the truth than the first ones."—Maimonides

THE BEAST OF REVELATION is possibly the most famous part of the book of Revelation. Who or what is the beast, and what does it mean that the number of the beast is 666? Below we will look at what the Sola Scriptura approach has to offer, looking at only what the scriptures have to say. But to give you an idea of how important the method of interpretation used is, below are some popular views of who or what the beast is claimed to represent. The beast has been said by theologians to be:

- All antichristian governments throughout history
- All religions and philosophies opposed to Christianity
- The beast that we each become when we don't follow God
- The entire Roman Catholic Papal system (all Popes)
- Hellenistic King Antiochus Epiphanes
- Roman Emperor Nero Caesar
- Roman Emperor Titus
- Pope Leo X
- A specific future pope
- Germany's Adolf Hitler
- Italy's Mussolini
- China's President Xi Jinping

- Russia's President Vladimir Putin
- A future leader of the European Union
- And many others...

Where do these various interpretations come from? As you should expect, they essentially boil down to our two fundamental questions we've explored throughout this book. Explanations for the beast range from an abstract concept like "all governments throughout history" to specific named individuals like Nero or Hitler. This range of views comes from the method of interpretation: literal vs. allegorical, and timing.

> Explanations for the beast range from an abstract concept like "all governments throughout history" to specific named individuals like Nero or Hitler. This range of views comes from the method of interpretation: literal vs. allegorical, and timing.

Allegorical interpretations say that the symbols used in Revelation, such as the beast, mean something other than what the plain sense of the text says. For example, although Rev 17:11 says that the beast is a specific king, and Rev 13:18 says the beast is a man, the allegorical interpretations say the beast is a system, government, or philosophy. An allegorical interpretation looks at the beast, which has similarity to the different beasts in the book of Daniel, and suggests that since the beast of Revelation is like a composite of multiple beasts in Daniel, then the beast represents multiple kingdoms.

The literal interpretation holds that the beast is a man, because that is what the scriptures actually say. Nowhere in the Bible is the beast said to be a philosophy, a religion, or a government, let alone multiple governments throughout all space and time. John is told directly that the beast is a man several times. A literal interpretation would go further to say that the beasts in Daniel are kingdoms that were yet to come because of the context when Daniel lived. He lived in the time of the first kingdom, Babylon, and its fall to the second kingdom, Persia. His vision of beasts included kingdoms still to come. Yet John lived at a much later time than Daniel. When Revelation was written, three of the kingdoms (Babylon, Medo–Persia, and Greece) had already passed, and the fourth kingdom (Rome) was in power. So, the vision of the beast to John looked different than in Daniel's vision because of this difference in point of time in writing, which explains the composite nature of the later vision.

Thus, the allegorical interpretation takes an approach of intellectual development (rationalization) to create assumptions about what the text means, while the literal approach holds only to what the text directly and plainly says. Moreover, the literal approach firmly places the text within its original context, how the original audience would have understood the text. You can see this really big difference in the above interpretations by those which say the beast is a system or more abstract concepts, versus those which say the beast is a specific person. The allegorical interpretation says the beast is a system of multiple kingdoms, not a man. The Bible says the beast is a man (Rev 13:18), a specific king in a succession of kings (Rev 17:11).

> The allegorical interpretation says the beast is a system of multiple kingdoms, not a man. The Bible says the beast is a man (Rev 13:18), a specific king in a succession of kings (Rev 17:11).

The next challenging interpretive question is timing. Since the events described in Revelation seem to possibly fit different time periods, like the persecution of Israel by the Seleucids, Romans, or Arabs, some interpretations see the events in Revelation as only in the past. Other interpretations point out that not all the details in the prophecies fit any past period exactly, so they are future events. And yet other interpretations hold that the events happen both in the past as a shadow of things to come, as well as in the future. Thus, you see governments of the past and even the future suggested above, as well as specific historical people (both present day people and unnamed future leaders).

What does the Sola Scriptura approach propose? It says we only look at what the scriptures say. Nowhere in the scriptures does it say the beast is a government system, philosophy, or antichristian religion. Nowhere in the scriptures does it give a name for the beast, neither a historical figure like Antiochus Epiphanes who lived before John wrote Revelation, nor a future named individual. Sola Scriptura would not name the Roman Catholic Papal system, Antiochus, Nero, Titus, Hitler, nor Putin, because the Bible does not name them. Only denominational interpretations, and sometimes political expediency, seem to do so.

For example, Martin Luther said that the beast was a specific person. In his commentary on the Bible, Martin named Pope Leo X as the Antichrist. Since Pope Leo X does not seem to have been thrown into a lake of fire by God, wars continue to this day, and Christ does not yet reign from a New Jerusalem in a New Heaven and a New Earth where all nations, people, tribes, and tongues come to honor him, then the scriptures are yet not completely fulfilled, and the Antichrist could not have been Pope Leo X. Yet Martin Luther was trying to reform the Roman Catholic church from within and ultimately could not do so. Pope Leo X excommunicated Martin Luther on January 3, 1521. It seemed to Martin that the battle with Christ was at hand, and the devil was empowering the Pope to teach unscriptural traditions. Politically, naming your opponent as the Antichrist certainly is effective in calling people to your side of a debate. For as much as Protestants love the Reformation, on the point of the Antichrist Luther was clearly wrong. Let's look closely at the relevant passages relating to this figure of the Antichrist.

Reference	Scripture (NIV)
Rev 13:18	This calls for wisdom. Let the person who has insight calculate the number of the beast, for *it is the number of a man.*
2 Thess 2:1–4	1 Concerning the coming of our Lord Jesus Christ and our being gathered to him, we ask you, brothers and sisters, 2 not to become easily unsettled or alarmed by the teaching allegedly from us—whether by a prophecy or by word of mouth or by letter—asserting that the day of the Lord has already come. 3 Don't let anyone deceive you in any way, for that day will not come until the rebellion occurs and *the man of lawlessness is revealed, the man doomed to destruction.* 4 He will oppose and will exalt himself over everything that is called God or is worshiped, so that he sets himself up in God's temple, proclaiming himself to be God.
Rev 17:11–14	11 *The beast who once was, and now is not, is an eighth king.* He belongs to the seven and is going to his destruction. 12 The ten horns you saw are ten kings who have not yet received a kingdom, but who for one hour will receive authority as kings along with the beast. 13 They have one purpose and will give their power and authority to the beast. 14 They will wage war against the Lamb, but the Lamb will triumph over them because he is Lord of lords and King of kings—and with him will be his called, chosen and faithful followers.
Dan 8:23–25	23 In the latter part of their reign, when rebels have become completely wicked, *a fierce-looking king, a master of intrigue, will arise.* 24 He will become very strong, but not by his own power. He will cause astounding devastation and will succeed in whatever he does. He will destroy those who are mighty, the holy people. 25 He will cause deceit to prosper, and he will consider himself superior. When they feel secure, he will destroy many and take his stand against the Prince of princes. Yet he will be destroyed, but not by human power.
Dan 7:17	*The four great beasts are four kings* that will rise from the earth.
Dan 7:23–27	23 "He gave me this explanation: 'The fourth beast is a fourth kingdom that will appear on earth. It will be different from all the other kingdoms and will devour the whole earth, trampling it down and crushing it. 24 *The ten horns are ten kings who will come from this kingdom. After them another king will arise*, different from the earlier ones; he will subdue three kings. 25 He will speak against the Most High and oppress his holy people and try to change the set times and the laws. The holy people will be delivered into his hands for a time, times and half a time. 26 But the court will sit, and his power will be taken away and completely destroyed forever. 27 Then the sovereignty, power and greatness of all the kingdoms under heaven will be handed over to the holy people of the Most High. His kingdom will be an everlasting kingdom, and all rulers will worship and obey him.

These passages speak of a specific man, a man of lawlessness, a man opposed to God, an eighth king in a succession of kings. If you refer back to the section on the book of Daniel, you'll recall that the Sola Scriptura method showed that Daniel speaks of a progression of specific kingdoms leading up to the Messianic Kingdom. From Babylon, which is Nebuchadnezzar, to the fourth kingdom of Rome, there are specific prophecies. Medo–Persia and Greece are specifically named as kingdoms that are represented by beasts. The kingdom of Rome was not yet a kingdom at the time of Daniel. From the fourth kingdom (Rome) come ten other kings. From them one king arises that subdues three others. This eighth king is the Antichrist, the man of lawlessness. The Bible plainly says the beast is a man, a man opposed to God, an eighth king in a line of succession, who leads many nations to wage war against the Messiah. He will oppress the people of God, be defeated, and then the everlasting Messianic kingdom will ensue.

> The Bible plainly says the beast is a man, a man opposed to God, an eighth king in a line of succession, who leads many nations to wage war against the Messiah. He will oppress the people of God, be defeated, and then the everlasting Messianic kingdom will ensue.

WHAT DOES THE BEAST ACTUALLY DO?

What does this Beast do? He rises to worldwide power and has authority for forty-two months. This forty-two months is forty-two months of the Hebrew lunar calendar (thirty) days, or 42x30 = 1,260 days. Forty-two months is three and a half years, or a time of one year, plus two times of a year, plus a half a year. Or a time, times, and half a time. Also, three and a half is half of seven. Notice how this same time period shows up numerous times in prophecy. In each of these cases either God is protecting his servants, or the Antichrist is reigning and oppressing the people of God.

Reference	Scripture (NIV)
Rev 13:5	The beast was given a mouth to utter proud words and blasphemies and *to exercise its authority for forty-two months.*
Rev 11:2–3	2 But exclude the outer court; do not measure it, because it has been given to *the Gentiles. They will trample on the holy city for 42 months.* 3 And I will appoint *my two witnesses,* and *they will prophesy for 1,260 days,* clothed in sackcloth."
Rev 12:4–6	4 Its tail swept a third of the stars out of the sky and flung them to the earth. The dragon stood in front of the woman who was about to give birth, so that it might devour her child the moment he was born. 5 She gave birth to a son, a male child, who "will rule all the nations with an iron scepter." And her child was snatched up to God and to his throne. 6 The woman fled into the wilderness to a place prepared for her by God, *where she might be taken care of for 1,260 days.*
Rev 12:14	The woman was given the two wings of a great eagle, so that she might fly to the place prepared for her in the wilderness, where *she would be taken care of for a time, times and half a time,* out of the serpent's reach.

Reference	Scripture (NIV)
Dan 7:23-25	23 "He gave me this explanation: 'The fourth beast is a fourth kingdom that will appear on earth. It will be different from all the other kingdoms and will devour the whole earth, trampling it down and crushing it. 24 The ten horns are ten kings who will come from this kingdom. After them another king will arise, different from the earlier ones; he will subdue three kings. 25 He will speak against the Most High and oppress his holy people and try to change the set times and the laws. The holy people will be delivered into his hands for *a time, times and half a time.*
Dan 9:27	He will confirm a covenant with many for *one 'seven.'* In the middle of the *'seven'* he will put an end to sacrifice and offering. And at the temple he will set up an abomination that causes desolation, until the end that is decreed is poured out on him."
Dan 12:7	The man clothed in linen, who was above the waters of the river, lifted his right hand and his left hand toward heaven, and I heard him swear by him who lives forever, saying, *"It will be for a time, times and half a time. When the power of the holy people has been finally broken, all these things will be completed."*

From the scriptures directly we learn that this blasphemous man is given authority to rule, and he will use that authority to oppress the people of God. This will last until the power of the holy people has finally been broken. During his reign, he will lead a coalition of nations to attack Jerusalem. He wages war against the Lamb and is defeated.

Scripture	Reference (NIV)
Rev 16:14-16	14 They are demonic spirits that perform signs, and they go out to the kings of the whole world, *to gather them for the battle on the great day of God Almighty.* 15 "Look, I come like a thief! Blessed is the one who stays awake and remains clothed, so as not to go naked and be shamefully exposed." 16 *Then they gathered the kings together to the place that in Hebrew is called Armageddon.*
Rev 17:11-14	11 The beast who once was, and now is not, is an eighth king. He belongs to the seven and is going to his destruction. 12 "The ten horns you saw are ten kings who have not yet received a kingdom, but who for one hour will receive authority as kings along with the beast. 13 They have one purpose and will give their power and authority to the beast. 14 *They will wage war against the Lamb,* but the Lamb will triumph over them because he is Lord of lords and King of kings—and with him will be his called, chosen and faithful followers."
Rev 19:19-20	19 Then I saw *the beast and the kings of the earth and their armies gathered together to wage war against the rider on the horse and his army.* 20 But the beast was captured, and with it the false prophet who had performed the signs on its behalf. With these signs he had deluded those who had received the mark of the beast and worshiped its image. The two of them were thrown alive into the fiery lake of burning sulfur. (NIV)

Scripture	Reference (NIV)
Dan 7:19-22	19 Then I wanted to know the meaning of the fourth beast, which was different from all the others and most terrifying, with its iron teeth and bronze claws—the beast that crushed and devoured its victims and trampled underfoot whatever was left. 20 I also wanted to know about the ten horns on its head and about the other horn that came up, before which three of them fell—the horn that looked more imposing than the others and that had eyes and a mouth that spoke boastfully. 21 As I watched, *this horn was waging war against the holy people and defeating them, 22 until the Ancient of Days came and pronounced judgment in favor of the holy people of the Most High, and the time came when they possessed the kingdom.*
Dan 9:27	He will confirm a covenant with many for one 'seven.' *In the middle of the 'seven' he will put an end to sacrifice and offering. And at the temple he will set up an abomination that causes desolation, until the end that is decreed is poured out on him."*
Dan 2:44-45	44 *"In the time of those kings, the God of heaven will set up a kingdom that will never be destroyed, nor will it be left to another people. It will crush all those kingdoms and bring them to an end, but it will itself endure forever.* 45 This is the meaning of the vision of the rock cut out of a mountain, but not by human hands—a rock that broke the iron, the bronze, the clay, the silver and the gold to pieces.
Dan 11:36, 40-45	36 *The king will do as he pleases. He will exalt and magnify himself above every god and will say unheard-of things against the God of gods. He will be successful until the time of wrath is completed, for what has been determined must take place.* 40 *At the time of the end the king of the South will engage him in battle*, and the king of the North will storm out against him with chariots and cavalry and a great fleet of ships. He will invade many countries and sweep through them like a flood. 41 *He will also invade the Beautiful Land.* Many countries will fall, but Edom, Moab and the leaders of Ammon will be delivered from his hand. 42 He will extend his power over many countries; Egypt will not escape. 43 He will gain control of the treasures of gold and silver and all the riches of Egypt, with the Libyans and Cushites in submission. 44 But reports from the east and the north will alarm him, and he will set out in a great rage to destroy and annihilate many. 45 *He will pitch his royal tents between the seas at the beautiful holy mountain.* Yet he will come to his end, and no one will help him.
Dan 8:21-25	21 The shaggy goat is the king of Greece, and the large horn between its eyes is the first king. 22 The four horns that replaced the one that was broken off represent four kingdoms that will emerge from his nation but will not have the same power. 23 In the latter part of their reign, when rebels have become completely wicked, a fierce-looking king, a master of intrigue, will arise. 24 He will become very strong, but not by his own power. He will cause astounding devastation and will succeed in whatever he does. *He will destroy those who are mighty, the holy people.* 25 He will cause deceit to prosper, and he will consider himself superior. When they feel secure, *he will destroy many and take his stand against the Prince of princes.* Yet he will be destroyed, but not by human power. (NIV)

Revelations About the Beast

Scripture	Reference (NIV)
Dan 12:7	The man clothed in linen, who was above the waters of the river, lifted his right hand and his left hand toward heaven, and I heard him swear by him who lives forever, saying, "*It will be for a time, times and half a time. When the power of the holy people has been finally broken, all these things will be completed.*"
Zech 12:3	*On that day, when all the nations of the earth are gathered against her*, I will make Jerusalem an immovable rock for all the nations. All who try to move it will injure themselves.
Zech 12:7–10	7 The Lord will save the dwellings of Judah first, so that the honor of the house of David and of Jerusalem's inhabitants may not be greater than that of Judah. 8 *On that day the Lord will shield those who live in Jerusalem*, so that the feeblest among them will be like David, and the house of David will be like God, like the angel of the Lord going before them. 9 *On that day I will set out to destroy all the nations that attack Jerusalem.* 10 And I will pour out on the house of David and the inhabitants of Jerusalem a spirit of grace and supplication. *They will look on me, the one they have pierced*, and they will mourn for him as one mourns for an only child, and grieve bitterly for him as one grieves for a firstborn son.
Joel 2:1–3	1 Blow the trumpet in Zion; sound the alarm on my holy hill. Let all who live in the land tremble, for *the day of the Lord is coming*. It is close at hand— 2 a day of darkness and gloom, a day of clouds and blackness. *Like dawn spreading across the mountains a large and mighty army comes, such as never was in ancient times nor ever will be in ages to come.*
Joel 2:18–20	18 *Then the Lord was jealous for his land and took pity on his people.* 19 The Lord replied to them: "I am sending you grain, new wine and olive oil, enough to satisfy you fully; *never again will I make you an object of scorn to the nations.* 20 *I will drive the northern horde far from you*, pushing it into a parched and barren land; its eastern ranks will drown in the Dead Sea and its western ranks in the Mediterranean Sea. And its stench will go up; its smell will rise." Surely he has done great things!
Joel 3:1–2	1 In those days and at that time, when I restore the fortunes of Judah and Jerusalem, 2 *I will gather all nations and bring them down to the Valley of Jehoshaphat. There I will put them on trial for what they did to my inheritance, my people Israel*, because they scattered my people among the nations and divided up my land.
Joel 3:14–16	14 *Multitudes, multitudes in the valley of decision! For the day of the Lord is near in the valley of decision.* 15 The sun and moon will be darkened, and the stars no longer shine. 16 The Lord will roar from Zion and thunder from Jerusalem; the earth and the heavens will tremble. *But the Lord will be a refuge for his people, a stronghold for the people of Israel.* 17 Then you will know that I, the Lord your God, dwell in Zion, my holy hill. Jerusalem will be holy; *never again will foreigners invade her.* (NIV)

Scripture	Reference (NIV)
Rev 20:7–10	7 When the thousand years are over, Satan will be released from his prison 8 and will go out to deceive the nations in the four corners of the earth—*Gog and Magog*—*and to gather them for battle*. In number they are like the sand on the seashore. 9 They marched across the breadth of the earth and *surrounded the camp of God's people, the city he loves*. But fire came down from heaven and devoured them. 10 And the devil, who deceived them, was thrown into the lake of burning sulfur, where the beast and the false prophet had been thrown. They will be tormented day and night for ever and ever.
Ezek 38:7–9	7 Get ready; be prepared, *you and all the hordes gathered about you*, and take command of them. 8 After many days you will be called to arms. *In future years you will invade a land that has recovered from war, whose people were gathered from many nations to the mountains of Israel, which had long been desolate.* They had been brought out from the nations, and now all of them live in safety. 9 *You and all your troops and the many nations with you will go up, advancing like a storm; you will be like a cloud covering the land.*
Ezek 38:14–18	14 Therefore, son of man, prophesy and say to Gog: 'This is what the Sovereign Lord says: In that day, when my people Israel are living in safety, will you not take notice of it? 15 *You will come from your place in the far north, you and many nations with you, all of them riding on horses, a great horde, a mighty army.* 16 *You will advance against my people Israel like a cloud that covers the land.* In days to come, Gog, I will bring you against my land, so that the nations may know me when I am proved holy through you before their eyes. 17 This is what the Sovereign Lord says: *You are the one I spoke of in former days by my servants the prophets of Israel.* At that time they prophesied for years that I would bring you against them. 18 This is what will happen in that day: *When Gog attacks the land of Israel,* my hot anger will be aroused, declares the Sovereign Lord.
Ezek 39:1–5	1 Son of man, prophesy against Gog and say: 'This is what the Sovereign Lord says: I am against you, Gog, chief prince of Meshek and Tubal. 2 I will turn you around and drag you along. *I will bring you from the far north and send you against the mountains of Israel.* 3 Then I will strike your bow from your left hand and make your arrows drop from your right hand. 4 *On the mountains of Israel you will fall, you and all your troops and the nations with you.* I will give you as food to all kinds of carrion birds and to the wild animals. 5 You will fall in the open field, for I have spoken, declares the Sovereign Lord.
Ezek 39:7–8	7 I will make known my holy name among my people Israel. *I will no longer let my holy name be profaned, and the nations will know that I the Lord am the Holy One in Israel.* 8 It is coming! It will surely take place, declares the Sovereign Lord. *This is the day I have spoken of.*
Ezek 39:17–19	17 Son of man, this is what the Sovereign Lord says: *Call out to every kind of bird and all the wild animals: 'Assemble and come together from all around to the sacrifice I am preparing for you, the great sacrifice on the mountains of Israel.* There you will eat flesh and drink blood. 18 *You will eat the flesh of mighty men and drink the blood of the princes of the earth* as if they were rams and lambs, goats and bulls—all of them fattened animals from Bashan. 19 At the sacrifice I am preparing for you, you will eat fat till you are glutted and drink blood till you are drunk. (NIV)

Scripture	Reference (NIV)
Rev 19:16–19	16 On his robe and on his thigh he has this name written: KING OF KINGS AND LORD OF LORDS. 17 And I saw an angel standing in the sun, *who cried in a loud voice to all the birds flying in midair, "Come, gather together for the great supper of God, 18 so that you may eat the flesh of kings, generals, and the mighty, of horses and their riders, and the flesh of all people, free and slave, great and small." 19 Then I saw the beast and the kings of the earth and their armies gathered together to wage war against the rider on the horse and his army.*
Matt 24:14–16	14 And this gospel of the kingdom will be preached in the whole world as a testimony to all nations, and then the end will come. 15 *So when you see standing in the holy place 'the abomination that causes desolation,' spoken of through the prophet Daniel— let the reader understand—* 16 then let those who are in Judea flee to the mountains.

The context of the Hebrew prophets is clear. Daniel had multiple dreams and visions of the end. Zechariah prophesied of the end of days. Joel spoke about the final kingdom before Messiah. And Ezekiel spoke of the end of the world as we know it. All of these prophets testify to a final attack on Israel, a war against God and his Messiah. A coalition of nations are led to wage war against the Messiah. This coalition of nations is defeated, and God establishes his Eternal Messianic Kingdom.

> All of these prophets testify to a final attack on Israel, a war against God and his Messiah. A coalition of nations are led to wage war against the Messiah. This coalition of nations is defeated, and God establishes his Eternal Messianic Kingdom.

SINGULAR DEFEAT OF THE BEAST

Notice that in the book of Revelation the beast is only defeated one time. Though there are many things that happen throughout the book, there is only one single mention of his defeat.

> "19 And I saw the beast and the kings of the earth and their armies assembled to make war against Him who sat on the horse and against His army. 20 And the beast was seized, and with him the false prophet who performed the signs in his presence, by which he deceived those who had received the mark of the beast and those who worshiped his image; these two were thrown alive into the lake of fire which burns with brimstone. 21 And the rest were killed with the sword which came from the mouth of Him who sat on the horse, and all the birds were filled with their flesh." (Rev 19:19–21, NASB)

This is the only place in the book where the beast is defeated. He is thrown into the fiery lake along with the false prophet. The rest of the people following the beast are killed by the Messiah and the armies of heaven. They die but are not thrown into the lake of fire. This singular occurrence of the beast being defeated gives us an anchor for other books in the Bible. We have the defeat in both the New Testament and the Hebrew Bible. In the New Testament we find the passages below.

Reference	Scripture (NIV)
Rev 19:20	But the beast was captured, and with it the false prophet who had performed the signs on its behalf. With these signs he had deluded those who had received the mark of the beast and worshiped its image. *The two of them were thrown alive into the fiery lake of burning sulfur.*
Rev 20:10	And the devil, who deceived them, was thrown into the lake of burning sulfur, *where the beast and the false prophet had been thrown.* They will be tormented day and night for ever and ever.
Rev 16:16–17	16 Then they gathered the kings together to the place that in Hebrew is called Armageddon. 17 The seventh angel poured out his bowl into the air, and out of the temple came a loud voice from the throne, saying, "It is done!"
Rev 11:15	The seventh angel sounded his trumpet, and there were loud voices in heaven, which said: *"The kingdom of the world has become the kingdom of our Lord and of his Messiah, and he will reign for ever and ever."*
2 Thess 2:8	And then the lawless one will be revealed, *whom the Lord Jesus will overthrow with the breath of his mouth and destroy by the splendor of his coming.*

Clearly the beast is defeated and thrown into the lake of fire. Later, Satan himself is defeated and thrown into the same lake of fire. The beast is defeated by Christ in that great battle in the place called Armageddon. The coming of Christ will see the defeat of the lawless one as Paul spoke of. And then the kingdom of the world will become the kingdom of Our Lord and of his Messiah, and he will reign for ever and ever.

What do we see in the Hebrew Bible? The same thing. Here are some interesting references:

Reference	Scripture (NIV)
Dan 7:11	Then I continued to watch because of the boastful words the horn was speaking. I kept looking until *the beast was slain and its body destroyed and thrown into the blazing fire.*
Dan 7:21–22	21 As I watched, this horn was waging war against the holy people and defeating them, 22 *until the Ancient of Days came and pronounced judgment in favor of the holy people of the Most High, and the time came when they possessed the kingdom.*
Dan 7:25–27	25 He will speak against the Most High and oppress his holy people and try to change the set times and the laws. The holy people will be delivered into his hands for a time, times and half a time. 26 "'But the court will sit, and *his power will be taken away and completely destroyed forever.* 27 Then the sovereignty, power and greatness of all the kingdoms under heaven will be handed over to the holy people of the Most High. *His kingdom will be an everlasting kingdom, and all rulers will worship and obey him.'*

As we can see in all these references, Christ will be victorious over the beast and his followers. There is a singular defeat of the beast before the everlasting kingdom of the Messiah is established. This defeat happens at the coming of Christ. In those final days leading up to Christ's return there will be a worldwide leader of many nations who oppresses the people of God. That is what both the Old and New Testaments plainly say. Christ has not yet returned, all rulers do not worship and obey Christ today, and so this points to a time of future fulfillment.

> There is a singular defeat of the beast before the everlasting kingdom of the Messiah is established. This defeat happens at the coming of Christ. In those final days leading up to Christ's return there will be a worldwide leader of many nations who oppresses the people of God.

THE NUMBER OF THE BEAST

The number of the beast may be the most well-known prophecy in the book of Revelation. People all over the world know of the number 666. It has appeared in countless secular books, movies, and conspiracy theories. Many people in history have been said to have their name equal to 666. And it is ironic that Revelation presents the number with a suggestion of a hidden meaning, without supplying the actual meaning. And so the traditions of men about the meaning have multiplied like weeds in a garden.

> "15 And it was given to him to give breath to the image of the beast, so that the image of the beast would even speak and cause as many as do not worship the image of the beast to be killed. 16 And he causes all, the small and the great, and the rich and the poor, and the free men and the slaves, to be given a mark on their right hand or on their forehead, 17 and he provides that no one will be able to buy or to sell, except the one who has the mark, either the name of the beast or the number of his name. 18 Here is wisdom. Let him who has understanding calculate the number of the beast, for the number is that of a man; and his number is six hundred and sixty-six." (Rev 13:15–18, NASB)

Gematria is an ancient Hebrew form of numerology, a pagan practice. The Bible testifies to pagan influences and practices in both the Old and New Testaments. We see God repeatedly warn the Israelites not to follow those evil practices, and we see Jesus and the Apostles warn Christians not to participate in the secret practices of darkness either. Yet, both groups did (and still do). In ancient Hebrew they used their alphabet letters to also represent numbers. For example, the first letter (aleph, א) also represents the number one. In this way you can assign a numeric value to any word by simply converting each letter to its equivalent number. You can also do the same thing with names of people, which are made up of letters, which can be converted into numbers. And so numerous attempts have been made at converting famous names into numbers looking for a match with 666.

This practice is still used today to connect different parts of the Bible together to reveal new meanings. For example, if one part of the Bible (a word or phrase) equals a particular number, then another part of the Bible with the same numeric value are said to be related. And the combination of these two (previously unrelated) passages is said to yield a new meaning. Since there are only twenty-two Hebrew letters, there is a limitation on the number of possible combinations of them. Given the breadth of the Bible we find many, many places that can be "connected" in this way. However, the knowledge of what these "connections" mean is supplied by the interpreters, not the Bible itself. This way of producing "new revelation" comes from outside the Bible, the traditions of men, and not what the Holy Spirit has revealed through the scriptures themselves. We will be mindful that later Rabbis interpreted the plain meaning of the scriptures to not sound like Jesus, and the Apostles fought repeatedly against the Gnostics who claimed to have secret knowledge of the scriptures. This practice of deriving new meaning from the original scriptures continues to the present day in both Judaism and Christianity. The Sola Scriptura method holds us to only what the scriptures say, so we will avoid any further exploration of this practice.

> The Bible nowhere explains the meaning of 666, but that verse reinforces the idea that the beast is a man. Numerology was a pagan practice, and the Bible speaks against those who claim secret knowledge of the scriptures. We should be careful here.

The Bible nowhere explains the meaning of 666, but that verse reinforces the idea that the beast is a man. Numerology was a pagan practice, and the Bible speaks against those who claim secret knowledge of the scriptures. We should be careful here. The suggestion that John practiced these dark arts creates many problems for the Christian. Are we suggesting John was gnostic, or practiced Kabbalah, or that those who do have a secret interpretation of the scriptures? Also, the number 666 occurs nowhere else in the book of Revelation, let alone in scripture. So why set doctrine based on a single verse? Let's look again at what the scriptures actually say.

> "Here is wisdom. Let him who has understanding calculate the number of the beast, for the number is that of a man; and his number is six hundred and sixty-six." (Rev 13:18, NASB)

The scriptures plainly say that the number is the number of a man. Think back on all the interpretations of the beast we reviewed earlier. Theologians have said it refers to specific people, or antichristian governments, or evil powers throughout history, or false religions and philosophies, or even the beast we each become when we don't follow God. But the number of the beast is a man, and he is the eighth king in a succession of kingdoms according to a plain reading of the scriptures as shown above.

Sola Scriptura will hold us to only what the scriptures say, and they plainly say he is a man. One result of calculating the number, having insight, is finding out that the beast is a man, not an abstract idea.

We could also spend time contemplating the meaning of various numbers, like seven meaning perfection, completion, wholeness, or God. And then six being less, suggesting one who is almost like God but not God, like the most beautiful angel of all (Lucifer) demanding that he be worshiped as God. Or we could look at the Hebrew letter for six, a vav (ו), which looks like a tent peg. We could see the tent peg as a nail driven into the ground. Digging a tent peg into the ground is the same kind of action Psalm 22:16 speaks of when it says the Messiah's hands and feet are "pierced" (ca'ari, כָּאֲרִי), a picture of the crucifixion. Three nails in the cross, three vavs, which is 666.

As interesting as all these theories are, the Sola Scriptura approach holds us to only what the scriptures directly say. And they say this number is the number of a man. The Bible repeatedly says the beast is a man. Nowhere does the Bible ever say the beast is a concept like all systems, governments, philosophies, or religions which are opposed to Christ throughout history.

> The Bible repeatedly says the beast is a man. Nowhere does the Bible ever say the beast is a concept like all systems, governments, philosophies, or religions which are opposed to Christ throughout history.

WHAT DID WE LEARN ABOUT THE BEAST?

From a plain reading of the scriptures, it is evident that the beast is a man, an eighth king, who will lead a group of ten other kings and their kingdoms in battle against the Messiah. He will oppress the people of God and attempt to establish himself as a god. He will attack Jerusalem and the final battle will happen when he and his followers are gathered together into the place called Armageddon, what Joel called the Valley of Decision, where God will decide against the blasphemous worldwide king. Judgment will be poured out on him like the visions Daniel, Ezekiel, Zechariah, Joel, Paul, and John spoke of. When Christ appears, he will defeat this beast and the beast will be thrown into the lake of fire. Afterward, Christ will finally defeat Satan and he will also be thrown into the same lake of fire.

#	Truth Claim	Primary Support	Secondary Support
12.1	The beast is a man.	Rev 13:18	Rev 17:11–14, 2 Thess 2:1–4, Dan 7:17,23–27, 8:23–25
12.2	The antichrist will oppress the people of God.	Rev 13:5–15	Rev 11:7, 12:3, 17:8,12, 19:19, Dan 7:7–8,19–25, 8:21–25, 9:27, 11:36, 12:7, 2 Thess 2:1–12

#	Truth Claim	Primary Support	Secondary Support
12.3	The antichrist will lead a coalition of nations to attack Jerusalem.	Rev 16:14–16	Rev 17:11–14, 19:16–20, 20:7–10, Dan 7:19–25, 9:27, 11:40–45, Zech 12:3,7–10, 14:2,3,13, Joel 2:1–3,18–20, 3:1–2,14–16, Ezek 38:7–9,14–18, 39:1–8,17–19, Matt 24:14–16
12.4	The beast will be defeated.	Rev 19:20	Rev 2:27, 11:15,18, 12:5, 14:10, 16:16–17, 17:12–14, 19:11–21, 20:10, 2 Thess 2:8, Dan 7:11,22,25–27, Mark 16:19

13

Revelations About Babylon

"Farewell unhappy, hopeless, blasphemous Rome! The Wrath of God has come upon you, as you deserve. We cared for Babylon, and she is not healed; let us then leave her, that she may become the habitation of dragons, spectres, and witches."—Martin Luther

THE MENTION OF BABYLON in the book of Revelation is one of the greatest points of theological controversy. For one thing, Babylon had already fallen centuries before the book was written so how could we understand John to mean it literally? Before we jump into this discussion, we should first recognize that not everything has been revealed to us.

> "When the seven peals of thunder had spoken, I was about to write; and I heard a voice from heaven saying, 'Seal up the things which the seven peals of thunder have spoken and do not write them.'" (Rev 10:4, NASB)

John was told not to write some things down, so some things are an intentional mystery. One of the mysteries we are told is Babylon.

> "and on her forehead a name was written, a mystery, 'BABYLON THE GREAT, THE MOTHER OF HARLOTS AND OF THE ABOMINATIONS OF THE EARTH.'" (Rev 17:5, NASB)

We are not meant to understand everything, for everything has not been revealed. Babylon is a mystery, according to the book of Revelation. Especially since at the time when John wrote down Revelation the ancient powers of Babylon had long been defeated. Babylon was overthrown by Persia. Then Persia by Greece. Then Greece by Rome. And it was during the time of the Roman Empire that Revelation was written. Babylon had been long gone by the time John wrote these famous words, so it truly was a mystery why this name was used again. When people heard the name Babylon, they must have been confused just like we are today.

This leads several commentaries to interpret Babylon as "spiritual Babylon" and identify her as something other than a literal Babylon. On the other hand, literal interpreters see Babylon as a literal city in the future that will be reinstated as a world power. The ancient city of Babylon today is known as Baghdad, Iraq. A palace of Saddam Hussein was constructed near the ruins of Nebuchadnezzar's city. The ancient pillars lay on the ground in the fields just outside the palace. The potential of a real future Babylon rising to power is realistically possible, as some of her descendants have dreamt of.

Different commentaries have suggested Babylon in Revelation represents:

- Rome, the seat of Papal authority and the worldwide Roman Catholic Church.
- Jerusalem, the great city where the prophets of God were ignored and tortured.
- A future city rebuilt in the end times.
- An allegory for all forces of evil throughout history.
- An allegory for the worldly influence inside the church itself.

What do the scriptures actually say? The Sola Scriptura method asks us to first look at what the text says for itself.

Reference	Scripture (NIV)
Rev 17:18	The woman you saw *is the great city* that rules over the kings of the earth.
Rev 18:10	Terrified at her torment, they will stand far off and cry: 'Woe! Woe to *you, great city, you mighty city* of Babylon! In one hour your doom has come!'
Rev 18:16b	'Woe! Woe to *you, great city*, dressed in fine linen, purple and scarlet, and glittering with gold, precious stones and pearls!
Rev 18:18–19	18 When they see the smoke of her burning, they will exclaim, 'Was there ever *a city like this great city*?' 19 They will throw dust on their heads, and with weeping and mourning cry out: 'Woe! Woe to *you, great city*, where all who had ships on the sea became rich through her wealth! In one hour she has been brought to ruin!'
Rev 18:21	Then a mighty angel picked up a boulder the size of a large millstone and threw it into the sea, and said: "With such violence *the great city* of Babylon will be thrown down, never to be found again.

As you can see above, the scriptures clearly say that Babylon is a city. This image of the prostitute is explained to John to be a great city that rules over the kings of the earth. The text does not say anywhere that Babylon is symbolic of all evil forces throughout history. The scriptures do not say Babylon represents worldly influence inside the church. Instead, the scriptures plainly speak of Babylon as an actual city. And this is a sinful city that leads the nations of the world:

Reference	Scripture (NIV)
Rev 17:2	With her *the kings of the earth committed adultery, and the inhabitants of the earth were intoxicated* with the wine of her adulteries.
Rev 17:15	Then the angel said to me, "The waters you saw, where the prostitute sits, are *peoples, multitudes, nations and languages.*
Rev 17:18	The woman you saw is the great city *that rules over the kings of the earth.*
Rev 18:3	For *all the nations have drunk* the maddening wine of her adulteries. *The kings of the earth committed adultery* with her, and *the merchants of the earth grew rich* from her excessive luxuries.
Rev 18:5	for *her sins are piled up to heaven*, and God has remembered *her crimes.*
Rev 18:23	The light of a lamp will never shine in you again. The voice of bridegroom and bride will never be heard in you again. *Your merchants were the world's important people.* By your magic spell *all the nations were led astray.*

Theologians that say Babylon is something other than a literal city are saying that, although an angel told John the meaning of the symbol of the prostitute, they know it means something else. Their "knowledge" comes from outside the Bible and from the traditions of men. And they are giving a meaning for the symbol of the prostitute that is different from the meaning that the angel told John. Are we to believe what an angel told John, or later theologians that came up with a different meaning? Are we to believe in the scriptures or in the traditions of men? And what about the warning in the book of Revelation itself not to add anything to what it says (Rev 22:18–19)? The Bible repeatedly says the symbol of the prostitute, Babylon, is a city. Nowhere does the Bible ever say Babylon is symbolic of all forces of evil throughout history. And nowhere does the Bible ever say Babylon represents worldly influence within the church.

> Theologians that say Babylon is something other than a literal city are saying that, although an angel told John the meaning of the symbol of the prostitute, they know it means something else.

The Sola Scriptura method shows us that Babylon is a great city that leads the rulers and important people of the world, makes people rich, and is full of sinful activities. Our next question then is what city is this mystery city? Could we say that John meant Jerusalem? When did Jerusalem make the world rich? When did Jerusalem ever sit as the leading city of all the rulers and important people of the world? Have the Chinese or Indians, for example, ever looked to Jerusalem as the leading world city? They have not, not in terms of religion, finances, nor political power. If the mystery city is Jerusalem, then it is not modern-day Jerusalem nor a Jerusalem of the past.

Could we say that Rome was ever leading the world and making it wealthy? One could envision that the world at the time of John and the seven churches to whom Revelation was addressed did see the Roman Empire as "the world." They could have understood Rome to be the city which the known world (in their part of the world) made people wealthy and was certainly not a city that espoused Judeo-Christian values in their day. At the same time, they did know about India and lands north of Britain. Rome never actually conquered the furthermost parts of the then-known world. While partially true, Rome is not a complete fulfillment of the prophecy either. Although one could argue it is a future Rome that will become the mysterious Babylon that Revelation speaks of.

Yet there is still a problem with identifying Rome as the Babylon of Revelation (either past or future). See if you can spot it in the following verses:

Reference	Scripture (NIV)
Rev 17:6	I saw that the woman was drunk with the blood of God's holy people, *the blood of those who bore testimony to Jesus.*
Rev 18:24	In her was found *the blood of prophets and of God's holy people*, of all who have been slaughtered on the earth.

The scriptures clearly say this city is where the prophets, God's holy people, and followers of Jesus are all murdered. While Rome did oppress the people of God and also killed Christians, it was not responsible for the deaths of the Hebrew prophets. It was Jerusalem that tortured and killed the prophets of God, not Rome.

Moreover, identifying Rome as the subject here during the destruction of Jerusalem in 70 AD is also problematic because the leaders of Rome do not line up with the specific prophecies about them.

> "9 Here is the mind which has wisdom. The seven heads are seven mountains on which the woman sits, 10 and they are seven kings; five have fallen, one is, the other has not yet come; and when he comes, he must remain a little while. 11 The beast which was and is not, is himself also an eighth and is one of the seven, and he goes to destruction." (Rev 17:9–11, NASB)

Roman Emperor Nero is often said to be the beast spoken of; however, he was the fifth and not the sixth emperor of Rome. The passage above clearly says at the time of Revelation five kings had fallen, one is (the sixth), and the other is yet to come. Also, the beast is an eighth king. Nero just does not line up with the scriptures. And as you saw in the last section, the beast is defeated when he wages war against the Messiah. Nero committed suicide on June 9th, 68 AD after the Roman Senate turned against him, not by losing a battle when waging war against the Messiah.

> Identifying Rome as the city of Babylon does not line up with the scriptures. Identifying Jerusalem in any time period to date also does not line up with the scriptures. It is a mystery, just like Revelation says it is.

Identifying Rome as the city of Babylon does not line up with the scriptures. Identifying Jerusalem in any time period to date also does not line up with the scriptures. It is a mystery, just like Revelation says it is. This city is one that leads the world, rulers and important people look to her for power, it makes people wealthy, and it is sinful. It also is the city that killed both the prophets of old and the followers of Jesus. If this is Jerusalem, then it must be a future version of Jerusalem.

The only other explanation is to take an allegorical view that Babylon represents all the forces of evil throughout history. The hesitancy with that view is that the scriptures speak plainly, and at length, about Babylon as an actual city. An angel explains the symbols to John and Babylon is said repeatedly to be a literal city. The allegorical view reinterprets the interpretation already given to John. Moreover, the allegorical view also suggests the beast represents worldly powers and influences. In the next section we will see that Babylon is destroyed by the beast. That makes the allegorical position untenable. It makes no sense to describe the beast as world powers opposed to God, and Babylon also as world powers opposed to God, and then say that the world powers attack the world powers before waging war on the Lamb. It is just way too confusing an explanation when compared to the plain and simple language that Babylon is an actual city that leads the nations, makes them wealthy, and is full of sin.

HOW IS BABYLON DESTROYED?

If the allegorical position that Babylon represents all world powers opposed to God throughout history is true, then the destruction of Babylon by the ten kings who follow the beast (also said to be allegorically world powers throughout history) does not make sense. According to the plain sense of the text, Babylon is destroyed one time. It is a singular defeat, and not a repeated event throughout all of history. Moreover, Babylon is distinct from the ten kings, which are themselves distinct from the beast. These are not all treated as the same thing in the scriptures.

Reference	Scripture (NIV)
Rev 17:9-10	9 This calls for a mind with wisdom. The seven heads are seven hills on which the woman sits. 10 *They are also seven kings.* Five have fallen, one is, the other has not yet come; but when he does come, he must remain for only a little while.
Rev 17:12-14	12 *The ten horns you saw are ten kings who have not yet received a kingdom*, but who for one hour will receive authority as kings along with the beast. 13 *They have one purpose and will give their power and authority to the beast.* 14 *They will wage war against the Lamb*, but the Lamb will triumph over them because he is Lord of lords and King of kings—and with him will be his called, chosen and faithful followers.
Rev 17:16-17	16 The beast and the ten horns you saw *will hate the prostitute.* They *will bring her to ruin* and leave her naked; they will eat her flesh and burn her with fire. 17 For God has put it into their hearts to accomplish his purpose by agreeing to hand over to the beast their royal authority, until God's words are fulfilled.

Revelation tells us that ten kings will follow the beast and destroy Babylon. This singular destruction shows the Allegorical interpretation to be false. The Preterist view is also shown to be false because of the facts of history. The Preterist view which holds that Babylon is Jerusalem and was destroyed by the beast, which is Rome, in 70 AD makes much more sense than the allegorical view for the scriptures above. Babylon is specifically named as a city, a name that is mysterious. And the beast and his followers literally destroy the city. However, if you recall from the prior section, the Jerusalem of 70 AD could not be what Revelation is referring to, for Jerusalem did not make the world rich at that time. Rome's wealth did not come from Jerusalem. Jerusalem was in a small Roman province far away from Rome. Jerusalem also did not have the leaders of the world, all the important people, look to her for leadership. At the time of the writing of Revelation, Jerusalem was oppressed by Rome, not leading the world.

> Revelation tells us that ten kings will follow the beast and destroy Babylon. This singular destruction shows the Allegorical interpretation to be false. The Preterist view is also shown to be false because of the facts of history.

THE TESTIMONY OF THE HEBREW PROPHETS

Did the Hebrew prophets speak of an attack on Jerusalem? Yes. As you saw in earlier sections of this book there are numerous prophecies about an attack on Israel. Daniel spoke of the "little horn" that attacks Jerusalem and oppresses the people of God (Dan 8:21–215, 11:36,40–45, 12:7). Jesus even reminded people of that prophecy by quoting Daniel directly.

> "15 'Therefore when you see the abomination of desolation which was spoken of through Daniel the prophet, standing in the holy place (let the reader understand), 16 then those who are in Judea must flee to the mountains.'" (Matt 24:15–16, NASB)

Zechariah spoke of the time when the nations of the world are gathered against Jerusalem (Zech 12:3). God will destroy those nations and the people of Jerusalem will look upon the one they have pierced and mourn for him as one mourns for an only son (Zech 12:7–10).

Joel spoke of the Day of the Lord when God defeats a large and mighty army, protecting Israel, never again allowing her to be an object of scorn to the nations (Joel 2:1–3,18–20). He defeats them as they are gathered together in the Valley of Decision. Never again will foreigners invade her (Joel 3:1–2,14–16).

Ezekiel prophesied about a future leader, Gog, who will lead the nations of the world in an attack on Jerusalem (Ezek 38:7–9, 38:14–18, 39:1–8, 17–19). The fall of Gog's armies is described as a feast for the birds and wild animals. Revelation also refers to Gog, as well as their defeat being a feast for the birds.

> "7 When the thousand years are completed, Satan will be released from his prison, 8 and will come out to deceive the nations which are in the four corners of the earth, Gog and Magog, to gather them together for the war;

the number of them is like the sand of the seashore. 9 And they came up on the broad plain of the earth and surrounded the camp of the saints and the beloved city, and fire came down from heaven and devoured them. 10 And the devil who deceived them was thrown into the lake of fire and brimstone, where the beast and the false prophet are also; and they will be tormented day and night forever and ever." (Rev 20:7–10, NASB)

"16 And on His robe and on His thigh He has a name written, 'KING OF KINGS, AND LORD OF LORDS.' 17 Then I saw an angel standing in the sun, and he cried out with a loud voice, saying to all the birds which fly in midheaven, 'Come, assemble for the great supper of God, 18 so that you may eat the flesh of kings and the flesh of commanders and the flesh of mighty men and the flesh of horses and of those who sit on them and the flesh of all men, both free men and slaves, and small and great.' 19 And I saw the beast and the kings of the earth and their armies assembled to make war against Him who sat on the horse and against His army." (Rev 19:16–19, NASB)

The Sola Scriptura view of Babylon being a future Jerusalem that is invaded does line up very well with the testimony of the Hebrew prophets. What about the reference to Babylon being a prostitute?

"and on her forehead a name was written, a mystery, 'BABYLON THE GREAT, THE MOTHER OF HARLOTS AND OF THE ABOMINATIONS OF THE EARTH.'" (Rev 17:5, NASB)

Does the Hebrew Bible ever call Jerusalem a prostitute? In fact, it does. In Ezekiel chapter 16 God tells the people of Jerusalem they are committing adultery by not worshipping him. They act like prostitutes, making shrines all over the place to other gods. They are unfaithful to him. Isaiah opens his book with the same condemnation.

"How the faithful city has become a harlot, she who was full of justice! Righteousness once lodged in her, but now murderers." (Isa 1:21, NASB)

Jeremiah joins Isaiah and Ezekiel in the very same condemnation.

"'At that time,' declares the Lord, 'I will be the God of all the families of Israel, and they shall be My people.'" (Jer 31:1, NASB)

Thus, the prophetic scriptures plainly say that Jerusalem has been a city of unfaithful people, like a prostitute. And the nations of the world will gather to attack her.

The prophetic scriptures plainly say that Jerusalem has been a city of unfaithful people, like a prostitute. And the nations of the world will gather to attack her.

WHAT DID WE LEARN ABOUT BABYLON?

By using scripture alone, the Sola Scriptura method, one can only conclude that Babylon is specifically a city. The symbol used is that of a prostitute, and an angel explains to John that the prostitute is a city. She is referred to as a city six times. To say she represents something else would be to say that a symbol which is explained actually stands for something other than what the angel said it meant. Even though an angel explains the meaning of this symbol to John, some theologians want to re-explain the explanation. This second "revelation" of the meaning of a symbol comes from men, not angels, and not what the scriptures actually say. Who are we to believe: what John said the angel told him, or what a theologian in later centuries decided it means? Are we to believe the scriptures, or the later traditions of men?

The scriptures also directly say that ten kings will follow the worldwide ruler (the beast) and will destroy this city. She is a city that makes the world wealthy, and the most important people of the world look to her for leadership. She is also the city where the Hebrew prophets were murdered as well as the followers of Jesus. The Sola Scriptura method leads us to view Babylon as Jerusalem. But never in the past has Jerusalem led the world, especially not during the Roman occupation at the time of Jesus. Revelation looks to a future time when Jerusalem is the seat of worldwide power. And then a worldwide leader will arise who will sadly lead many nations in war against her to destroy her. Once the earthly Jerusalem has been destroyed, then a New Jerusalem will come down out of Heaven to replace the old one.

> "And I saw the holy city, new Jerusalem, coming down out of heaven from God, made ready as a bride adorned for her husband." (Rev 21:2, NASB)

#	Truth Claim	Primary Support	Secondary Support
13.1	Babylon represents an actual city.	Rev 17:18	Rev 18:10,16,18–19,21
13.2	Babylon leads the nations (leaders, merchants, and important people) astray into sin.	Rev 17:2	Rev 17:15,18, 18:3,5,23
13.3	God will punish those who oppress his people.	Rev 16:5-6	Rev 6:10, 18:2,6, 19:1–3, Isa 2:4, 9:6–7, 13:11, 21:9, 47:5–15, Dan 7:11–14,18,22,26–27, Joel 3:9–21, Ezek 38:14, Zech 9:9–17, 12:8, Ps 2:2,9, 96:13, 98:9, 110:6
13.4	Babylon will fall.	Rev 18:1–24	Jer 50:39, 51:8,37,45, Isa 13:11, 21:9, 47:5–15
13.5	Babylon will be destroyed by the ten kings who previously followed her ways.	Rev 17:16–17	Rev 17:9–10,12–14

14

Revelations About Judgment

"There will be three groups of people on the great Day of Judgment at the end of days: one of wholly righteous people, one of wholly wicked people, and one of middling people. Wholly righteous people will immediately be written and sealed for eternal life. Wholly wicked people will immediately be written and sealed for Gehenna, as it is stated: 'And many of those who sleep in the dust of the earth shall wake, some to eternal life and some to shame and everlasting contempt' (Daniel 12:2). Middling people will descend to Gehenna to be cleansed and to achieve atonement for their sins, and they will cry out in their pain and eventually ascend from there."—Talmud Rosh Hashanah 16b:15–17a

THERE ARE OFTEN TWO really big discussions around judgment in the book of Revelation. First, there is a question about if God will really judge all people and for how long? Does anyone get punished forever, in an eternal Hell with unending torture? Or does everyone eventually go to Heaven? Or perhaps, are some people so bad that their souls are burned up and nothing is left, thus their torture ends because they cease to exist? You may be surprised to know that the answers about what happens after we die vary greatly across Christianity, they also vary across different movements within Judaism.

Second, do the seven seals, seven trumpets, and seven bowl judgments describe twenty-one different things or are they parallel visions of the same seven things? Interpretations, commentaries, and denominations disagree on these things, but what does a Sola Scriptura approach conclude? If you set aside the various conflicting church traditions and the ruminations of theologians, what do the scriptures themselves directly say? Let's take a look.

IS JUDGMENT ETERNAL?

Eternal judgment is a complicated and difficult topic to discuss. On the one hand, some denominations are notorious for preaching "hellfire and brimstone," scaring their congregation into doing things to avoid going to hell. On the other hand, some denominations teach that God is love and the only real hell is the one we create for ourselves while we are alive on earth. And other denominations are somewhere in between.

For the denominations that use scare tactics, it is hard for people to feel the love of God when you feel incredible guilt and shame for being a sinful person. For some people the self-loathing is so overpowering that they live very unhappy lives and never really hear the "Good News." The good part being that: although we are actually sinful people, Jesus came to save us from sin. If we truly believe he died to pay the price for our sins, then we no longer should hold onto the guilt of past sins we already confessed. In fact, we should recognize that it is the devil himself that wants to keep us bound up in shame, loathing of our self, and feeling separate from both God and others. The devil tries to make God a liar when we are told we are forgiven. Not only does God forgive us, but our sins are as far from him as the east is from the west. If you have already repented of a past sin, then just let it go. When Satan sends you reminders of it, tell Satan to go away. Between the scare tactics some use, and the reminders of past sin from Satan, one may never hear the Good News and instead live in constant fear of eternal judgment.

On the other end of the spectrum are the denominations that teach that there is no hell, and all souls eventually go to heaven. They believe that God is love, and a loving God would never punish someone forever. Perhaps there is some amount of punishment after death, but after a period of purging you of your sins you would surely eventually have paid the price and be set free. People don't want to hear that stuff about punishment at church. There has already been enough judgment in the world. We can all be viewed as hypocrites, and no one has the right to judge anyone else. People want to feel good. If they're not happy and clapping along with the church service, then they won't come back. People only want to hear motivational speeches and not think about any kind of eternal judgment. But what does the Bible actually say about eternal judgment? Is there really such a thing?

> "And the smoke of their torment goes up forever and ever; they have no rest day and night, those who worship the beast and his image, and whoever receives the mark of his name.'" (Rev 14:11, NASB)

> "And the devil who deceived them was thrown into the lake of fire and brimstone, where the beast and the false prophet are also; and they will be tormented day and night forever and ever." (Rev 20:10, NASB)

> "11 Then I saw a great white throne and Him who sat upon it, from whose presence earth and heaven fled away, and no place was found for them. 12

> And I saw the dead, the great and the small, standing before the throne, and books were opened; and another book was opened, which is the book of life; and the dead were judged from the things which were written in the books, according to their deeds. 13 And the sea gave up the dead which were in it, and death and Hades gave up the dead which were in them; and they were judged, every one of them according to their deeds. 14 Then death and Hades were thrown into the lake of fire. This is the second death, the lake of fire. 15 And if anyone's name was not found written in the book of life, he was thrown into the lake of fire." (Rev 20:11–15, NASB)

> "2 Many of those who sleep in the dust of the ground will awake, these to everlasting life, but the others to disgrace and everlasting contempt. 3 Those who have insight will shine brightly like the brightness of the expanse of heaven, and those who lead the many to righteousness, like the stars forever and ever." (Dan 12:2–3, NASB)

> "44 Then they themselves also will answer, 'Lord, when did we see You hungry, or thirsty, or a stranger, or naked, or sick, or in prison, and did not take care of You?' 45 Then He will answer them, 'Truly I say to you, to the extent that you did not do it to one of the least of these, you did not do it to Me.' 46 These will go away into eternal punishment, but the righteous into eternal life.'" (Matt 25:44–46, NASB)

The Sola Scriptura approach will hold only to what the scriptures directly say. The book of Revelation, the prophet Daniel, and the words of Jesus clearly indicate that just as there is eternal life, there is also eternal punishment. Daniel describes it as everlasting contempt.

Daniel uses the same word for "contempt" that Isaiah uses in his final chapter, *lediron* (לְדִרְאוֹן). In Isaiah's final chapter he uses the word to describe the state of those who rebel against God.

> "22 'For just as the new heavens and the new earth which I make will endure before Me,' declares the Lord, 'So your offspring and your name will endure. 23 'And it shall be from new moon to new moon and from sabbath to sabbath, all mankind will come to bow down before Me,' says the Lord. 24 'Then they will go forth and look on the corpses of the men who have transgressed against Me. For their worm will not die and their fire will not be quenched; and they will be an abhorrence to all mankind.'" (Isa 66:22–24, NASB)

As much as this is a hard message to share with others, if you think about it: what it really says to us is that we truly need the Blood of Jesus. Every one of us. There is no one who is without sin. If there was no judgment and no punishment, then there would be no need for the atoning work Jesus did on the cross. If you don't need to make things right with God because of your sins, because you don't believe in sin, then you also don't see any value in believing in the Blood of Jesus. And that is why the

Holy Spirit convicts us of our sins. So that we will know we need Jesus, so that we will repent, and so that we will change our ways, living in a holy fear of the God who will one day judge everyone. Even the preachers who yell at their congregations are sinners and will be judged. Notice that Revelation clearly describes everyone being judged, believers and unbelievers alike. You and I will both be there one day.

The Hebrew Bible and New Testament are both clear that all people, great and small, living and dead, will one day stand before the Throne of God and be judged. Some will receive everlasting life, and others shame and everlasting contempt. Everlasting lasts forever.

> "And I saw the dead, the great and the small, standing before the throne, and books were opened; and another book was opened, which is the book of life; and the dead were judged from the things which were written in the books, according to their deeds." (Rev 20:12, NASB)

> The Hebrew Bible and New Testament are both clear that all people, great and small, living and dead, will one day stand before the Throne of God and be judged. Some will receive everlasting life, and others shame and everlasting contempt. Everlasting lasts forever.

SEALS, TRUMPETS, AND BOWL JUDGMENTS

There are similarities between the seals, trumpets, and bowls which lead some interpreters to conclude they are parallel descriptions of the same things. For example, there are seven of each and they describe terrible things happening like those seen in the time of Moses (turning water into blood, plagues, and death).

In the view of some theologians, these parallel events describe a single sequence of events. Take for example, the singular destruction of Jerusalem in 70 AD. They use historical events to explain each of the seals, trumpets, and bowls. They suggest John was afraid of Rome and so used secret codes to write what he really meant. With this interpretation, though already imprisoned and exiled for his beliefs, suddenly John was afraid of men rather than God and obscured God's message which Jesus told him to send to the seven churches.

In the view of other theologians, these parallel events repeat in the lives of all people throughout history, and the seals, trumpets, and bowls are how God deals with unbelievers. In this view God warns people when they are doing wrong, represented by the trumpets, and God punishes people with calamities, represented by the bowls of wrath.

Still other theologians see these as chronological and separate events. The seven seals bring a partial destruction as warning, the seven trumpets bring a further (but still partial) destruction as even more warning, and the seven bowls unleash the final and complete wrath of God. Altogether there are twenty-one separate events.

While there are similarities, the seals, bowls, and trumpets are very different from a Sola Scriptura perspective. The seals bring a partial destruction of up to a fourth, the trumpets bring up to a third, and the bowls bring a final and complete destruction.

> "7 When the Lamb broke the fourth seal, I heard the voice of the fourth living creature saying, 'Come.' 8 I looked, and behold, an ashen horse; and he who sat on it had the name Death; and Hades was following with him. Authority was given to them over a fourth of the earth, to kill with sword and with famine and with pestilence and by the wild beasts of the earth." (Rev 6:7–8, NASB)

Notice that as the seals are opened the ensuing destruction is only up to a fourth of the earth.

> "7 The first sounded, and there came hail and fire, mixed with blood, and they were thrown to the earth; and a third of the earth was burned up, and a third of the trees were burned up, and all the green grass was burned up. 8 The second angel sounded, and something like a great mountain burning with fire was thrown into the sea; and a third of the sea became blood, 9 and a third of the creatures which were in the sea and had life, died; and a third of the ships were destroyed. 10 The third angel sounded, and a great star fell from heaven, burning like a torch, and it fell on a third of the rivers and on the springs of waters. 11 The name of the star is called Wormwood; and a third of the waters became wormwood, and many men died from the waters, because they were made bitter. 12 The fourth angel sounded, and a third of the sun and a third of the moon and a third of the stars were struck, so that a third of them would be darkened and the day would not shine for a third of it, and the night in the same way." (Rev 8:7–12, NASB)

However, notice that the trumpets allow more destruction than the seals, and the bowls allow for even more. This is an increasing progression of judgment: seals (25 percent), trumpets (33 percent), and bowls (100 percent).

> "2 So the first angel went and poured out his bowl on the earth; and it became a loathsome and malignant sore on the people who had the mark of the beast and who worshiped his image. 3 The second angel poured out his bowl into the sea, and it became blood like that of a dead man; and every living thing in the sea died." (Rev 16:2–3, NASB)

> "8 The fourth angel poured out his bowl upon the sun, and it was given to it to scorch men with fire. 9 Men were scorched with fierce heat; and they blasphemed the name of God who has the power over these plagues, and they did not repent so as to give Him glory. 10 Then the fifth angel poured out his bowl on the throne of the beast, and his kingdom became darkened; and they gnawed their tongues because of pain, 11 and they blasphemed the God of heaven because of their pains and their sores; and they did not repent of their deeds." (Rev 16:8–11, NASB)

Not only do the seals, trumpets, and bowls progress from partial destruction to complete, but they affect mostly different things. In the seals we see partial destruction through wars, famine, and death (Rev 6). In the trumpets we see more partial destruction of the earth, waters, and stars, along with torture of people in more wars (Rev 8–9). In the bowls, which are the seven last plagues, we see complete destruction of every living thing in the waters, a scorching heat from the sun that burns people, destruction of Babylon the Great, and the agony of painful sores from plagues (Rev 16).

The only real exact parallel between the seals, trumpets, and bowls is that there is lightning, thunder, and an earthquake associated with all three (Rev 8:5, 11:19, and 16:18). Other than a general "bad time" for people of the earth, the set of things affected and the degree to which they are affected are different. As an aside, lightning, thunder, and earthquakes happen in many other places in the Bible too. So that is not enough of a parallelism to support a doctrinal position and teach that to others.

> The only real exact parallel between the seals, trumpets, and bowls is that there is lightning, thunder, and an earthquake associated with all three (Rev 8:5, 11:19, and 16:18). Other than a general "bad time" for people of the earth, the set of things affected and the degree to which they are affected are different.

Moreover, the bowls are actually described as "last." "Last" in Greek is *eschatos* (ἐσχάτας) and means the furthest, the extreme-end, and at the last. This is where we get the name of our study of the End Times, called "Eschatology." With these last plagues God's wrath is "completed" (*etelesthe*, ἐτελέσθη), finished, accomplished.

> "Then I saw another sign in heaven, great and marvelous, seven angels who had seven plagues, which are the last [ἐσχάτας], because in them the wrath of God is finished [ἐτελέσθη]." (Rev 15:1, NASB)

We also see that this revelation of God will bring all nations to acknowledge and worship the one True God.

> "'Who will not fear, O Lord, and glorify Your name? For You alone are holy; for all the nations will come and worship before You, for Your righteous acts have been revealed.'" (Rev 15:4, NASB)

Since all nations today do not worship the one true God, then these "last" plagues must not have happened yet. The Preterist view must be dismissed. God's wrath has not yet been "completed." Unbelievers and those choosing to revel in sin still need to be warned. Judgment is still coming. Faith in Jesus' Blood as atonement for our sins still matters, for God's wrath is not yet complete.

THE FOUR HORSEMEN AND THE HARVEST

Ignoring what the text plainly says, some interpretations give wildly different interpretations of these seals, trumpets, and bowls. For example, one allegorical interpretation holds that the Four Horsemen of the Apocalypse refer to the reception of the Gospel by the people of earth. The white horse represents the original pure church, the red horse represents wars over doctrine and interpretation, the black horse represents the scarcity of people in no longer knowing the true Gospel, and the pale horse represents the spiritual death of most people not knowing the Word of God. But Sola Scriptura asks: where does the Bible say any of that? Nowhere. Here is what it actually says:

> "Then I saw when the Lamb broke one of the seven seals, and I heard one of the four living creatures saying as with a voice of thunder, 'Come.' 2 I looked, and behold, a white horse, and he who sat on it had a bow; and a crown was given to him, and he went out conquering and to conquer. 3 When He broke the second seal, I heard the second living creature saying, 'Come.' 4 And another, a red horse, went out; and to him who sat on it, it was granted to take peace from the earth, and that men would slay one another; and a great sword was given to him. 5 When He broke the third seal, I heard the third living creature saying, 'Come.' I looked, and behold, a black horse; and he who sat on it had a pair of scales in his hand. 6 And I heard something like a voice in the center of the four living creatures saying, 'A quart of wheat for a denarius, and three quarts of barley for a denarius; and do not damage the oil and the wine.' 7 When the Lamb broke the fourth seal, I heard the voice of the fourth living creature saying, 'Come.' 8 I looked, and behold, an ashen horse; and he who sat on it had the name Death; and Hades was following with him. Authority was given to them over a fourth of the earth, to kill with sword and with famine and with pestilence and by the wild beasts of the earth." (Rev 6:1–8, NASB)

Nowhere in the text do you find mention of the original church, argument over doctrine, or people losing the true Gospel, as an Allegorical view states. The Sola Scriptura approach can only accept what the text actually says. The text literally describes wars, famine, and death.

> Nowhere in the text do you find mention of the original church, argument over doctrine, or people losing the true Gospel, as an Allegorical view states. The Sola Scriptura approach can only accept what the text actually says. The text literally describes wars, famine, and death.

The Bible plainly says that there will be increasing warnings from God, signs of the times, which increase until the time of wrath, the time of harvesting the earth. And that time of wrath will be a great punishment brought on the unbelievers.

> "16 Then He who sat on the cloud swung His sickle over the earth, and the earth was reaped. 17 And another angel came out of the temple which is in

heaven, and he also had a sharp sickle. 18 Then another angel, the one who has power over fire, came out from the altar; and he called with a loud voice to him who had the sharp sickle, saying, 'Put in your sharp sickle and gather the clusters from the vine of the earth, because her grapes are ripe.' 19 So the angel swung his sickle to the earth and gathered the clusters from the vine of the earth, and threw them into the great wine press of the wrath of God. 20 And the wine press was trodden outside the city, and blood came out from the wine press, up to the horses' bridles, for a distance of two hundred miles." (Rev 14:16–20, NASB)

WHAT DID WE LEARN ABOUT JUDGMENT?

The reality of our own impending judgment is made clear in the book of Revelation, as well as throughout the entire Bible. From the prophets of old, to the Gospels, to the Epistles, to the book of Revelation, we see repeatedly that all the dead will be judged. Unlike some interpretations that teach that all souls eventually go to Heaven, the Sola Scriptura approach holds only to what the Bible directly says, namely that at the time of judgment some will inherit everlasting life and others will receive shame and everlasting contempt. Everlasting is forever, unending, and eternal. Clearly this is the background context for our need for salvation. We are all sinners and will be judged. Have we broken any of the laws, even the least of them? If so, how do we find atonement? How do we make things right with God? Some sins seem to be repairable, like returning something you have stolen. But what about the things you can't undo? How to you undo murder, or taking God's name in vain, or forgetting the Sabbath, or being jealous and coveting what other people have? Or what about the things we have left undone, like feeding the poor, helping the oppressed, visiting the sick, caring for the immigrants, or just loving all of our neighbors no matter who they are? Who among us is truly perfect? Who really doesn't need the forgiveness, the atonement, that Christ offers? Who can stand on their own two feet before the throne of God in the Day of Judgment? Not me.

As we look at the passages regarding judgment, we also see that leading up to the Day of Judgment are "woes." It is not a good time on the earth. The coming wars, famines, and destruction get progressively worse up until the day of the Second Coming. And there are false prophets, false messiahs, and false teachers that will arise along the way leading up to the end of things as we know them. But we should take heart because when Jesus returns everyone will know it. He won't return in secret. He won't be revealed as a hidden child born in a remote part of Tibet. He won't arise through political campaigns to bring a peace deal to the Middle East. He won't be a popular Evangelist with a Megachurch in Korea. He won't be a charismatic leader of a cult down in Texas. He won't be a Caliph that builds the largest Muslim nation ever seen before. He won't be some relatively unknown Rabbi out helping the lepers somewhere in Israel, until he is "found out." He won't be the chief fundraiser for building a Third Temple in Jerusalem. No, when Jesus appears everyone on Earth will know it, just like when you see lightning flash across the sky. There is no doubt of what you have seen. Even small children know the truth of lightning and don't question it. Everyone will see it. It will be obvious to the entire world. There won't be any controversy or doubt. There will be no need for faith anymore, time will be up, and all things will be revealed.

> "21 For then there will be a great tribulation, such as has not occurred since the beginning of the world until now, nor ever will. 22 Unless those days had been cut short, no life would have been saved; but for the sake of the elect those days will be cut short. 23 Then if anyone says to you, 'Behold, here is the Christ,' or 'There He is,' do not believe him. 24 For false Christs and false prophets will arise and will show great signs and wonders, so as to mislead, if possible, even the elect. 25 Behold, I have told you in advance. 26 So if they say to you, 'Behold, He is in the wilderness,' do not go out, or, 'Behold, He is in the inner rooms,' do not believe them. 27 For just as the lightning comes from the east and flashes even to the west, so will the coming of the Son of Man be." (Matt 24:21-27, NASB)

#	Truth Claim	Primary Support	Secondary Support
14.1	All the dead will be judged.	Rev 20:11-15	Matt 13:43, 16:27, 19:28, 25:41-46, John 4:36, 5:24-29, 11:24, Acts 24:15, Jude 1:14-15,23, Luke 10:20, 14:14, 1 Thes 4:16, 1 Cor 15:20-57, Rev 2:11, 3:5, 9:4-19, 11:18, 14:7-20, Joel 2:2,3:13,11,30-31, Isa 2:10-11,19-21, 13:9-13, 26:19-21, 34:4,8, 53:11, 57:2, 66:24, Ezek 32:7-8, 37:12, Hos 10:8, Jer 30:7, Dan 7:9-10, 12:1-3, Ps 69:28
14.2	Woes precede the Day of Judgment.	Rev 6:16-17	Matt 24, Mk 13, Lk 21, 2 Thess 2, Rev 6-18, Isa 24:17-23, Dan 12:1, Joel 2:1-11,28-32, Amos 5:16-20, Zeph 1:14-2:3
14.3	All nations will worship the one True God.	Rev 15:4	Rev 2:27, 12:5, 19:15, Mark 16:19, Ps 86:9, Isa 66:23, Jer 10:7

15

Revelations About Eternity

"You should not believe your conscience and your feelings more than the Word which the Lord Who receives sinners preaches to you."—Martin Luther

IN THE BOOK OF Revelation, we get many insights about eternity for believers. There are numerous promises made to the seven churches who were the original audience of this book. And there are beautiful promises and visions at the end of the book.

PROMISES TO THE SEVEN CHURCHES

In the first part of the book of Revelation each of the seven churches are given promises of the future. Those who are victorious, those who follow Jesus, those who don't follow the ways of the world will receive the following:

1. The right to eat from the tree of life which is in the paradise of God (Rev 2:7b)
2. Eternal life as the victor's crown (Rev 2:10b)
3. Eternal life, not dying in the second death (Rev 2:11)
4. Hidden manna, and a white stone with a new name known only to you (Rev 2:17b)
5. Authority over the nations (Rev 2:26b–27a)
6. The morning star (Rev 2:28)
7. White clothing and eternal life (Rev 3:5)
8. Escape from the hour of trial to come on the whole world (Rev 3:10)
9. To become a pillar in the temple of God and never again leave it (Rev 3:12)

10. Will have written on them the name of God, the new Jerusalem, and Jesus' new name (Rev 3:12)
11. Will be with Jesus and eat with him (Rev 3:20)
12. The right to rule with Jesus (Rev 3:21)

VISIONS OF ETERNITY

At the end of Revelation, we see beautiful promises of that future time when God will make all things new. Those who are victorious, those who follow Jesus, those who don't follow the ways of the world will live in this place.

1. A new Heaven and a new Earth (Rev 21:1)
2. A new Jerusalem which comes down out of Heaven from God (Rev 21:2)
3. God will dwell there directly with his people (Rev 21:3)
4. God will wipe away every tear (Rev 21:4)
5. There will be no more death or mourning or crying or pain (Rev 21:4)
6. Everything will be made new (Rev 21:5)
7. The thirsty will receive water without cost from the spring of the water of life (Rev 21:6)
8. A new Jerusalem that is a massive city and shines brightly because of God (Rev 21:9–27)
9. The Tree of Life flowing from the river of the water of life for healing of all (Rev 22:1–2)
10. The throne of God and of the Lamb, where we will see him face to face (Rev 22:3–4)
11. The light of God will shine everywhere (Rev 22:5)

WHAT DID WE LEARN ABOUT ETERNITY?

In hearing all these promises of the future, we should consider what they mean for us. The Sola Scriptura approach takes these promises seriously and does not add anything to them or take anything away. The promises stand just as they are. To those who are victorious in this world, those who follow Jesus even in the midst of the pain and trouble in this world, those who do not follow the ways of the world, they will receive eternal life.

This eternal life will be one where you will see God face to face. You will live in a new creation where everything is made new. It will be a paradise that is beautiful, full of light, and made of the most precious jewels and metals. God will wipe away every tear and there will be no more death, mourning, crying, or pain.

Those troubles in your life that still linger, those friends and family with life challenges, that pain that keeps you up at night, and the things that worry us every day will all pass away. Mourning will be turned into joy. The former things will be remembered no more. Our sins will be as far from us as the east is from the west. We will all know the feeling of being without sin, without guilt, and without pain. No one will look down on us, and we will not be tempted to look down on anyone else. No hands will be against us, not even those of the devil, for he will be no more. There will be no more oppression, no more injustice of any kind, no more poverty, no more hunger, and no more unending thirst. Physically or spiritually.

We should all look forward to that great time of the future, after the resurrection of the dead, where we will live in God's beautiful new creation that is without the influence of evil. Blessed are those who wash their robes in the Blood of the Lamb. For they are the ones who will be able to eat from the Tree of Life and go through the gates into that new city.

#	Truth Claim	Primary Support	Secondary Support
15.1	The victorious will eat from the Tree of Life.	Rev 22:12–14	Rev 2:7,11, 3:5,12, 22:2, Luke 23:43, Gen 2:9, 3:22
15.2	Be faithful even to the point of death and you will not be hurt by the second death.	Rev 20:6	Rev 2:7,10–11,17, 3:5,12, 20:6, 14, 21:8, Matt 10:28, 25:46, Luke 12:5, John 5:28–29, 11:17–27
15.3	The victorious will receive everlasting life.	Rev 3:5	Rev 2:7,10–11,17, 3:12, 20:6, 14, 21:8, Matt 10:28, 25:46, Luke 12:5, John 5:28–29, 11:17–27
15.4	God will wipe away every tear and there will be no more death.	Rev 21:4	Rev 7:17, 20:14, 21:4, 1 Cor 15:26, Isa 25:8, 30:19, 35:10, 51:11, 60:20, 65:19, Jer 31:12
15.5	God's servants will drink Living Water.	Rev 22:17	John 4:10–14, 7:38, Rev 7:13–17, 21:6–8, 22:1–3,17, Ps 23:2, 36:8–9, 42:2, 46:4, 143:6, Zech 14:8, Jer 2:13, 17:13, Isa 12:3, 41:18, 44:3, 55:1, Prov 9:5, Ezek 47:1,9, Joel 3:18

16

What Does All This Mean for Us Today?

"The Bible is a remarkable fountain: The more one draws and drinks of it, the more it stimulates thirst."—Martin Luther

A STUDY OF SCRIPTURE should move us further along in our own spiritual development. It should help us understand how to be better people. It should lead us in the paths of righteousness, for the sake of God's name. In other words, the world around us will see how we behave. Those who are believers in Jesus and profess his name to others, are watched for what they do. If we do not walk in an upright way, then others will see that and be skeptical of Christianity. If we do not walk in the paths of righteousness, then the name of God gets ridiculed by others. Just look at what happens to the church because of a scandal. There are numerous scandals throughout history, as well as in our day. These scandals plague the church, inhibit our young people from wanting to be a part of the church, and cause good people to divide themselves. A popular preacher that falls from grace doesn't fall alone. They take some of the people around them down too. Either people who are directly involved may fall, or their supporters who are shocked at the scandal. How much does it grieve God when we Christians make huge mistakes and cause damage to his Kingdom? Though we may excuse it because we're all broken people, the damage in the eyes of the unbelievers is already done. We must be very careful with anything that may cause division within the church, or worse: lead to scandal.

PRAISE AND WARNINGS TO THE SEVEN CHURCHES

As we seek to understand what the book of Revelation means for our lives today, we should look at what it meant to the original audience first. The seven churches to whom it was addressed received both praise and warnings from Jesus. We should take these admonitions seriously. Imagine if Jesus sent a letter to your church, what would it say? These seven churches each received one. Here are some things that the people in the seven churches were doing well:

1. They were hard workers and persevered in their faith (Rev 2:2–3).
2. They did not tolerate wicked people and tested the claims people made (Rev 2:2).
3. They hated the practices of the Nicolaitans (Rev 2:6).
4. They did not renounce their faith in Jesus even under persecution (Rev 2:13, 3:8).
5. They served others with good deeds, love, and faith (Rev 2:19, 3:8).
6. They did not learn occult practices and secrets (Rev 2:24b).
7. They endured patiently (Rev 3:10a).

Here are some things that the people were not doing well and were warned about:

1. Some lost their initial love and zeal for God (Rev 2:4).
2. Some were sexually immoral and ate food sacrificed to idols (Rev 2:14–15, 20).
3. Some left their good works incomplete and did not finish what they started (Rev 3:1b–3a).
4. Some were lackluster in their good works, lukewarm and neither hot nor cold (Rev 3:15–16).
5. Some trusted in riches and wealth for their security (Rev 3:17–18).

HOW DOES THIS APPLY TO US TODAY?

Not only does the book of Revelation give beautiful visions of the Eternal Kingdom of Messiah, as well as warnings against following the wicked ways of this world, but we see a direct calling on the lives of the people to whom the book was written. As we look at the praise and warnings given to the seven churches, we can see that there are Biblical principles that still apply to our lives today.

Here are some of the big takeaways for you and me:

1. We should be hard workers in the Kingdom of God.
2. We should serve others with good deeds, love, and faith.
3. We should have a passionate zeal, full of love and mercy toward others.
4. We should keep our faith, even under trials and persecution, never denying Christ.

5. We should test the teachings of others, to see if they are true and faithful to Christ.

6. We should avoid wicked practices, unfaithful teachers, and occult teachings.

7. We should endure all things patiently.

Think about these things. Are you working hard to really understand Revelation, or depending on others to do the work? Are you serving others, or arguing with others? Are you loving and merciful to others? Do you keep the faith even when the work becomes hard? Do you test the things others say the scriptures mean? Do you test what you read, even in this book? Do you avoid trying to learn occult explanations of Revelation, secret teachings, and teachers who seem to have some other motive other than faithfully following Christ? Are you enduring this complex study of Revelation patiently without giving up?

Moreover, do these attributes Jesus was looking for in the seven churches characterize our lives today? How is our faith doing? What are the fruits of our faith? Have the words of God, the seeds of love and mercy, been sown on good soil in us? Have we grown up to be trees that bear good fruit? Do our tree branches support others, like birds looking for somewhere safe to rest? Is our life characterized by patience, love, faith, endurance, and perseverance? Are we as joyful and productive for the Lord today as we once were a long time ago, or have we grown tired and perhaps a little cold?

If Jesus were to write your church a letter today, what would he say about it? If he were to write you a personal letter today, what would he say about you? We all have work to do. We should be about our Father's business right here and now. We should decide right now that things are going to change. We should repent of times where our hearts grew a little colder, where our faith has been challenged, and where we have not served others as Christ asked us to. We should repent of the things we have done, the things we have left undone, and the things we did not complete. We should lean forward again and put our shoulder to the wheel, working hard, persevering, and enduring all things patiently. Let our faith guide us, let the love of God lead us, and let the Holy Spirit of God work through us. We should be the kind of people God asks us to be.

> "19 Every tree that does not bear good fruit is cut down and thrown into the fire. 20 So then, you will know them by their fruits." (Matt 7:19–20, NASB)

> "Our people must also learn to engage in good deeds to meet pressing needs, so that they will not be unfruitful." (Titus 3:14, NASB)

> "'I am the true vine, and My Father is the vinedresser. 2 Every branch in Me that does not bear fruit, He takes away; and every branch that bears fruit, He prunes it so that it may bear more fruit. 3 You are already clean because of the word which I have spoken to you. 4 Abide in Me, and I in you. As the branch cannot bear fruit of itself unless it abides in the vine, so neither can you unless

you abide in Me. 5 I am the vine, you are the branches; he who abides in Me and I in him, he bears much fruit, for apart from Me you can do nothing. 6 If anyone does not abide in Me, he is thrown away as a branch and dries up; and they gather them, and cast them into the fire and they are burned." (John 15:1–6, NASB)

RESPONDING TO DIFFERENT INTERPRETATIONS

Given the broad range of interpretations for the book of Revelation we have seen, what should our response be? Should we take all the knowledge presented in this book and go and fight with people who hold a non–Sola Scriptura view? Should we take all the truth claims presented here and beat other people over the head with the scriptures? Should we accuse them of syncretism, conflation, or heresy? Should we be divisive and wipe the dust off our feet if they don't succumb to our reasoning? Is that walking in the paths of righteousness? What does that do to the body of Christ, the believers, who don't have time to study all the scriptures but hear the confusing arguments of the theologians? Does it build up the faith of others to hear all these arguments? If you took the time to read all of this book, then you are way ahead of most other Christians. But don't forget that others have not had the time to look so deeply into this subject area. You have a responsibility not to use your knowledge to damage the faith of others. Use your knowledge for good, not to shame or hurt other people.

> The purpose of this book is to help others better understand Revelation, not to empower arguments and cause further division.

The purpose of this book is to help others better understand Revelation, not to empower arguments and cause further division. Most people do not have the time to understand all the different viewpoints, their advantages and disadvantages, nor to think through the implications. Even some of my college professors had not heard about all the different views and were surprised by the questions I brought up stemming from studying other viewpoints. Now that you have read this book, you must choose what you will do with all this knowledge. Knowing that many people do not know all the different viewpoints, you should recognize the fear that can set in for people when they hear an explanation they've never heard before. Sometimes this unsettles people. Sometimes it causes them to get angry. I experienced all these things in my own study. Some people will be argumentative, while others may be confused. But almost all will become emotionally engaged. How we care for the emotions of our sisters and brothers in Christ is of paramount importance. We don't want anyone to feel shamed, rejected, ridiculed, or beaten down by our explanations. Paul told Timothy how to teach others about the scriptures in his second letter.

> "23 But refuse foolish and ignorant speculations, knowing that they produce quarrels. 24 The Lord's bond-servant must not be quarrelsome, but be kind to all, able to teach, patient when wronged, 25 with gentleness correcting those who are in opposition, if perhaps God may grant them repentance leading to the knowledge of the truth, 26 and they may come to their senses and escape from the snare of the devil, having been held captive by him to do his will." (2 Tim 2:23-26, NASB)

Look at the instructions from Paul: don't have anything to do with foolish arguments. If you find yourself talking about the book of Revelation with someone and they want to reinterpret what an angel told John or Daniel the symbols of a vision meant, is that a foolish argument? When a person wants to cling to an explanation that directly conflicts with what the scriptures say, then they are not placing the scriptures above the traditions of theologians. You won't unseat their views by showing them scriptures, because they cling to traditions instead. Famous theologians can carry more weight than the original Disciples.

Paul says not to quarrel but be kind. That is very hard to do. Some people like to shame others when arguing. They sometimes throw out their status, education, experience, or some other kind of appeal to their authority to try to win their argument. However, this is another form of depending on something outside the scriptures themselves. You won't win an argument with them either, even if you have better education, experience, or a fancy man made title. Quarrels only end in shame and hurt.

Paul says not to be resentful. That will prevent you from loving the other person. Resenting another person for having a good argument, not listening to you, or shaming you won't help you to be kind to them. Don't engage in foolish arguments, don't quarrel, and be kind. What if famous theologians were like that? The debates would be less exciting, but perhaps there would be less division and discord among the followers of Jesus? Lastly, Paul says to gently instruct others. It is up to God to lead others in their knowledge of the truth. It is the devil that holds us captive to wrong thoughts and wrong motives, all to just do his will. And what is that?

The will of the devil is that the church would be defeated. The will of the devil is that there would be great quarrels, great division, and endless arguments within the church. The will of the devil is to have the church be unattractive to newcomers, and to become something believers no longer want to be a part of. A win for the Kingdom of God is not when one theologian sounds smarter than another. A win for the body of Christ is not when a church splits and the "heretics" go to a different gathering place next Sunday because they misunderstand the book of Revelation. Division, discord, anger, mistrust, and accusation are all part of the kingdom of the devil, not the Kingdom of Christ. The will of the devil is that Christianity would fail. That it would be unappealing and seem ridiculous. A win for the Kingdom of God is when people look more deeply into the scriptures. Even if they don't agree with your interpretation. Let go, and let God do the work on the hearts of others (as well as your own).

> Division, discord, anger, mistrust, and accusation are all part of the kingdom of the devil, not the Kingdom of Christ. The will of the devil is that Christianity would fail. That it would be unappealing and seem ridiculous. A win for the Kingdom of God is when people look more deeply into the scriptures. Even if they don't agree with your interpretation. Let go, and let God do the work on the hearts of others (as well as your own).

I expect there will be ongoing disagreement over the interpretation of Revelation, and the Bible itself, until Christ returns. That's why Jesus said one day he would separate the goats from the sheep (Matt 25:31–46). We will not be able to convince everyone of our view, period. But in trying to teach others, or at least explain our own view, we should be extremely careful not to push anyone out of faith. We should never shame anyone or cause them to feel like we treated them harshly. We should be gentle with others and leave it up to God to work his truth into all of our lives. We should all live our lives as peacemakers, mourning for the trouble in this world, meekly seeking unity with others, hungering and thirsting for righteousness for every one of us, showing mercy to those who oppose us, and accepting persecution if it happens rather than taking vengeance on others. We should all begin on the same page: Jesus Christ is Our Lord and Savior. He will return to judge the living and the dead. We should live our lives following in his teachings. We should love God with all our heart, all our mind, all our soul, with all our strength. And let us truly love our neighbor, everyone around us, even those opposed to us.

Remember that we moderns did not start these arguments. As you read in the first part of this book the disagreements go all the way back to the early church. The earliest Christian scholars living in Antioch took a literal view and claimed their authority from the disciples of John (Ignatius and Polycarp), the author of Revelation. A rival school developed in Alexandria and took the Greek philosophical approach to explaining scripture which we now know as the Allegorical view. Famous early adherents included Origen and Augustine who influenced much of early church theology. The Protestant Reformation did nothing to settle the disputes, for we see the different early branches of Methodists, Anglicans, Presbyterian, Lutheran, and others continuing to argue over these very same issues. Martin Luther, John Calvin, John Wesley, and others simply did not agree on eschatological matters. Since we didn't start these arguments then we don't have to defend any of them. Arguments over Revelation go all the way back to the early church and have not been resolved down through the ages. No one can claim to truly have the original view of the Apostles believed by most of the church throughout history. Historical writings show us otherwise. Though different traditions have developed over time, we should be able to start a conversation by looking only at the scriptures themselves. And any interpretation that cannot be backed up with direct quotes in scripture should give us pause.

> Arguments over Revelation go all the way back to the early church and have not been resolved down through the ages. No one can claim to truly have the original view of the Apostles believed by most of the church throughout history. Historical writings show us otherwise.

The most important thing in any discussion of Revelation is the truth of the saving power of the Blood of Jesus. No matter which interpretation one takes, the fact that Jesus fulfilled the prophecies to give his soul as an offering for our sins remains. All interpretations agree with this point. We should do nothing to scare people away from this truth. If our message isn't about recognizing our own brokenness and need for Jesus' help to fix things, then we are missing the biggest message of the Bible. If we don't see this Gospel, then we are off the path of truth. Since all interpretations agree on this main point, we should repeatedly return to it in our conversations. It should be a common touchpoint we can all agree on. And it should be the overarching doctrine we teach others. The identification of the beast, the meaning of 666, the meaning of the Four Horsemen, are all interesting discussions. But the answers to those questions do not save, only the Blood of Jesus saves. We need salvation from all potential scenarios that may arise from any of the interpretations. And the answer in all of them is the same: keep the faith in Jesus and do not conform to the ways of the world. Do not get off the straight and narrow path, turning neither to the left nor to the right. Keep your eyes fixed on Jesus. All mainstream interpretations agree on a literal interpretation of the role of the Messiah. We should always begin there and keep returning to it. Jesus came into the world to save sinners. He offered his soul as the perfect sacrifice for our sins. And not for ours only, but for the sins of the whole world.

> All mainstream interpretations agree on a literal interpretation of the role of the Messiah. We should always begin there and keep returning to it. Jesus came into the world to save sinners. He offered his soul as the perfect sacrifice for our sins. And not for ours only, but for the sins of the whole world.

CONCLUSIONS

Revelation is a confusing book. Because of this we naturally turn to commentaries for explanations of what is going on. Sadly, most commentaries only teach a specific interpretation without even mentioning other possible interpretations. This leads to placing the teachings of commentaries above what the scriptures themselves say. To make matters worse, there are at least four traditional ways of interpreting scripture and the New Testament itself uses all of them. In the second century Origen introduced allegorical biblical interpretations using the Greek philosophical method of Hellenism. Those new teachings directly opposed the older literal interpretations of the first Christian school in Antioch which was led by the students of the Apostles. So from the beginning of Christianity there has been a vast theological divide over how to interpret Revelation, and the views have only evolved and splintered. We can see that the same thing happened in Judaism when looking at the very same Hebrew Bible prophecies. How are modern people to respond to the millennia of arguments?

The Sola Scriptura approach has us begin with only the scriptures themselves. It does not follow any of the traditions which have been introduced or evolved over time since the scriptures were written. While there are numerous and conflicting traditions about the meaning of the scriptures, we should all be able to hold to at least what the scriptures directly say. Since all interpretations claim to be rooted in the scriptures, but yet there are so many conflicting views, we should go back to that root to understand exactly what it does say. The details of God's Word are promised to be fulfilled and the Bible warns us against a time when people will turn away from God's Word and replace it with myths (untruths). It also warns us that the words of true prophets will come to pass, so if we hold the prophets of the Bible to be true, then we must also hold their words to be true.

Christians generally hold that Jesus fulfills most of the prophecies about the Messiah, and those unfilled will be fulfilled at a future time at his Second Coming. The beliefs about his Second Coming and his role while here at the First Coming are generally taken as literal interpretations of scripture. Jesus literally gave his life to make atonement for the sins of others. Jesus was literally rejected by his own people. And Jesus will literally come again, appearing on the clouds in glory.

Mixed in with these literal interpretations of the Messianic prophecies are prophecies regarding the end times. Just as we take the Messianic prophecies literally, so too should we take the end times prophecies. It is also apparent from how God speaks through the prophets, the expectations of the prophets themselves, as well as Jesus himself, that scriptures are to be taken literally. We see this throughout the New Testament in how Jesus, Peter, and Paul refer to the Hebrew Bible prophecies of the end times. Moreover, when symbolism is used the Bible frequently directly explains that symbolism. Any tradition that provides an alternative explanation for symbols which are already explained in the Bible is an interpretation outside of scripture itself. Though they may argue using general principles, the argument should be about what the text actually says and not about general principles which are in fact true. As we think through all these things, we should remember the parable Jesus taught about how people accept the words of scripture.

> "18 Hear then the parable of the sower. 19 When anyone hears the word of the kingdom and does not understand it, the evil one comes and snatches away what has been sown in his heart. This is the one on whom seed was sown beside the road. 20 The one on whom seed was sown on the rocky places, this is the man who hears the word and immediately receives it with joy; 21 yet he has no firm root in himself, but is only temporary, and when affliction or persecution arises because of the word, immediately he falls away. 22 And the one on whom seed was sown among the thorns, this is the man who hears

the word, and the worry of the world and the deceitfulness of wealth choke the word, and it becomes unfruitful. 23 And the one on whom seed was sown on the good soil, this is the man who hears the word and understands it; who indeed bears fruit and brings forth, some a hundredfold, some sixty, and some thirty." (Matt 13:18–23, NASB)

Clearly there is confusion about the meaning of the book of Revelation, and so there is opportunity for the evil one to come and snatch away what has been sown in our hearts. The love of God, his teachings on how we are to live, and the path of salvation can all slip away from people if they see arguments and division among God's people. And the evil one can use some interpretations as a way to have Christians ridicule and shame each other. Worse, they can cause church splits, heresies, and drive people away from Christianity. None of those things are edifying. None of these things build up the Kingdom.

The root of the seed is the foundation of the scriptures. Without an understanding of the context of the Hebrew prophets a person misses a great deal of the background necessary to approach the book of Revelation. When trouble or persecution comes because of explanations outside the scriptures, a person without a solid background in the Hebrew Bible prophecies can quickly become lost and confused. They also may become fearful or angry. Sometimes they may even hold others in contempt and try to shame them.

The modern world clearly provides all kinds of opportunities to choke out our study of the Word. As you have seen in this book there is a large amount of background context to study as you engage with the book of Revelation. Few people make the time to go into a verse-by-verse study of Revelation, looking at all the Hebrew Bible references in their own context. The thorns of day-to-day life choke us.

The good soil is someone who hears the word, understands it, and produces a crop. We should take a good look at what crop is produced from our study of the book of Revelation. What do the different denominations teach, if anything at all? And is it producing the kind of people God would have us become, or only further division and shame? What is the result of the various teachings out there about Revelation? Money-making movies, fantasy book series, numerous comic strips and memes about the end of the world, ridicule of Christians, doomsday cults, etc.? What is the result of the teachings about Revelation within your own church? What about what you think about them in your heart of hearts? Do they make you afraid and cause you to worry, or inspire you and push you deeper into the study of scripture?

Are we good soil? Do we hold the seeds closely or let them blow away? Do we nourish the Word in study and contemplation, or are we just "in one ear and out the other"? Do the thorns around us grow up and choke the Word? Do people disparage others, shame us, or make us fearful in our study because they claim some sort of authority? God has no respect for people's earthly positions. We all stand alone in judgment. Martin Luther, Pope Leo X, David Guzik, Pope Francis, John Wesley, nor

John Calvin will be defending you at judgment. It's just you and God. Don't let the thorns of the world choke out your study of the scriptures. Don't be afraid of what other people may think or say about you if you read the scriptures with your best intention to understand. Don't let the endless commentaries blow you from place to place like the wind. Be the good soil. Hold onto the seed, the Word. Nourish it, study it, water it, and let the light shine upon it.

Our whole approach to scripture should be consistent. We should not take part of a passage and interpret it literally, for example about the Messiah, and another part of the very same passage non–literally. When an angel explains the meaning of symbols to a prophet, we should not provide a different meaning for the symbols. We should let scripture interpret scripture, for all that God intended for us to know has been explained. And as we have seen there are specific prophecies God has not yet revealed and told the prophets to keep hidden. So we should not expect to have answers for everything, as that was not the will of God.

The full expectation about the events of the end times was explained through several Hebrew prophets. When you put these ancient prophecies together you can see them as the background context for the book of Revelation. In order to truly understand Revelation, you must begin with the Hebrew prophecies themselves. Just like in order to truly understand the Messiah, you must be familiar with the Hebrew prophecies about the Messiah. As Jesus walked along the road to Emmaus with the two disciples, he explained the scriptures about the Messiah to them beginning with Moses and all the prophets (Luke 24:27). The New Testament repeatedly references the Hebrew scriptures and shows how they are fulfilled in Christ. We should seriously consider the Hebrew prophecies before we begin to understand the New Testament. All scripture is profitable for instruction.

You should remember that your view of the end times prophecies does not impact your salvation. Only your faith in Christ will save you. It's not holding to an allegorical, literal, futuristic, dispensational, millennial, historic–grammatical, or any other interpretation of prophecies that will save you. Only your faith.

> "For God so loved the world, that He gave His only begotten Son, that whoever believes in Him shall not perish, but have eternal life." (John 3:16, NASB)

Since faith in Christ is the most important thing, and the only necessary thing for salvation, then it's not worth arguing about various interpretations of Revelation. It's certainly not worth becoming divisive, causing church splits, or declaring secret knowledge and setting dates for Christ's return. We should be about the work of the Kingdom, not the work of arguments. Our faith is shown through our deeds, and by our deeds others will know who we truly follow. Some trees will bear good fruit while others will not.

We should be about the business of Our Father Who Art in Heaven, and not do the business of the devil. We should remember to praise and hallow his Name, singing

What Does All This Mean for Us Today?

Hallelujah for all that he has done in our lives. We should praise God and not curse one another. One day his Kingdom will come, and his will is going to be done here on Earth as it is in Heaven. We will see the complete fulfillment of the book of Revelation, and all that the prophets have spoken. We should pray for all we need him to provide every day, including both forgiveness for our sins as well as the ability for us to forgive others. We should pray for a way out of temptation and for deliverance from evil. And we should remember that his is the real kingdom, the real power, and he deserves all the glory, forever and ever. Amen!

Bibliography

Albertz, Rainer, and Becking, Bob. *Yahwism after the Exile*. Van Gorcum, 2003.

Ashi and Ravina II, eds. *The Babylonian Talmud (Talmud Bavli)*. Babylon, 500.

Beale, G.K., and Campbell, David. *Revelation: A Shorter Commentary*. Grand Rapids: Eerdmans, 2015.

Calvin, John. *Preface to the Book of Joel*. Grand Rapids: Christian Classics Ethereal Library, 1557.

Easton, Matthew. *Easton's Bible Dictionary*. Nashville: Thomas Nelson, 1897.

Ezra, Abraham. *Commentaries on the TaNaKh*. Lucca, 1145.

Frishman, Elyse. *Mishkan T'filah: A Reform Siddur*. New York: Central Conference of American Rabbis, 2016.

Henry, Matthew. *Concise Commentary on the Whole Bible*. Chicago: Moody, 1989.

Jacobs, Louis. *The Jewish Religion: A Companion*. Oxford: Oxford University Press, 1995.

Jacobs, Rick. "What is Reform Judaism?" Union for Reform Judaism (URJ), 2020. https://reformjudaism.org/what-reform-judaism.

Keil, Carl Friedrich, and Delitzsch, Franz. *Commentary on the Old Testament*. Leipsic, 1866.

Kogan, Shmuel. *Atonement in the Absence of Sacrifices*. Chabad-Lubavitch Media Center, Brooklyn, 2018.

Luther, Martin. *Preface to the Revelation of Saint John (Initial)*. Wittenberg: Hans Lufft, 1530.

———. *Preface to the Revelation of Saint John (Revised)*. Wittenberg: Hans Lufft, 1546.

Nestle, Eberhard. *Η ΚΑΙΝΗ ΔΙΑΘΗΚΗ. Text with Critical Apparatus*. London: British and Foreign Bible Society, 1904.

Rashi. *Commentary of the Entire Tanach*. Troyes, 1107.

Rambam. *Commentary on the Mishnah*. Fayyum, 1158.

Reddish, Mitchell. *Revelation - Smyth and Helwys Bible Commentary*. Macon: Smyth and Helwys, 2005.

Sahgal, Neha, et al. *Israel's Religiously Divided Society*. Pew Research Center, Washington, DC, 2016.

Shurpin, Yehuda. "Why Isn't the Book of Daniel Part of the Prophets?" Chabad Media Center, 2012. https://www.chabad.org/library/article_cdo/aid/1735365/jewish/Why-Isnt-the-Book-of-Daniel-Part-of-the-Prophets.htm.

Smith, William. *Smith's Bible Dictionary*. Grand Rapids: Christian Classics Ethereal Library, 2022.

Thompson, John Christopher, and Macchia, Frank D. *Revelation - Two Horizons New Testament Commentary*. Grand Rapids: Eerdmans, 2016.

Wesley, John. *Explanatory Notes on the Whole Bible*. London: William Pine, 1765.

BIBLIOGRAPHY

Wilson, Mark. *Revelation - Zondervan Illustrated Bible Backgrounds Commentary*. Grand Rapids: Zondervan, 2016.

Wolvaardt, Bennie, et al. *How to Interpret the Bible*. Harpenden: Veritas College and the Good Book Company, 1999.

www.ingramcontent.com/pod-product-compliance
Lightning Source LLC
Chambersburg PA
CBHW081145230426
43664CB00018B/2808